British Armoured Divisions and their Commanders, 1939–1945

To all who served in armour, especially those who lost their lives.

For heroes have the whole earth for their tomb; and in lands far from their own, where the column with its epitaph declares it, there is enshrined in every breast a record unwritten with no tablet to preserve it, except that of the heart.

British Armoured Divisions and their Commanders, 1939–1945

Richard Doherty

Pen & Sword
MILITARY

First published in Great Britain in 2013 by
Pen & Sword Military
an imprint of
Pen & Sword Books Ltd
47 Church Street
Barnsley
South Yorkshire
S70 2AS

ISBN 978-1-84884-838-2

A CIP catalogue record for this book is available from the British Library

Typeset in Ehrhardt by
Mac Style, Driffield, East Yorkshire
Printed and bound by CPI Group (UK) Ltd, Croydon, CR0 4YY

Pen & Sword Books Ltd incorporates the imprints of Pen & Sword
Archaeology, Atlas, Aviation, Battleground, Discovery, Family History,
History, Maritime, Military, Naval, Politics, Railways, Select,
Social History, Transport, True Crime, and Claymore Press,
Frontline Books, Leo Cooper, Praetorian Press, Remember When,
Seaforth Publishing and Wharncliffe.

For a complete list of Pen & Sword titles please contact
PEN & SWORD BOOKS LIMITED
47 Church Street, Barnsley, South Yorkshire, S70 2AS, England
E-mail: enquiries@pen-and-sword.co.uk
Website: www.pen-and-sword.co.uk

Contents

Acknowledgements

Once again I express my thanks to Brigadier Henry Wilson, publishing manager of Pen and Sword Books, at whose suggestion I researched and wrote this book and whose encouragement and enthusiasm ensured that it was completed.

Along the way I also had the support and assistance of many individuals and organizations to make the book possible. Not least of these was the Tank Museum at Bovington where the encyclopaedic knowledge and infectious enthusiasm of David Fletcher MBE, the resident historian, provided answers to many questions and produced copies of obscure documents.

The records of the armoured divisions and their constituent formations and units reside at the National Archives at Kew. As ever the staff of the Reading and Search Rooms were courteous, professional and knowledgeable. Likewise, the staff of the Imperial War Museum at Lambeth were helpful and professional; the assistance of Mr Roderick Suddaby, head of the Department of Documents, was especially appreciated.

Bob O'Hara and his team at the National Archives have often helped me with my research, especially when a trip to Kew has not been possible while he and I have often put the world to rights over a cup of tea in the cafeteria. My thanks are due to Bob and his team for all their work.

In tracking down titles that were long out of print but essential for my research I was able to call on the help of the Londonderry Central Library and the Belfast Central Library, as well as the Linen Hall Library in Belfast. To all three I offer sincere thanks. Particular thanks for obtaining rare titles are also due to Valerie Jamieson, Head Librarian, Library and Information Services, HQ 38 (Irish) Brigade and to the Prince Consort's Library, Aldershot, as well as to Major (Retd) Noel Nash MBE.

Andy Shepherd was kind enough to read the manuscript at various stages and to offer informed comment that kept me focused on the main effort, and to Andy I offer a special word of thanks.

Frank Small was helpful with information on the armament of tanks and in providing an image for the photographs section of the book and I am grateful for his help. The maps were drawn by Tim Webster, whose patience, understanding and interest is much appreciated. David Rowlands, military artist *extraordinaire*, provided images of a number of his excellent paintings for use in the book as well as for the jacket, for which I am indebted to him. David also allowed his painting of 1st Royal

Tank Regiment at Beda Fomm to be used on the jacket and I am especially grateful for this kindness.

The Pen and Sword team are always able to turn a manuscript into a well presented book and deserve much praise for their efforts. To Matt Jones and the production team and to Jon Wilkinson for his jacket design I extend my gratitude.

Finally, I am always grateful for the patient support of Carol, my wife, our children, Joanne, James and Catríona, and our grandson Cíaran, without which it would have been impossible for me to write this book.

Richard Doherty
Co. Londonderry
January 2013

Maps

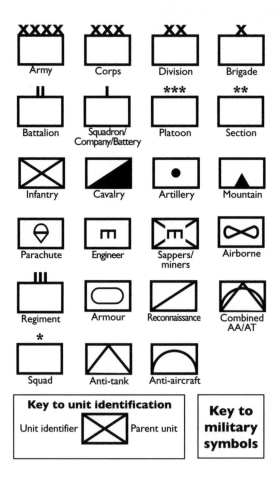

Army	Corps	Division	Brigade
Battalion	Squadron/Company/Battery	Platoon	Section
Infantry	Cavalry	Artillery	Mountain
Parachute	Engineer	Sappers/miners	Airborne
Regiment	Armour	Reconnaissance	Combined AA/AT
Squad	Anti-tank	Anti-aircraft	

Key to unit identification

Unit identifier — Parent unit

Key to military symbols

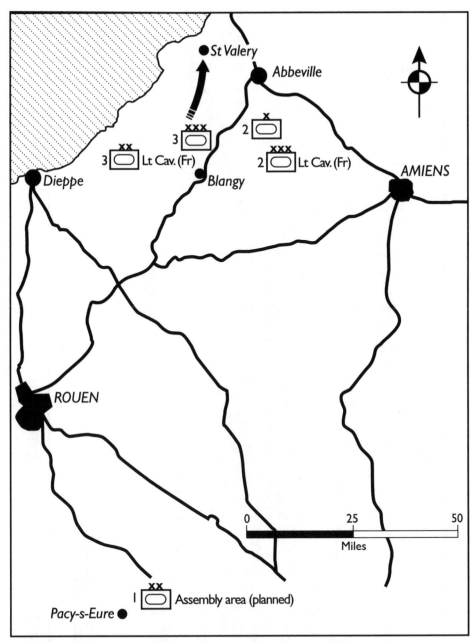

**MAP 1 France 1940: 1st Armoured Division
under French command south of the Somme**

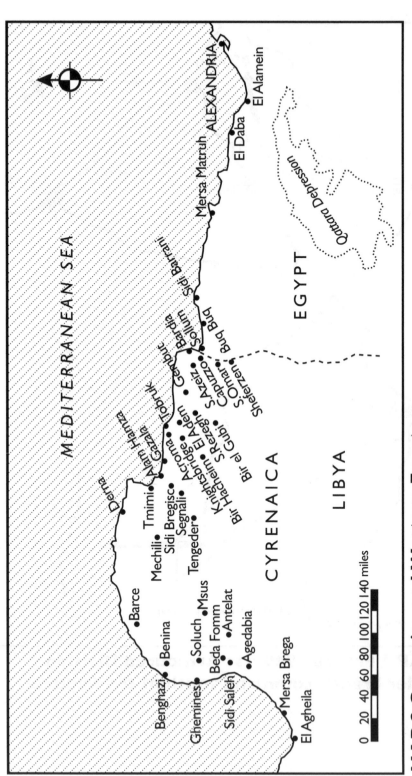

MAP 2 Cyrenaica and Western Egypt

MEDITERRANEAN SEA

EGYPT

Qattara Depression

El Alamein

El Daba

ALEXANDRIA

Mersa Matruh

Sidi Barrani

Sollum

Bardia

Gerabub

Buq Buq

Capuzzo

S.Azeiz

S.Omar

Sheferzen

Tobruk

Acroma

El Adem

Knightsbridge

S.Rezegh

Bir el Gubi

Bir Hacheim

El Gazala

Alam Hamza

Tmimi

Derna

Mechili

Sidi Bregisc

Segnali

Tengeder

Barce

Benina

Soluch

Msus

Beda Fomm

Antelat

Agedabia

Benghazi

Ghemines

Sidi Saleh

Mersa Brega

El Agheila

CYRENAICA

LIBYA

0 20 40 60 80 100 120 140 miles

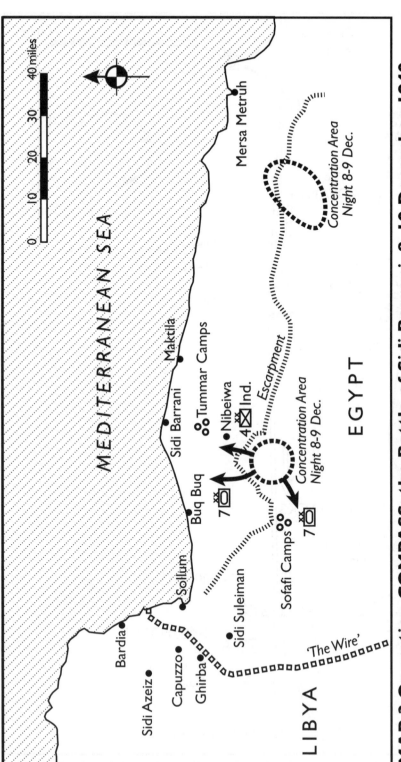

MAP 3 Operation COMPASS: the Battle of Sidi Barrani, 8–10 December 1940

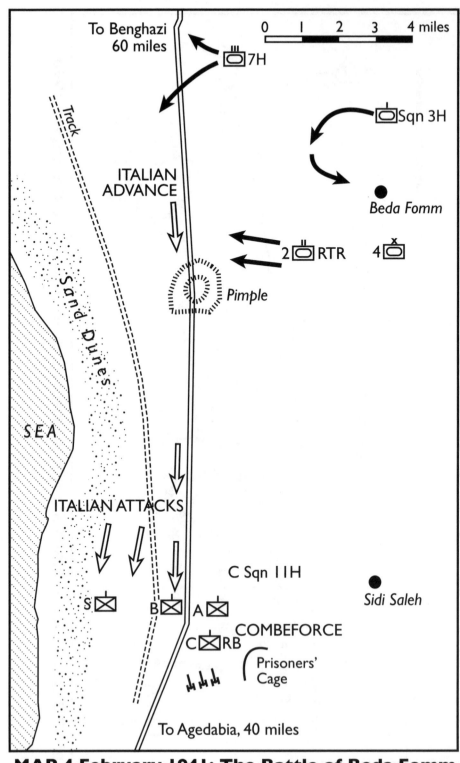

To Benghazi
60 miles

7H

0 1 2 3 4 miles

Sqn 3H

Track

ITALIAN
ADVANCE

Beda Fomm

2 RTR 4 ×

Sand Dunes

Pimple

SEA

ITALIAN ATTACKS

C Sqn 11H

Sidi Saleh

S B A

COMBEFORCE

C RB

Prisoners'
Cage

To Agedabia, 40 miles

MAP 4 February 1941: The Battle of Beda Fomm

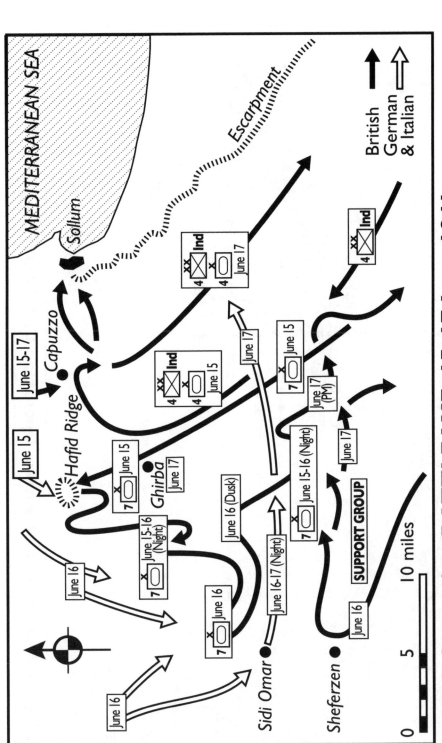

MAP 5 Operation BATTLEAXE, 15-17 June 1941

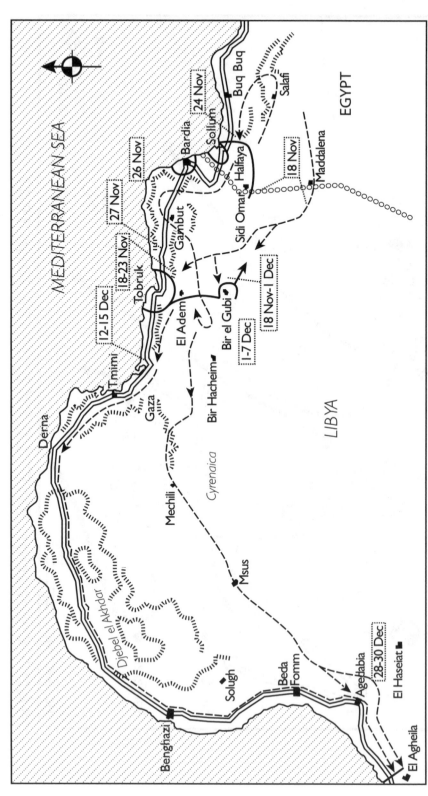

MAP 6 Eighth Army's first offensive: Operation CRUSADER

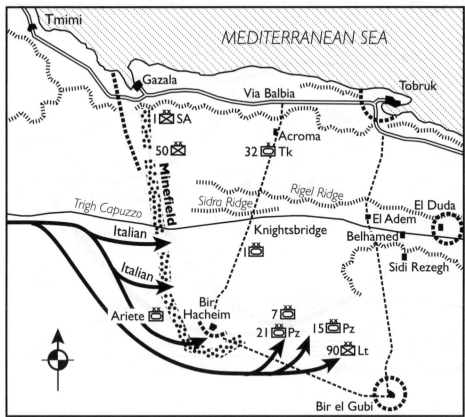

MAP 7 The Gazala Battlefield May-June 1942

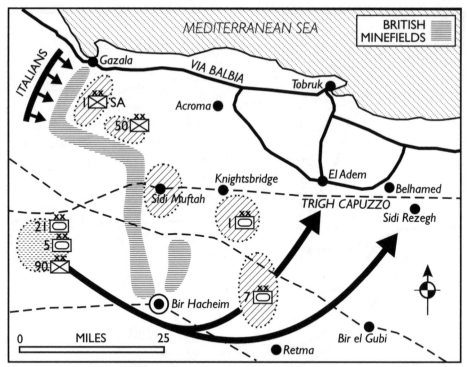

MAP 8 (a) Gazala Battles. Phase A, 27-28 May 1942

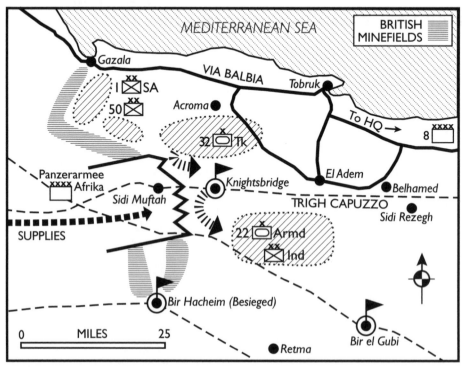

MAP 8 (b) Gazala Battles. Phase B, 31 May - 5 June 1942

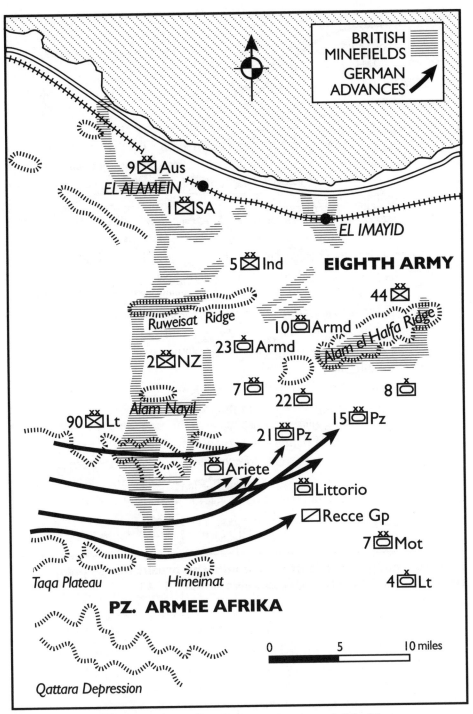

MAP 9 The Battle of Alam el Halfa,
30/31 August - 7 September 1942

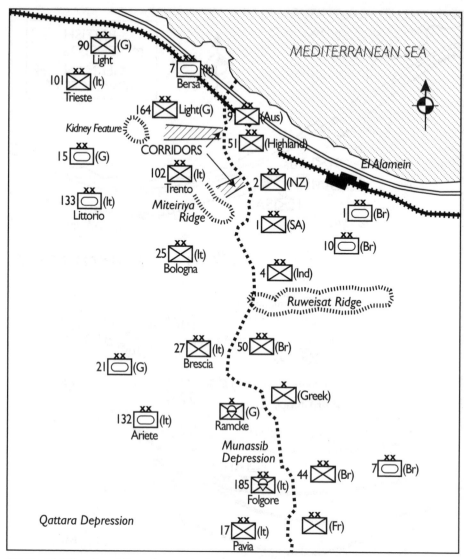

MAP 10 The final Battle of El Alamein, the breakthrough plan, Operation LIGHTFOOT, October-November 1942

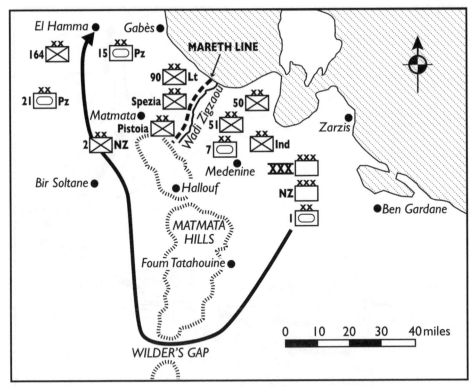

MAP 11 The Battle of Mareth, March 1943

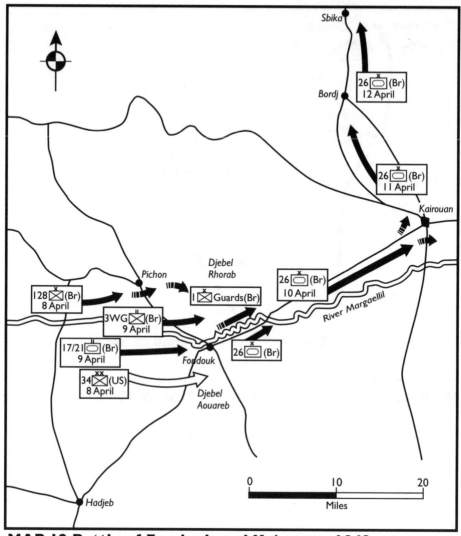

MAP 12 Battle of Fondouk and Kairouan, 1943

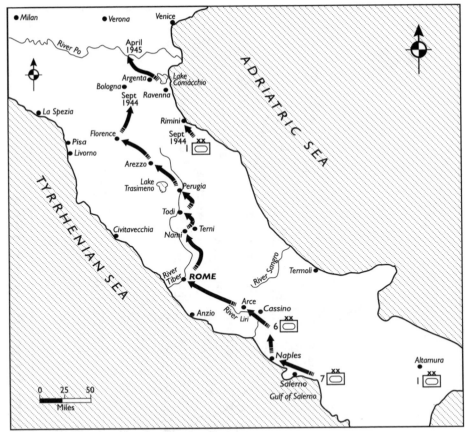

MAP 13 Italy: the Armoured Divisions

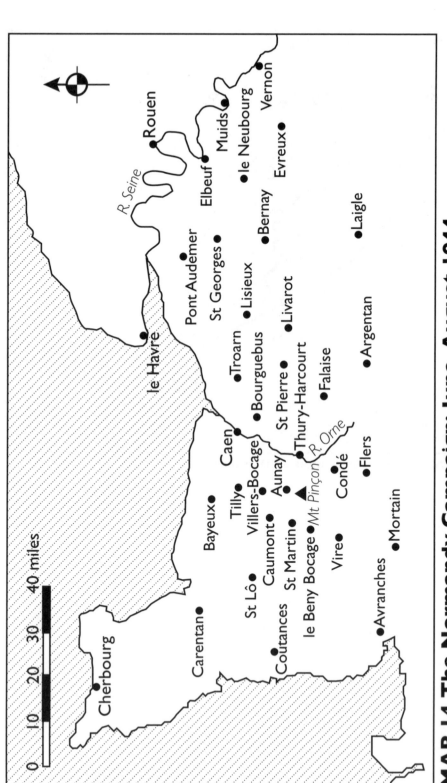

MAP 14 The Normandy Campaign: June–August 1944

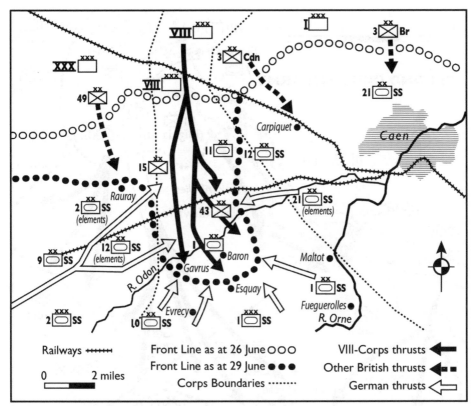

Railways ┼┼┼┼┼

0   2 miles

Front Line as at 26 June ○○○
Front Line as at 29 June ●●●
Corps Boundaries ·········

VIII-Corps thrusts ◀━━
Other British thrusts ◀■■
German thrusts ⬅

MAP 15 Operation EPSOM - creating the Odon Bridgehead
and German counterattacks of 29 June 1944

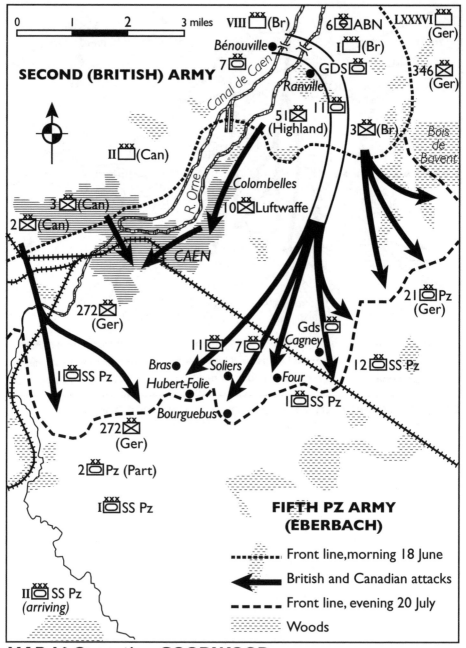

MAP 16 Operation GOODWOOD

Within the map:

0 1 2 3 miles

VIII (Br)   6 ABN   LXXXVI (Ger)

Bénouville   I (Br)

SECOND (BRITISH) ARMY   7   GDS   346 (Ger)

Canal de Caen

Ranville

51 (Highland)   11   3 (Br)   Bois de Bavent

II (Can)

R. Orne

Colombelles

3 (Can)   10 Luftwaffe

2 (Can)   CAEN

272 (Ger)   21 Pz (Ger)

Gds   Cagney

1 SS Pz   11   7   12 SS Pz

Bras   Soliers

Hubert-Folie   Four

Bourguebus   1 SS Pz

272 (Ger)

2 Pz (Part)   FIFTH PZ ARMY (EBERBACH)

1 SS Pz

.... Front line, morning 18 June

◄──── British and Canadian attacks

II SS Pz (arriving)   ── ── Front line, evening 20 July

▓▓▓ Woods

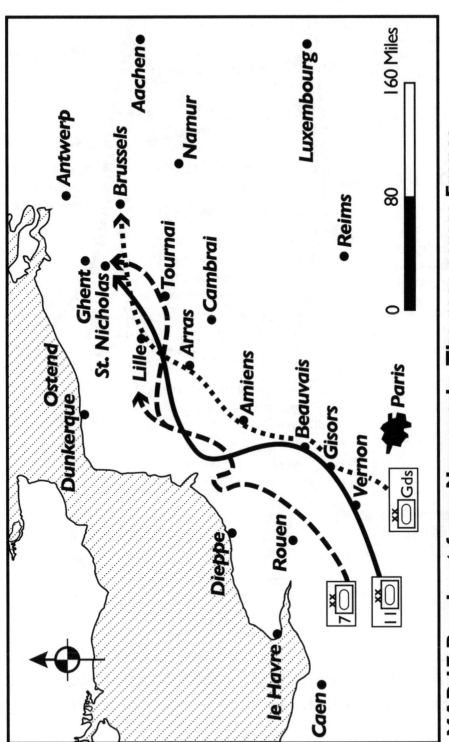

MAP 17 Breakout from Normandy. The race across France

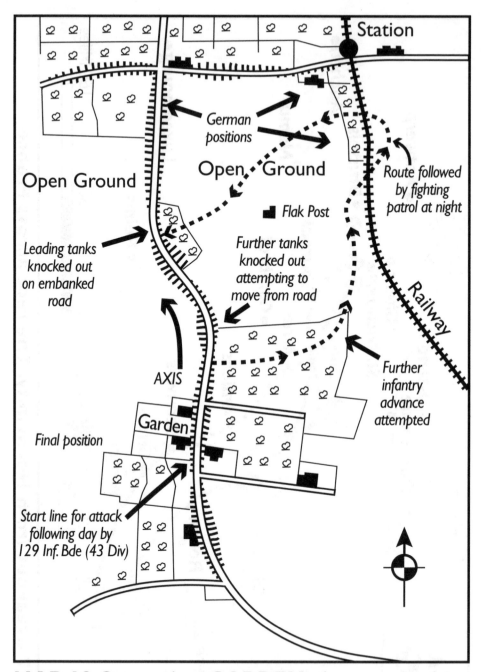

MAP 18 Operation GARDEN: the unsuccessful attempt to reach the airborne bridgehead at Arnhem

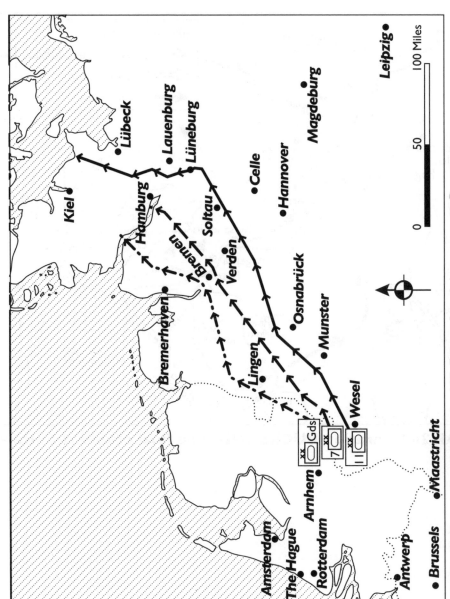

MAP 19 From the Rhine to VE Day: the drive across Germany

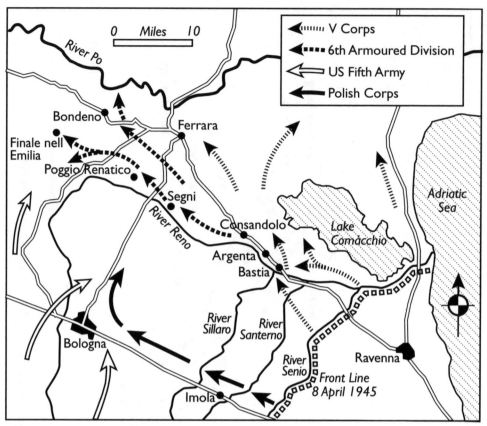

MAP 20 Operation BUCKLAND: The final offensive in Italy

Prologue

Across the land tanks rumble on their way to victory. Artillery roars in support and infantry engage enemy positions. In the sky above aircraft swoop to attack the enemy while other planes report the positions of the enemy artillery and strongpoints. Although the advance is opposed the attacking armies have the advantage of manoeuvre and firepower and the ability to disrupt the foe's communications. Ahead of them confusion in the enemy ranks and its high command aids the attackers.

France 1940, and the onslaught of Hitler's panzers, panzergrenadiers and stukas? No, France 1918 and the advance of the Allied armies with the British Expeditionary Force in the lead. This was the first campaign in which armour played a significant, and battle-winning, role. Most of that armour was British and the concept was entirely British. This was 'lightning war', or as the media would dub it in 1940, *blitzkrieg*. A British 'invention', by 1940 it seemed that the British army had forgotten the lessons it had taught the world in 1918 while the vanquished foe had absorbed them.

Since 1945 there has been a popular perception that British armour did not perform well in the Second World War while its performance at the end of the First has been all but forgotten. But was British armour really handled so badly between 1940 and 1945?

Introduction

The aim of this book is to examine the role of British armoured divisions during the Second World War, assessing performance and achievements, especially in light of the problems besetting British tank design. Eleven armoured divisions were formed: Guards, 1st, 2nd, 6th, 7th, 8th, 9th, 10th, 11th, 42nd and 79th. However, neither 9th nor 42nd Divisions ever saw action, being disbanded in the United Kingdom, 8th did not fight as a complete formation, and 79th was re-organized in 1943 to command all British specialized armour in north-west Europe. While many independent armoured brigades were formed, and frequently assigned to infantry divisions, their role is outside the scope of this book, although some of them will be referred to in the narrative.

The first campaign in which a British armoured division was involved was in 1940 in France, during which elements of 1st Armoured Division saw brief action. However, the division's arrival in France was too late and its story is not typical of the British experience with major armoured formations. With the withdrawal from France British land forces were engaged only in North Africa, initially against the Italians but, later, also against the Germans in a campaign that lasted until May 1943 with the deployment of considerable armoured forces. The earlier phases of the campaign were fought in the deserts of Egypt and Libya, an almost ideal battleground for tanks and a training ground for British armour, which learned many painful lessons.

By the time the North African campaign had moved into Tunisia, six British armoured divisions had been deployed: 1st, 2nd, 6th, 7th, 8th and 10th. However, 2nd, 8th and 10th were disbanded in North Africa, 8th never having fought as a division. Of the others, 1st and 6th went on to fight in Italy, where 1st Armoured Division was disbanded after the battle of Coriano Ridge but 6th served until the end, providing Eighth Army's spearhead in the final Allied advance to the Po in April 1945. Seventh Armoured fought briefly in Italy but was withdrawn for the invasion of north-west Europe, where it served throughout the campaign, together with Guards and 11th Armoured Divisions. The 'funnies' of 79th Armoured Division fought for the first time on D Day and were an essential asset for Second British and First Canadian Armies until the end of the war; they also supported American forces on numerous occasions.

Although ideas for armoured warfare strategy and tactics had been formulated and tested in the interwar years, it took several years of war before the British Army became an effective user of armour. It is often claimed that one reason for this was the presence of many cavalry officers who continued to employ outdated tactics, but it has to be said that the 'modern' officers of the Royal Tank Corps were guilty of preaching a deeply flawed message that was responsible for many of the travails suffered by British armour in the early years. Although the cavalry had been grouped into the Royal Armoured Corps together with the Royal Tank Regiment in 1939, it took the hard experience of the battlefield to forge a new concept of armoured warfare – and all too often the tutors were the Germans who had learned their lessons at the hands of the British in the First World War and whose concept of armoured warfare in the 1930s was much more realistic.

Moreover, the British concept of two classes of tank – an infantry-support, or I, tank and a fast-moving 'cruiser', or cavalry, tank did not help. Nor did the failure to create an effective British tank until the later stages of the war, forcing a reliance on American tanks. One major failing in British doctrine was the lack of an effective tank gun, with earlier tanks relying on weapons defective in hitting power and range. (Some prophets of armoured warfare, including Percy Hobart, must shoulder blame for this.) Although this failing was mirrored in early German tank design, the Germans were much quicker to resolve it than the British.

It was also mid-war before an ideal armoured divisional order of battle was achieved, even though an experimental training force, and exercises, between the wars had indicated just such an orbat. By 1943 the armoured division included: an armoured brigade of three armoured regiments and a motorized infantry battalion; an infantry brigade of three battalions, carried in lorries (later half-tracks); an armoured reconnaissance regiment; two field artillery regiments, of which one, equipped with self-propelled guns, deployed with the armoured brigade; anti-tank and light anti-aircraft regiments; two field squadrons and a field park squadron of Royal Engineers; and other support and service units. This orbat was altered in Italy where the terrain demanded a second infantry brigade. By the late summer of 1944 in north-west Europe the units of the armoured and infantry brigades in British armoured divisions deployed in battlegroups, a more effective system allowing greater co-operation between armour and infantry.

The book will examine how British armoured thinking evolved during the war, how that translated into the strategic and operational picture, how it was affected by the attitudes of commanders at various levels, and how enemy operational policy helped reshape ours. Since the contribution of commanders was critical, their role will also be considered.

The evolution of the tank will be studied too, from the early cruisers and I-tanks through to the successful Comet and its successor, Centurion, which was just too late to see active service in Europe. In addition the book will explore some long-held ideas about the effectiveness, or otherwise, of British armoured divisions and some of the actions in which they were involved and the theatres in which those actions occurred.

Chapter One

A New Weapon

Lieutenant John Gorman MC, 2nd (Armoured) Battalion Irish Guards in Guards Armoured Division, sat in the turret of his Sherman as shells from the guns of ten field regiments, three medium regiments and a heavy regiment of Second British Army roared overhead. Also in the air above the young officer were Hawker Typhoon fighter-bombers of the Allied Tactical Air Forces. In all, eleven squadrons of Typhoons operated a 'cab rank', ready to answer calls for support from any of the ground forces. It was 2.25pm on 17 September 1944.

> There was a huge artillery bombardment to get us out from the Escaut canal. In front of me … were eighteen tanks … and one, two, three, four, five, six, seven, eight, nine were knocked out and all these bodies tumbled out, burning, some of them. The Germans hit the first nine with great speed and accuracy. That was the kind of effect that their superior anti-tank guns had. They were in turn knocked out by Typhoon rocket-firing planes … We advanced then to a place called Valkenswaard, to another bridge which was captured and we were there by dusk that evening.[1]

Gorman was describing the opening phase of Operation GARDEN, the ground element of the offensive to capture and hold bridges over the Lower Rhine. Overhead the transport aircraft and gliders carrying men of First Allied Airborne Army passed en route to their objectives in Operation MARKET, the airborne element of the attack. Operation MARKET GARDEN, remembered best for the failure to seize and hold the bridge at Arnhem, is one in which British armour is said to have failed. However, the reasons for the failure of the operation lay in its planning stages, and with those who commanded at the highest levels, rather than with those who executed it. John Gorman and his fellow armoured guardsmen were no more guilty of failure than anyone else who fought in MARKET GARDEN. But the perceived failure, or sluggishness, of Guards Armoured Division has become one of the sticks with which to beat the British armoured divisions of the Second World War, to advance the argument that, even so late in the war, the British Army had still not grasped all the essentials of armoured warfare. Is this argument true? Did Guards Armoured Division fail on the road to Arnhem and did British armour still have much to learn in September 1944? To answer those questions we must look back on the evolution of British armour from 1916 until the outbreak of the war.

Britain invented the tank. And the British Army invented armoured warfare. The second statement does not flow naturally from the first. It would have been quite possible for British scientists and soldiers to have invented the tank and then fail to find a proper role for it. Indeed the later perceived masters of armoured warfare, the Germans, saw no role for tanks in the Great War and, therefore, failed to respond to the presence of British and French tanks on the battlefield by building their own: German tank production was minuscule whereas Britain and France produced thousands.

Although Winston Churchill laid claim to being the man behind the tank, he had not been alone in its development. The concept grew from an idea from Major Ernest Dunlop Swinton, a Royal Engineers' officer, for an armoured machine-gun destroyer. During the Boer War Swinton had been impressed with the power of the machine gun, then a relatively new weapon. In South Africa Swinton also met a mining engineer called Marriott with whom he maintained contact and from whom, in July 1914, he learned of an American innovation, the caterpillar tractor, produced for agricultural purposes by the Holt Company. According to Marriott, this tractor 'had a remarkable cross-country performance' which might suit it to military purposes. There the idea might have languished had it not been for a serendipitous decision by Field Marshal Lord Kitchener that sent Swinton, by then a lieutenant colonel, to GHQ of the British Expeditionary Force. Kitchener decided that Swinton, whose post was Deputy Director of Railways to the BEF, should become official media correspondent for the Force. Having banned all press correspondents from France, this was Kitchener's response to the general outcry about the absence of news from the front. With no job description to adhere to, Swinton created his own and travelled freely to observe the situation. As the war stalled in the autumn, and trench warfare developed, Swinton turned his mind to means of breaking what was already being identified correctly as linear siege warfare. With efforts to break through the German lines stopped by machine-gun fire and barbed wire, Swinton envisaged an armoured vehicle to provide protection against bullets, destroy machine guns and wire, and cross trenches. Remembering Marriott's letter about the Holt tractor he thought the vehicle could be the answer.

At the same time the Royal Naval Air Service, which operated armoured cars, wanted a mobile bridge to traverse obstacles where bridges had been destroyed, and this is where Churchill, then First Lord of the Admiralty, entered the picture. Admiral Bacon had proposed the production of a 15-inch howitzer to be towed on land; this captured Churchill's imagination as he had been impressed by the heavy artillery that the Germans were using in Belgium. Both Admiralty proposals, the mobile bridge and the howitzer, drew Churchill's attention to the caterpillar tractor, prompting him to establish the Admiralty Landship Committee. Needless to say, their Lordships were not best pleased.

Unable to see Kitchener to put his idea to him, Swinton had proposed to Sir Maurice Hankey, Secretary to the Committee of Imperial Defence, that some Holt tractors be used to build experimental fighting vehicles. Although Hankey was enthusiastic, there was no similar reaction from Kitchener or GHQ. However, Hankey broke the stalemate with a memorandum to Prime Minister Asquith in which he reflected on the difficulties of either side breaking through the trench system with conventional forces and weapons. He suggested that siege engines adapted to the modern era could be deployed. Such engines might include:

> Numbers of large heavy rollers, themselves bullet-proof, propelled ... by motor engines, geared very low, the driving wheel fitted with caterpillar driving gear to grip the ground, the driver's seat armoured and with a Maxim gun fitted. The object of this device would be to roll down barbed wire by sheer weight, to give some cover to men creeping up behind, and to support the advance with machine-gun fire.

In this 'device' may be seen the tank's origins. Hankey's note was also seen by Churchill who wrote to Asquith proposing a similar idea and then set up his Admiralty Landship Committee. Some Holt caterpillar tractors had already arrived in Britain, purchased by the War Office's transport department, which had been trying to obtain the funds to buy them since 1909. However, the Holt tractor played no further part in the development of the tank. While it looked as if the Admiralty was going to produce the siege machine to end the stalemate of trench warfare as working examples of the landship began to appear, Churchill was sacked as a result of the Gallipoli tragedy and his disagreements with the First Sea Lord, Sir Jackie Fisher. It appeared that the project might be killed off by the Admiralty. However, it was taken over by the War Office although Carver suggested that this was 'apparently more out of pique that the Admiralty was interfering in army affairs than anything else'.

Major Ralph Glyn then entered the picture. A liaison officer between the War Office and BEF GHQ, Glyn knew of the work of the Admiralty Landship Committee and, while visiting GHQ in May 1915, told Swinton about it. This was news to the latter but, encouraged by Hankey, who visited GHQ with the prime minister in late May, he drafted a paper, described by Carver as 'highly significant and very remarkable', which he submitted to GHQ on 1 June.

This paper, entitled 'The Necessity for Machine-gun Destroyers', examined why previous attacks had failed to overcome machine guns and obstacles and provided a detailed account of how the proposed new fighting vehicles could succeed.

> These machines could be petrol tractors on the caterpillar principle of a type which can travel up to 4 miles an hour on the flat, can cross a ditch up to 4 feet in width without climbing, can climb in and out of a broader cavity and can scramble over a breastwork. It is possible to build such tractors. They should be armoured with hardened steelplate, proof against the German steel-cored, armour-piercing and reversed bullets, and armed with – say – two Maxims and a Maxim 2-pounder gun. It is suggested that they should be employed as a surprise in an assault on the German position on a large scale. To enable the element of surprise to come in, these machines should be built at home secretly and their existence should not be disclosed until all are ready. There should be no preliminary efforts made with a few machines, the result of which would give the scheme away.

The first British tanks went into action during the Battle of the Somme on 15 September 1916. Only two dozen took part in the assault, instead of the fifty planned, the others having suffered mechanical or other problems. Thus Glyn's proposal that they should first be used on a large scale had been ignored. Although the Germans were taken by surprise by the appearance of the first tanks, they also discovered that the armoured vehicles were vulnerable to direct or indirect artillery fire while heavy machine-gun rounds could penetrate their armour. By 1917 many more tanks were available and over 200 British tanks were deployed at Ypres during the summer; the French army had deployed over a hundred in April. While the Battle of Cambrai, in November 1917, is often seen as the first large-scale British use of tanks that was not true. Nor is it true that they proved a battle-winning weapon. In fact, once again the Germans exploited their weaknesses with artillery and infantry defences and most of the tanks were out of action by the second day of battle.

Nonetheless, the British Army was learning many valuable lessons which became clear in 1918 when, in the final offensive that led to victory, tanks played a significant role. British operational practice had evolved to improve co-operation between all arms – artillery, infantry, aircraft and armour all played their part in bringing about the German defeat. The tank had arrived as a new battlefield weapon and the British Army's Tank Corps had earned its reputation of fighting 'from mud, through blood to the green fields beyond', as well as four Victoria Crosses. One historian of the Tank Corps wrote that the last tank action of the war occurred on 5 November when eight Whippet tanks supported 3 Guards Brigade near Mormal Forest. By then, he commented:

> The Tank Corps was virtually at the end of its tether. It had been fighting non-stop for 96 days, with nearly 2,000 tanks and armoured cars in almost continuous action. Nearly half had been knocked out or damaged beyond local repair and sent to salvage, while over 3,000 officers and men had been lost, a grievous price to pay out of a Corps whose total strength was only 10,500. Nevertheless ... warfare would never be quite the same again. The tank was not yet 'Queen of the Battlefield', but the Tank Corps had shown what armoured forces were capable of achieving when properly led and given half a chance.

In the aftermath of war the Tank Corps was placed on the Army's permanent establishment and, in 1923, received Royal approval as the Royal Tank Corps. The Corps adopted the motto 'Fear Naught', although the unofficial motto 'From Mud, through Blood to the Green Fields Beyond' was also used and was reflected in the Corps' official colours.

The years following the Great War saw a great debate on the role of the tank in war. Much of this centred round the thinking of Major 'Boney' Fuller who, in May 1918, when it seemed that the war would last into 1919, had proposed what he dubbed 'Plan 1919'. Shaping Fuller's thinking were four main factors. The first was his belief that the Battle of Cambrai might have resulted in a decisive breakthrough had there been tanks sufficient to maintain the offensive's momentum and if, to coincide with the armoured attack, a diversionary attack had been launched on another sector of the front to draw off German reserves. Secondly, Fuller had been influenced by the Allied decision to maintain a defensive posture in 1918 while preparing for a major offensive in 1919 when the American Expeditionary Force would have attained its intended strength. This 'pause' would allow time for industry to produce the tanks necessary for the British, French and US armies 'and an army based on tanks would need less manpower than one relying primarily on infantry and artillery'. His awareness of the confusion which the German Operation MICHAEL offensive in March 1918 had caused in the Allied command led Fuller to consider that the true target for an Allied offensive should be the German command organization. This was the third factor influencing his thinking, of which he wrote:

> I began to turn from the purely frontal attack to the possibilities of flanking operations, and a little later on to a definite rear attack effected by depositing groups of machine gunners in rear of the enemy's fighting front in order to cut its garrisons off from their reserves. The next step was a simple, though dramatic, one – ... to cut an entire army or group of armies off from its command. The argument was a perfectly logical one, namely as a government depends on its power on a national will, so does an army depend for its power on the will of its commander and his staff: cut that will off, and the army will be paralyzed.

Fuller's final influencing factor was the Medium A, or Whippet tank, which was lighter and faster than existing designs. Examples of Whippet were in France when Fuller wrote his paper and another proposed light tank, Medium D, would weigh less than twenty tons, and travel at 20mph with a range of 200 miles. As well as being the first tank to feature sprung suspension, Medium D was central to Fuller's Plan 1919: he foresaw some 2,000 of them being deployed in an offensive including a total of almost 5,000 tanks.

Who was Fuller? Known as 'Boney', he had quickly recognized the tank's potential. Although tanks made their battlefield debut on the Somme in September 1916, not until Cambrai in 1917 did they show their full potential. In between, Fuller had joined the staff of Lieutenant Colonel Hugh Elles, commander of all tanks in France. Fuller wrote the first training memorandum on tank warfare before producing Plan 1919, proposing the use *en masse* of Allied tanks in an offensive in 1919, when the Allies would move over from their defensive posture. He proposed a breakthrough by 790 of the new Medium D tanks, supported by aircraft, aimed at the enemy's major headquarters to create panic and confusion. At the same time artillery and infantry, together with 2,592 heavy tanks and another 390 Medium Ds, would attack along a ninety-mile front before a pursuit, intended to destroy the enemy high command and communication centres and disrupt his reserves, was launched by 1,220 medium tanks. Fuller's plan demanded some 5,000 tanks, about half of them British; the French and Americans would provide the remainder in equal proportions. At the War Office Fuller's paper was refined by General Capper to become a proposal that was tabled to the Supreme Allied War Council under General Foch in July, by which time the number of tanks needed had increased to 10,500.

Plan 1919 was never implemented as the Allies achieved victory in the hundred days' campaign that began in August 1918. In that final campaign the Allies used all arms, including air forces, to defeat the German armies in the field. The medium tanks, so important in Fuller's thinking, proved their value as mechanized cavalry and not simply as machines for breaking the stalemate of trench warfare, or as siege machines, the intended role of the earlier heavy tanks. Although never tested in the laboratory of action, Plan 1919 achieved considerable credibility, which it did not merit. Macksey described as 'a flight of fancy' Fuller's imagery of companies of Medium Ds using naval tactics in the manner of a fleet at sea. That industry could have produced so many tanks in the time required was yet another 'flight of fancy' on Fuller's part.

The *RUSI Journal* published Fuller's essay on tank warfare* which earned him RUSI's Gold Medal for 1919; there had only been one other contender. The essay sparked controversy which created a divide between those who identified the tank as critical to future battlefield planning and operations, and opponents of mechanization. Fuller's opponents corrupted his arguments to suggest that he was proposing an all-tank army rather than a balanced all-arms mobile force. For the large number of believers in Plan 1919, Fuller's Gold Medal added to their perception of it as the Holy Grail of modern, mechanized warfare. Fuller, Plan 1919 and the *RUSI Journal* essay all influenced the thinking of many between the wars.

In Britain one of the most significant decisions was the creation of the Experimental Force on 1 May 1927. Commanded by Colonel R. J. Collins, this included armoured cars and light tanks for reconnaissance, a medium tank battalion deploying forty-eight Vickers medium tanks, a mechanized machine-gun battalion, a battery of Birch self-propelled guns and a mechanized engineer company. The Force's manoeuvres on Salisbury Plain that summer were attended by many observers but although the CIGS, Field Marshal Sir George Milne, waxed eloquent about the future of armoured forces – and the Experimental Force had trounced 3rd Division, supported by cavalry, in a major trial – it was disbanded in November 1928. However, it may be regarded as the father of all the armoured formations that followed while its work was noted in the armies of other nations, including the USA, USSR and Germany. Some of its personnel were to become noted proponents of armoured warfare, especially Tim Pile who would command the UK's anti-aircraft defences during the Second World War, Giffard le Q. Martel, who would command the Royal Armoured Corps, and Percy Hobart, the future commander of 79th Armoured Division. Although Milne's support proved temporary, and the Force 'was both first light and false dawn', it did point the way to the future.

---

* 'The War on Land: The application of recent developments in the Mechanics and other scientific knowledge to Preparation and Training for Future War on Land.'

There followed Brigadier Charles Broad's official publication *Mechanised and Armoured Formations*, issued in 1929, based on the Experimental Force's work. Known as the *Purple Primer*, from the colour of its covers, it described what armoured forces could do and what their limitations were, how they could best be organized, and their employment in action. Broad assumed that such formations would be controlled by radio in any future war, an extremely daring prediction in 1929. Within two years his prediction was proved accurate when he took command of 1 Tank Brigade, the Army's first such formation, and gave a demonstration on Salisbury Plain, in front of the Army Council, in which the entire formation manoeuvred in perfect formation under radio control in fogbound conditions.

Britain might have been at the forefront of developments in armoured warfare at this point but its lead was soon lost. By the mid-thirties a resurgent Germany had created a *Panzerwaffe* of three armoured divisions and was experimenting with new tanks while the Red Army was looking towards the development of tanks suitable for deep operations akin to those the Germans would carry out in 1940. Not until 1936 did the War Office agree to establish Britain's first armoured division, the Mobile Division. Born out of a decision to replace the Cavalry Division with a new mechanized formation based on the experience of recent exercises, the Mobile Division later became 1st Armoured Division.

The creation of the Mobile Division was a landmark in the creation of British armoured forces, but it was formed against the prevailing background of a re-armament programme in an era when the harsh economic climate meant that all three services were scrambling for shares of a limited defence budget. The Army came third in the battle for funding with the Royal Navy and the Royal Air Force receiving priority. But, even then, armour was not *the* priority for funding within the Army. Given the concerns about strategic bombing and air attack on the United Kingdom, anti-aircraft defences were considered more important than tanks. Moreover, the Army was still perceived as an imperial gendarmerie with its principal role the defence of Britain's overseas possessions and, especially, of the Indian empire. Thus it was that, in this decade, Britain lost its lead in the development of tanks.

Although that loss was due to a lack of development funding there were other reasons, not least the early deaths of some leading tank designers, especially Sir John Carden of Vickers, killed in a 1935 air crash. Shortage of funding meant that there were only two centres of research and development, the Royal Ordnance Factories and Vickers Ltd, neither with large design staffs. The meagre annual budget for tanks (between £22,500 and £93,750 in the years 1927 to 1936) meant that they were just about kept in work. There was nothing to persuade other companies to become involved in tank design and construction. J. P. Harris summed the situation up:

It was impossible to interest other firms in tank design and development without giving a definite guarantee of orders later and this had not been practicable until the beginning of a serious rearmament effort in 1936. There had consequently been a dearth of ideas and 'a very narrow field of research and experiment'.

Such factors lay behind the prevailing situation in October 1936 when the Committee of Imperial Defence (CID) learned the sad state of Britain's armoured strength: fewer than 400 tanks in service (166 medium and 209 light), most of them obsolete, a judgement that included all the mediums. Britain was still operating tanks that had been effective AFVs in their heyday, but that heyday was far behind them. Even 1936's light tanks would be hopelessly outdated by the outbreak of war.

In spite of all the pioneering work, Britain lagged behind Germany. There had been no shortage of ideas on the development of tank warfare, some unrealistic, which had inspired the tank arms of other nations. Heinz Guderian, for example, praised Percy Hobart and is even said to have proposed a toast to him. That the Germans had looked to Britain for ideas on armoured warfare is not surprising. No one else was developing such a doctrine, except the Russians, who were being very secretive; the Americans, retreating into isolation after the Great War, had disbanded their tank units while the French saw tanks only as a support to infantry and, in any case, felt secure behind their Maginot Line. However, the Germans had some idea of Red Army thinking as German tanks and formations were training secretly in the Soviet Union. German officers became aware of armoured formations at corps strength in the Red Army which must also have had an effect on their thinking. (Von Mellenthin asserted that Britain fell 'about ten years behind Germany in the development of tank tactics' before the outbreak of war.)[2]

Strangely there was a view in British political circles that the Germans would not develop an armoured force. On 15 March 1933 a Cabinet meeting was told that:

> In stressing the danger of Germany starting to build unlimited tanks you will of course not overlook that tanks are very expensive and that Germany has many other immediate requirements, including aircraft, as mentioned in Minutes of last Cabinet meeting.[3]

Such thinking may have influenced government decisions on the development of armoured forces as, four years later, a report on comparative strengths of 'certain other nations' and the UK could still claim that:

> Unless German construction of heavy tanks has already been carried out in secret on a large scale she will not in January 1939 possess tank units of a type or in the numbers necessary to give her a prospect of breaking through the French or Belgian frontier fortifications by means of AFVs.[4]

That same report stated that equipping Germany's regular (thirty-nine) and reserve (fifteen) divisions would be complete by January 1938 with the 'possible exception of medium and heavy tanks'. The threat of the German armoured forces was not recognized.[5]

And yet the Committee for Imperial Defence had presented to the Cabinet on 26 November 1934 a report which included this comment:

Tank training centres are reported at Zossen, Döberitz and Wünsdorf. Mechanical transport training centres are known to be located at the first two camps. Cavalry personnel in large numbers are apparently being transferred to mechanical transport units; our Military Attaché, Berlin, has seen … cavalry personnel still in breeches and boots but wearing the piping of mechanical transport troops. Two cavalry regiments are reported to be completely mechanized, but no details are available.[6]

By 1934 Percy Hobart was arguably the foremost proponent of armoured warfare in the British Army, and in Europe. In that year he took command of 1 Tank Brigade and the formation was given a permanent place on the Army List; Hobart was also Inspector, Royal Tank Corps. There is no doubt that he was wedded absolutely to the idea of the tank being the dominant battlefield factor. During the interwar period he devoted much time to developing a tank philosophy and planning for the future, as well as training. In training he was a mentor par excellence. Field Marshal Lord Carver, a junior Royal Tank Corps officer in 1936, recalled how:

Every summer the Tank Brigade concentrated in camp … on Salisbury Plain for three months of training. Here we exercised under the eagle eye of the fierce brigade commander, the great 'Hobo', Percy Hobart. He was a merciless trainer, who drove us all hard and overlooked no detail, his intensity matched by his keen interest in all ranks under his command. He was universally respected, admired and served with enthusiasm.[7]

However, Hobart's ideas on doctrine were not on a par with his qualities as a trainer. In the 1920s and 1930s he developed a concept of tank warfare in which may be seen some shadow of Fuller's Plan 1919. Also, there was the influence of Basil Liddell Hart who had written, in the early 1920s, of the 'expanding torrent' of an exploitation force once a breach had been created in an enemy's front. Hobart had written that 'The object is to destroy the enemy's will to resist': this could be achieved by striking at the heart or brain of that enemy and when that blow fell the fight would be over. Here may be seen the influence of Fuller. Hobart opined that 'a supreme effort and heavy casualties' would be worthwhile if a war or campaign was shortened. He saw a fast-moving armoured force as the means of achieving this.

And he formulated just such a force: a division of five basic elements: a Reconnaissance Group, with armoured cars, light tanks, motorcycle-mounted troops and anti-tank guns; a Fire Group, with light tanks, mobile artillery, infantry with machine guns and anti-tank guns; a Tank Group, with medium tanks, scout tanks and tracked artillery; a Divisional Troops Group, with three aircraft squadrons, engineers, including bridging equipment, and communications elements; a Maintenance Group, providing the administration for the entire division. This was a blueprint for a future armoured division. However, Hobart was to develop his thinking and to assert a doctrine that would not have worked in practice since the balance of the force was wrong. By 1937 he was advocating two types of armoured formation: the first was an 'army reconnaissance formation', a division of two cavalry brigades each of three cavalry tank regiments, while the second was a 'tank division' with three integral formations, a 'tank brigade', a 'cavalry brigade' with one or two cavalry tank regiments and a 'holding group' with mobile infantry, medium, anti-aircraft and anti-tank artillery, and engineers. Later still, when he was in Home Guard, he proposed a discrete 'armoured army' of ten armoured divisions fielding 10,000 tanks.

While Hobart was a man of vision, his vision was not always sound: although he acknowledged the need for artillery, engineers and infantry, he did not realize how important these arms would be to the overall formation. Much has been written about the sacking of Hobart as GOC of the Mobile Division, Egypt and, while there was almost certainly an element of personal dislike in that incident, the GOC British Troops Egypt, General Sir Henry Maitland Wilson, believed that Hobart's 'tactical ideas are based on the invincibility and invulnerability of the tank to the exclusion of the employment of other arms in correct proportion'. Hobart's biographer, Macksey, would note that 'Time would show the truth of that'.

Hobart not only got these factors wrong but also erred in two other areas: he did not see the anti-tank gun as being the threat that it was; and nor did he foresee the need for a tank gun larger than a 2-pounder (although he later realized his error and called for a 6-pounder). In 1935 he wrote that the future tank should have all-over armour, 360-degree-traverse for the main gun, ability to fire on the move, wireless control, and good cross-country speed. This was accepted by Colonel Giffard le Q. Martel, Assistant Director of Mechanization at the War Office from 1936. Acknowledging the need to compromise between the needs for mobility and armour, the resultant specification called for a tank with 'one high velocity gun, say 2 pounder'. It also added that a bigger projectile was 'not required' as this would 'mean fewer rounds to carry'. This specification led to the 'cruiser' line of British tanks. Martel had visited Russia and had seen tanks that rode on an American suspension system, designed by J. Walter Christie. The US Army had not bought Christie's suspension, considering it too expensive, but the Soviets had recognized its value. So did Martel who persuaded the Nuffield Organization to buy the rights from Christie and design a tank with the new suspension. In so doing, Martel not only set the scene for the cruiser line but broke the duopoly of tank design and production residing with Vickers and Woolwich Arsenal.

In contrast, Germany had designed lightly-armed and lightly-armoured tanks but with dimensions that meant they could be up-gunned and up-armoured. Their three panzer divisions were all-arms formations, but strong in tanks, owing something at least to the British mobile division concept. Germany had ignored completely the French model which would not stand the test of war in 1940. Thus German industry could concentrate its resources since there was no split in tank philosophy whereas in Britain the War Office demanded a heavily-armoured infantry support tank, or I-tank, which also carried only a light gun (in fact, early I-tanks were armed simply with machine guns), as well as the cruiser. For the *Panzerwaffe* there would be a light tank for reconnaissance and protection duties and a medium tank with versatile combat ability and good range.

These errors were bad enough. The situation was exacerbated by the problems that afflicted the tanks. As noted earlier, the majority of tanks, including all the mediums, in service in 1936 were obsolete. Little improvement had occurred by 1939 when many outdated light tanks still equipped armoured units. The I-tank/cruiser division did not help since it led to two lines of development, neither armed with anything heavier than a 2-pounder. In January 1939 the first A9 Cruiser Mark 1 tanks were issued. Designed by Sir John Carden shortly before his death, the prototype A9 emerged in April 1936. With a 2-pounder and 14mm (just over a half inch) of armour, it had a decent performance and, for its time, good anti-tank performance. Initially, two small machine-gun turrets were fitted to the hull, on the front corners, but were eliminated from the production version because they trapped fumes when the guns were fired. However, A9's suspension was bad, the ride was uncomfortable for the crew, and its maximum speed of 25mph (40km/h) was unimpressive. Even so, 125 examples were ordered.

But the War Office had also ordered two other cruiser tanks. A10, Cruiser Mark 2, resembled A9 but was produced by Vickers to the same specification. Vickers opted for a single machine gun, beside the driver, and for heavier armour at 30mm (about 1.18-inch); A10 also mounted the 2-pounder. Since the weight was heavier – 14 tons compared to A9's 12 – the speed was significantly lower at 15mph (25km/h). Nonetheless, Vickers received an order for A10 and 170 were built eventually. Both A9 and A10 saw service in France in 1940 and in North Africa. Since the speeds offered by A9 and A10 did not really match the concept of fast-moving tanks, capable of high-speed flanking movement, the War Office ordered yet another cruiser: A13 (Cruiser Mark 3). Its design was radically different and its manufacturer was not a traditional tank builder. A13 was designed by Nuffield Mechanization and Aero Limited, a company established by Lord Nuffield (Sir William Morris Bt had been ennobled as Lord Nuffield in 1934) as a branch of Morris Motors to build both tanks and aeroplanes in 'shadow factories'. As we have seen, Nuffield had been persuaded by Martel to buy the rights to J. Walter Christie's suspension. Not only did Nuffield license the suspension, he also bought an American tank which was subjected to close and detailed examination by his engineers. Christie's suspension, with large-diameter road wheels and large coil springs, became the basis for Nuffield's entry into the cruiser-tank market. With design work on A13 finished in January 1937 the first tank was ready before the year was out. Cruiser Mark 3 also mounted the inevitable 2-pounder and single machine gun, was powered by a Nuffield version of the American Liberty aero-engine and, since it was protected by only 14mm of armour, could exceed 30mph (48km/h). Thus it seemed that this newcomer to the production of tanks had created the machine most closely matching the cruiser concept.

However, it was felt that a tank should have better protection than that offered by A13 and so the War Office ordered another version, A13 Mark 2, with 30mm of armour, dubbed Cruiser Mark 4, production of which began in 1938. In all, 665 were built and some saw service in France in 1940 while many equipped armoured units in North Africa. Armament was the same 2-pounder main gun and machine gun and speed a maximum 28mph (45km/h) with a ninety-five-mile range which was a little less than Mark 3's 108 miles. Cruiser Mark 4 was plagued by mechanical problems throughout its service life, which did nothing for crew morale. In spite of Cruiser Mark 4's improved armour, and the fact that both it and Mark 3 met the requirements for a cruiser tank, the War Office considered that they should be supported by a heavier tank and set about trying to develop such a machine, under the titles A14 and A15. Both were abandoned in 1939 as neither showed any real advantages over A13, but still the War Office longed for a heavier cruiser and the London Midland and Scottish Railway Company (LMSR) was asked to build a revised heavy A13, or A13 Mark 3 which would appear under the guise of Cruiser Mark 5, or Covenanter, one of the worst examples of British tank design of the war.

Although the Nuffield Organization assisted in designing Covenanter the company chose not to become involved in its production. Instead Nuffield began work on a successor to its own A13 which became A15, or Crusader. The basic A13 layout was retained, with Christie suspension, and 2-pounder main gun in a lozenge-shaped turret that Nuffield had helped develop for Covenanter. It also mounted two machine guns, one for the driver, who would surely have been too pre-occupied with his own job to use it, and one in a small turret on the left front of the hull. As with similar turrets in A9, this was removed because fumes from the gun affected the gunner. Improvements to the tank's ride were also made with an additional road wheel being added on either side. Armour was to be 40mm (1.57 inches) but thicker armour was called for before production began.

The other basic type of tank in 1939 was the I-tank but there was not quite the same selection as with the cruiser. General Sir Hugh Elles, Master General of the Ordnance (MGO), had believed that the next war would be fought on much the same lines as the Great War and, therefore, the infantry would need a heavily-armoured tank to support them as they attacked across no man's land. He drew up a specification that included sound protection, machine-gun armament, and a maximum price of £6,000. Carden drew up the design but was dead before it was transformed into a not very impressive tank. When Elles saw the prototype being put through its paces he observed that it waddled like the popular strip-cartoon duck 'Matilda', and the tank had its name: Infantry Tank A11 became Matilda.

Since Matilda had been designed 'down to a price' rather than to an operational requirement, Carden had been forced to create a two-man tank, a concept already known to be wanting; the price precluded a three-man crew. The result was a narrow, well-armoured body topped by a one-man turret carrying a single machine gun. With 'spindly suspension' Matilda's waddling was limited to 8mph (13km/h), 'an expensive and complex method of taking one machine gun to war'. The Royal Tank Corps was not impressed and argued successfully for a three-man tank with a heavier gun that could be used as protection against other tanks. Thus was born a heavier model, A12, which became known as Matilda 2, although it was not a development of the original Matilda. The new tank made its appearance in 1938 and had the distinction of being the sole British tank to serve, in varying forms, throughout the Second World War.

Matilda 2 was superior to Matilda 1 in every respect: better designed, it had heavy armour and a 2-pounder gun in a one-piece cast, hydraulically-rotating turret, while its improved suspension was protected. Only 136 Matilda 1s were built, many serving in France where their lack of effective armament was a deadly disadvantage. Thereafter, surviving examples were used only for training. Matilda 2 went on to serve in North Africa and did sterling service until superseded by American-built M3 Grants and M4 Shermans; dubbed 'Queen of the Desert', its reign as such did not survive the introduction of German tanks to the theatre. Subsequently, Matildas filled several specialist roles, including mine-clearing, bridge-carrying and flame-throwing, although the Australian Army used them operationally in the Pacific where their heavy armour remained impervious to Japanese anti-tank guns. With armour of up to 78mm (3 inches) and a speed of 15.5mph (25km/h) Matilda 2 was, for a significant time, the best British tank.

Whereas Matilda was a War Office inspired design, another I-tank was in production when war broke out. Valentine was a product of Vickers Armstrong, who drew on their experience with cruisers and incorporated cruiser features. The company believed that they could design a tank superior to Matilda and took their concept to the War Office in the hope of gaining an order. Since the design was submitted on 14 February 1938 it is believed that this is why the resulting I-tank came to be called Valentine (it is more likely to be an acronym from the manufacturer's address: Vickers Armstrong Ltd, Engineers, Newcastle upon Tyne). War Office prevarication meant that over sixteen months passed before a decision to order was reached. Needless to say, the War Office also called for the earliest possible delivery of the 275 tanks ordered.[8] In May 1940 Vickers Armstrong delivered the first Valentines, too late to see service in France. However, the tank saw considerable service in North Africa. As with its contemporaries, it was armed with the 2-pounder and a machine gun, but some were fitted with 3-inch howitzers as close support tanks; Valentine would later carry the 6-pounder gun. It was reliable and tough, if a challenge for drivers. In general it was popular with crews even though the turret was cramped and did not offer the best all-round vision – defects common to other contemporary British tanks. With armour up to 65mm (2.55 inches) and a maximum 15mph speed, Valentine's range was ninety miles. One unusual source of praise for it was the Red Army, to which over 2,600 Valentines were supplied; most were Canadian built, a version described by the Soviets as 'the best tank we have received from any of our Allies'. With sound hull design and reliable running gear, Valentine went on to be the basis of several specialized armoured vehicles, including the Archer self-propelled 17-pounder anti-tank gun. Although it passed the operational mantle to other tanks, Valentine proved the concept of the DD swimming tank and such engineer support roles as bridgelaying and was also used in experimental work with flame-throwers and mine-clearing. Despite being obsolete by mid-war, Valentine was built in greater numbers than any other British tank: 8,275 in the UK and 1,420 in Canada.

With the exceptions of Crusader and Valentine, which were to be upgunned with 6-pounders, none of these tanks could carry anything other than a 2-pounder as their designs did not permit the necessary modifications. British tanks also suffered from what now seems a strange restriction: to save track wear, tanks were transported by rail and had to fit within the limits of railway loading gauges (the side-mounted air louvres on Churchills had to be removed for rail travel) whereas the continental gauge was wider and higher. Moreover, since British forces would operate overseas in the event of war, weight was a greater consideration since tanks would have to be carried by ship whereas the Germans did not consider this factor in their designs.

One piece of equipment common to all early cruiser and I-tanks was the 2-pounder gun. Initially intended as a tank gun, this also became the 2-pounder anti-tank gun and when formally approved, on 1 January 1936, was 'undoubtedly the best anti-tank gun in the world'.[9] Firing a standard 2-pounder anti-tank round, the muzzle velocity was 2,650 feet per second (806 metres per second), maximum range was 8,000 yards (7,315 metres) and it could penetrate 42mm (1.65 inches) of armour sloped at 30 degrees at 1,000 yards (914 metres). When introduced into service it could penetrate the armour of any German tank and remained an effective weapon even in 1940, although it was nearing the end of its useful life. Many writers have commented that no high explosive (HE) round was available for the 2-pounder but this is not so.[10] A shell with a small TNT filling was produced for use against soft-skinned vehicles and static defended positions but it appears that this round was not issued to tank units. The lack of HE rounds was to put British tanks at a disadvantage on many occasions.

By the time war broke out the successor to the 2-pounder had been designed and its prototype built. This was the 6-pounder, orders for which were placed in June 1940, but the first guns were not produced until November 1941. (The delay was occasioned by the decision to concentrate production on the 2-pounder, over 500 of which had been lost in France. It was felt that much time would have been lost in setting up 6-pounder production which would have left the Army without anti-tank guns. The need to have equipment was considered greater than the need for better equipment.) Of course, this meant that the tanks, both cruiser and infantry, had to soldier on with their 2-pounders. As far as most contemporary tanks were concerned, up-gunning to the 6-pounder would have been impossible since there was insufficient room to fit the new guns in existing turrets. The exception was Crusader, which could accept the new gun in its more spacious turret.

Another major change in 1939 was the creation of the Royal Armoured Corps (RAC) which came about following the work of a committee established by the Army Council in early 1938. Chaired by Lieutenant General Sir Bertram Sergison-Brooke, the committee considered the organization of the mechanized cavalry units and the Royal Tank Corps 'in the light of the difficulties of peace training and the provision of the reserves of personnel for war'. By now many Cavalry of the Line regiments had been mechanized and equipped with armoured cars and light tanks. The Royal Tank Corps had also been expanded with its centre at Bovington becoming the Army Armoured Fighting Vehicles School on 1 April 1937. Royal Tank Corps personnel were involved heavily in training not only their own RTC personnel, but those of the mechanized cavalry regiments and Indian Army cavalry regiments that were also becoming mechanized. By the time the Sergison-Brooke Committee settled to its task, there were eighteen mechanized cavalry regiments and eight RTC battalions. The committee heard evidence that the Cavalry was experiencing difficulties in recruiting, due to uncertainty about the future of its units. Many avoided the Cavalry because it was horsed and perceived to be outdated while the RTC was seen as more modern and its ranks were full. Moreover, the RTC was creaming off the best of those joining the Army. Cavalry and RTC training also differed widely: each cavalry regiment did most recruit training 'in house' whereas RTC recruits went to Bovington for twenty-seven weeks' training before joining a battalion. The committee eventually concluded that the mechanized cavalry and RTC should be brought together in one corps. However, the recommendation stopped short of advocating complete amalgamation, although the committee believed that this would happen eventually.

The final recommendation was to create a Royal Armoured Corps with all recruits wearing the same cap badge and uniform until completion of training and posting to units. Although a new depot was desirable, Bovington would fill that need in the meantime while an RAC Pay and Records Office would also be established. Among recommendations rejected were those suggesting that I-tanks should become an Infantry responsibility and the adoption of the title 'Armoured Cavalry'. Since a corps within a corps was not considered appropriate the Royal Tank Corps would become the Royal Tank Regiment. On 4 April 1939 the Secretary of State for War, Leslie Hore-Belisha MP, announced the creation of 'a Royal Armoured Corps with precedence in the Army immediately before the Royal Regiment of Artillery'.

When war broke out in September 1939 the German Army could field six armoured divisions, although most of their equipment was obsolete. The British Army had only two armoured divisions, one of them in Egypt, which also deployed obsolete equipment. The plans of those German generals who advocated armoured warfare had not been pursued with the necessary fervour by their fellow generals and some ninety per cent of German tanks were obsolete by late 1939. Ironically, the German army made its reputation for fast armoured warfighting with tanks that were hardly worthy of the name: the planned light and medium main battle tanks, which became PzKw III and PzKw IV, had been delayed by 'design and production problems [and] it had been necessary to introduce a stop-gap training tank'. This became PzKw I, a six-ton machine with only two machine guns which, when it appeared in 1934, was already obsolete. Another interim light tank was called for: PzKw II was introduced but, weighing only nine tons and with a 20mm gun, was also hardly fit for purpose. By 1939 PzKw II was outclassed by foreign machines with its armour unable to offer its crews adequate protection against modern anti-tank guns, including the British 2-pounder. It was only in 1936 that production models of PzKw III and IV left the factories. Weighing twenty tons each, PzKw III mounted a 37mm anti-tank gun (instead of the 50mm gun that Guderian had asked for to deal with the heavier armour he foresaw being fitted to opponents' tanks) while PzKw IV had a short-barrelled 75mm low-velocity weapon that could fire both armour-piercing and high explosive rounds. However, when German forces crossed the Polish border on 1 September

1939, there were only 309 PzKw IIs and IIIs in total, with but ninety-eight being IIIs, from a total of 3,195 tanks on strength. Rather than the PzKw III providing seventy-five per cent of Germany's front-line tanks, only one tank in thirty-two was a PzKw III. (Of the tanks in service in September 1939, 1,445 were PzKw Is, little more than machine-gun carriers like Matilda 1, with 1,226 PzKw IIs; another 215 PzKw Is were in use as command tanks. The Germans also deployed significant numbers of Czech LT-35 and LT38 light tanks.)

The German armoured division of the period usually included a tank brigade of eight battalions in two regiments, a motorized infantry brigade of one regiment, a motorcycle battalion, an artillery regiment, anti-tank, reconnaissance and engineer battalions, and medical, signal, supply and administration units. Strength averaged 11,790 men manning 328 tanks, 101 armoured cars, 226 machine guns, of which forty-six were heavy, forty-eight light or medium mortars, eight light infantry guns, forty-eight anti-tank guns, twenty field howitzers, eight of which were heavy, four 100mm cannon and twelve light anti-aircraft guns.

Let us look now at the British counterpart. As already noted only two British armoured divisions were in existence in September 1939. In Britain was the senior of these formations, 1st Armoured Division, while its companion was stationed in Egypt. Formed in 1937 with Alan Brooke, the former Director of Military Training and future CIGS, as its commander, by the outbreak of war it had been renamed 1st Armoured Division and included two armoured brigades, one light and one heavy, each of three regiments or Royal Tanks' battalions, and a Support Group comprising a Royal Horse Artillery (RHA) regiment, a light anti-tank/anti-aircraft regiment, two infantry motor battalions, a field squadron and field park of the Royal Engineers with medical, signals and other support units. The division deployed 349 tanks, twenty-one more than its German counterpart and was commanded by Major General Roger Evans. The second formation, the Mobile Division, Egypt, formed under Major General Percy Hobart in September 1938, was renamed the Armoured Division (Egypt) when war broke out and would become 7th Armoured Division on 16 February 1940. Since it was far from the expected seat of war, it is no surprise that it was not up to strength. Although it ought to have disposed the same order of battle as its counterpart at home, its heavy tank brigade had only two tank regiments – the third did not arrive until October 1940 – and no support group. Not until January 1940 did the support group form; in September 1939 the divisional troops included 1st King's Royal Rifle Corps (1 KRRC), M Battery 3rd Regiment Royal Horse Artillery (3 RHA) and C Battery 4 RHA, with M Battery in the anti-tank role. Nor were there any divisional engineers until April 1940. The division deployed fewer than 300 tanks, including many obsolete Vickers Lights.[11]

While the Germans outnumbered the British in terms of armoured divisions, they had no great superiority in tank quality. Both armies relied heavily on obsolete or obsolescent designs but the Germans held the advantage in that they had a well-defined doctrine for armoured warfare. Or had they?

Leading German proponents of armoured warfare, such as Guderian, found opposition to their ideas in the ranks of the high command. Guderian had argued that the armoured branch should include all other arms, which would adapt their tactical doctrine to that of the tank. He wrote in 1936 that infantry, artillery and engineers would be motorized and partially armoured 'within the framework of the armoured division and the motorized infantry division'. Accordingly, they would 'adjust their new tactical programme and employment to their new speed'. Speed, above everything else, was to be the hallmark of the armoured division. There should be no parcelling out tanks amongst the infantry divisions, wrote Guderian, as this would revert to the early, failed, British tactics of 1916–17. Not until they deployed tanks *en masse* at Cambrai had the British achieved any success with the new weapon. Thus mass and speed were what would give the armoured divisions the advantage in future wars. In Fuller's words, 'speed, still more speed, and always speed' was critical.

Steeped in tradition, the German general staff believed in rapid movement leading to decision in battle with the use of new armaments and technology to achieve these. Central to their thinking was the concept of *Vernichtungsgedanke*, 'the idea of annihilation', a term originating with Alfred von Schlieffen, meaning the complete destruction of an enemy's forces by blows delivered swiftly and without warning from the flanks and rear. German thinking aimed at concentrating force at the decisive point on the battlefield and in engaging the enemy in *Kesselschlachten* or 'cauldron battles' through rapid manoeuvre in the shape of concentric encircling movements. History provided lessons to prove this doctrine. There was the classic example of the Battle of Cannae – still being quoted in 1991 by the American General Norman Schwartzkopf, commander of Coalition forces in the First Gulf War – in which Hannibal's Carthaginian army had carried out a quick double envelopment of a stronger Roman army in 216BC and the more recent, but very apt, example of Frederick the Great's defeat of an Austrian army that outnumbered his Prussian army by two-to-one at Leuthen in 1757. All this would suggest that the revolutionary new ideas of Guderian and his fellow armoured leaders would fall on fertile ground in the German High Command. It was not to be.

While *Vernichtungsgedanke* was still central to strategic thinking, the factor that militated against an immediate acceptance of the new ideas based on armour was the importance of the infantry in German thinking. Even in January 1940 the German army was stating plainly that 'The infantry is the main arm. All other arms are subsidiary to it'. Nor did this concept fade over the next two years as OKW's document *Glückhäfte Strategie*, published in 1942, included a chapter entitled 'Infantry, the Queen [of the battlefield]', the concluding paragraph of which read:

Each new weapon, so say the wiseacres, is the death of the infantry. The infantryman silently pulls on his cigarette and smiles. He knows that, tomorrow, this new weapon will belong to him. There is only one new factor in the techniques of war which remains above all other inventions. This new factor is the infantry, the eternally young child of war, the man on foot, even as Socrates himself was, the only and the eternal, who sees the whites of the enemy's eyes.

Although it is safe to assume that this piece of purple prose was written by an infantryman it contains an essential truth: the Germans saw armoured units and formations only as another tool with which to achieve *Vernichtungsgedanke*. Mechanized formations could counter the increased firepower that had been seen on the Western Front in the Great War. Thus the German High Command failed to see the true potential of armoured formations. As Matthew Cooper expressed it, they:

> failed to recognize what von Moltke had understood in the 1860s: that contemporary inventions may revolutionize the form of warfare, that they may offer possibilities, not only for the strengthening of traditional strategy, but also for its complete transformation – as with the railway, the telegraph, and the rifled weapon in the mid-nineteenth century, so with the lorry, the tank and the aeroplane in the early twentieth century. Out of these was to emerge a new idea of war so revolutionary in its implications that few could comprehend it, and even fewer dared to use it. There was all the difference in the world between a traditional strategy using modern weapons to further its precepts, and a novel strategy based on the potential offered by those weapons to revolutionize war. This new concept may be called the 'armoured idea'.

The 'armoured idea' had been born in Britain but had not been nurtured well. The Germans – or, at least, some of them – had adopted the infant and offered it some nourishment but not all that it needed to develop to full maturity. Nonetheless, the German infant had developed more than the British by the time both nations stood in arms against each other again in 1939.

Notes

The account of the origin and development of tanks and armoured warfare is based on the following: Carver, *The Apostles of Mobility*; Forty, *Royal Tank Regiment* and *World War Two Tanks*; Macksey, *The Tank Pioneers*, *A History of the Royal Armoured Corps* and *Armoured Crusader*; Harris, *Men, Ideas and Tanks*; Hogg and Weeks, *The Illustrated Encyclopaedia of Military Vehicles*. Information on the German army is from Cooper, *The German Army, 1933–1945* with other sources as follows:

1. Sir John Gorman, Interview with author, Feb 1995
2. Von Mellenthin, *Panzer Battles*, p.11
3. NA Kew, CAB23/75, pp.298–9
4. NA Kew, CAB24/273, p.21
5. Ibid
6. NA Kew, CAB24/251
7. Carver, *Out of Step*, pp.29–30
8. Foss, *Illustrated Encyclopaedia of the World's Tanks and Fighting Vehicles*, p.34
9. Hogg, *British and American Artillery of World War 2*, p.73
10. Ibid
11. Joslen, *Orders of Battle*, pp.13–15, 19–21

Chapter Two

First Blood: France 1940

There was no immediate clash of arms between British and German armies. The latter were engaged in overrunning Poland while the former were mobilizing to cross the Channel and join the French armies. While the Royal Navy and Royal Air Force were engaged almost immediately, ground forces would have to wait until the following spring before meeting their opponents. Meanwhile the British Expeditionary Force (BEF) prepared positions and lines of communication for the first clash of arms. Such was the lack of action in the early months of war that the media dubbed this period Phoney War, while soldiers would recall it as the *Sitzkrieg*.

Although the British Army of 1939 was the world's only fully mechanized army, the BEF did not take an armoured division to France initially. While 1st Armoured Division had been created as the Mobile Division in late 1937 it was not ready to deploy to the mainland in the autumn of 1939. Not fully equipped, it was held back in England. (Overall, on 11 July 1939, orders for 2,000 tanks had been placed against the Army's requirement for no fewer than 2,231.)

Thus, even in the new year, the division's two brigades lacked sufficient tanks with which to go to war. While the units trained for war many of their soldiers must have wondered if they would ever see action. Their greatest enemy seemed to be the weather of that foul, wet winter of 1939–40 or the inevitable toll of tragic training incidents: one man destined never to go to war but to become 5th Royal Tanks' first casualty of the war was twenty-one-year-old Trooper Louis Gliddon, killed in an accident involving a light tank.[1]

Plans to deploy 1st Armoured Division to France did not go smoothly. The exigencies of war – that great catch-all phrase to cover all forms of frictions – meant that the division lost both infantry motor battalions in mid-April to help form a War Office mobile reserve during the Norwegian campaign, thus leaving it bereft of its support group. A re-organization in March converted the light and heavy armoured brigades into 2 and 3 Armoured Brigades respectively, but did little other than change titles. Re-organization was still under way in May. However, 2 Armoured Brigade's cavalry regiments – Queen's Bays, 9th Royal Lancers and 10th Royal Hussars – had been provided with cruisers, many 'still short of equipment such as wireless, telescopes, and armour-piercing ammunition'. The division lost even more strength when a mixed force of tanks and infantry was sent to Calais on 22 May; this included the cruiser and light tanks of 3rd Royal Tanks (3 RTR). The infantry deployed to Calais was 30 Brigade, originally cobbled together as the War Office reserve for Norway with the two motor battalions of 1st Armoured's Support Group. All this before the division even left England.

Lord Gort, the BEF commander, had pressed for the deployment of the division to France but the first elements did not begin landing at le Havre until 15 May, five days after the German attack on France and the Low Countries had brought the Phoney War to an end. Advance parties moved to Arras but the Germans were already threatening that town, prompting a change of plan. With le Havre under heavy enemy air attack, and its sea approaches mined, the landing of the division's main body had to be made at Cherbourg where it began unloading on 19 May. From Cherbourg units were to move to Pacy-sur-Eure, some thirty-five miles south of Rouen, where the training area would become the divisional assembly area. Not only did 1st Armoured lack its infantry and 3 RTR, but it also lacked its divisional field artillery, some wireless equipment, any reserve of tanks, and bridging equipment. Its tank state totalled 257 tanks, including 143 cruisers. These inadequacies did not prevent General Headquarters from sending General Roger Evans orders on the evening of 21 May. He was:

(a) to seize and hold crossings of the Somme from Picquigny to Pont Remy inclusive. This task was to be regarded as most urgent and ... to be undertaken as soon as one armoured regiment, one field squadron, one Field Park troop and one Light Anti-Aircraft and Anti-Tank Regiment were available.
(b) to concentrate the remainder of the leading brigade in rear of the Somme;
(c) when this had been done, to be prepared to move either eastwards or northwards according to circumstances in order to operate in the area of the British Expeditionary Force.

Even had 1st Armoured Division been complete, complying with such orders would have been difficult, especially as the Somme crossings were already in enemy hands. Moreover, German forces were threatening the Seine crossings near Rouen. A further revised plan was called for. To safeguard the Seine crossings, the proposed jumping-off area for an advance to the Somme when the armoured units arrived, Evans deployed 101st Light Anti-Aircraft/Anti-Tank Regiment with a Royal Engineer field squadron. (Although the anti-tank element of 101st Regiment was equipped with 2-pounders, the AA batteries had only Lewis machine guns rather than the intended Bofors 40mm guns.) Next morning, elements of the division, including the Queen's Bays, arriving by rail south of the Seine, were ordered to move quickly to Forêt de Lyons, east of Rouen, to prevent German armour either breaking through the line of the lower Andelle towards the city or interdicting the arrival of additional British units scheduled to arrive next day.

That next day Evans ordered the Bays to move up to the Bresle river from Aumale to Blangy. As the tanks trundled off, Evans met with Lieutenant Colonel R. Briggs in Rouen; Briggs had arrived by plane on the 21st with confirmation of the earlier orders. He had fresh information that, due to the fog of war, was far from accurate. According to Briggs' information, the Germans were:

Acting defensively on the southern flank 'as far west as Péronne and possibly further still'; that only 'the mangled remains of six panzer divisions' appeared to have come through the gap between Cambrai and Péronne, to have carried out reconnaissances south of the Somme, found nothing and withdrawn to the river. The main German tank attack then taking place appeared to be on St Omer and on Arras.

Some of this may be described as wishful thinking while the description of 'six mangled panzer divisions' was woefully wide of the mark. There were ten panzer divisions operating between the BEF and the Somme and, by the 23rd, the Germans had brought forward *Panzergrenadier* – motorized infantry – divisions to hold the Somme crossings and bridgeheads south of Amiens and Abbeville. But Colonel Briggs believed that the French Seventh Army had engaged the enemy on the Somme on the night of 22/23 May and would cross the Somme on the 23rd. Accepting this, and believing that Franco-British counter-attacks at Arras on 21/22 May marked the opening of operations to seal the gap, GHQ of the BEF issued fresh orders to 'safeguard the right flank of the BEF during its southern advance to cut German communications between Cambrai and Péronne'. Evans was to advance immediately with whatever of the division were ready. 'Action at once may be decisive; tomorrow may be too late.'

Those who issued that order were blissfully unaware that even yesterday would have been too late. Unaware of the scale of the disaster facing the Allied forces, Evans considered that he had no option but to comply with the order, even though he appreciated that 'an operation to secure a crossing over an unreconnoitred water obstacle, attempted without artillery and infantry of my support group and carried out by armoured units arriving piecemeal direct from detrainment, was hazardous and unpromising of success'.

The situation was complicated even more by the French General Georges. He had other plans for 1st Armoured and informed the British mission at his HQ that, while Seventh French Army advanced across the Somme to the north, Evans' armour should mop up elements of the enemy south of Abbeville. Evidently, Georges had little idea of an armoured division's role and less of the operational situation. Lord Gort was informed of Georges' desire and responded that the division should 'not be used to chase small packets of enemy tanks'. Gort ordered that the division should carry out the task already assigned to it and 'make itself felt in the battle'. Needless to say, Gort had no information about the situation on the Somme.

Nor were those the only ideas on what 1st Armoured Division should do. General Robert Altmayer, commanding the left wing of Seventh Army, issued an order placing Evans' division under his command and instructing it to cover his left flank in an attack on Amiens. This was countermanded by the British Mission at General Georges' HQ which clarified that Altmayer had no authority over Evans, who ordered 2 Armoured Brigade, under Brigadier Richard McCreery, to make for the Somme that night. This brigade, which included 9th Lancers and 10th Hussars as well as the Bays, was still dispersed. Brigade HQ and the Bays were on the Bresle river, between Aumale and Blangy, having disembarked at Cherbourg on the 20th. However, the other two regiments had only disembarked at Cherbourg on the 22nd/23rd. Detraining south of the Seine on the 23rd they made best speed to link up with Brigade HQ and the Bays. They did so on the morning of Empire Day, 24 May, at Hornoy and Aumont, between Aumale on the Bresle and Picquigny on the Somme, having travelled sixty-five miles by road since detraining. In that same twenty-four hours they had also to prepare for battle.

When McCreery's units reached the Somme they found the crossings in German hands. On the five-mile front between Dreuil and Picquigny, three crossings were attacked but, with assaulting forces limited to a troop of tanks and a company of infantry in each case, all were seen off.

While 2 Armoured Brigade was moving up to the Somme, 3 Armoured was landing at Cherbourg. Brigadier John Crocker had only two units, 3 RTR having been despatched to Calais. By noon on 25 May 3 Armoured Brigade was in position, preparing for action. Both brigades were about to be committed to battle under French command as Altmayer was given operational command of 1st Armoured, and 51st (Highland), to support his Tenth Army, which also included three French divisions. Altmayer planned to attack the German bridgehead at Abbeville on the 27th with the British armoured brigades supporting his 2nd and 5th Light Cavalry Divisions. McCreery's brigade was to spearhead 2nd Light Cavalry Division's advance on the right flank while Crocker's performed the same role for 5th Light Cavalry Division on the left. Without success, Evans had tried to explain to the French commanders that a British armoured division was designed for a mobile manoeuvring role while its tanks were neither designed nor heavily enough armoured to make frontal assaults on well positioned anti-tank defences.

Under command of Colonel Berniquet, and in conjunction with his division, 2 Armoured Brigade was to capture high ground south of the Somme from Bray to les Planches. At the same time 3 Armoured Brigade, under command of General Chenoine was, with his division, to attack and seize the high ground from Rouvroy to St Valéry sur Somme. French artillery and infantry would provide support for both attacks. The Blangy–Abbeville road was to be the centre-line, with 2 Armoured Brigade east of the road and 3 Armoured to the west. Information on the enemy was patchy and made worse by the fact that German armoured-car and motorcycle patrols were dominating actively the area between the Somme and Bresle rivers. However, the country over which the advance was to be made was generally open and rolling, although there were some small woods and valleys with steep sides, neither of which favoured tanks, and several villages, some hidden partially by the woods. Due to inadequate reconnaissance little was known about German dispositions and numbers.

After some delay due to the French artillery not being ready, Altmayer's attack began at 4.30am on the 27th. The lack of adequate reconnaissance and preparation soon made itself felt. The right wing of the attack, including 2 Armoured Brigade, found that some of the small woods and villages hid anti-tank guns and the tanks made little progress, as they lacked effective artillery and infantry. 'Co-operation with the French divisions was ineffective, and close mutual support almost non-existent.' The result was heavy tank losses in 2 Armoured Brigade as German anti-tank guns took their toll.

Crocker's tanks had a very different experience. With much less opposition outside Abbeville good progress was made and the tanks reached the high ground overlooking the Somme close to Cambron, Saigneville and St Valéry sur Somme, the last-named at the mouth of the Somme. Nonetheless, German anti-tank guns claimed several casualties: 2 RTR lost six tanks near Abbeville and 5 RTR also suffered, although most of its losses were attributed to 'mechanical breakdown rather than enemy action'. Fifth Royal Tanks pushed through to St Valéry and mounted a 'moderately successful' attack 'gallantly carried out but not supported by the French'. No French infantry appeared to secure the ground taken by the tanks. When news arrived that afternoon that the French were digging in behind the high ground at Behen, Quesnoy and Brutelles the tanks were withdrawn.

It seemed as if 1st Armoured Division's work had been in vain. The Germans still held their bridgeheads and had a firm grip on the line of the Somme. British losses had been heavy, the result of pitting thinly-armoured cruiser tanks, without proper artillery and infantry support, against well-defended positions. Enemy action had claimed sixty-five tanks, some of which were later recovered, while fifty-five had suffered mechanical failures, often due to inadequate time to prepare them or carry out maintenance since they had landed in France. Damaged or broken-down tanks presented a problem as only basic repairs could be carried out at brigade workshops; for major repairs tanks needed to be moved to the divisional workshops south-west of Rouen which suffered from a shortage of spare parts.

Neither brigade of 1st Armoured Division was committed to action the following day, although the French divisions made another attempt to reach the Somme. Although some elements reached the river the German grip could not be broken. McCreery and Crocker's men spent the day re-organizing what was left of 1st Armoured's tanks: the Bays and 10th Hussars had been so reduced that they were formed into a composite regiment. A French heavy armoured division then arrived, 4th Armoured under Major General de Gaulle, which, although a powerful formation, had taken considerable punishment.

De Gaulle's division launched another attack on the 29th. Advancing astride the Blangy–Abbeville road, it met well-sited anti-tank guns in woods and along the ridge running north-west from Villers sur Mareuil. Once again the French artillery provided only token support while there were no infantry to consolidate any ground taken. Even so, de Gaulle tried again the following day but, once more, the attack failed. 'Against prepared positions, now strongly held, armour alone could achieve little. At the end of four days' fighting the enemy's bridgeheads remained untaken and the Somme and its crossings were still his.' De Gaulle, now remembered best for his time as French President in the post-war era, had been the leading advocate of armoured warfare in France in the late 1930s, although 'his views had not been heeded [and] his own chance to apply them came too late, and was too limited'.

The French had made little use of 1st Armoured after the first day of action, a situation which the British official historian considered a result of an instruction issued by Georges on the 28th. In turn, this appears to be the result of Evans, Colonel Briggs and General Swayne convincing Georges of the difference between British and French armoured divisions. Georges' instruction (No.1809) emphasized to French commanders 'the characteristics and proper employment of the British division'.

> The British division therefore bears a closer resemblance to a light mechanized division than to an armoured division. It is, in short, composed of light tanks, very lightly armoured and therefore vulnerable against enemy anti-tank guns.
>
> It is possible that during the recent period of crisis material may have had to be used in unfavourable conditions; it is none the less true that the employment of this division should not be contemplated except within the limits allowed by the nature of its equipment unless battle conditions make other arrangements vitally necessary.
>
> Further, we should be ready to use, as soon as possible, the Evans Division within the framework of a tactical group comprising in particular the 51st Division and the British Armoured Division – a group whose role on our left flank will be determined according to its capabilities.

Major General Victor Fortune's 51st (Highland) Division was then arriving south of the Somme from the Saar front. Already under French command, the Highland Division was grouped with 1st Armoured in the French IX Corps, commanded by General Ihler. However, the British generals could also receive orders from the War Office, via the Swayne Mission or by direct contact. Although operationally under French command, their logistic support was through the BEF's lines of communications (LoC). Other British troops in the area were grouped into an improvised division on 31 May, dubbed Beauman Division after its commander, General Beauman, including previous improvised groupings such as Beauforce, Vicforce and the aptly-named Digforce, composed of reservists in the Auxiliary Military Pioneer Corps. With the BEF's main body being evacuated from Dunkirk, 1st Armoured and 51st (Highland) Divisions were taking over positions along the Bresle to prepare for another attack on the enemy's Somme bridgehead in co-operation with French divisions. In the meantime, Beauman Division held a defensive line behind the Bresle and along the Andelle and Béthune rivers, defending Rouen, Dieppe and le Havre, from all of which non-fighting troops, equipment and surplus stores were being evacuated.

In the early days of June 1st Armoured Division was much diminished with the survivors of 2 Armoured Brigade formed into a composite regiment which, together with what remained of 1st Support Group, was placed under command of 51st (Highland) Division. Crocker's brigade was withdrawn to Rouen to refit. The Germans were making ready for the next phase of operations. The panzer divisions had been pushing towards the channel coast and ports but were now being switched to move southward and eastward with scarcely a pause. Such speed and flexibility of movement was the essence of mechanized manoeuvre warfare and there could be no doubt that the Germans had mastered it.

With the bulk of the BEF evacuated from Dunkirk, the Germans switched to delivering the final blows against the French armies with a new offensive on 5 June. Bock's Army Group attacked along the Somme with three of the five panzer corps (each including two panzer and a motorized division) assigned to it. Bock deployed one corps between Amiens and Abbeville while the others moved east of Amiens. A bold strike by Major General Rommel's 7th Panzer Division – including a river crossing that Liddell Hart described as one that 'would hardly have been given credit as practicable' – created a wedge in the French positions, taking Rommel beyond the Somme on the first day and twenty miles beyond by the following morning. With French defences breaking down, he was speeding towards the Seine on the 7th.

Until that day General Evans had little idea of the strategic situation, having received scant information from the French. Realizing that the situation was serious he called McCreery and Crocker together to make a plan that called for a composite force, under Crocker, to take up position near Gournay on the Dieppe–Paris road. With little left of 2 Brigade, the force would be formed largely from 3 Brigade, including those tanks ready for action, together with a squadron of light tanks from the Bays. While Crocker's composite force deployed, 2 Armoured Brigade and the rear echelons withdrew over the Seine.

That afternoon Evans met the Allied Commander-in-Chief, General Weygand, who ordered 1st Armoured Division to hold a twelve-mile line along the Andelle river astride the axis of the German breakthrough. Two British LoC battalions would be in the sector, with nine such battalions altogether stretched out in the sixty miles between Dieppe and the Seine south of Rouen. When Evans pointed out how weak his formation was, Weygand told him that he must stop the enemy with his hands and 'bite him like a dog' before finally conceding to Crocker's withdrawal southward should the position prove untenable. There must have been something of the atmosphere of the Mad Hatter's tea party at Tenth Army HQ that afternoon.

Evans reinforced Crocker with some more tanks to bring the composite force up to ninety-two, including forty-three cruisers, forty-two light tanks and seven I-tanks intended as replacements for 1 Tank Brigade. Thus Crocker's force had the muscle of only two understrength armoured regiments. From the light tanks Crocker created a reconnaissance squadron under Captain Pat Hobart, nephew of the famous Percy Hobart, to patrol across the Andelle. All 2 RTR deployed across that river, reinforced by a squadron of 5 RTR. Standing patrols were established to provide early warning of an enemy advance. However, at 7.45pm on 7 June, Crocker was told to take up position behind the Andelle and, therefore, ordered 2 RTR to withdraw.

Before that order could be acted upon, Rommel struck. His tanks had moved at what might best be described as 'Rommel speed', covering thirty miles that day. The patrols had been caught up in their onward rush with one patrol losing two tanks while its commander, Lieutenant Derek Barker, was wounded fatally. Pat Hobart had a narrow escape when confronted head-on with a German tank at 300 yards. Eluding the German, having engaged him with his .50 machine gun which kept stopping, he also lost contact with his own tanks but eventually made his way back, encountering another German tank en route.

Support Group, deployed near Forges-les-Eaux, was overrun while withdrawing, with those who escaped capture forced to retire northwards. While the Bays' light tanks and the Matildas covered the crossings south of Sigy, 2 RTR spent the night at Bosc Edeline, mounting patrols on the Andelle from Sigy northward. Rommel was Sigy-bound next morning as he sped to seize the Seine bridges at Elbeuf. Less than an hour before noon some of his panzers crossed the Andelle at Sigy, using a ford. When Rommel learned that a reconnaissance troop had seized intact a bridge at Normanville he switched his advance there to cross the Andelle before thrusting westward in twin columns, using side roads and by-passing villages to maintain speed by avoiding the refugee-crowded main roads. Meanwhile the British infantry along the Andelle were withdrawing. With the infantry safely away, 2 RTR withdrew. 'But the roads were crowded with refugees, as well as a French division that made no attempt to stand and fight. Thus the withdrawal was outstripped by Rommel's advance.'

At about 4.00pm Crocker decided to withdraw southward to cross the Seine at les Andelys or Gaillon before Rommel, en route for Rouen, could cut off his troops. Although the tails of both British and German formations brushed in this southward move, the withdrawal was carried out without interference: Crocker was heading for bridges farther south than those to which Rommel was making.

Crocker extricated his brigade successfully and, on the 9th, some pressure was relieved when Rommel's division was pulled back to undertake another rapid advance, one that would see 51st (Highland) and four French divisions cut off and captured. That evening Evans sent 3 Armoured Brigade back to refit while 2 Armoured remained to support the French. Neither had any real strength, McCreery's brigade deploying only two weak squadrons while Crocker's had only sixteen cruiser and nineteen light tanks. The refit was cut short on 12 June when Crocker was ordered to Conches, some thirty miles behind the Seine. He was not caught unawares since he had prepared for such an eventuality by organizing two composite squadrons. On reaching Conches with his thirty-two tanks he relieved McCreery's brigade, now only fifteen tanks strong, and found that 157 Infantry Brigade was arriving from England.

The overall situation in France was deteriorating rapidly with German thrusts in several sectors. With Tenth Army falling back westward and its neighbour retreating southward, Rommel's division was again brought into play. Its task on the coast complete, 7th Panzer was sent westward to seize Cherbourg. Crocker's command was ordered back sixty miles to Courtomer, between Laigle and Alençon where he learned that the rear part of his brigade was among British elements moving to Brest to embark for home.

In fact 3 Armoured Brigade would be diverted from Brest. McCreery's 2 Armoured Brigade, however, continued to there and evacuation, 'getting away with time to spare'.[2] When, on the 16th, Crocker was ordered south-westward again, he found himself near Alençon where he received fuel and rations. With petrol for only

225 miles he reported his situation to General Marshall-Cornwall, commanding the remaining British troops with Tenth Army, and was ordered to make for Cherbourg.

At midnight his small force – 409 personnel, twenty-nine tanks and sixty other vehicles – set off, diverting via Mortain to avoid XII French Corps, which was retreating across his route. Once through Mortain, the roads were less congested and he made better time. During a brief afternoon stop near St Lô he heard a radio report that the French government was suing for peace which hastened his steps. In spite of further delays, he reached Cherbourg that night. In twenty hours his tanks had covered 175 miles; in the previous six days the mileage was about 400. All fourteen A13 cruisers reached Cherbourg with the sole A9 abandoned just outside the city, and only two of his fourteen light tanks failed to reach their destination. (The tanks and key vehicles were loaded on the quayside although other vehicles were left there, having been sabotaged to prevent the enemy using them.) In his subsequent report, Evans had this to say of Crocker:

> The highest credit is due to the Brigade Commander, who displayed the cool determination and steadfast endurance which have always marked his conduct in the field and have inspired the confidence of those about him. A full share of the credit falls to the crews and unit fitters, also.

The experience of one tank of 5 RTR is worth recording. The battalion's composite squadron was dubbed Z Squadron, under Major Winship, and Ron 'Titch' Maple was one of its soldiers.

> Titch Maple's tank was commanded by Captain Le Mesurier ... Z Squadron finally received the message that they were to make their way to Cherbourg. The Squadron Commander studied the map, issued his instructions to the crew commanders and gave the order to his driver to advance. Fifty-six hours later, after driving almost non-stop, often under attack from the air – Titch received a minor head-wound when the column was machine-gunned – and always fighting for space on the roads with the pathetic columns of refugees, all the tanks in Z Squadron reached Cherbourg, as did their support transport ... It was 0400 hours on 16 June 1940: Sunday, but far from being a day of rest. There was no sign of the Navy but there were some transports. The orders were to abandon or destroy everything but the tanks and special vehicles, such as command vehicles, workshop lorries and wireless trucks. The Z Squadron tanks were loaded, with a great deal of haste and rather less than good order, on what appeared to be the last ship to leave Cherbourg. As they cleared the harbour they were bombed but this was not enough to wake the men who slept where they dropped on the deck.

Although strictly speaking outside the ambit of this book, it is worth taking a short look at an armoured action involving not the cruisers of 1st Armoured, but the I-tanks of 1 Tank Brigade. This action, often referred to as the 'Arras counter-attack', took place on 21 May. Had it not been for the persistence of Brigadier Vyvyan Pope, RAC adviser at BEF HQ, it might never have taken place. As it was, two RTR battalions – 4th and 7th – with two infantry battalions sallied forth to attack 'an unknown number of panzer divisions'.[3] En route to the start line 4 RTR lost touch with their infantry and went into action alone while 7 RTR took the wrong road, became mixed up, lost the infantry and, eventually, went into battle piecemeal. Of the seventy Matildas deployed, only sixteen were Mark 2s. Even so the I-tanks wrought havoc. When German anti-tank gunners opened fire on the Matildas their 37mm rounds made no impression on the British tanks whose machine guns took a heavy toll of the gunners. Something approaching panic swept through the ranks of the infantry of Rommel's 7th Panzer Division. With the tanks some miles distant on a different axis of advance, the infantry had no armour support and so 4 and 7 RTR punched through to the German gun lines, some three miles distant. But it was there that the attack faltered. Deployed with 7th Panzer were some Luftwaffe 88mm anti-aircraft guns, which were ordered into action against the Matildas. Even Matilda 2's armour was not proof against 88 rounds, although the German guns engaged at over 1,000 yards. With no infantry or artillery support and no HE rounds for their own guns, the Matildas had to withdraw.

Nevertheless, they had shown that the Germans were not invincible and had demonstrated what tanks, well handled and well led, could do. They had also taught the Germans a valuable lesson as a result of which panzers would be both up-armoured and up-gunned. And the legend of the 88 had been born. This weapon would plague Allied armour throughout the war, either as an anti-tank weapon or as a tank gun mounted in the later Tiger heavy tanks. However, the lessons do not seem to have been learned quite so well by the British.

The remnants of 1st Armoured Division reached Britain safely. Only thirteen tanks (six lights and seven cruisers) were brought back, the sum total of BEF tanks recovered to Britain, of a total of 704 sent to the continent. Most, it was reckoned, had succumbed to mechanical problems; seventy-five per cent fell into this category.[4] Personnel losses had been heaviest in the light tank units which Pope described as 'a washout'. Uncertain that he would get home, Pope sent the following letter to Brigadier Kenchington, Deputy Director Staff Duties (AFVs) at the War Office; it was delivered by Brigadier Pratt, commander 1 Tank Brigade, on 26 May. (Pope returned to Whitehall on 30 May.)

Will you please impress upon all concerned the following facts which we have – or at any rate I have – learned as a result of bitter experience.

There must be a *Commander* RAC in the Field with an adequate staff to enable him to command, and he must control all movements of RAC troops as directed by the General Staff. Unless this is done, we shall continue to fritter away our tanks. We must model ourselves upon the German lines in this connection. You will be staggered to learn that 1 Army Tank Brigade marched and counter-marched the better part of 300 miles to fight one action. Pratt will give you details. Similarly, 3rd RTR has been thrown away. You will learn the details later.

We must have thicker armour on our fighting tanks and every tank must carry a cannon. The 2-pdr is good enough now, but only just. We *must* mount something better and put it behind 40 to 80mm of armour.

All of our tanks must be mechanically simple and reliable. 75 % of our casualties have been due to mechanical failures and slow repairs.

We want the highest road speed compatible with the above. The A.12 Mk II is too slow. The A.13 is OK in this respect.

Moves by rail cannot be relied upon. The Boche can always cut the lines by air attack. All our tanks must, therefore, be capable of moving long distances at reasonably high speeds by road.

Armoured cars are invaluable for recce, and 12 L. have done marvels, but the Morris is not tactically or technically good enough. The armour must not be very thick – though the thicker the better – but the car must mount a gun: 2-pdr will do.

The Armd Reconnaissance Brigade is a wash-out. It might be able to carry out recce alone, but cannot fight a delaying action. Cruiser tanks or light tanks carrying guns are essential. I would, however, far rather have extra armoured divs.

2. The RAC has done extraordinarily well in the most arduous circumstances, but has suffered enormously. With suitable tanks it would have mopped up the Boche. As it is, the Boche tanks have suffered heavily.

1 Army Tank Brigade walked through everything it met, but mechanical failures have wrecked it.

I fear Cruisers Mk I and II and A.13 will prove to be too thin-skinned.

3. I do hope the Powers that be realize that the Boche has succeeded solely because of his mass of tanks supported by air attacks. Man for man we can beat him any day and twice a day, but dive-bombing followed by tank attack is too much on our very extended fronts.

If only 1st Armoured Division had been out here in time, it might have made all the difference.

Pope had identified the major flaws in British tanks and their employment but it took some time for such flaws to be rectified and British tank crews continued to pay for them in blood, sweat and frustration. In the aftermath of Dunkirk a committee under Major General Bartholomew was established to examine the lessons from the campaign. Pope gave evidence to the Bartholomew Committee that armour needed to be concentrated for best effect in both offence and defence and re-iterated his views on the flaws in British tanks and their employment.[5]

With the United Kingdom now standing alone in Europe and threatened with invasion, Benito Mussolini, Italy's dictator, against the advice of his senior service officers, declared war on a country most Italians regarded as a friend. From Italy's North African colony of Libya, British forces defending the Canal Zone and the port of Alexandria in Egypt could now expect attack. And it is to Egypt that we turn our attention, to 7th Armoured Division, the former Mobile Division, Egypt.

Notes

This chapter is based on Ellis, *The War in France and Flanders* in the Official History of the Second World War series, Liddell Hart, *The Tanks (Vol II)*, Wilson, *Press On Regardless*, and war diaries of GHQ BEF, 1st Armoured Division, 2 Armoured Brigade and 3 Armoured Brigade with other information as follows:

1. www.cwgc.org accessed 27 Apr 2012
2. Macksey, *A History of the Royal Armoured Corps*, p.79
3. Ibid, p.74
4. Ibid, pp.79–80
5. NA Kew, WO106/1775, Bartholomew Report

Chapter Three

War in the Desert

In March 1938 Leslie Hore–Belisha, Secretary of State for War, announced the formation of a mobile division in Egypt. Percy Hobart was offered the command. With the division to be formed not later than October its GOC arrived in Egypt on 27 September. He found the elements of his new command to be a mechanized cavalry brigade, which became the Light Armoured Brigade, of three hussar regiments, and a tank group, which became the Heavy Armoured Brigade, of two RTC battalions. The mechanized cavalry brigade included 7th Queen's Own Hussars in light tanks, 8th King's Royal Irish Hussars in trucks, but scheduled to convert to light tanks, and 11th (Prince Albert's Own) Hussars, the Cherrypickers, in Great War vintage Rolls Royce armoured cars. The RTC battalions of the tank group-cum-heavy armoured brigade were 1st and 6th with light tanks and Vickers mediums. There was also a Pivot Group including 3 RHA, with 3.7-inch howitzers, and a King's Royal Rifle Corps battalion. A second infantry battalion was due to join the Pivot Group and Hobart also had to establish a divisional HQ, a task eased by the fact that he was also responsible for Abbassia Garrison, where he identified four capable staff officers.

Although perceiving the HQ in Egypt as 'complacent and pathetic' Hobart was determined to build a cohesive formation. While his units were organized as two brigades there had been little training at formation level and, overall, little knowledge of what operating as armoured formations entailed. There were cavalry officers aggrieved at losing their beloved horses, but there were also many, especially in the ranks of the younger men, enthusiastic about mechanization. And some senior officers felt a similar enthusiasm, chief among them the brigade major of the Cavalry Brigade, Charles Keightley, who would achieve distinction in the war that loomed. Keightley had spent time in Germany with one of the new panzer divisions and appreciated fully the task that British armour would face when opposed by such a formation.

With the support of Keightley, and others, Hobart devised a training programme and, by March 1939, organized major exercises for his command. These were witnessed by the GOC-in-C, British Troops Egypt, who, in spite of not having wanted Hobart in Egypt at all, noted his satisfaction. A group of disparate units had become a well-drilled formation, familiar with the need for all-arms co-operation in battle. It had also learned how to live in, and with, the desert, using the terrain to advantage. Hobart's attention to detail ensured that such basic points as the need for tank commanders and crews to dismount and inspect their vehicles immediately at every halt were emphasized. In such fashion, the lesson was driven home that minor problems, such as loose bolts or leaks, could be spotted and rectified before becoming major problems that caused breakdowns and reduced the division's effectiveness. As a trainer Hobart had few equals and, although his persistent ramming home of what might have seemed minor matters may have caused frustration if not anger on many occasions, this produced rich dividends when the division went into action in 1940.

Hobart was not to command the Mobile Division, Egypt, by then renamed 7th Armoured Division, in action. His differences with senior officers led to his dismissal and recall to Britain. But he had trained the division intensely in how to operate in the desert, based on personal experience in Mesopotamia in the Great War. The lesson that the deeper one could operate into the desert the greater the opportunity for obtaining surprise was best illustrated in the destruction of Tenth Italian Army in Operation COMPASS. Hobart's plans for operating deep in the desert also led to the establishment of large supply dumps to meet the needs of a corps fighting in the desert. In fact, restyled field maintenance centres (FMCs), such dumps were a major element of that success against the Italians in 1940 and became a standard element in British corps' logistical support chains in north-west Europe in 1944–45.

When Hobart left Egypt in November 1939 he was cheered lustily by his men, some of whom must surely at times have wished him far away during his exercises and under his verbal lashings. Those who expressed their appreciation of their GOC as he left for home included gunners, cavalrymen, tankmen and infantrymen. The commander of Western Desert Force, Richard O'Connor, considered the Mobile Division, Egypt as 'the best trained division I have ever seen'. And it was under O'Connor's command that the division was to perform such sterling service in Operation COMPASS.

Although war was declared on 3 September 1939 there was no immediate outbreak of hostilities in North Africa. Italy did not declare war on Britain, although Mussolini, Italy's dictator, was keen to go to war. His senior officers warned him that Italy would not be ready for war until 1943 – and many, in common with a majority of their countrymen, had no wish to go to war with Britain, a country they regarded as a friend. Thus the Mobile Division, Egypt had more time to prepare. On the outbreak of war it had moved up to the 'wire', the frontier between Egypt and the Italian colony of Libya where, as soon as it was clear that Italy had no immediate warlike intentions, rigorous training resumed. When Hobart left, he bequeathed a formation that would soon become a legend at home and across the world.

Major General Michael O'Moore Creagh MC, commissioned in 7th Queen's Own Hussars in 1911, took command on 4 December 1939. Also arriving was new and better equipment and new designations for the component formations: the Heavy Armoured Brigade became 4 Armoured Brigade and the Light Armoured Brigade's new title was 7 Armoured Brigade; the Pivot Group became the Support Group. Commanding 4 Armoured Brigade was Brigadier J. A. L. Caunter with Brigadier H. E. Russell at the helm of 7 Armoured while Brigadier W. H. E. Gott led the Support Group. Gott's command expanded with the arrival of 2nd Rifle Brigade, a motor battalion; each tank regiment had its full complement of fifty-two tanks.

More changes followed. On 16 February 1940 the division became 7th Armoured Division. At much the same time the original divisional emblem, a white circle on a red ground, was replaced by probably the most famous example of British military 'heraldry', the image of a *jerboa* or desert rat. After a close study of a jerboa in Cairo Zoo the GOC's wife drew a design for the new emblem that was agreed by the officers and men. The final design to be applied to tanks, vehicles and uniforms, was drawn by Trooper Ken Hill of 50 RTR, later killed in a booby-trapped tank in Libya. That the new emblem was popular was exemplified by the soubriquet adopted by the soldiers of 7th Armoured Division who began calling themselves the 'Desert Rats'. There can be no doubt that esprit de corps was strong in the division created by Hobart and when war came to North Africa the Desert Rats were ready to play their part.

Italy finally declared war on Britain and France on 10 June 1940. Elements of 7th Armoured Division were already on the frontier with Libya. Squadron leaders from 11th Hussars, the divisional reconnaissance regiment, had carried out discreet observation of the Italian frontier posts; 'there were strict orders that in no circumstances was action to be taken that might be considered provocative'. However, most of the division was at Gerawla when news of Italy's declaration of war on France and Britain was received. As part of Lieutenant General O'Connor's Western Desert Force, the division concentrated at Mersa Matruh with 11th Hussars deployed closer to the frontier at Sidi Barrani. Facing Western Desert Force was an Italian army estimated at some 215,000 men.

It was a mark of the confidence felt by the men of 7th Armoured Division that, even though the division was understrength (8th Hussars were still training on their new tanks), they took the fight to the enemy immediately. Support Group and 11th Hussars penetrated the frontier wire, took Fort Capuzzo and Fort Maddalena, attacked the camp at Sidi Azeiz and interdicted traffic on the Bardia-Tobruk road. In a week over 200 prisoners were taken, many Italian tanks and other vehicles were destroyed and the first tank-versus-tank battle of the desert war took place, at Ghirba, where an Italian infantry battalion, two tank companies and an artillery battery were wiped out. The overall effect of this flurry of activity was to prompt Marshal Graziani, the Italian commander-in-chief in Libya, to assess British strength in Egypt as much greater than it really was. In turn, this made him even more cautious about invading Egypt. Between Mussolini's declaration of war and Tenth Army's invasion of Egypt, Italian casualties totalled 3,500; British losses were just over 150.

In the following weeks units of the Desert Rats, especially 11th Hussars, harassed the Italian frontier forces in a series of raids that put Tenth Italian Army on the defensive and gave the moral ascendancy to the outnumbered British. In his *Despatch*, General Wavell mentioned especially the work of 11th Hussars which:

> was continuously in the front line, and usually behind that of the enemy, during the whole period; its tireless and daring search for information and constant harassing of the enemy showed a spirit and efficiency worthy of the best traditions of this fine regiment.[1]

Other units were also mentioned. Wavell commended the 'eagerness to take opportunities and skill to make the most of them' of the light tank regiments – 7th and 8th Hussars – the efficient back-up provided by 1 and 6 RTR, the 'dash' and effectiveness of the RHA batteries of Support Group,

> and the skill of the infantry battalions, 3rd Coldstream, 1st King's Royal Rifle Corps and 2nd Rifle Brigade who 'gained a complete mastery of the ... area between themselves and the enemy by active night patrolling'. Of course, the GOC merited mention and Wavell noted how O'Moore Creagh 'directed these operations with admirable skill and initiative, and was ably seconded by his brigade and regimental commanders'.[2]

Eventually, Italian commanders in Libya had to conform with Il Duce's plans by invading Egypt. On 13 September an Italian force of over five divisions with 200 tanks moved into Egypt. For the previous month the frontier had been held by Gott's Support Group with 1 RTR guarding the southern flank. As Gott's command fought rearguard actions that inflicted considerable loss on the Italians, 1 RTR harried the flank before moving north to oppose Graziani's main force. By the time the regiment had reached its new operational area it was too late for the fighting. Tenth Army had stopped at Sidi Barrani. The Italian advance had covered less than sixty miles in four days; they were not even halfway to Mersa Matruh, where Western Desert Force awaited their onslaught. It soon became clear that no early attack was to be made on the Matruh positions as the invaders began building fortified camps between the coast and the northern edge of the escarpment that reaches the coast in Cyrenaica before slanting to the south-east from Sollum. That chain of camps was inherently weak with each too far from its neighbours to provide mutual support. In the following weeks, British mobile patrols slipped between them to reconnoitre the rear area, with, once again, 11th Hussars prominent.

While Tenth Army stood on the defensive on the Barrani line, reinforcements for 7th Armoured Division arrived in Egypt in the shape of 3rd Hussars and 2 RTR while 7 RTR, equipped with Matildas, also arrived. By late October 3rd Hussars and 2 RTR had brought the armoured brigades of the Desert Rats up to strength; the Hussars still had light tanks while 2 RTR had cruisers, largely A13s but with some A9s and A10s. Although 2 RTR joined 4 Armoured Brigade and 3rd Hussars 7 Armoured, squadrons were interchanged so that every unit in the division had a cruiser squadron.

From then until early December all units were involved in training, with the new arrivals practising desert movement and 7 RTR exercising with the infantry of 4th Indian Division. Wavell had decided that, if the Italians did not push forward towards Matruh, Western Desert Force would take the offensive. Planning was under way for such an attack, intended as a large-scale raid, although its effect was to be much more than might be expected of any raid. In fact Wavell had considered that the attack might open strategic opportunities, including 'converting the enemy's defeat into an outstanding victory'. By so doing, Wavell showed considerable foresight. For this attack, codenamed Operation COMPASS, Lieutenant General O'Connor's Western Desert Force was to include 7th Armoured and 4th Indian Divisions, two additional brigades of infantry (from the Australian 6th Division) and 7 RTR as corps troops, a total strength of 30,000. Against him Tenth Army deployed 80,000. However, Western Desert Force had 275 tanks against 120 Italian and 7th Armoured Division had trained for mobile armoured operations in the desert whereas the Italian armour lacked such training.

When a major rehearsal of the original plan for COMPASS was criticized heavily, O'Connor accepted the views of the critics – Alec Gatehouse and Brigadier Eric Dorman-Smith – and their arguments that the enemy camps should be attacked indirectly from the rear, and revised his plans accordingly. The Royal Air Force was to ensure that Italian reconnaissance aircraft did not spot Western Desert Force's preparatory movements, allowing the attackers to gain the critical element of surprise. By 8 December most of Western Desert Force was in position about ten miles from the Italian camps. Tummar East, Tummar West and Nibeiwa, about twenty miles south of Barrani, were assaulted early on the 9th by 4th Indian Division, supported by Matildas of 7 RTR. All were taken in a matter of hours. Complete surprise had been achieved. Cooks were preparing breakfast and soldiers were awakening to the new day when the attackers struck. In spite of being taken off balance the Italian gunners showed great courage, manning their guns to tackle the lumbering Matildas. But to no avail. Their rounds bounced off the British tanks and many Italian gunners perished as their guns were crushed by the Matildas.

As the infantry and the Matildas dealt with the camps, 7th Armoured Division had been on the move. Horace Birks, commanding 4 Armoured Brigade, had orders to drive north-west towards the coast, while Gott's Support Group moved west to prevent the Rabia and Sofafi garrisons launching counter-attacks. That the Italians were recovering their equilibrium was demonstrated emphatically to Birks' men early in their advance as they passed through a bottleneck under the guns of Nibeiwa and Rabia. Birks commented that he and 'Pip' Roberts, his Brigade Major, 'seemed to spend our time sticking our heads in and out of the turret' while making for Azzaziya to attack and destroy the enemy tank force. As the Italian tanks were not to be found the brigade continued to the coast road where the telegraph lines and pipeline were cut, columns of transport shot up and several hundred prisoners taken. British armour, of 6 RTR, was now astride the Italian escape route from Sidi Barrani.

Next day 6 RTR handed over to 2 RTR and deployed eastward to prevent the Maktila garrison reinforcing Sidi Barrani. Meanwhile, elements of 7th Armoured Division were being fed into the attack on Sidi Barrani. When O'Connor asked that the division support 4th Indian's attack by assaulting from the west, 2 RTR deployed with 7 RTR's seven remaining Matildas and went into action under cover of a sandstorm. Resistance collapsed quickly with over 2,500 prisoners taken and more than a hundred guns overrun.

That sandstorm also screened 6 RTR's move eastward, helping to protect it from artillery fire. Excellent wireless communication ensured that the tanks kept together. That evening and next morning the battalion dealt blows to the enemy: some 5,000 prisoners were taken while only one tank commander was wounded and the supporting infantry's casualties numbered only thirty.

At the end of the second day of battle – 10 December – it was obvious that a major victory had been achieved and O'Connor was keen to exploit his gains. Brigadier Caunter, acting GOC as O'Moore Creagh was ill, suggested a thrust to cut off the enemy retreat at Buq Buq, to be carried out by 7 Armoured Brigade which had been held in reserve. Four Armoured Brigade was to withdraw, refuel, carry out maintenance and deploy south onto the escarpment to cut off enemy troops trying to escape. A major advance, that would end with the destruction of Tenth Army and O'Connor's command wresting Cyrenaica from Italian control, was under way.

Buq Buq fell on the 11th, the Italians slipping out as 7 Brigade approached. There followed an encounter not far west of Buq Buq with an Italian force of near divisional strength. The light tanks of A Squadron 3rd Hussars attacked at speed across a saltpan in the face of heavy fire. All were knocked out but their crews continued to fire until the tanks caught fire. B Squadron, detached to 2 RTR, also attacked the Italian flank with two troops tackling the gun positions and silencing some two dozen artillery pieces. At this stage the Italians broke, some 3,000 to 4,000 being taken prisoner with fifty-eight guns and many dead. A Squadron 3rd Hussars lost their squadron leader, Major William Ritson, and two officers dead, with twenty officers and men wounded and thirteen tanks destroyed.

Support Group was mopping up in the Sofafi area while 4 Armoured Brigade prepared for a pursuit into Cyrenaica. That pursuit began on the evening of the 13th with 11th Hussars leading. Next morning the brigade was astride the coast road twenty miles west of Bardia where there was a pause while 6th Australian Division came forward to assault the town. By 15 December all Italian troops were back in Cyrenaica, save those who were prisoners, of whom there were 38,000, including a corps and four divisional commanders. No fewer than 240 guns, seventy tanks and stocks of fuel and equipment were also in British hands. Small wonder that Churchill commented that the events of the previous week 'constituted a victory of the first order'. In a message to Wavell, the Prime Minister said the 'the Army of the Nile has rendered glorious service to the Empire and our cause'.

The advance continued with Sidi Omar taken by 7th Hussars and 2 RTR, aided by the guns of 4 RHA, on the 16th but divisional tank strength was diminishing. By 18 December only thirty-one cruisers and fifty-five lights remained in 4 Brigade while 7 Brigade had twenty-eight cruisers and fifty-three lights. Other problems included the loss of fuel being transported to the forward units. This was not due to enemy action but to that of pre-war politicians and civil servants who had decided, in the interests of economy, that fuel should be carried by road in 4-gallon 'expendable' drums that were so flimsy that leakage and evaporation accounted for a one per cent loss for every ten miles travelled. Before long only half of each container was reaching forward units. Ironically, the Italian logistic system provided some help: fuel captured from Tenth Army was carried in much more robust, Italian, drums which proved a godsend to the advancing tanks and supporting vehicles. (Not until 1942 was the scandalous British flimsy container replaced by a drum based on that used by the Germans and called, accordingly, a jerrycan.)

Capturing the coast road, the Via Balbia, was a tremendous boon to Western Desert Force as it eased the supply problem. Even so, the number of troops that could be maintained so far forward was limited, which led to the withdrawal of 4th Indian Division after the fall of Sidi Barrani. Although that had been planned, the operational situation would have justified keeping both Indians and Australians in the desert, but maintenance problems militated against this. Other assistance was provided by the Royal Navy, including transporting many prisoners to Alexandria. O'Connor paid tribute to the work of 7th Armoured Division's Royal Army Service Corps (RASC) men who ensured that the forward elements were supplied in spite of difficult terrain and dust storms. Even so, at one point the daily water ration had to be reduced from one gallon per man to half that.

On 1 January 1941 Western Desert Force was restyled XIII Corps (perhaps reflecting 7th Armoured and 6th Australian Divisions which then made up the corps) and was making ready for the next phase. Two days later the Australians attacked Bardia which fell on the 5th. No fewer than 45,000 prisoners, 462 artillery pieces and 129 tanks were taken. Now it fell to 7th Armoured Division to isolate Tobruk prior to another Australian assault. Again the operation was successful. Assisted by the surviving Matildas of 7 RTR and a feint attack by the Support Group, Australian infantry took the town on 22 January with another 30,000 prisoners, 236 guns and eighty-seven tanks. Against this level of success must be noted the wear and tear on tanks with 7th Armoured reduced to 145 tanks, only fifty of which were cruisers. As a temporary measure two units were dismounted (6 RTR in 4 Brigade and 8th Hussars in 7 Brigade) with their tanks distributed to the other regiments of their brigades.

Meanwhile 4 Armoured Brigade had moved off towards Mechili which was reached on the 23rd. Eleventh Hussars patrolled between Mechili and the Australians at Derna while preparations were made for the next phase of operations. About thirty miles south-west of Mechili, a field supply depot was established – the division's most forward unit– and the three Light Recovery Sections were brought forward, having already been occupied heavily in recovering and repairing tanks. Water was a particular problem for, although the Water Tank Company brought water forward daily, and wells and cisterns had been discovered nearby, there was still a dearth of water since some of that found locally had been contaminated deliberately.

By now it was clear that Marshal Graziani planned to evacuate Cyrenaica completely, which left the British commander with two alternatives: pursue the Italians along the coast in strength, or use the more mobile element of the corps to cut off Tenth Army south of Benghazi. Although coastal pursuit would be easier for logistic support, and naval guns could also be employed, it would be slow as the mountains come down close to the sea between Derna and Benghazi, which would assist delaying actions. On the other hand, sending 7th Armoured Division across the chord of the Cyrenaican bulge could lead to the total destruction of Tenth Army but would entail a 150-mile journey across uncharted desert with all the difficulties of supplying fuel, food and, especially, water. Moreover, when the force established itself across the road south from Benghazi it could be attacked from behind by Italian forces in Tripolitania.

Such was the prize on offer that Wavell flew to the front to consult with General Wilson, commanding British Troops Egypt, O'Connor and O'Moore Creagh 'and the decision was made to take the bold course and try to cut off the Italians south of Benghazi'.

Led by 11th Hussars, followed by 4 Armoured Brigade, the advance began on the morning of 4 February; behind the tanks travelled the artillery and 2nd Rifle Brigade. The first bound was to Msus, whence it was planned to go west. But when news was received that the Italians were already withdrawing from Benghazi, Creagh amended the orders, sending the attackers south-west. O'Connor approved the decision which 'was to have far-reaching consequences in the coming battle – indeed, it was to make the difference between great success and overwhelming victory'.

Once it was appreciated just how bad was the going and how slow progress would be, it was decided to send the Rifle Brigade's wheeled vehicles and an artillery detachment ahead to join 11th Hussars as a flying column. The gunner element included C Battery 4 RHA with three guns of 155th Light Anti-Aircraft (LAA) Regiment and a section of 106th Anti-Tank Regiment; eight guns of 106th travelled with the Rifle Brigade.

With the addition of these elements, 11th Hussars became Combeforce.

The going continued to be extremely bad; tracked vehicles here were less handicapped than wheeled, with the result that the armour caught up with, and were at one time held back by the Flying Column in front of them. This stretch of bad going lasted for about twenty miles and must be one of the longest stretches of almost impassable country that a mechanized force has ever been ordered to cross. So soon as the going improved, the wheeled column, of course, speedily went away from the tracked portion of the Division, and in view of subsequent events the decision of the Divisional Commander to reorganize his order of march, even though it cost much time, was amply vindicated.

Among difficulties faced in this trek across the unknown were attacks by the *Regia Aeronautica* (the Italian Royal Air Force), radiators boiling, the carriers of the Rifle Brigade running out of petrol (which ruled them out of the subsequent battle) and 'thermos bombs' dropped by Italian aircraft.

Once on better ground the Flying Column was able to move at high speed with C Squadron 11th Hussars leading. Combeforce also included an RAF armoured car squadron and a squadron of King's Dragoon Guards (in place of a Cherrypickers' squadron deployed with the Australians; A Squadron 11th Hussars was with Support Group.) Reaching Msus, Combeforce cleared the area and resumed the advance. On the morning of 5 February the leading squadron reached the coast road near Sidi Saleh, with the rest of 11th Hussars and the Flying Column soon joining. Combeforce deployed 2,000 men with twenty artillery pieces of various types but no tanks. The Rifle Brigade had set out with 140 trucks, only one of which failed to reach the coast.

Combeforce's timing could not have been better. With the KDG squadron deployed to the south to provide warning of an attack from Tripolitania, the main force had not long arrived astride the road than, at 2.30pm, the first Italian column retreating from Benghazi was engaged by a single Rifle Brigade company. About 20,000 men, with tanks and artillery, came upon the Green Jackets. Surely this should have meant the end of Major Pearson's company? Instead of attacking from the flanks and pinching out the British position, the Italians launched a series of unco-ordinated frontal attacks, each of which was beaten off. Meanwhile, a monumental traffic jam built up behind on the road from Benghazi.

Late on the afternoon of the 5th the leading elements of 4 Armoured Brigade's column reached Beda Fomm, north of Sidi Saleh, from where attacks could be launched on the stream of lorries coming from Benghazi. Caunter ordered 7th Hussars to move quickly to the road at Beda Fomm while the cruisers of 2 RTR and the RHA battery deployed to Beda Fomm itself. B Squadron 7th Hussars reported Beda Fomm clear of enemy at 5.15pm and, a little over forty-five minutes later, B and C Squadrons surprised enemy troops at their evening meal. The ensuing action scattered the Italians but darkness put paid to the pursuit, although a blazing Italian petrol lorry provided illumination for much of the night. A Squadron 2 RTR was also in action until dark while the remainder of the battalion laagered at Beda Fomm. During the night Trooper Hughes of A Squadron captured two Italian tanks that approached the squadron positions by climbing onto the turrets and forcing their commanders to surrender at gunpoint.

By the morning of 6 February 4 Armoured Brigade was positioned firmly to the north and north-east of Sidi Saleh, securing the right flank and ensuring that any Italian outflanking movement would be westward. However, Italian attacks were piecemeal, the first coming from three columns, totalling some 900 vehicles, at about 10.45am. Two columns, one on the track west of the main road, the other on the coastal area, were stopped by anti-tank and small arms fire and surrendered almost immediately. The third column, on the main road, put up more of a fight as it included tanks and guns. However, after an hour's fighting, it also surrendered. More resolution was shown in the following three or four attacks but the Green Jackets and their gunner comrades held firm and the tally of prisoners mounted.

Another three-column attack, with tank support, hit the British line at about 9pm. This time there were casualties amongst the gunners and the line was penetrated,

> With the result that the close support that had been so admirably supplied by the gunners temporarily became limited. Nevertheless, the line still held and the enemy within the area, about five hundred, were rounded up. An hour later, two more guns of 106th RHA arrived and were immediately placed at Colonel Renton's disposal. Their appearance was most timely and greatly strengthened the anti-tank defences about the main road. More mines were laid and the leading vehicle of the next attack was blown up with the result that another 150 prisoners were roped in.

Another column was broken up at midnight while two tanks were captured during the night.

At Beda Fomm A and C Squadrons of 2 RTR had taken a grievous toll of Italian tanks as they launched attacks on the British positions. F Battery RHA added to that toll. In spite of the courage of the Italian tankmen, each attempt to break through the British line cost them heavily. Some eight miles to the north 7th Hussars had also been inflicting loss on the Italians while 3rd Hussars and D Battery 3 RHA added to the purgatory of the Italian troops. Meanwhile, 1 RTR from 7 Armoured Brigade were en route to add their weight to the fight.

By midday on 6 February 4 Armoured Brigade faced a crisis at the Pimple feature since only six tanks were still battleworthy, the remainder having been knocked out or broken down. However, the Italians failed to appreciate that they had an opportunity to break through. Their chance to exploit ended with the arrival of two squadrons from 1 RTR during the afternoon. As the day progressed the Italians suffered the loss of more tanks but so, also, did 7th Armoured Division. By evening 2 RTR had only seven cruisers, including two from RHQ, with which to face more than a dozen enemy tanks, while another thirty Italian tanks, with artillery, followed. Behind the Italians, Benghazi fell to Australian troops.

The end came on the 7th when General Virginio, Chief of Staff of Tenth Army, with his staff, arrived at HQ 4 Armoured Brigade to surrender. Not long afterwards, General Bergonzoli also surrendered. Tenth Army was broken. Prisoners numbered over 20,000 at Sidi Saleh, including no fewer than six generals, while 112 tanks, 216 artillery pieces and some 1,500 lorries, as well as large quantities of weapons, stores and other equipment, fell into 7th Armoured Division hands. And the cost in men to 7th Armoured? Nine had been killed and fifteen wounded. The divisional historian summed up the reasons for the victory at Beda Fomm.

> To the staunch fighting qualities of the Rifle Brigade and their supporting gunners under Colonel Combe's overall command was added the skilful fighting of the armour and especially the accurate gunnery of the 2nd Royal Tanks from hull-down positions. The fighting of the Armoured Brigade held much weight off the slender defences at Sidi Saleh, and their battle has been described as a textbook example of an armoured battle, Cruiser tanks using their mobility and firepower to deal with enemy tanks, light tanks screening the flanks and front and Horse Artillery to deal with the enemy infantry. But all this would have been in vain if it had not been for the Rifle Brigade and their Gunners who stood firm and fought it out and held the head of that immense column. Between them, these two forces of Colonel Combe and Brigadier Caunter under General Creagh's direction beat the very heart out of the enemy and totally destroyed his Army.

O'Connor's command had advanced 700 miles, destroyed Tenth Army, taken 130,000 prisoners, 400 tanks and 1,290 guns. Seventh Armoured Division had been a constant factor in that advance with its training and professionalism a major part of the British success. O'Connor had shown that he appreciated fully the potential of armoured forces in concert with other arms and his willingness to take risks had paid magnificent dividends. The prophets of armoured warfare had spoken and written of the potential of fast-moving armoured forces to cut off command and control of an enemy force, disrupt its communications and destroy its morale. The Battle of Beda Fomm had, like the German advance of 1940, proved that theory. Had the Italian Tenth Army been able to maintain its cohesion and morale, and its commanders their control of the army, there would have been a very different outcome to Operation COMPASS. As it was, British troops stood poised to strike into Tripolitania and take Tripoli itself, thus completing the destruction of Mussolini's African empire.

Even as 7th Armoured Division advanced across the Cyrenaican bulge, events elsewhere in the Mediterranean conspired to ensure that the final prize of victory in North Africa would not be had in 1941. Mussolini had attacked Greece which led to a British intervention and formations being taken from O'Connor for the expeditionary force to Greece. (On 10 February the Defence Committee met to review their Middle East policy, followed by Foreign Secretary Anthony Eden's mission to Greece and the Greek acceptance of British support – something they had earlier rejected.) Rather than pressing on to Tripoli, XIII Corps was to hold its ground and a static Cyrenaica Command was created. O'Connor also left, returning to Cairo for hospital treatment. After its COMPASS exertions 7th Armoured Division, too, needed rest and re-equipment and was ordered back to Egypt. Before the move to Cairo began, 11th Hussars advanced to Agedabia and thence to El Agheila with Support Group following and moving to Mersa Brega. A patrol of 11th Hussars encountered an omen of things to come when they were attacked, on St Valentine's Day, by Luftwaffe aircraft, one of which was shot down and its pilot captured by Lieutenant Cranshaw.

Second Armoured Division moved to Cyrenaica to relieve 7th which, on arrival in Cairo, drove through the Egyptian capital, its tanks 'bedecked with captured flags'. However, three units were left behind in Cyrenaica: 1 RHA, 3rd Hussars and 2 RTR, the Hussars with all the remaining light tanks and 2 RTR in captured Italian tanks. Although 2nd Armoured Division was to relieve its sister formation, the two could not be considered as equals. Whereas the Desert Rats had been in existence since before the war and had undergone thorough preparation and training, the same could not be said for 2nd Armoured. Formed in Egypt after the outbreak of war – Divisional HQ came into being on 15 December 1939 – the new division had as GOC an officer whose armoured credentials were not in doubt. Major General Frederick Elliott 'Boots' Hotblack had transferred to the Tank Corps during the Great War and was awarded the DSO, a Bar to the DSO as an operational Tank Corps officer and the Military Cross as a staff officer when he took command of tanks and infantry while on a visit to the front. However, Hotblack suffered a stroke in April 1940 and was succeeded by Willoughby Norrie as acting GOC. The next GOC, Major General Justice Tilly DSO MC, took command in May 1940. An experienced tank officer who had transferred to the Royal Tank Corps in 1927, he had commanded at battalion and brigade level and been Chief Instructor at the RTC Central School, Bovington and the Gunnery Wing of the Army AFV School, Lulworth. However, Tilly was killed in an accident in Egypt on 5 January 1941.[3] Following his death Brigadier H. B. Latham held the reins temporarily until Major General Michael Gambier-Parry took over on 12 February 1941. A superstitious soldier might have opined that 2nd Armoured Division was not destined to be a lucky formation. What happened to the division would have confirmed him in his superstition.

Not only did 2nd Armoured suffer the loss of two commanders in a short period but the division was far from complete on moving into Cyrenaica. The *Official History* describes it as little better than a 'weak armoured brigade, not fully mobile, and likely to waste away altogether if it did much fighting, and an incomplete Support Group.' Two of the division's regiments had deployed in the pursuit of Tenth Italian Army and its tanks had suffered accordingly. That left 1 and 3 Armoured Brigades with only two cruiser and two light tank regiments. As the *Official History* notes, 'The cruisers were in a particularly bad mechanical state, and their tracks were almost worn out.' Worse was to follow since 1 Armoured Brigade was assigned to the expeditionary force for Greece as the core of an armoured brigade group including elements of Support Group (a motor battalion, field regiment, anti-tank battery and machine-gun company). For its part, 3 Armoured Brigade was no more than a hastily assembled formation, having only one original regiment, 5 RTR, available. To complete the brigade it was assigned 3rd Hussars and 6 RTR. No regiment was at full strength: 5 RTR had cruisers, but only twenty-three of its complement of fifty-eight[4] while 6 RTR had a mix of cruisers and Italian M-13s, which had to be fitted with British No.11 wireless sets; 3rd Hussars also included a squadron of M-13s. The last of these units joined the brigade only in March, having journeyed from El Adem with many mechanical breakdowns en route. That left 1st King's Dragoon Guards, the reconnaissance regiment, which had converted to armoured cars from horses as recently as January but had deployed a squadron in 7th Armoured Division's operations in Cyrenaica.

None of this might have mattered had 2nd Armoured Division been given time to prepare fully and train for desert operations. That was not to happen. Hitler had come to the aid of Mussolini in both Greece and North Africa. In the latter theatre the Führer had decided to deploy a German armoured corps under Major General Erwin Rommel, who had commanded 7th Panzer Division in France. The new Lieutenant General Rommel's command was dubbed *Deutsches Afrikakorps* (German Africa Corps) or DAK, more commonly known as the Afrika Korps, and had begun landing in Libya. Rommel himself arrived in Tripoli on 12 February, the day Gambier-Parry took command of 2nd Armoured Division. The German commander was two days ahead of the first elements of his combat troops, men of Major General Streich's 5th Light Motorized Division, created from a cadre of elements drawn from 3rd Panzer Division. Initially, Hitler had intended only to send a *Sperrverband* (blocking detachment) but, while 5th Light was forming, he told Mussolini that he would add an armoured division to this force if the Italians held the Sirte area. Thus was born Afrika Korps: 15th Panzer Division was to follow 5th Light to Libya. The Afrika Korps and its commander were destined to become more famous in Britain than in Germany.

Cyrenaica Command was established under Lieutenant General Sir Henry Maitland Wilson, who was also designated Military Governor. The Australian General Thomas Blamey's I Australian Corps relieved XIII Corps but the Australian Corps HQ was destined for Greece, as were Generals Wilson and Blamey, and thus 2nd Armoured Division and 6th Australian Division came under control of Cyrenaica Command; Lieutenant General Sir Philip Neame VC succeeded Wilson as C-in-C. Cyrenaica Command was a static headquarters and 'Its lack of the trained staff and signal equipment required to control mobile operations over large distances was later to prove a serious handicap'. Not only was 2nd Armoured Division seriously understrength but it, and 9th Australian Division (which began relieving 6th Division in early March), was spread over too broad a front and without an adequate command structure. Obviously, the two formations could not 'permanently secure the desert flank'. However, the slim intelligence available to General Wavell in Cairo was sufficient to suggest that the earliest date for a serious threat to Cyrenaica was May. Meanwhile, Wavell planned to have two more divisions in Cyrenaica with stronger artillery support; the breathing space would also allow 2nd Armoured to complete training.

Before long the intelligence picture was changing, suggesting an Axis attack much earlier than May. Neame was also drawing Middle East HQ's attention to the weaknesses of his situation in Cyrenaica. Since defence would depend upon mobile operations by 2nd Armoured Division, this formation was critical to meeting any enemy thrust. However, as Neame noted, 2nd Armoured could hardly be described as a mobile formation and, if it had to move any great distance, would lose many tanks to mechanical failures. He considered that the minimum defence of Cyrenaica should include a complete and fully mobile armoured division, two fully-equipped infantry divisions and proper air support. He was told that it would be early April before reinforcements could be sent to Cyrenaica, and then only in small numbers.

A brigade of 9th Australian Division held the forward British positions at Mersa Brega but was virtually immobile and its withdrawal was authorized. New tactical instructions were issued from Cairo: the open ground between El Agheila and Benghazi was to be defended by armoured action, it being suitable for such operations, while ground could be given up as far as Benghazi and even that port could be evacuated, as its value was greater in the propaganda sphere than the military. Even at this stage it was felt that the Axis forces' logistical difficulties would work to their disadvantage. Moreover, it was now clear that no British reinforcements could be sent to Cyrenaica before May. On 20 March responsibility for the forward area switched from 9th Australian to 2nd Armoured. As plans were laid for defensive action there was one piece of good news – the arrival of 3 Indian Motor Brigade, due at El Adem on the 29th. The brigade included three Indian Army cavalry regiments mounted in trucks. Although with no heavy weaponry and short of wireless sets, it was tactically mobile. Before the Indians arrived, however, the enemy struck.

On 24 March Axis troops occupied El Agheila and, six days later, Wavell told Neame that, since no reinforcements could be provided for two months, he was to delay the enemy during that time. The dispositions of the two divisions were: 3

Armoured Brigade south-east of Mersa Brega with Support Group holding a front of about eight miles at Mersa Brega; and five battalions of 9th Australian Division defending the Jebel area. A shortage of communications meant that the Australians had no direct contact with Gambier-Parry's HQ.

Rommel had concluded that the British 'had no offensive intentions and ... were probably thinning out the forward area'. This emboldened him in his plans, which he had agreed with his Italian superior, General Gariboldi, for an attack into Cyrenaica to recover the ground lost to the British, followed by an attack into Egypt and to the Suez Canal. As he would need reinforcements for this he travelled to Berlin to put his case. However, he met with no great enthusiasm and was told that he would receive only 15th Panzer Division, as already arranged, and should, therefore, act with caution because of the difficulties of supply and transport. This was emphasized in a written order, dated 21 March, pointing out that he was to follow the instructions of the Italian command, to defend Tripolitania and prepare for the recapture of Cyrenaica, which could begin when 15th Panzer arrived in mid-May. Rommel's concept of caution differed from that of OKH in Berlin. Seeing an opportunity to retake Cyrenaica he planned to take it. On 30 March Major General Streich was ordered to take Mersa Brega next day, which he duly did. Rommel also ordered a reconnaissance towards Jalo oasis for 2 April, to prevent any British flanking movement from that direction. Gariboldi had approved Rommel's plan but forbade any advance beyond Mersa Brega without his approval.

In numbers of tanks the opposing forces were almost evenly balanced as 5th Light Division's panzer regiment had only two battalions with 130 tanks, of which only two thirds were gun-armed. In fact, when Rommel advanced on 31 March he did so with only fifty effective tanks but these formed a well-trained team that was well led in contrast to the ad hoc British force with inadequate communications and insufficient training, as well as, in the cases of the crews manning captured tanks, unfamiliar equipment. Moreover, the Germans advanced on a wide front, creating the impression of greater numbers, but prepared to concentrate when striking. In the air the Luftwaffe and Regia Aeronautica enjoyed local superiority, thus denying the British command information on the true strengths – or rather weaknesses – of their opponents.

First to encounter the Germans were the men of 5 RTR, who had already met them in France. That clash occurred between a patrol of A Squadron 5 RTR and enemy tanks advancing from El Agheila to Mersa Brega. Although the patrol, of six tanks, claimed to have hit two or three of the foe, it suffered two casualties through mechanical failures and another tank damaged by enemy action. Later in the day enemy infantry attacked the Mersa Brega line held by Support Group. The attack was checked but the Germans subsequently made a small breakthrough close to the sea. Support Group began withdrawing and 3 Armoured Brigade's leading elements fell back next day to avoid being outflanked. While this accorded with Wavell's instructions to give up ground, it meant that a strong position had been abandoned in favour of a fluid situation that worked to Rommel's advantage. One effect of this withdrawal was to allow Rommel to exploit across the chord of the Cyrenaican bulge, as O'Connor had done, while it also encouraged him to follow up the retreating British. He was now disregarding the instructions for caution that he had received both from OKH and Gariboldi, but doing so to take advantage of a favourable tactical situation.

The retreat continued with Axis forces hustling 2nd Armoured: part of Support Group was cut off by an advance party of eight tanks on 2 April while the main body of Streich's panzer regiment overran the rearward line of those who had been cut off, precipitating further retreat. In an engagement with German tanks 5 RTR lost twenty-three men killed and five tanks knocked out. By that night the battalion's strength was down to twelve tanks and, although it claimed to have accounted for ten enemy tanks, enemy losses were only three. Gambier-Parry ordered a retreat to Antelat, ninety miles from Mersa Brega. Support Group reached there on the evening of the 2nd. Meanwhile, 6 RTR, ordered from Beda Fomm to Agedabia, found traffic 'streaming northward' and so the commanding officer chose to move east to Antelat to cover the retreat.

All this caused confusion in the British ranks and played into Rommel's hands. A small armoured thrust had achieved a breakdown in cohesion and loosened whatever grip Neame had on the situation. Rommel, sensing that the British had no intention of standing for a serious fight, 'decided to stay on the heels of the retreating enemy and make a bid to seize the whole of Cyrenaica at one stroke'. It was boldness of the same stamp as shown by O'Connor only months before and would bring the same scale of rewards. Thus 5th Light Division's reconnaissance battalion was sent towards Benghazi with a small detachment pushing through the desert to Mechili and Gazala while the transport was sent back to collect fuel, ammunition and rations for the planned deep strike. That strike began on the morning of 4 April and, once again, confusion in the British ranks came to Rommel's aid. On 3 April a series of setbacks exacerbated the British situation. Communications were breaking down frequently, due to problems in keeping batteries charged, while orders were being countermanded – 6 RTR was sent south towards Agedabia to act as rearguard but discovered the remainder of the division heading in the opposite direction, towards Sceleidima, north of Antelat. Then a large enemy force was reported approaching Msus and 2nd Armoured Division's main fuel and supplies dump. Confirmed by aerial reconnaissance as some hundred tanks with motor transport, this led to an order to destroy the dump, which was done before it was discovered that the 'enemy force' was a patrol of the Long Range Desert Group with 3 Armoured Brigade's Recovery Section.

As the retreat progressed so confusion deepened with 6 RTR again the victim of conflicting orders on 4 April. Nor could the battalion obtain diesel for its M-13s at Msus, and it had to abandon some tanks to use their fuel for the remainder. The rearguard of 5 RTR fought their way out of a trap at Derna on the 7th – where the brigade commander, Brigadier Rex Rimington, and part of his HQ had been captured earlier in the day by an advanced detachment of 5th Light.

That evening Gambier-Parry was ordered to withdraw to the east, a move he planned to make next day. However, his position at Mechili had been surrounded by enemy forces, although these were much lighter than Gambier-Parry believed, the bulk of Rommel's tank column having been disoriented in a sandstorm. At first light on the 8th several breakout attempts were made but were greeted with machine-gun and shellfire. Then the Germans attacked under cover of a duststorm with only a few tanks and lorries. Gambier-Parry, duped into believing he was being attacked by a large German force, surrendered, although some groups managed to escape.

Such was the disaster that had befallen 2nd Armoured Division that the formation was never to see action again. A month later, on 10 May, its name was stricken from the order of battle. It had never got into its stride in the desert, its command, control and communications had been wanting from its arrival in Cyrenaica and it had been knocked off balance by Rommel's opportunistic attack. Following the success of O'Connor's offensive this marked a major setback for British arms, a setback made even worse on 7 April when Generals Neame and O'Connor and Brigadier Combe were captured by a German reconnaissance detachment, having taken a wrong turning in the desert. O'Connor had been brought up from Egypt by Wavell to assist Neame in the operations against Rommel. The best general the British had in North Africa was to spend the next thirty months as a prisoner of war.

Rommel's advance continued, although he failed to take Tobruk where Australian troops held out. He reached the Egyptian frontier, seizing the Halfaya Pass. British forces retreated to Mersa Matruh but, now at the end of a very long supply line, Rommel's plan to push on to the Suez Canal was set aside. In less than a month Rommel had retaken Cyrenaica with a force including Streich's 5th Light Division, two Italian divisions – one armoured and one motorized – and the artillery of the Italian formations. It was a remarkable achievement, but even Rommel had to concede that an advance to the Nile was not possible without major reinforcements.

Such reinforcements were unlikely, although 15th Panzer Division, the other main element of Afrika Korps, was arriving – and being hustled up to Tobruk. In Berlin plans were being refined for the invasion of the Soviet Union and considerable German forces were already committed to Greece; German air support was also being lent to a pro-Nazi rebellion in Iraq. Moreover, Rommel had a nemesis in Berlin in General Franz Halder, chief of the general staff, who hated the Afrika Korps commander and described him as a 'soldier gone mad'. Halder sent General Paulus to visit Rommel, giving him authority to command Rommel as necessary. Paulus arrived as an assault on Tobruk was being planned, approved the launch of the operation, and then stopped any further attacks after a three-mile stretch of the perimeter was captured. He ordered Rommel to maintain his positions and ensure that he had adequate supplies of fuel, ammunition, food and water for future operations, thus granting the British a breathing space.

Pressure to mount an offensive was applied to Wavell from 10 Downing Street. Churchill knew, through Ultra, Rommel's situation – although he still failed to appreciate that the normal rules of warfare meant little to this German general – and the War Cabinet wanted the airfields between Sollum and Derna recaptured as soon as possible, lest the Germans, now with air bases in Greece and soon to have more in

Crete, should cut the Mediterranean sea route. Thus the prime minister took a major risk: a convoy, codenamed TIGER, was to be sent through the Mediterranean with tanks and fighter aircraft for Egypt. TIGER passed through the straits of Gibraltar on 5 May and reached Alexandria a week later, carrying more than 200 tanks – dubbed 'Tiger cubs' – and forty-three Hawker Hurricanes. One ship, *Empire Song*, was lost to a mine with fifty-seven tanks, ten Hurricanes and a number of lorries going to the bottom.

Churchill was determined that Wavell should seize the initiative at the earliest possible moment. Lieutenant General Sir Noel Beresford-Peirse, commanding the reborn Western Desert Force (it would become XIII Corps again in the autumn), was to plan an offensive. At his disposal he had one armoured formation – 7th Armoured Division; 2nd Armoured had been disbanded. Beresford-Peirse's offensive was codenamed Operation BATTLEAXE but before it took place a smaller offensive, Operation BREVITY, was launched on 15 May under command of Brigadier 'Strafer' Gott, whose formation was dubbed the British Mobile Force.

Wavell defined BREVITY's main objectives as: acquiring ground in the Sollum area from which to launch a further offensive towards Tobruk; and inflicting as much loss as possible on Axis forces in the area. Intended as a rapid blow, all available armour was allocated to it; the few battle-ready units available following Rommel's race into Cyrenaica were placed under Gott's command. An indication of just how low British fortunes had sunk is given by the strength Gott deployed for BREVITY. His attacking force included three groups: his left column, on the desert flank, was 7 Armoured Brigade Group, a misnomer as the 'group' included only 2 RTR with no more than twenty-nine cruisers and three columns of the Support Group; the centre group was 22 Guards Brigade, which had to borrow transport to make itself mobile, and twenty-four Matildas of 4 RTR; the third group (known as the Coast Group) included 2nd Rifle Brigade with 8th Field Regiment RA.

It was the Guards' Group that took Halfaya Pass against determined opposition from its Italian defenders, especially the gunners, before pushing on to capture Fort Capuzzo. The Coast Group was to fix the enemy defenders in Sollum before taking the lower reaches of Halfaya Pass and Sollum. The left group, including 2 RTR's cruisers, made good progress towards Sidi Azeiz, pushing back light enemy forces. The Germans had expected an attack, having intercepted radio traffic, and the opening phase of BREVITY caused them some concern. They saw it as the beginning of an attempt to lift the siege of Tobruk and Rommel had not sufficient transport to bring up reserves to deal with such an operation. He did strengthen the eastern flank of the besieging force and prepared to block any attempt to break out by the Tobruk garrison. Although German commanders on the ground overestimated British strength – one believed that he was facing two British armoured divisions – Rommel soon came to a more realistic appreciation, ordered a counter-attack and promised reinforcements of a tank battalion by dawn on the 16th.

The German counter-attack regained Fort Capuzzo and inflicted heavy casualties on its British defenders. Gott realized that he had lost the initiative. Concerned that the Guards Brigade Group was in danger of being attacked by Axis armour on open ground he conducted a withdrawal to the Halfaya Pass with 7 Armoured Brigade in covering positions near Sidi Azeiz. Thus ended Operation BREVITY. Although Halfaya Pass remained in British hands, the operation had emphasized to Rommel its importance as a supply route. It would be recaptured in a German counter-attack less than a fortnight later.

BREVITY had hardly been a good omen for BATTLEAXE. However, the arrival of the TIGER convoy allowed the rebuilding of 7th Armoured Division to begin as the merchant ships had brought in eighty-two cruisers, including some of the new A16 Crusaders, as well as 135 Matildas and twenty-one light tanks. Since it was known that the enemy had administrative problems – partly as a result of Rommel's rapid advance – it followed that he would be unlikely to 'do more than reconnaissances in force' for the time being. Gott was to hold the Halfaya Pass and operate as far to the west as he could, thereby providing a more westerly start-line for BATTLEAXE. Holding the pass would also permit use of the coast road to Sollum in the early stages of the advance. Thus 3rd Coldstream, with I-tanks, field, anti-tank and anti-aircraft artillery, defended the pass while mobile columns from 7th Support Group patrolled the southern flank.

Halfaya Pass was lost to the Germans as the result of a bluff. Colonel Herff, who had commanded the German counter-attack during BREVITY, believed a display of force might induce the British to relinquish the plateau above the escarpment. Although he had tanks available – Rommel could call on 160 in all – there was an acute shortage of fuel, precluding any major armoured move. Herff's display of force metamorphosed into an attack by a force greatly outnumbering the Coldstream group defending the pass. Although the British fought tenaciously, Gott decided to withdraw on the 27th and Lieutenant Colonel Moubray led a skilful operation to escape Herff's clutches. In the process the force suffered 173 casualties and lost twelve guns (four field and eight anti-tank) plus five I-tanks.

Although the forward start-line for BATTLEAXE had been lost, planning continued with Wavell issuing orders for the offensive a day after the loss of Halfaya Pass. Having defeated the enemy on the frontier and secured the Bardia–Sollum–Capuzzo–Sidi Azeiz area, Western Desert Force was to defeat Axis forces around Tobruk and El Adem before exploiting to Derna and Mechili. At all phases of the operation, Beresford-Peirse was to decide the role to be played by the Tobruk garrison which, Wavell noted, was to be 'vigorous'.

The critical factor in deciding the date for BATTLEAXE was the time needed to re-equip 7th Armoured Division. In fact, the division had to be re-formed as it had not existed as a battleworthy formation since February and the withdrawal from Cyrenaica and many officers and men had been posted out. Thus the division not only had to be re-equipped but re-organized and trained. Its new order of battle included 7 Armoured Brigade with two regiments of cruisers, 4 Armoured Brigade with two regiments of I-tanks, and Support Group. In contrast to the intensive training undertaken earlier, it was allowed only five days to train for BATTLEAXE. When added to the time taken to unload the tanks at Alexandria docks, carry out modifications for desert warfare and overhaul those needing major work (many cruisers had over 700 miles on their clocks and were, therefore, well worn, while some light tanks had to be all but rebuilt), the earliest date for D Day for BATTLEAXE was set as 15 June.

This did not please Churchill. Although he had been a soldier, that had been in a different era and he did not appreciate fully the complexities of modern warfare. Churchill believed that a tank, once unloaded at Alexandria, could go into action in the desert immediately. The fitting of sand filters and other work seemed to him to be only so many excuses – as also was the need to train the tank crews. In this case, he had to wait, impatiently, for BATTLEAXE.

Wavell had good intelligence on enemy strength in the area from which 5th Light Division had been withdrawn and relieved by 15th Panzer, under General Walter Neumann-Silkow. The recently-arrived division took over the frontier zone except for the Sollum–Musaid–Capuzzo area, held by three Italian infantry battalions and a regiment of artillery from Trento Division, the remainder of which was at Bardia. The Axis positions were designed for all-round defence and were well-camouflaged, although short of ammunition, fuel and water.

To break through, Beresford-Peirse planned to use the largest force that could be maintained in action: 7th Armoured Division, the HQ and artillery of 4th Indian Division, 11 Indian and 22 Guards Brigades. Major General Frank Messervy's 4th Indian Division would have under command, as well as the two infantry brigades, 4 Armoured Brigade, equipped with Matildas. While Messervy's command would destroy Axis forces in the Bardia–Sollum–Halfaya–Capuzzo area, the Desert Rats would cover its left flank and assist in destroying the enemy in the frontier area. Capturing the Halfaya area was assigned to 11 Indian Brigade, supported by a squadron and a half of Matildas, while the remainder of 4 Armoured Brigade and 22 Guards Brigade attacked Point 206 and Capuzzo from the south-west, an indirect route chosen after aerial reconnaissance revealed a newly-constructed anti-tank obstacle on the direct line of approach. On the left flank, under Creagh's command, 7 Armoured Brigade and Jaxo Column of Support Group (a company of 1st King's Royal Rifle Corps with troops of 25-pounders and anti-tank guns) were to advance to Hafid ridge and beyond, while the remainder of Support Group provided a screen against attack from the Sidi Omar direction. If the advance attracted German armour and a tank battle seemed likely then 4 Armoured Brigade would revert to Creagh's command.

The availability of communications with Air Commodore Raymond Collishaw's Striking Force Group (as No. 204 Group RAF had been renamed by Air Marshal Arthur Tedder, acting Air Officer Commanding in Chief, Middle East) forced Beresford-Peirse to locate his headquarters at Sidi Barrani, some five hours' drive from the front. The RAF had been urged to 'accept great risks elsewhere in order to provide the maximum air support'. Tedder noted that, on 15 June, 'we enjoyed effective though not numerical air superiority' with the enemy managing only six air attacks that day.[5] Wavell had impressed upon Beresford-Peirse the need for 'utmost boldness and resolution' although, privately, telling General Dill, the CIGS, that there might be insufficient strength left at the end of the first phase – the defeat of the enemy on the frontier – to permit the second phase, the advance to Tobruk, to be launched.

Wavell's misgivings were well founded. A strong anti-tank gun defence at the Halfaya Pass position defeated 11 Indian Brigade and their supporting Matildas; eleven tanks were knocked out by gunfire with another four trapped in minefields. On the left flank 7 Armoured Brigade was stalled at Hafid ridge by a series of well-sited defensive positions that threw back three British attacks supported by the 25-pounder troop of Jaxo Column. Although part of the defences was penetrated there was no cracking of the remainder of the German line. Initially, only a squadron of 8th Panzer Regiment was in the area but the real damage to the British tanks was inflicted by anti-tank guns, including a quartet of 88mm anti-aircraft guns deployed in a ground role. By evening only forty-eight of 7 Armoured's cruisers were still runners. By then a battalion of 5th Panzer Regiment had replaced the squadron of 8th.

In the centre, Messervy's attack had begun at 10.30am with 4 RTR advancing towards Point 206. Enemy reaction was sharp with a battalion of 8th Panzer Regiment tackling the British tanks and a fierce skirmish developing. While this battle was under way, Messervy attacked Fort Capuzzo, sending 7 RTR against it. Faced with a two-pronged attack by 4 Armoured Brigade, the German tanks moved to the north-east and Point 206 fell. At Fort Capuzzo 7 RTR broke through and prepared to continue but the infantry who should have consolidated the ground had fallen behind, due to communications problems, and the tanks had to await them instead of re-organizing. The Germans launched a series of counter-attacks, all of which were beaten off. By then the day was almost over. It ended with success in the centre, defeat at Halfaya and a bloody nose at Hafid ridge. The enemy had bought time, and aerial reconnaissance indicated much transport moving along the Trigh Capuzzo. Rommel was reinforcing his front.

For D Day plus 2, Beresford-Peirse planned that Messervy should renew that attack on Halfaya Pass while improving his position around Capuzzo and exploiting towards Bardia. However, 4 Armoured Brigade was to rejoin 7th Armoured Division, which was to destroy the enemy armour around Hafid while continuing to protect the desert flank. But Rommel's HQ had been monitoring British radio traffic and had deduced that an attack was imminent, even though it was felt that the British did not have the forces necessary for an offensive. Preparations had been made to react and Axis forces were at a high level of readiness. In spite of the losses of the 15th, uncertainty about Point 206 and the isolation of Halfaya, Axis reinforcements were en route with the first detachment of 5th Light Division reaching the Hafid area; the remainder reached Sidi Azeiz at midnight. Captured documents and wireless intercepts gave Rommel a solid impression of British dispositions and strengths, leading him to order 8th Panzer Regiment to attack at Capuzzo at dawn on the 16th while 5th Panzer Regiment was to flank through the desert to hit at Western Desert Force's flank and rear.

The second day of BATTLEAXE saw the initiative begin to pass to Rommel, although 8th Panzer Regiment's planned attack was beaten off by 4 Armoured Brigade, the guns of 31st Field Regiment and 1st Buffs of 22 Guards Brigade. With the Scots Guards having taken Musaid, and Sollum barracks, it was not immediately obvious that the balance was swinging to the Axis. Nonetheless, Messervy's assessment of 4th Indian Division's tactical situation was such that he judged that 4 Armoured Brigade could not be returned to command of 7th Armoured Division. His assessment proved accurate.

Two attacks by 11 Indian Brigade were repulsed below the escarpment while 7 Armoured Brigade and elements of Support Group were entangled in a day-long mauling with 5th Light Division, a battle that crabbed its way from the Hafid area along the frontier in the direction of Sidi Omar and the remainder of Support Group. This allowed Support Group's guns to join in. Throughout the battle the panzers tried to work their way around 7 Armoured Brigade's western flank to create a wedge between 2 and 6 RTR. Their efforts came to naught but both British units lost many tanks with no more than twenty-one still battleworthy that evening.

Still maintaining hopes of success, Beresford-Peirse urged Creagh and Messervy to continue as planned. The divisional commanders, knowing that 22 Guards Brigade was secure at Capuzzo, planned that 4 Armoured should rejoin 7th Armoured Division next day so that the division could launch an attack to destroy the enemy armour. Wavell visited the front during the day but made no changes in the corps commander's plans. Collishaw's aircraft were contributing significantly to the battle by disrupting enemy transport along the Trigh Capuzzo while 15th Panzer Division was concerned about a possible British attack from Capuzzo. Rommel remained calm, assuring Neumann-Silkow that the battle was shifting in their favour, although a planned attack towards Sidi Suleiman was to be delayed until the morning of the 17th. He had also worked out what Beresford-Peirse intended to do the following day and laid plans to thwart him with dawn attacks by 5th Light and 15th Panzer towards Halfaya, the former striking via Sidi Suleiman and the latter through Alam Abu Dihak.

Both German attacks caught Western Desert Force off balance although 4 Armoured Brigade, about to move off on its new task, fought off 15th Panzer. However, 5th Panzer Regiment drove back 7 Armoured Brigade and reached Sidi Suleiman by about 8am, placing the Germans in a position to cut off 22 Guards Brigade and threaten the British force at Halfaya. Moreover, the few Matildas still with the Guards were very low on ammunition. Exacerbating the situation was a breakdown in wireless communications that prevented Creagh from contacting Beresford-Peirse until 9.30am by which time the Desert Rats' tank strength was reduced to twenty-two cruisers and seventeen Matildas. Wavell was still at Sidi Barrani and, realizing that a major decision had to be made, determined that the responsibility was his, boarded a plane with Beresford-Peirse and flew to Creagh's HQ where he found that Messervy had ordered the Guards Brigade to begin withdrawing at 11am. Having studied the situation, Wavell cancelled his own order for a counter-attack at Sidi Suleiman, decided to break off operations and ordered that all formations withdraw and refit, recovering as many damaged tanks as possible.

Western Desert Force broke off from battle with the support of the RAF, whose fighters (including some of the Hurricanes of the TIGER convoy) provided excellent protection and whose bombers, from about 10am, kept up harassing attacks on enemy vehicles, delaying pursuit. Such was the quality of the air cover that only one enemy dive-bombing attack got through, causing almost 100 casualties. What was left of the armoured brigades acted as rearguard to the retreating infantry. By the end of the day, Western Desert Force's forward troops were back on the line from Sidi Barrani to Sofafi. Losses included 122 dead, 588 wounded and 259 missing. Although only four guns had been lost the armour suffered heavily: of ninety cruisers and about 100 Matildas committed to battle, twenty-seven of the former and sixty-four of the latter were lost. RAF losses included thirty-three fighters and three bombers. Axis losses were ninety-three Germans dead, 350 wounded and 235 missing (Wavell commented that 220 Germans had been captured[6] while about 350 Italian prisoners were released by their British captors before withdrawing.) About fifty German tanks were damaged or broke down but many were recovered and repaired; the Germans also repaired some British tanks and put them into service. German tank losses numbered no more than twelve destroyed, although the British claimed to have destroyed almost a hundred (Wavell reduced the estimate to forty to fifty). Ten Luftwaffe aircraft were lost.

It might be claimed that the result was a draw but that would be to ignore the fact that Western Desert Force had failed to destroy the enemy armour and had lost tanks that the British could ill afford. Losses were such that it would be months before offensive action could be contemplated. Rather than being a draw, BATTLEAXE was closer to a disaster for British arms. Wavell noted that the main cause of failure was:

> the difficulty in combining the action of cruiser and I-tanks, and the cramping effect on manoeuvre of having only two regiments in each armoured brigade and the lack of training in 7th Armoured Division. Had tank crews had more practice with their weapons they would have destroyed a much larger number of enemy tanks; and had they all been more experienced in maintenance there would have been fewer tanks out of action through mechanical breakdown; so that instead of being so outnumbered at the end of the battle, we should have been in sufficient strength to have defeated the enemy.[7]

While Wavell was right in this assessment, and in judging that the enemy 'manoeuvred his forces skilfully' and had a healthy respect for the British anti-tank guns (still the 2-pounder) and 25-pounders which were frequently deployed against tanks, he was wrong in stating that the Germans 'showed little boldness or inclination to close' other than when deployed defensively. He was failing to see that Rommel was not looking for a tank-versus-tank battle; German doctrine was for anti-tank guns to deal with tanks while panzers dealt with the infantry. Although it was believed that large numbers of British tanks were lost in tank-to-tank combat, the majority fell to German anti-tank guns. By now Rommel was able to deploy the new 50mm Pak-38, a more powerful weapon than the British 2-pounder, and had about a dozen 88mm anti-aircraft guns operating in the anti-tank role. The latter had taken a heavy toll of the Matildas while the Pak-38s played a significant part, numbering more than one-in-three of Afrika Korps' anti-tank guns. However, British tank crews whose tanks were knocked out generally considered themselves to have been the victims of enemy tanks whereas, in most instances, they had been hit by anti-tank rounds.

Verney's history of 7th Armoured Division notes that 'for the most part, the German tanks were capable of knocking out British tanks at 2,000 yards, while the 2-pounder guns of the latter were not effective beyond six or eight hundred yards'. Verney goes on to comment that German tanks had to be dealt with by 25-pounder guns, 'the crews of which were devoid of armour protection'. In fact, the German tanks did not outgun their British rivals: the Panzer III's 50mm gun was no better than the 2-pounder, being able to penetrate 39mm of armour at 1,000 yards; the 2-pounder could penetrate 40mm at the same range. It was, of course, 88s that were knocking out British tanks at 2,000 yards. Liddell Hart noted that the British after-battle reports emphasized the quality of the 2-pounder (as did Wavell in his *Despatch*, although referring to the anti-tank version) and 'made no complaints about armament being inferior to the Germans'.

When tanks fought tanks the British 'often had the better of the exchange' and their handling was generally competent as was that of their commanders on the ground. It was at the higher levels that British commanders were failing, particularly through their inclination to disperse armour to support infantry operations rather than planning for close co-operation. When armour deployed in small packets as an adjunct to the infantry, losses were excessive.

In fairness to the planners of BATTLEAXE, however, they had sought to use all arms in partnership as well as seeking to seize vital ground. That their plans did not work out was due to a combination of factors, one of them the problem of British wheeled artillery becoming bogged in soft sand on 15 June. As Ronald Lewin commented, 'the naked 25-pounder had to be employed in armoured battles, towed into action by an unarmoured vehicle with the gun pointing in the wrong direction'.[8] With British artillery unable to support the Halfaya attack the 88s were able to pick off the Matildas at long range. The answer to the field artillery problem had been around since the mid-1920s when the Birch gun, an 18-pounder mounted on a tank body, had been tested in the Experimental Armoured Force. A successor to the Birch gun was still some months in the future. In the meantime, some anti-tank gunners were firing their 2-pounders from the beds of the lorries on which they were carried *en portée*. They, too, would benefit from self-propelled weapons in the future.

When the British armour remained concentrated it could achieve its objectives, especially when the artillery provided co-ordinated supporting fire. But without HE shells for their guns the tanks had to come to close quarters with the enemy to allow their machine guns to engage, a tactic that took them within killing range of enemy anti-tank guns. Nor was the lorry-borne infantry always able to keep pace with the tanks.

Arthur Tedder, the new AOC-in-C, saw BATTLEAXE from a different perspective and was highly critical of the army. Although the RAF was prepared to support the ground forces, he told Portal, Chief of the Air Staff that:

The main difficulty ... had been the almost complete lack of information from the ground. Arrangements had been made for communication and recognition between our air and ground forces. Calls from the air for acknowledgement of the recognition signal were never answered. In such circumstances close-support bombing became impossible. Indeed, Army Headquarters had great difficulty even in giving a bombing line. Wavell's statement, 'we are not organized or trained', was correct. It appeared to me that the troops had been quite untrained, and apparently unable to keep their own commanders informed, much less to keep the air forces informed.[9]

The need for better co-operation with the air was one of many lessons from the failure of BATTLEAXE. Before long the level of co-operation between ground and air forces in North Africa would become a model for the Allied powers. Tedder played a major part in that development, but so also did ground commanders, including the new C-in-C, Middle East.

Notes

This chapter is based on Playfair et al, *The Mediterranean and the Middle East. Vol I* from the Official History series, Liddell Hart, *The Tanks (Vol II)*, Macksey, *Armoured Crusader* and *A History of the Royal Armoured Corps*, Neillands, *The Desert Rats: 7th Armoured Division 1940–1945*, Verney, *The Desert Rats: The 7th Armoured Division in World War II* and the war diaries of Western Desert Force, 2nd Armoured, 7th Armoured Division, 4 Armoured Brigade, 7 Armoured Brigade, 22 Guards Brigade and 4 RTR.

1. *London Gazette,* 13 June 1946, p.3002
2. Ibid
3. Smart, *Biographical Dictionary of British Generals of the Second World War*, pp.160–1 & p.310
4. In *Press On Regardless*, p.38, Wilson states twenty-eight
5. Tedder, *With Prejudice*, p.124
6. Wavell's Despatch, *London Gazette*, 3 July 46, p.3443
7. Ibid
8. Lewin, *Man of Armour*, p.71
9. Tedder, op cit, p.127

Chapter Four

The Struggle Continues

The failure of BATTLEAXE had an immediate effect on the command of Middle East Forces: Churchill decided that Wavell must go. To succeed him, the C-in-C, India, General Sir Claude Auchinleck, was appointed; Wavell would take over Auchinleck's position in India. The 'Auk' would soon come under pressure from the prime minister for action in the desert.

Not least amongst Churchill's reasons for demanding action was his belief that the ration strength of Middle East Command's ground forces represented its effective fighting strength. At the beginning of 1941 that ration strength was almost 336,000 and was to rise considerably – to over 490,000 – by the middle of the year but the prime minister failed to grasp that, in an undeveloped region, any army's support elements had to be much larger than in a European country. Thus it can be said, fairly, that the prime minister and his generals in North Africa did not see the same picture.

It was fortunate that Rommel had his problems, too. On 22 June Germany launched Operation BARBAROSSA, the invasion of the Soviet Union. The invasion forces had priority for equipment, fuel, ammunition and all the other matériel of war. Rommel was at the tail end of Germany's supply chain and his problems were exacerbated by British naval and air attacks on convoys between Italy and Libya. Thus Afrika Korps' commander was forced to sit on the frontier, continue the siege of Tobruk and rebuild his forces before renewing the offensive. He received more tanks but no new tank units, although 5th Light Division was renamed 21st Panzer, but managed to cobble together a new formation, which he called the Afrika Division, later to be restyled 90th Light Division, by bringing together independent infantry battalions and some artillery units. Alongside General Navarrini's Italian XXI Corps, Afrika Korps became part of Rommel's new command, Panzergruppe Afrika, with the Italian Savona Division incorporated in Afrika Korps. In addition, the Italian XX Corps, including Ariete Armoured and Trieste Motorized Divisions, was available, but remained outside Rommel's command.

For his part Auchinleck was also re-equipping and rebuilding his field force, which grew to 115,000 troops. Three new motorized infantry divisions arrived and ten new armoured regiments were added. Of the armoured regiments, three formed 1 Army Tank Brigade which, on arrival in Egypt, found that its tanks had been issued to other units for use in BATTLEAXE and thus 8, 42 and 44 RTR had to wait for three months before being re-equipped, this time with the Valentine. A new armoured brigade – 22 – arrived in October, made up of 2nd Royal Gloucestershire Hussars (2 RGH) and 3rd and 4th County of London Yeomanry (CLY) Regiments and equipped with Crusaders. Meanwhile, 4 Armoured Brigade was re-constituted with 8th King's Royal Irish Hussars and 3 and 5 RTR. The brigade, commanded by Gatehouse, was equipped with American M3 light tanks, known as Honeys in British service, although officially christened Stuarts. The Stuart was fast – 36mph – was smaller and lighter than Crusader but had similar armour (and a 37mm gun that was slightly superior to the 2-pounder in penetrative power) and was liked by its crews; the nickname 'Honey' was a mark of affection. Crusaders also provided the main equipment of 7 Armoured Brigade (7th Hussars, 2 and 6 RTR) but there were still many A13s and twenty-six A10s.

Although Rommel attempted a reconnaissance in force by 21st Panzer Division on 14 September he could not mount a major offensive due to operations by the RAF and the Royal Navy from Malta. Nonetheless, a new offensive was being planned, although the date was likely to be in early 1942. Meanwhile, Italian intelligence – always much better in Egypt than their allies – warned that the British were preparing a large-scale offensive. The Italian sources provided news of the arrivals of convoys delivering artillery, lorries, tanks and personnel while air reconnaissance confirmed that the British were building supply dumps close to the frontier.

Auchinleck was indeed preparing for a fresh offensive, although he had resisted Churchill's demands that it should be an early one. He was restructuring his forces which now included two corps, XIII and XXX. XIII Corps included 2nd New Zealand Division, 4th Indian Division and 1 Army Tank Brigade, with Matildas and some Valentines, and was commanded by Lieutenant General A. F. Godwin-Austen. XXX Corps was an armoured corps which included 7th Armoured Division and 1st South African Division as well as 22 Guards Brigade. The Desert Rats included three armoured brigades – 4, 7 and 22 – while the South African formation was a motorized infantry division of two brigades. Commanding XXX Corps was Lieutenant General Vyvyan Pope, who had been RAC Adviser at BEF HQ in France in 1940, the man who had identified the faults in British tanks and the flaws in their handling and had given evidence to the Bartholomew Committee on the necessity of concentrating armour. (He also foresaw that the Germans would up-gun their tanks and strengthen their armour and that a 6-pounder anti-tank gun was needed as soon as possible.) By 1941 Pope was among the leading proponents of armoured warfare in Britain. Appointed Major General AFVs at Middle East HQ on 20 September 1941, four days later he was told by Auchinleck that he would have XXX Corps. His appointment contradicts the oft-expressed opinion that Auchinleck was a bad picker of commanders. His Brigadier General Staff (BGS), Hugh Russell, was another expert in the field of armour, having previously commanded 7 Armoured Brigade. Their appointments augured well for XXX Corps and the new army of which it was part. This was Eighth Army, to which Auchinleck had appointed General Sir Alan Cunningham, victor in the recent East African campaign, as commander. While Eighth Army was to become arguably the most famous British field army in history, Cunningham would not rank among the great commanders.

Tragically for Eighth Army, Pope and Russell, who had quickly established a staff for XXX Corps HQ, with Brigadier Eric Unwin, their Assistant Quartermaster

General, boarded a Hudson on 5 October to fly to Cunningham's first Eighth Army conference on the forthcoming offensive. Almost immediately the Hudson got into difficulties and crashed into the Mocattam Hills, killing all on board.[1] Pope's death had grave repercussions on the course of the battle that lay ahead. Willoughby Norrie, GOC 1st Armoured Division, which was en route to Egypt, was given command of XXX Corps (he had arrived ahead of his division to prepare for their deployment). Although a brave soldier with Great War experience in the Tank Corps, he did not have Pope's understanding of armour.

The British offensive was codenamed Operation CRUSADER and preparations had been thorough. Auchinleck had resisted Churchill's pressure for an early offensive and, at a meeting at Chequers in August, had impressed the PM and the Defence Committee of the need to delay an offensive to have the greatest chance of success.[2] Central to those preparations was 7th Armoured Division, now commanded by Strafer Gott as Major General Creagh had been sent back to the UK in September; his tenure as GOC was the longest in the division's wartime history. Succeeding Gott as commander of Support Group was Brigadier 'Jock' Campbell, a Gunner who was to distinguish himself in the coming battle, earn the VC and later become divisional GOC before being killed in a car crash.

As already noted, 7th Armoured Division included three armoured brigades and its total tank strength on the eve of battle was 453 tanks, with 166 in 4 Armoured Brigade, 129 in 7 and 158 in 22. (The last named belonged to 1st Armoured Division which, as we have already noted, was en route to North Africa.) The disposition of tanks meant that 4 Brigade was equipped entirely with the Stuart light tank while the other brigades had mostly cruisers. Each brigade deployed three armoured units; 4 Brigade also included 2 RHA and 2nd Scots Guards.

The plans for CRUSADER went through changes in detail but were finalized as having two objectives: to pin down the enemy in the frontier defences and clear the Capuzzo–Tobruk sector; and to destroy the enemy's armour. As a result the siege of Tobruk would be lifted. These objectives would be achieved by XIII Corps, including 1 Tank Brigade (of 126 tanks), carrying out operations along the frontier, holding the Axis defences on the line Halfaya–Sidi Omar while 2nd New Zealand Division outflanked those defences from the south. Meanwhile, the armour of XXX Corps was to arc around the enemy's left, or southern, flank and, as well as destroying the Axis armour, was to ensure that that armour did not engage XIII Corps; 4 Armoured Brigade was to protect XIII Corps' flank. At 'the earliest possible moment' the Tobruk garrison was to sally forth to join in the battle, to which end 32 Tank Brigade was built up within the perimeter.[3]

That then was the plan. Eighth Army had 118,000 men, 860 tanks, 849 medium, field and anti-tank guns and air support from 512 aircraft.[4] This gave the British numerical superiority over the Axis in most respects: Italo-German strength was 102,000 men, 380 medium tanks (although one XIII Corps staff officer put the figure at 550 German and Italian tanks), 1,140 medium, field and anti-tank guns and a strong air element that was, however, smaller than the RAF. Brigadier Freddie de

Butts, then at HQ XIII Corps commented that these figures of Axis strength were 'misleading since we were soon to discover that the German armour was superior to ours in almost every aspect: mechanical reliability, armour and gunnery, quite apart from the skill and dash with which it was used'.[5]

Nonetheless, there was considerable optimism in the British ranks. Eighth Army had one inestimable advantage that cannot be overstated: complete surprise. The enemy were unaware of the intensive preparations – the three field maintenance centres (FMCs) that had been established to hold about 30,000 tons of ammunition, fuel and other supplies[6]– nor of the many tanks concentrating in the frontal area. A simple camouflage measure, known as sunshades, made tanks look like lorries from the air. Heavy rain, unprecedented in its intensity according to von Mellenthin, on the eve of CRUSADER grounded enemy aircraft, which had already failed to detect Eighth Army's build-up.

Rommel, preparing for an attack on 23 November, was in Rome when Eighth Army's assault began and, for once, was taken off balance. For his part, Auchinleck had set the date for D Day for CRUSADER as 18 November, delayed somewhat to allow final training for the South African infantry. On the 17th German preparations for the attack on Tobruk were entering their final phase with 15th Panzer Division moving up to the south-east of the perimeter while Afrika Division was already in its forming-up area. When the British wireless net fell silent that day, von Ravenstein, commanding 21st Panzer, added an anti-tank company to his reconnaissance screen at Tobruk. The Germans were in the wrong positions for the battle that was about to break out.

Fighting in Operation CRUSADER lasted until the turn of the year. Not only was it intense and brutal, it was also some of the most complicated fighting of the war. Major General 'Pip' Roberts, then a staff officer at HQ XXX Corps, commented that it 'turned out to be the most difficult to follow in the whole of the war in any theatre'.[7] Part of that was due to the fact that the battles were fought over an area of 2,500 miles in which 'map-reading was difficult'.[8] For this study it is not necessary to describe those battles in detail but the overall role of 7th Armoured Division will be summarized.

After a night of heavy rain, CRUSADER began at dawn on 18 November and, at first, XXX Corps' armour made good progress, meeting only light enemy reconnaissance elements. Nor did German or Italian aircraft put in an appearance as they were still grounded on waterlogged airfields. By the end of the first day 4 and 7 Brigades were on their objectives across the Trigh el Abd, while 22 Brigade was just short of its objective. At first Axis commanders believed the British advance to be no more than a reconnaissance in force, which is what Rommel, returning to Cyrenaica from Rome, also believed. It took some time for him to appreciate the true British intention.

On the 19th Rommel agreed to move a battlegroup of 21st Panzer southwards while 15th Panzer deployed to Gambut. This deployment occurred after he had received reports of the British advance, including news that the Italian Ariete Division was under attack. Ariete were dug in at Bir el Gubi and gave 22 Armoured

Brigade a bloody nose, forcing the British to break off the attack after a day-long battle. Although 22 Armoured Brigade claimed to have destroyed forty-five Italian tanks they had lost an equal number of their own.

Elsewhere 4 Armoured Brigade had been in bloody conflict with a German battlegroup of about 100 tanks that had moved south towards the frontier, supported by aircraft, including Ju87 Stuka dive-bombers. The tanks and their air support fell on HQ 8th King's Royal Irish Hussars. With the panzers opening fire beyond the effective range of the 37mm guns of the Hussars' Stuarts, the Germans held the upper hand. Although 5 RTR moved to aid the Hussars, the latter had lost twenty tanks by the time the action ended, many to the new German 50mm anti-tank gun, a highly effective weapon with a very low profile. Not surprisingly the British view was that German tank guns had done the damage.

In the centre 7 Armoured Brigade had also been in action and, in the early afternoon, attacked Sidi Rezegh airfield which they seized, capturing nineteen planes on the ground with eighty personnel and many vehicles. Sidi Rezegh was to be the pivot of the first phase of fighting. But already British commanders had committed the cardinal error of failing to concentrate their armour. As Macksey commented in his history of the Royal Armoured Corps:

> In the opening phases, units of the RAC were dispersed in a chase after elusive enemy tank formations, and in the act were offered up as separate targets for Rommel's selected counter strokes. Faced with the familiar dilemma of how to destroy pin-point, hard targets and still lacking a gun which enabled tanks to stand off and shell the enemy with high explosive, tank commanders were compelled, time and again, to indulge in Balaclava-like charges in the hope of overrunning emplaced guns.

Rommel may have been caught off-balance and failed initially to concentrate his own armour but he soon regained that balance and took advantage of the British dispersion of armour. Generally he was happy to allow the British armour to attack, picking them off with his anti-tank guns in their 'Balaclava-like charges'. On two occasions, however, he was also guilty of making foolish charges, the first at Sidi Rezegh on the 22nd and the other three days later when he raced for the frontier, outflanking his foe to strike them in the rear. Neither attack led to success but instead caused the loss of many tanks as the British 25-pounders dashed Rommel's hopes of smashing XXX Corps. However, by the 25th there was little left of 4 and 22 Armoured Brigades and the total strength of 7th Armoured Division was but fifty tanks, less than a tenth of the original British tank strength. At this stage of the war the German practice of recovering and repairing damaged tanks was generally better than the British but, on this occasion, the British mastered the art of recovery and repair, aided by Rommel himself in his desperate dash to the frontier since that allowed British units to hold the critical ground at Sidi Rezegh and repair many tanks that had suffered minor damage or had broken down. This helped rebuild Eighth Army's tank strength.

In this first phase of the battle 7th Armoured Division had earned three Victoria Crosses, two of which were posthumous, on 21 November. Rifleman John Beeley of 1st King's Royal Rifle Corps, in Support Group, was in a company that was pinned down by heavy enemy fire as it attacked Sidi Rezegh airfield. With his officers killed or wounded, Beeley took the initiative and charged an enemy position containing an anti-tank gun and two machine guns. Armed only with a Bren gun, Beeley knocked out the position, enabling his platoon to advance, but suffered mortal wounds and fell dead across his gun. His comrades took the objective, and many prisoners.

Later in the action some fifty enemy tanks attacked 2 RTR and S Company 2nd Rifle Brigade but were repulsed by fire from 2-pounders of 3 RHA and 25-pounders of 60th Field Regiment. Having refuelled and replenished ammunition the panzers returned. This time their only opposition came from two portée-mounted 2-pounders of 3 RHA under Second Lieutenant George Ward Gunn and a single Bofors 40mm anti-aircraft gun. The enemy concentrated their fire on the British guns which fought back desperately. The Bofors was knocked out, as was one 2-pounder while the other was damaged. But Ward Gunn got the damaged gun into action again and continued the struggle. After firing a few rounds, Ward Gunn was killed and the gun damaged beyond repair, but the portée was driven out of action, a new gun mounted and the detachment returned to the fray. Ward Gunn became the second VC of that November day.

The third VC also went to a Gunner, Brigadier Jock Campbell, Commander, Support Group. As the light faded, at about 5pm, HQ Support Group came under attack with the enemy closing to within 1,000 yards. It was then that Campbell led a counter-attack from his unarmoured staff car. Hanging on to the car's windscreen he led 6 RTR's surviving tanks and, when the car began to fall behind, leapt on a tank to direct the battle from there. For his sustained gallantry that day Campbell was also awarded the Victoria Cross.

On that day also the Tobruk garrison broke out, a sally leading to another two VCs, one to Captain Pip Gardner of 4 RTR in 32 Tank Brigade on the 23rd and the second two days later to Captain Bernard Jackman of the Royal Northumberland Fusiliers, who was killed in action.

Gradually the British wore Rommel down but it was, as Wellington would have put it, a close-run thing. And it was British superiority in logistics that swung the balance. On 3 December a re-supply convoy en route to the Axis garrison of Bardia was forced to turn back. For Rommel that was the last straw. He retreated to the Derna area prior to a withdrawal to El Agheila. But the fighting was far from over. That it was Rommel who was retreating and not Eighth Army was due to the personal intervention of Auchinleck.

On the 23rd, as he began to realize his true tank losses, Cunningham's earlier sense of optimism evaporated. He saw Eighth Army as unprepared to meet any possible Axis advance into Egypt – the same picture that Rommel was seeing – and refused to be re-assured by Godwin-Austen's report that XIII Corps' front was stable and that XXX Corps could still provide support from south of Sidi Rezegh. Asked by Cunningham to come to the front to decide CRUSADER's fate, Auchinleck flew from

Cairo and arrived at Eighth Army HQ at Maddalena in the early evening of the 23rd. Cunningham outlined a situation of German superiority and, since he felt that XXX Corps' armour could no longer guarantee the infantry's security, expressed his concern that his troops east and south of Sidi Rezegh might be cut off and that Eighth Army would be left with no reserves with which to stop Rommel thrusting into Egypt.

Auchinleck decided to continue the offensive. He noted that:

I was in no doubt myself at any time as to the right course, and at once instructed General Cunningham to continue his offensive with the object of recapturing Sidi Rezegh and joining hands with the Tobruk garrison. It looked as if the enemy was hard pressed and stretched to the limit, and this was borne out by his behaviour at this period of the battle: he was thrusting here, there and everywhere in what seemed to me a desperate effort to throw us off our balance, create chaos in our ranks, and so pave the way for regaining the initiative. The enemy, it is true, had temporarily succeeded in seizing the local tactical initiative, but the strategical initiative remained with us: we were attacking, he was defending. This general initiative it was at all costs essential to retain.[9]

In his history of the Second World War, Churchill was to record that 'By his personal action Auchinleck thus saved the battle and proved his outstanding qualities as a leader in the field.'[10] In fact, Auchinleck did more than instruct Cunningham to continue his offensive: he relieved Cunningham and took command of Eighth Army himself. He appreciated that the enemy was as bruised and confused as was Eighth Army, and that the latter could still prevail. And he was to provide the leadership that led to a British victory. Paradoxically, on the day that Auchinleck arrived at Cunningham's HQ, Rommel wrote to his wife to tell her that 'The battle seems to have passed its crisis. I'm very well, in good humour and full of confidence. Two hundred enemy tanks shot up so far. Our fronts have held.'

Although what was left of 7 Armoured Brigade and 1st King's Royal Rifle Corps were withdrawn to Cairo to re-organize on the 27th, 4 Brigade still had sixty tanks and was in action against the enemy, as was 22 Brigade, even though reduced to a composite regiment of only thirty tanks. Norrie pooled the tanks of both brigades and amalgamated them as 4 Brigade under Brigadier Gatehouse. Accounts of the actions of that and subsequent days note that the British tanks 'were consistently out-matched by the armour and guns of the Germans' with one NCO of 5 RTR, Jake Wardrop, commenting that the 'great thing' about an early encounter 'was the fact that we had fought back the crack German division and they had *bigger* guns and *thicker* tanks'[author's italics].[11] But Wardrop also gives an indication of why Eighth Army was gaining the upper hand when he wrote: 'The big experiment of guns, tanks and infantry was proving a huge success.'[12] It was no experiment but a proven tactic that had been drilled into 7th Armoured Division but seems to have been forgotten or ignored by 1941.

As Eighth Army added to its local successes, what Verney terms the second battle of Sidi Rezegh came to an end on 1 December. Rommel had failed to break British resistance and had to accept 'the conclusion that he could no longer carry on the investment of Tobruk'. Over the next nine days the enemy withdrew from the Tobruk perimeter, leaving the Axis garrisons to the east isolated. Seventh Armoured Division, now reduced to 4 Armoured Brigade, supported by 4th Indian Division, a South African brigade and five armoured-car regiments, thrust from Bir el Gubi towards Acroma while XIII Corps, with 70th Division from Tobruk, also attacked. During the fierce fighting that followed, Rommel's attempt to re-supply Bardia came to naught and he made his decision to withdraw, a retreat aided by the stout defence of Bir el Gubi by its Italian garrison. Rommel's withdrawal 'was well conducted … and never became a rout, and the German armour was handled with skill, generally behind a screen of anti-tank guns which our armour could not penetrate.' By dusk on 10 December Axis forces had withdrawn to the Gazala Line. There followed a few days of comparative rest for 7th Armoured Division.

Early on the morning of 15 December 4 Armoured Brigade was back in action, attempting to work around the southern flank of the Gazala Line but, next day, Rommel ordered a withdrawal and began a retreat that would take him back to Agedabia. This ended what von Mellenthin described as the battle of Gazala. He also noted that Rommel decided to withdraw as the Italian soldiers were suffering heavily and 'their fighting power had decreased to an alarming degree' while his command was 'in danger of exhausting our last stocks of ammunition'. Even so, Italian officers wanted to continue the fight and even Kesselring was taken aback by Rommel's decision.

Heavy rain, with occasional flooding, made pursuit difficult and attempts to cut off the enemy in his retreat from Benghazi failed. Throughout the withdrawal the enemy maintained his balance and deployed rearguards strong enough to strike back at the pursuers. This period is described by Jake Wardrop as:

> the period at which the steeplechase really began, from now until 20 December we chased them until they were right back behind the Agheila salt flats. We ran round them, over them and underneath them. It was cold and most nights we moved sweeping across the blue to head somebody else off. On those night marches, the drivers drove half asleep and the operators slept with the phones on their ears.[13]

On 26 December it was learned that 7th Armoured Division was to be relieved by 1st Armoured Division and would return to Cairo to re-organize. On 3 January 1942 Divisional HQ arrived in Cairo. Three days later 22 Armoured Brigade (which, reconstituted, had taken over from 4 Brigade) was relieved at the front by 1st Armoured Division, having suffered a double blow from two German counter-attacks on the road to El Agheila on 27 and 30 December in which the brigade lost sixty tanks. CRUSADER was over and with it 7th Armoured Division's role. Auchinleck's strategic plan was for a follow through from CRUSADER, codenamed ACROBAT, to take Tripolitania and remove the Axis presence from North Africa. First Armoured Division was to spearhead ACROBAT.

For Eighth Army it had been a pyrrhic victory with 2,908 dead, 7,300 wounded and 7,400 missing while 270 tanks had been lost. Against this Axis forces had suffered 33,000 casualties and lost 300 tanks. But another casualty on the British side was that they persisted in the belief that German tanks were better gunned and better armoured than their British counterparts. We have already noted the comments of Verney and Wardrop in this respect. Macksey has this to say in respect of Wardrop's comments.

> In reality the short 50mm in the Mark III was no better than the 2-pounder, and the short 75mm in the Mark IV only a rather inaccurate infantry support weapon whose effect on armour was greatly exaggerated. And, of course, the German 30mm armour was thinner than most British; simply (and fatally) the British teams investigating captured German tanks had as yet failed to find out that their armour was face-hardened and therefore proof against the uncapped 2-pounder shot except at the closest range. The deadliest threat remained the long 50mm anti-tank gun and the 88mm whose powers were still not fully realized.

There were still lessons to be learned, especially in terms of all-arms co-operation. Verney quotes an article, written by an officer who had experienced CRUSADER, which appeared in the *Royal Armoured Corps Journal* seven years later.

> To those who took part a bitter taste remained; those who fought in tanks cursed those who sent them into battle, inferior in armour and equipment and in tanks that broke down endlessly. The infantry, with a sprinkling of useless anti-tank guns, looked to the tanks to protect them against enemy tanks, and were bitter at their failure to do so. The armoured commanders, hurrying from one spot to another to protect infantry from the threat of enemy tanks which did not always materialize, blamed the infantry for wearing out their tanks and crews by the misuse of the decisive arm in Desert warfare.

The crews of the Crusaders had a valid point when talking about reliability – or the lack of it. Crusader earned a reputation for problems that it never shook off, some of which were exacerbated by desert conditions. One armoured regiment considered it lucky not to have six Crusaders a day break down on the march. The tank's Liberty engine was made up of separate sets of cylinders rather than a single block and tended to start disassembling itself when worked hard and fast across country in the desert, leading to oil leaks and major seizures, while the water pump contained soft white-metal components that were worn away by the ingestion of sand, leading to more leaks. On top of that the cooling fans were driven by exposed chains which also wore out more quickly in desert conditions.[14] On the plus side, Crusader's turret was capable of accepting a 6-pounder gun and the tank was up-gunned with the larger weapon with the first examples arriving in the Middle East in mid-1942.

Also due to reach artillery units in the Middle East at much the same time was the first self-propelled gun since the Birch gun of the 1920s. The lessons of 1941 of the 'naked 25-pounder' had been taken to heart and, in October, an improvised self-propelled armoured variant of the 25-pounder had been ordered. This was Bishop, or 'Ordnance, QF, 25pdr Mks 2 or 3, on Carrier, Valentine, 25pdr Gun Mk 1'. Bishop used the chassis and hull of the Valentine from which the turret was removed and replaced by an armoured barbette – a large metal box would be a more accurate description – housing a modified 25-pounder top carriage, complete with gun. The nature of the beast reduced the 25-pounder's performance as the barbette restricted elevation to 15 degrees, thereby almost halving range to 6,400 yards. Little thought seemed to have been given to the comfort of the detachment who, especially in desert conditions, had to work in very cramped conditions. Although an Ordnance Board Mission to North Africa in 1943 would comment that 'Nothing good can be said of the Valentine SP, although the detachments are efficient', Bishop did provide a useful interim weapon for the artillery regiments of the armoured divisions. Bishop, of which 100 were ordered in October 1941, remained in service throughout the rest of the North African campaign and through the Sicilian campaign into the early months in Italy. It also allowed gunner units to train in handling SP guns and learn the operational art of using them in conjunction with armour.

We have already noted that 2-pounder anti-tank gun detachments were mounting their weapons on lorries in order to provide mobility. Although the need for a 2-pounder replacement had been recognized early in the gun's life, the requirement for immediate replacements for 2-pounders lost in France had delayed the introduction of the replacement 6-pounder 57mm gun. Eventually the 6-pounder began leaving the factories in November 1941 and, by May 1942, was being built at a rate of over 1,500 per month. Thought was given to a self-propelled version, which led to Deacon, a turntable-mounted gun on the flat bed of a semi-armoured Matador lorry. Of the 175 models built most were sent to the Middle East but, although mechanically sound and effective, it suffered from much too high a profile and poor cross-country performance, being prone to bogging in sand. Deacon was withdrawn at the end of the North African campaign (remaining examples were later sold to Turkey) and anti-tank regiments had to wait a little longer for the American M-10 Wolverine SP 3-inch anti-tank gun, which was later up-gunned with the British 17-pounder anti-tank gun as Achilles, and Archer, a Valentine mounting a 17-pounder.

Mark Twain commented that history does not repeat itself but that it often rhymes. The truth of his aphorism was to be demonstrated in January 1942. Remember when 7th Armoured was relieved on the Cyrenaican frontier in early 1941 by 2nd Armoured Division, which was soon thrown into the maelstrom of battle by Rommel's unexpected offensive? Now, for a second time, 7th Armoured had been withdrawn from that same frontier and relieved by a formation with no experience of battle in North Africa and only limited experience of battle in France in 1940. In fact, scarcely had 1st Armoured arrived than it lost its GOC, Major General Herbert Lumsden, an advocate of armoured warfare, wounded in a strafing attack. Frank Messervy, an Indian cavalryman, was appointed in Lumsden's place.

After the fighting of the CRUSADER battles, Eighth Army needed a rest but, more importantly, re-equipment and supplies for a renewed offensive, the thrust into Tripolitania and the final defeat of Axis forces in North Africa. Initially, Rommel, expecting the British to resume their pursuit, applied his mind to meeting such an attack. He was relieved when a small convoy reached Tripoli and one of the ships unloaded twenty-three tanks. Just before Benghazi fell a German freighter had delivered another twenty-two tanks there. This reinforcement was welcome news, as was the arrival of armoured half-tracks and guns from the workshops at Tripoli. Then came another convoy with no fewer than fifty-four tanks, crews and fuel. This was manna from heaven for Rommel and a welcome boost to his forces awaiting a fresh British offensive (which Auchinleck expected to resume between 10 and 15 February). Rommel was enjoying the fruits of a period of Axis success in the naval war: the Mediterranean Fleet had lost the carrier *Ark Royal* and the battleship *Barham* to U-boat action in November while the Italian Decima MAS had damaged severely the battleships *Queen Elizabeth* and *Valiant* at anchor in Alexandria harbour in December; the cruisers *Galatea* and *Neptune*, the destroyer *Kandahar* and the sloop *Parramatta* had also been lost to mines or submarines, effectively putting the Royal Navy's Force K out of action for a time. Coupled with heavy bombing of Malta by Luftflotte II, which had been transferred from Russia to Sicily, Axis convoys could sail to Tripoli in much greater safety than before.

However, the British command believed that the Germans were not capable of offensive action and that Eighth Army had time to re-organize before resuming the march on Tripoli, a dangerous assumption to make when Rommel was about, but perhaps the British command was not yet tuned to Rommel's wavelength. As a result the front was held only lightly: a small, largely infantry, force that included two battalions of 1st Armoured Division's Support Group, another two from 200 Guards Brigade group and a composite squadron from 3rd and 4th County of London Yeomanry, with two dozen Stuarts, together with a reconnaissance squadron of 11th Hussars. (Elements of Eighth Army were also engaged in suppressing the Axis garrisons of Bardia and Halfaya.) Behind the front-line troops lay Brigadier Raymond Briggs' 2 Armoured Brigade (Bays, 9th Lancers and 10th Hussars) but they were ninety miles away, busily repairing their Crusaders and Stuarts and training. The brigade's tanks needed repair and maintenance as they had travelled the 450 miles from the railhead at Mersa Matruh on their tracks since there were no tank transporters. Each regiment had twenty-six Crusaders and eighteen Stuarts, and no personnel familiar with the desert.

The true situation on the other side of the line was revealed to Rommel by wireless intercept: the British were tired and needed reinforcement before resuming the offensive. He also knew that the British armoured formation in Cyrenaica was new to the desert. For Rommel this was an invitation to seize the initiative and attack. And he did just that. On 21 January Axis forces surged forward and took the British completely by surprise. The defensive screen was pushed aside but 2 Armoured

Brigade was quick to react. At 5am on the 22nd its three regiments were ordered 'to move at first light to an area, known as "Well with Wind-pump", some 30 miles to our south',[15] in what was considered to be a precaution rather than an immediate counter-attack from the desert flank. When 2 Armoured Brigade set off 10th Hussars were in the lead with the other two regiments echeloned to their flanks. At midday the brigade, halted south of Saunnu, learned that the enemy had broken through the Guards Brigade and were advancing rapidly along the Via Balbia. Briggs' formation was to swing westwards and intercept. However, instead of keeping his armour concentrated Briggs broke his brigade into regimental groups to respond to orders from above and calls for support from the infantry. Thus each regiment was thrown into action separately.

The first of Briggs' regiments in the subsequent advance was 9th Lancers, the 'Delhi Spearmen', the change of direction having placed them at the front. There was no contact with the enemy throughout the rest of that day, although Axis aircraft were seen to the south, and the brigade laagered for the night with B Echelon and the workshops in the Saunnu Depression where, under cover of darkness, a mixed Italo-German column attacked. As a battle broke out, Briggs sent the Bays to Saunnu and the other two regiments to deploy across the Antelat–Saunnu track.

About eight miles south-east of Antelat the Lancers clashed with the enemy and before long the Hussars were also engaged. Both had lost tanks due to breakdown after the long drive of the previous day and fuel was being used up rapidly. The Lancers suffered badly when they charged at enemy positions and some tanks even ran out of fuel in action and later had to be towed away. The Hussars lost twenty-seven tanks in the course of the day. One of their squadron leaders, Major Rex Wingfield, was awarded the MC for his leadership and courage that day (although recommended for the DSO) when his squadron, then in the lead, was attacked by twelve German tanks from the left while anti-tank guns opened up at short range from the right flank.

> With skilful use of smoke and by brilliant handling of his squadron Major Wingfield not only extricated his squadron from a delicate position, but by his initiative overran and destroyed several anti-tank guns and killed their crews. He subsequently engaged the enemy tanks which were forced to withdraw after several had been hit. Later, he personally returned in his own tank under fire and collected the crews and the wounded of his disabled tanks.[16]

While there were many acts of gallantry such as that shown by Wingfield, the bald fact remained that the British armour had again been committed piecemeal. Radio communication breakdowns compounded the problems and even though this was improved as armoured cars from the Royals and 11th Hussars entered the action 2 Armoured Brigade was now scattered and, failing to combine, 'soon fell victim to ambush and chance engagements with a concentrated foe'. With 1st Armoured Division in retreat, the Bays deployed as rearguard and lost many tanks. Although there was a proposal that 4th Indian Division should attack southward from Benghazi to stabilize the situation this was not acted on due to lack of information about enemy locations and strength. Moreover, 4th Indian's only armour was 8 RTR's Valentines which had just been driven over eighty miles from Mechili and needed time for the crews to recover and the tanks to be made fit for action.

Rommel never let go of his advantage and forced Eighth Army back to the Gazala Line by 4 February. The Desert Fox, as he was dubbed in the British forces, had shown his skill and daring yet again. Eighth Army, now commanded by Lieutenant General Neil Ritchie, had been outfoxed. But Rommel's forces were also exhausted and in no state for an immediate continuation of their advance. Both sides settled down to rebuild their strength. For Eighth Army that would mean new and better tanks – and more of them – and the excellent 6-pounder anti-tank gun as well as the arrival of the Bishop SPG and the 6-pounder-armed Crusader, although the last two mentioned would not appear in time for the next battles. However, although British numbers would exceed those of their opponents, the lack of training and experience in all-arms fighting was still a critical factor that would continue to plague them for some time yet.

On 27 February Auchinleck told Churchill that he planned:

1. To continue to build up armoured striking force in the Army forward area as rapidly as possible. 2. Meanwhile to make Gazala-Tobruk and Sollum-Maddalena positions as strong as possible and push railway forward towards El Adem. 3. To build up forward area reserves of supplies for renewal of offensive. 4. To seize first chance of staging limited offensive to regain landing grounds in area Derna-Mechili provided this can be done without prejudicing chances of launching major offensive to recapture Cyrenaica or safety of Tobruk base area.[17]

Auchinleck was also making strenuous efforts to increase the effectiveness of the forces under his command, especially Eighth Army. Conscious that all-arms co-operation lagged well behind that practised by the Germans, he established a Higher War course at Sarafand to train officers who might become divisional commanders as part of an effort to improve the quality of leadership and training and bring about better co-operation on the ground. At Haifa the Staff College had been expanded with an RAF element included to ensure greater inter-service co-operation while all tactical and weapon training schools in Middle East Forces were 'to ensure that a uniform doctrine, which took account of the characteristics of all three arms [artillery, armour and infantry] and was attuned to modern conditions, was taught under a single direction'.[18]

Ritchie had been appointed as Eighth Army commander as an interim measure but Churchill had announced that appointment to the House of Commons, thus giving it an undeserved imprimatur. Since Ritchie had shown himself as not fully able for the job Auchinleck now considered sidelining him by creating a GHQ Reserve with Ritchie as commander; this came to naught due to the shortage of formations; it might also have brought Montgomery to the desert as commander of Eighth Army.

Both sides sat along the Gazala Line – a series of defended localities linked by a long belt of wire and minefields from the coast near Gazala to Bir Hacheim, forty miles to the south-east – facing each other and gathering strength for a fresh offensive. Much had changed. Rommel now commanded Panzerarmee Afrika, in which the former Afrika Division had been re-equipped and renamed 90th Light Division, while German air superiority had neutralized Malta, forcing the Royal Navy to move its submarine flotilla from the island and placing the RAF on the defensive. In late April Hitler promised Mussolini that Malta would be invaded in June in an operation involving airborne forces. Rommel wanted to attack Tobruk and then push into Egypt to the Suez Canal and beyond. Initially the German high command wanted him to delay this attack until Malta had fallen but eventually gave permission for an offensive in May. Hitler's main interest lay in the Soviet Union and thus Germany's main effort was concentrated there, leaving Rommel very little with which to pursue the campaign in North Africa although he believed that a great strategic benefit could be reaped from the North African campaign. He envisaged his attack into Egypt carrying the Axis army on to conquer the entire Middle East and 'bring about the complete defeat of the entire British forces' in the theatre, as well as freeing Germany from all its worries about oil.

Appreciating that Eighth Army was being reinforced for an offensive, Rommel wanted to make his move first. In fact, he had underestimated his opponent's strength. Von Mellenthin commented that, had he known the true British strength, 'even Rommel might have baulked at an attack on such a greatly superior enemy'. Rommel's intelligence service was unaware of 22 Armoured and 32 Tank Brigades, or of the existence of the Knightsbridge box, held by 201 Guards Brigade, while 29 Indian Brigade at Bir el Gubi, and 3 Indian Motor Brigade south-east of Bir Hacheim were also missing from the Axis picture. Nor was it realized that 'the main Gazala minebelt had been extended from the Trigh el Abd as far south as Bir Hacheim. Our lack of information is a tribute to the security and camouflage of Eighth Army.'

As Rommel appreciated, Auchinleck also planned an offensive and was suffering intense pressure from Churchill to launch it before Eighth Army was ready. For the British the strategic situation had changed immensely. The Japanese had entered the war in December, invading Malaya and then Burma; British forces in the Far East were retreating while Malaya and Singapore had been lost. Reinforcements for North Africa and Eighth Army had been diverted to fight the new enemy – one division, 18th, had been lost when it was sent to Singapore shortly before the island fell – while formations and units in North Africa had been sent eastward, as had elements of the RAF; these included 70th Division and 7 Armoured Brigade from 7th Armoured Division. Two Australian divisions had been withdrawn from the Middle East because of the threat to their homeland; 9th Australian Division remained for the time being.

Nonetheless, Eighth Army continued to grow. The British defences were held by 1st South African Division in the north and 50th (Northumbrian) in the south while a Free French brigade under General Koenig garrisoned Bir Hacheim. Behind the defended localities, or 'boxes', were the armoured divisions, with Lumsden's 1st in the north and Messervy's 7th in the south, each deploying an armoured brigade (2 and 4 respectively) while 7th Armoured had no fewer than four infantry brigades under command, which would create its own problems. In addition, 22 Armoured Brigade was included in the order of battle, under Lumsden's command, as were two tank brigades, 1 and 32, with a mixture of Matildas and Valentines. Eighth Army was also well provided for with artillery and co-operation with the Desert Air Force, already good, was improving constantly. Air support had been excellent during the CRUSADER battles and Rommel's offensive, with the Desert Air Force representing the RAF's tactical element in North Africa.

The face of the armoured brigades had changed considerably with the arrival of the American M3 Grant medium tanks. The M3 had been developed following US Army study of the 1939–40 campaigns in Poland and France, as result of which it was decided that a 75mm gun should be standard tank armament. However, the turret of the new M2A1 tank could not take a 75mm and a new turret was needed. In the meantime a temporary solution was necessary until a new tank with a 75mm turret-mounted gun could be produced. That interim solution was to mount the 75mm in a side sponson on the tank's hull, retaining the M2A1's 37mm in the turret. Thus was born the M3 Lee/Grant tank, which looked like a combination of contemporary thinking with a throwback to early British Great War tanks. The M3 Lee was adopted by the US Army, but used mainly for training, while the M3 Grant had a turret designed to mount a radio, reflecting British practice. The Grants were about to be blooded for the first time. Crews had undergone training and were happy with a tank that carried a gun which could fire a high-explosive shell to deal with enemy anti-tank gun crews. The Grant's great drawback was that the sponson mounting meant that the 75 could not be fired from a hull-down position; its traverse was also limited to 20 degrees. (At first crews did not realize that the turret-mounted 37 was better at penetrating enemy armour than the 75.) Another drawback was its riveted hull; those rivets had an unpleasant propensity to ricochet around inside if the tank was struck by an enemy round. Nonetheless, the appearance of the Grants was a shock to their opponents. In 7th Armoured Division the three regiments of 4 Armoured Brigade each deployed two squadrons of Grants and one of Stuarts. In the other two armoured brigades each regiment had a single Grant squadron and two of Crusaders or Stuarts; the 6-pounder-armed Crusader had yet to arrive.

Another shock to the enemy armour was provided by the arrival in front-line units of the new 6-pounder anti-tank gun. Known as 'Roberts' to conceal their identity as long as possible, these could penetrate 74mm of armour sloped at 30 degrees at a range of 1,000 yards, an ability that would increase as improved ammunition became available. (The 6-pounder was also to go into service with the US Army as their 57mm anti-tank gun.) Although few in number in the coming battles (112 had reached units) the 6-pounder was to wreak havoc on enemy tanks later in the summer. Had more been available at the end of May Axis armour would have suffered many more losses.

XIII Corps held the northern part of the Gazala Line with 1st South African Division deployed from Gazala to Alam Hamza and 50th (Northumbrian) from there to south of the Trigh Capuzzo. XXX Corps was to meet and deal with Rommel's armoured assault which, it was expected, would take one of two forms: exploitation along the Trigh Capuzzo, or a drive into the desert to outflank the Bir Hacheim position. Should the attack come through the British centre Ritchie's armour would have time to concentrate as the enemy would have to breach the minefields. Since an attack around Bir Hacheim would present different operational problems, the armoured brigades were to deploy in positions from which they could concentrate as rapidly as possible. Auchinleck emphasized to Ritchie the need to keep the armour concentrated and not to disperse it as before. Nonetheless, Eighth Army's commander disposed 2 Armoured Brigade astride the Trigh Capuzzo west of El Adem and eight miles north-east of 22 Armoured. The latter was deployed close to Bir el Harmat, north of the Trigh el Abd and some fifteen miles north-west of 4 Armoured, which was about twelve miles east of Bir Hacheim. These dispositions proved Eighth Army's undoing; the British brigades were offered up piecemeal to Rommel.

Another factor telling against the British was summarized by Liddell Hart:

The basic defect in the British dispositions was that they had been planned primarily with a view to an offensive – under pressure from the War Cabinet … They were better suited to provide a pivot for an attack westwards, than to meet an attack by Rommel. Moreover, the vast accumulation of supplies in the forward base at Belhamed (just north of Sidi Rezegh) weighed on the minds of the British commanders, making them hesitate to manoeuvre their armour in any way that might uncover their base.

Rommel was aware that he was taking a risk as he had fewer tanks than his foe: he assessed his own tank strength as 320 German and 240 Italian and the British strength at 900. His figure for British tanks is close to Ritchie's true figure of 849 tanks of which 573 were in the armoured divisions with a further 276 equipping two army tank brigades.[19] Thus the initial balance was about three-to-two in Ritchie's favour while the scales were weighed even more to his advantage by the 240 poor Italian tanks and fifty Panzer IIs, which would have little chance in any tank-versus-tank battle. As far back as 8 February Auchinleck had emphasized the need for training to achieve better co-operation in battle but there had not been enough time or, in some cases, willingness, to change how things were done on the British side. Thus another advantage was conceded to Rommel.

Early in the afternoon of 26 May Rommel opened his offensive, Operation THESEUS. In the Gazala-Sidi Muftah area, to the north, an infantry attack was launched on 1st South African Division. But this was a diversion since the main attack was being made by armour under General Walter Nehring, commander of Afrika Korps, at the French in Bir Hacheim. At the same time the Italian Ariete Armoured and Trieste Motorized Divisions were to advance through the gap north of Koenig's position; both formations formed Gruppe Crüwell, commanded by General Ludwig Crüwell, formerly commander of Afrika Korps. The southern element of the attack was codenamed Operation VENEZIA.

Von Moltke declaimed that no plan survives first contact but Rommel's did not even reach that point. He lost the element of surprise when British reconnaissance elements spotted the dust cloud of the VENEZIA formations and he added confusion by deciding to change those formations' tasks, switching the attack on Bir Hacheim from Afrika Korps to Gruppe Crüwell. But his orders were not picked up by Trieste, which continued on its original axis; Ariete headed alone for Bir Hacheim. And Afrika Korps, instead of having a relatively easy race around the southern flank of the British line, ran into much tougher opposition than expected in the form of Grants and 6-pounder anti-tank guns. Rommel's intelligence staff had been completely unaware of the presence of either new weapon.

The confusion created by Rommel was compounded next day. Neither side gained an advantage on the 27th with the French at Bir Hacheim holding off Ariete, and Afrika Korps splitting by detaching 90th Light. Nehring's decision allowed British columns to strike through the gap in Afrika Korps and harass the supply columns. Meanwhile the panzer divisions crossed the Trigh Capuzzo and came under attack from British armour. However, Ritchie had come to Rommel's aid because, in spite of Auchinleck's orders to concentrate his armour, Eighth Army's commander 'had thrown his armour into the battle piecemeal and thus given us the chance of engaging them in each separate occasion with just about enough of our own tanks. This dispersal of the British armoured brigades was incomprehensible.'

South of Bir Hacheim the commander of 3 Indian Motor Brigade reported to Messervy at 7th Armoured Division HQ that he was facing 'a whole bloody German armoured division'. In fact he was being attacked by Ariete. Although the Italians were surprised to find the Indians across their axis of advance they recovered rapidly and hit 3 Indian Brigade so hard that it had ceased to exist within thirty minutes. More of the same followed. At the Retma Box, which had yet to be finished, 7 Motor Brigade was caught unawares and all but crumpled under an attack by 90th Light. Meanwhile, 4 Armoured Brigade had been ordered to support 7 Motor and 3 Indian Brigades but, as it was preparing to move off, Brigade HQ was struck by 15th Panzer Division. Then 7th Armoured Division HQ was also overrun. Messervy was among those captured, although he subsequently escaped.

The leading unit of 4 Armoured, 3 RTR, met 15th Panzer almost head-on. But the tanks were deployed for action and the Grants, and supporting anti-tank guns of the Chestnut Troop RHA took a heavy toll of the Germans, as Rommel would note. Bill Close, recently commissioned from the ranks, was in B Squadron, equipped with Grants. He recalled that B and C Squadrons formed a line taking 'as much shelter from the ridge as the low 75mm sponson would allow' until, at a range of about 1,200 yards, the order to fire was given.

The 15th Panzer Division ... must have experienced a severe shock. They were using their normal tactics with anti-tank guns up to 88mm calibre deployed behind the advancing waves. Believing they were facing tanks armed only with two-pounders – they may even have assumed after seeing the Recce Squadron that the Grants were Honeys – they slowed at a distance which under normal circumstances would have required us to close with them and suffer the inevitable consequences. Instead they met concentrated and destructive fire.

The Grant's 75mm … gun fired a fourteen-pound shell which could cause severe damage at 1,500 yards and penetrate the thickest armour of a Mark III at 1,200 yards.

Furthermore the Grants had the additional firepower of their 37mm turrets, equal in this case to two squadrons of Honeys or Crusaders. As flame spurted from the line of tanks, a positive blizzard of high grade steel whipped over the level ground.[20]

This encounter stopped 15th Panzer temporarily. But a German counter-attack, supported by some 88s, knocked out a number of British tanks and it became clear that 3 RTR faced a large enemy formation. The battalion withdrew smartly to the north. The Irish Hussars were not so fortunate. The panzers hit them before they got into battle formation and the regiment was all but wiped out, for the second time; only two Grants survived, the commanding officer was captured and many men were killed, wounded or captured. About four miles north, the brigade's other unit, 5 RTR, encountered 21st Panzer Division and, in the ensuing battle, lost a number of tanks but inflicted significant casualties on the enemy; Macksey wrote that the battalion 'had a good day, catching enemy columns with their 75s and causing immense damage'. By the end of the day 4 Armoured Brigade had ceased to be an effective formation. The same could be said of 7th Armoured Division, which was to be without a GOC until the afternoon of the 29th.

First Armoured Division had also engaged Afrika Korps with 22 Armoured Brigade losing thirty tanks in as many minutes when it clashed head-on with the two panzer divisions, prompting Lumsden to order the brigade back to the Knightsbridge area to regroup. Lumsden then ordered both 2 and 22 Armoured Brigades to make co-ordinated strikes on Afrika Korps' right flank. Supported by the divisional artillery, that attack forced the panzer divisions to stop after which the Matildas of 1 Army Tank Brigade joined in. The British attackers penetrated between Rommel and his armour, cutting him off for some time, and also wrought havoc in the Axis rear echelons, knocking out much soft-skinned transport.

Confusion may have reigned in Eighth Army that evening but it is interesting to note Rommel's appreciation of the day's fighting:

it was clear that our plan to overrun the British forces behind the Gazala line had not succeeded. The advance to the coast had also failed and we had thus been unable to cut off the 50th British and 1st South African Divisions from the rest of the Eighth Army. The principal cause was our underestimate of the strength of the British armoured divisions. The advent of the new American tank had torn great holes in our ranks. Our entire force now stood in heavy and destructive combat with a superior enemy.

The shock of meeting the Grants and suffering unexpected losses to them had the effect of causing Rommel to underestimate the effect his forces had had on the British armour. Moreover, the British had failed signally to appreciate and exploit Panzerarmee's weaknesses. In such fashion did Ritchie hand the advantage to Rommel. Messervy must also take part of the blame: 'Had all his tanks been positioned in their previously reconnoitred defensive positions on the left at Bir Hacheim, then they could have dealt Rommel a mortal blow.'[21] Pip Roberts, CO of 3 RTR, described those positions, writing that:

> a particularly good battle position was selected some three miles SE of Bir Hacheim, where the whole brigade could take up hull–down positions – or as hull–down a position as is possible with the Grant. ... We felt that if the German panzers ran their heads up against this position they were in for a very nasty shock, particularly as it would be the first time they would encounter the 75mm guns from the Grant.[22]

Rommel's comments on the day might have been very different if both Ritchie and Messervy had implemented Auchinleck's orders to concentrate the armour. Since the hitting power of the Grant's 75 allowed the British to engage the Germans at a range at which the latter would have considered themselves safe, Roberts' 'very nasty shock' might well have been a battle-winning episode for Eighth Army.

But the opportunity to smash Rommel's offensive was thrown away and Eighth Army was pitched into a major battle that would cost many lives on both sides. Next morning Rommel advanced again but only with 21st Panzer Division as 15th was almost out of fuel and ammunition. The British position dubbed Commonwealth Keep fell to 21st after a determined fight while Ariete, advancing northwards from Bir el Harmat, found itself in combat with two British brigades – 2 Armoured engaged from the east and 1 Army Tank Brigade from the north-west – from which the British emerged with less damage and fewer losses. At El Adem the rump of 4 Armoured Brigade – 5 RTR and a composite unit of Irish Hussars and 3 RTR – attacked 90th Light and drove it off. While 21st Panzer was moving north that day, General Lumsden had intended that 2 and 22 Armoured Brigades should attack it from the flank but 22 Armoured had to be deployed to watch 15th Panzer, leaving 2 Armoured to harass the Germans but unable to block their advance. The immobile Germans also came under attack from the Desert Air Force, which did outstanding work in spite of poor visibility.

The second day of battle ended with Ritchie 'still satisfied with the progress of the battle. He considered rightly that Rommel's plan, which had been revealed by captured orders, had been badly upset.' Eighth Army's commander felt that he could still destroy the Axis forces completely as he could concentrate 240 cruisers and ninety I-tanks with another forty cruisers and thirty I-tanks due to arrive next day, the 29th. Auchinleck, accepting Ritchie's reports, was also optimistic but emphasized the need to strike quickly before Rommel regained his equilibrium. Ritchie seems never to have grasped this need. Meanwhile two Italian divisions, Pavia and Trieste, having discovered locations not under continuous fire, were creating gaps in the minefields near the Trigh Capuzzo and Trigh el Abd.

Rommel was indeed anxious at the end of the 28th. His force was dispersed, he had suffered some 200 tank casualties, and his supply situation was precarious as he was depending on a route around Bir Hacheim that was vulnerable to attack while minefields still blocked the Trigh Capuzzo and Trigh el Abd. He decided to concentrate his force on the 29th. Then, late in the day, he learned that the two Italian divisions had created breaches in the minefields through which supplies could be brought by shorter and safer routes.

On 29 May Gruppe Crüwell continued pushing against the South Africans, although Sabratha Division achieved nothing and lost 400 men captured. That same day Crüwell became a prisoner himself when his Storch aircraft was shot down over the battlefield. But Rommel showed his skill as a leader by taking great personal risks to lead supply vehicles through to Afrika Korps from Bir el Harmat, thus alleviating 15th Panzer's problems and allowing the division to rejoin the battle by mid-morning. By then 21st Panzer was in action against 2 Armoured Brigade which had launched an attack earlier in the morning. Into the fray were drawn 15th Panzer and Ariete as well as two units of 22 Armoured Brigade while 4 Armoured would also have joined but for a fierce sandstorm. This battle lasted throughout the day and by nightfall 'both sides were severely battered and completely exhausted, but the Axis formations had partly succeeded in concentrating; even the 90th Light Division had joined up'. Once again the Desert Air Force had provided staunch support.

Rommel's regrouping saw 15th and 21st Panzer, Ariete and 90th Light Divisions west of the British Knightsbridge position and between Trigh Capuzzo and Trigh el Abd. He now recast his plans by going on the defensive while he regained his balance. However, his new positions, in the area dubbed the Cauldron, gave Ritchie the impression that Eighth Army had scored a tactical success as Rommel had already lost about 200 tanks and seemed confined to an area no more than four miles by two in size. Nothing could be further from the truth since Rommel had the two gaps through the minefields for resupply and a screen of anti-tank guns to protect his front. For the Desert Fox there was one complication: the presence of a British box at Sidi Muftah held by 150 Brigade. Since this menaced one of Panzerarmee's supply routes, Rommel decided to eliminate it. This led to desperate fighting in which 150 Brigade held out courageously, refusing to surrender, until German and Italian troops finally overran the box on 1 June. Rommel summed up the fighting thus:

The attack was launched on the morning of 31 May. German–Italian units fought their way forward yard by yard against the toughest British resistance imaginable. The defence was conducted with considerable skill and, as usual, the British fought to the last round. They also brought a new 57mm anti-tank gun into use in this action. Nevertheless, by the time evening came we had penetrated a substantial distance into the British positions.

The 'new 57mm anti-tank gun' was 'Robert', the 6-pounder. This appears to be the first German mention of the gun in action although it may have been encountered elsewhere and not identified; examples were, of course, captured at Sidi Muftah.

Opportunities to catch Rommel off-balance had been lost even though Ritchie had been planning an offensive, Operation LIMERICK, by XIII Corps. But, on 5 June, Ritchie did launch a counter-offensive, Operation ABERDEEN, in which some objectives were taken before infantry/armour co-ordination broke down and a German attack inflicted heavy losses on Eighth Army's infantry. Moreover, the British artillery had failed to cause significant damage to the enemy's positions, principally because their fire was directed on the wrong locations; von Mellenthin noted that 'Ariete signalled that the British shells were falling well short of their positions, and in fact the preliminary bombardment was completely wasted on empty desert'. Thus the enemy escaped the full weight of British guns. Ritchie continued to believe that Eighth Army had done well, claiming that the enemy had taken heavy losses and was in bad shape. This was simply not true: 22 Armoured Brigade had lost sixty tanks, four British field regiments had also been lost and the second prong of ABERDEEN, an attack by I-tanks ran into trouble when 21st Panzer hit the British tanks from the flank, driving them into a minefield and fire from anti-tank guns. And Messervy had been captured for a second time during a German counter-attack although, once again, he escaped quickly. Thus it can only be said that the battle of the Cauldron was a German victory.

Fighting rumbled into the following day with Messervy trying to rescue those British troops still inside the Cauldron. By evening, however, it was all over. ABERDEEN had cost Eighth Army heavily with 200 tanks, four field regiments (ninety-six guns) and an infantry brigade lost. With this phase of the battle over, Rommel was in a better position than at any time since crossing his start line. 'Over an undeveloped country, a great area lacking in landmarks'[23] the armoured clash had been fought at considerable speed. There had been confusion, piecemeal fighting and exhaustion on both sides but Rommel's force was concentrated, had kept its supply routes open and was now confident. By contrast morale in Eighth Army was shaken after a series of 'swift retreats and some disasters' and infantry soldiers began wondering about their armoured comrades. There were stories of armoured formations arguing against orders and leaving the infantry in the lurch. As one eminent soldier-historian has summarized it:

It was the old cry from Waterloo: 'Where are our Cavalry?' The fault lay not with the brave soldiers of the tank units themselves so much as with the commanders who had become accustomed more to discussion than obedience; and lost time and initiative thereby. It also lay with inadequate tactical doctrine, and an habitual failure to grasp the best methods of attack.[24]

In his *Despatch* Auchinleck identified this battle as the point at which Eighth Army lost its chance of turning the tide:

The failure of Eighth Army's counter-attack on June 5 was probably the turning-point of the battle. Until then our chances of putting the enemy to flight and even of destroying him had seemed good.[25]

Although XXX Corps had suffered heavily, XIII Corps, save for 150 Brigade, remained intact and, on the morning of 11 June, Ritchie swung its left flank onto the line of the Trigh Capuzzo, parallel to Eighth Army's main lines of communication, and at ninety degrees to what was left of the Gazala Line. East of XIII Corps stood the strongpoints of Knightsbridge, El Adem and Belhamed, covering Tobruk and continuing the defensive line. Eighth Army still outnumbered its foe in tanks: 1st and 7th Armoured Divisions could muster about 200 tanks while there were eighty I-tanks in the tank brigades. Against this, Rommel had only 150 tanks in the two panzer divisions and a further sixty Italian tanks. Irrespective of the setbacks of recent days, and the losses of tanks, Ritchie still held the advantage. But Ritchie was no Rommel who would never have countenanced his command being pinned against the coast, with the possibility of being hammered to destruction, the situation in which Ritchie was placing Eighth Army.

Rommel chose that evening to take his armour out of the Cauldron with 15th Panzer, 90th Light and Trieste making for El Adem while 21st Panzer and Ariete struck towards Acroma. An Eighth Army move to repel 15th Panzer's advance was foiled when Rommel sent 21st Panzer into the rear of 7th Armoured. Once again Messervy went missing involuntarily. Having run into 90th Light while en route to Army HQ he was forced to take cover in a dry well and so Lumsden, arriving with 1st Armoured, was asked to take command of 7th as well. Lumsden proposed that the armour should fall back into the Knightsbridge box but Norrie ordered him to break through 15th Panzer.

The ensuing battle was yet another disaster for Eighth Army. The action lasted throughout the afternoon of the 12th and about 120 British tanks were lost, with the German anti-tank guns doing most of the damage. This was the worst defeat yet inflicted on British armour and left XXX Corps but a shadow of itself and incapable of action. By evening the surviving British tanks were east of Knightsbridge. That afternoon the Germans had shown up the inadequacy of British tactics and leadership. The Grants, with their 75mm guns, may have outmatched the Mark IIIs and IVs but the Crusaders, still with 2-pounders, needed a three-to-one advantage to match the Mark IIIs while the Valentines, also with 2-pounders, were slow and the Stuarts were only 'very good armoured reconnaissance vehicle[s]'. Furthermore those regiments with a mix of Grant and Crusader squadrons had failed to develop a common battle drill.[26] Even the availability of replacement tanks had not helped XXX Corps (at the beginning of the day there had been 330 British tanks, more than twice the number under Rommel's command).

Although Auchinleck had spent the day at Ritchie's HQ he had not interfered with the conduct of the battle, believing that Ritchie had not lost his nerve – which was true – and that he could hold Rommel. He accepted Ritchie's assessments, but these and the situation reports that Auchinleck received at Army HQ were already out of date when he read them. The situation at the front was worsening. Unaware of that, Auchinleck flew back to Cairo next day.

Rommel put such pressure on 201 Guards Brigade at Knightsbridge that Gott ordered the evacuation of the box on the evening of the 13th. With Eighth Army being pressed northwards and threatened with extinction between Gazala and Tobruk, XXX Corps down to fifty tanks, with only twenty I-tanks still in action, Ritchie issued orders for XIII Corps to move eastwards to the Egyptian frontier. Those orders were given in the early hours of 14 June: Ritchie realized that he could not stop Rommel from cutting off XIII Corps.

During one action to slow Rommel's advance on Knightsbridge in the evening of 13 June, 15th Panzer was engaged by the remnants of the British armour. Although 2 Armoured Brigade had run out of ammunition a relieving effort was made by a combined 7/42 RTR, under Lieutenant Colonel Henry Foote, that allowed the Guards to withdraw. Such was Foote's courage and leadership on this and other occasions that he was awarded the Victoria Cross. (Foote's battalion was in 32 Army Tank Brigade, which would shortly be captured in Tobruk.)

As the crisis deepened Ritchie considered that Tobruk could be held, although Auchinleck thought otherwise since the Navy was reluctant to carry out resupply, as it had done the previous year, and the landward defences had been denuded with the minefields lifted to be replanted in the Gazala Line. Crucial to Tobruk's survival was support from a force operating in the area El Adem–Belhamed but such support was killed off on 17 June with the final tank battle of the Gazala struggle. That day Messervy ordered the survivors of 4 Armoured Brigade to attack the German armour concentrated between Sidi Rezegh and El Adem. Their pennants fluttering proudly, ninety British tanks charged the two German armoured divisions. There would be but one result. More than thirty tanks were lost. Messervy was removed from command of 7th Armoured Division and Eighth Army was left without an armoured arm. What was left of 4 Armoured Brigade made for Egypt.

Tobruk fell on 21 June, Auchinleck's birthday. In its death throes there had been a demonstration of what might have been had British commanders adapted the 3.7-inch heavy anti-aircraft gun to the anti-tank role. In the defence of Tobruk gunners of 68th HAA Regiment used their weapons, dug in deeply as protection against dive-bombing attacks, to great effect. One gunsite held out for four hours until swarming infantry overwhelmed it. The guns accounted for at least four enemy tanks.[27]

Rommel was promoted to field marshal, the youngest in the German army, and given permission to strike into Egypt and destroy, finally, British forces in the country. Although short of supplies, he struck out. Ritchie had planned to hold Egypt on a line anchored on the pre-war seaside resort of Mersa Matruh but Auchinleck relieved him as commander of Eighth Army and ordered withdrawal to the line of defended localities from El Alamein to the edge of the Qattara Depression.

On 27 June an exchange of telegrams between the Chiefs of Staff and the Commanders-in-Chief, Middle East, on operations in Cyrenaica was presented to the War Cabinet. It was noted that:

the only tank capable of meeting German tanks on anything approaching equal terms is the Grant. We deployed 138 Grants against 320 Mark III and IV German tanks. All other tanks, Crusader, Stuart, Valentine, Matilda, now hardly count in armoured battle, for lack of a more powerful weapon than the 2-pounder ...

[The Grant] ... stands up to heavy punishment; its main defect is that its 75mm gun has a very limited traverse. To that extent it is not entirely satisfactory. This defect is remedied in later models not yet available in the Middle East.[28]

The 'later' model referred to was the new American tank, the M4 Sherman. Churchill, who was in Washington, was assured by Roosevelt that 300 Sherman tanks would be transferred from the US Army to Eighth Army. Before long those tanks were loaded on ships for the Middle East.

Also on the high seas en route to Egypt and Eighth Army were the first of the 6-pounder-armed Crusader tanks while Bishop self-propelled guns were being produced and American M7 self-propelled 105mm howitzers would soon follow. Meanwhile, another two armoured divisions were preparing to join Eighth Army's order of battle: 8th Armoured Division was formed in the UK in late 1940 and, with 23 and 24 Armoured Brigades, was en route to join Middle East Forces as Eighth Army retreated into Egypt; 10th Armoured Division was formed in Palestine in August 1941 by re-designating and re-organizing 1st Cavalry Division. With Major General Alec Gatehouse as GOC and including 8 and 9 Armoured Brigades, 10th Armoured joined XXX Corps' order of battle on 19 June.[29]

In spite of Rommel's genius, Gazala was a battle that Eighth Army could, and should, have won. In a defensive role, in which, as Rommel noted, British soldiers excelled, with considerable numerical superiority in tanks and more artillery than the Axis, Eighth Army had every opportunity to defeat Rommel, but the failure to concentrate armour and to co-ordinate properly armour and infantry outweighed the advantages. Pip Roberts wrote:

we had a magnificent opportunity of inflicting a heavy defeat on the Germans, but our armoured divisions were spread about the battlefield and were defeated in detail and then further decimated by small attacks against [the Axis] positions which were well defended by anti-tank guns.[30]

Notes

This chapter is based on Playfair et al, *The Mediterranean and the Middle East. Vols II and III* from the Official History series, Liddell Hart, *The Tanks (Vol II)* and *The Rommel Papers*, Macksey, *A History of the Royal Armoured Corps*, Verney, *The Desert Rats: The 7th Armoured Division in World War II*, von Mellenthin *Panzer Battles*, and the war diaries of Eighth Army, Western Desert Force, XIII Corps, XXX Corps, 1st and 7th Armoured Divisions, 4 Armoured Brigade, 7 Armoured Brigade and 22 Guards Brigade. Information on artillery and tanks is taken from Hogg, *British and American Artillery of World War 2* and Hogg and Weeks, *Illustrated Encyclopaedia of Military Vehicles*, except where otherwise noted. Other sources are as follows:

1. Lewin, *Man of Armour*, p.139
2. Connell, *Auchinleck*, pp.266–7
3. NA Kew, WO201/358: Report of Operations, Eighth Army, Sep-Nov 1941
4. Ibid
5. de Butts, *Now the Dust has Settled*, p.30
6. NA Kew, WO201/358, op cit
7. Roberts, *From the Desert to Baltic*, p. 56
8. Ibid
9. *London Gazette*, No. 38177, 15 January 1948, Despatch, p.31
10. Churchill, *The Second World War* Vol III, p.505
11. Wardrop, *Tanks Across the Desert*, p.32
12. Ibid, p.36
13. Ibid, p.37
14. Fletcher, *Crusader*, pp.19–20
15. IWM, Wingfield Memoir, p.67
16. *London Gazette* 21 Apr 1942; NA Kew, WO373/19
17. Butler, *Grand Strategy*, iii, p.450
18. NA Kew, CAB44/97, p.10
19. Doherty, *A Noble Crusade*, p.59
20. Close, *A View from the Turret*, pp.73–4
21. Forty, in Wardrop, *Tanks across the Desert*, p.40
22. Roberts, op cit, p.65
23. NA Kew, CAB44/97, Intro
24. Fraser, *And We Shall Shock Them*, p.200
25. *London Gazette* No. 38177, op cit, Despatch, p.50
26. NA Kew, CAB44/97, p.11
27. Routledge, *Anti-Aircraft Artillery*, p.140
28. NA Kew, CAB66/26/2, pp.1–2
29. Joslen, *Orders of Battle*, pp.22 & 25–6
30. Roberts, op cit, p.89

Chapter Five

Eighth Army Turns the Tables

As Eighth Army retreated to the El Alamein–Qattara Line, Sir Claude Auchinleck pondered the situation. Rommel could be held on that line whereas Ritchie's planned stand at Mersa would have thrown away Eighth Army, allowed the Axis to overrun the Delta and changed completely the strategic balance of the war, threatening the Russian southern flank and even India. As Eighth Army commander, as well as C-in-C, Middle East, Auchinleck's burden was great but he was able to bear it, withdrawing his troops from action at Mersa Matruh and bringing them back to the new line. It was not an easy withdrawal: 1st Armoured Division clashed twice with Afrika Korps and once with two Italian divisions while British stragglers were intermingled with Panzerarmee's leading elements. Even so, Auchinleck got his men back and Eighth Army was waiting for Rommel when he hit the Alamein Line on 1 July. The first battle of El Alamein had begun.

Auchinleck had been aware of Eighth Army's problems and had plans to cure them, including, as noted in Chapter Four, that Higher Command course at Sarafand, expansion of the Staff College at Haifa, adding an RAF element to ensure closer air-ground co-operation (already very good thanks to Auchinleck and Tedder's close personal relationship), and ensuring the teaching of a uniform doctrine at all Middle East Command tactical and weapon training schools.[1] While these were longer-term solutions Auchinleck also modified Eighth Army's operational shape. Aware that immobile infantry in the Alamein defended localities (he did not like the term 'box') presented a hostage to fortune, he 'thinned them out so that no more remained in the line than could be carried by allocated transport'[2] and applied Rommel's battlegroup system by breaking the divisional organization into brigade-sized battlegroups.

The change to the battlegroup system created much controversy, especially from Montgomery, but Auchinleck had identified the nature of desert warfare:

Swift turning movements are the essence of desert warfare. To do this you must be strong in 'armour', stronger than the enemy or at least as strong. If this requirement is absent you have had it – infantry and artillery are helpless in the Desert without armour, however brave they are – useless mouths who can be outflanked, surrounded and mopped up.[3]

Moreover, it was always his intention that the battlegroups would be co-ordinated by the divisional commanders who would make their presence felt in action. Auchinleck also ensured that the artillery was concentrated and created a new form of armoured brigade in 2 Light Armoured Brigade, equipped with armoured cars. These wheeled vehicles could move more swiftly than tanks and were intended for rapid exploitation of breakthroughs. Of his personal resolve to win there was no doubt. He told his chief of staff, Dorman-Smith, that 'The British pride themselves on being good losers. I'm a damn bad loser. I'm going to win'. That was Auchinleck the Gael speaking.

Rommel attacked the El Alamein positions on 1 July to meet a severe rebuff. His plan, based on inadequate reconnaissance, had been too hasty. Intended to bluff and hustle the British out of their positions it did not work against Eighth Army under Auchinleck. With fewer than a hundred tanks, and already exhausted infantry, Rommel's hammer broke on the anvil of Eighth Army's defence. Infantry, artillery, hull-down tanks and the Desert Air Force all took their toll of the Panzerarmee. There were some gains but the overall picture showed failure. The advance into the Nile Delta was going no farther.

Eighth Army had two fresh armoured divisions as 10th (previously 1st Cavalry) had finished conversion and 8th had arrived from Britain. However, 10th lost its tanks to provide replacements for the losses of 1st and 7th Armoured Divisions while 8th's two brigades were detached to support other formations. The arrival of the first M4 Sherman tanks was still in the future but the 6-pounder-armed Crusader was about to enter service. Soon there would be no shortage of equipment; but there were other problems, chief among them the breakdown in trust between infantry and armour, best summed up by Brigadier Howard Kippenberger, a New Zealand officer:

> At this time there was throughout Eighth Army, not only in New Zealand Division, a most intense distrust, almost hatred, of our armour. Everywhere one heard tales of the other arms being let down; it was regarded as axiomatic that the tanks would not be where they were wanted in time.

Kippenberger recounted how, on 2 July, during Eighth Army's first counter-attack, he 'was distressed to find several very slightly damaged Crusader tanks making no attempt to get back into the battle. One officer asked me if he should and was disappointed by my emphatic reply'. But the armoured crews were having great doubts themselves. Macksey noted how tankmen were 'disgruntled, among other things, with their machines'. Most tank crews, having been in action for almost five weeks, were suffering extreme fatigue, according to a medical report of 2 July, which ascribed the situation to lack of rest, poor crew comfort, inadequate clothing and lack of proper nutrition: the diet was generally cold bully beef and hard army biscuit.

The Intelligence Officer of 4 CLY described how, on the night of 30/31 May:

> at the Colonel's conference in the back of his truck, I noticed with a shock how worn and tired the Officers present looked. Red-eyed, haggard, bearded men, with matted hair huddled round the map I had marked. ... Lack of sleep had sharpened features and lined every face into a sad caricature. Eye lids felt dry and sore, limbs ached with the longing for rest.[4]

Matters did not improve during the July battles. On the 18th the war diary of 9th Lancers noted that 'for once we had sausages instead of AP shot for breakfast'[5] while, five days later, the same officer wrote that:

It is apparent that the length of time which the regiment has now been in the desert (seven months), combined with the constant battles and lack of sleep, is having its effect; most of us are at the extreme limit and it is getting hard to even think clearly. Yesterday three men – all normal, stout-hearted men – went temporarily out of their minds and others were showing the same signs of mental and physical strain.[6]

This was, he commented, 'a factor which is easily forgotten'.[7]

In the course of the July battles elements of the armoured divisions were committed in two significant attacks. One was with the New Zealanders at Ruweisat ridge on the 23rd but before discussing the action it is worth recording comments made by Kippenberger to Major General Harding, Director of Military Training, prior to the operation. Asked his opinion of the cause of the recent setbacks:

I spoke without reserve. For what it was worth, my opinion was that we would never get anywhere until the armour was placed under the command of infantry brigadiers and advanced on the same axis as the infantry. Under command and on the same axis. In some operations I conceded that the armour commander should control and that the infantry employed should be under him and still both arms should operate on the same axis. We fought one more unsuccessful battle on the old lines and then the principle, for which I argued and which must have had some very much more influential protagonists, was adopted.

That unsuccessful battle was the attack on Ruweisat. The armour involved were the three fresh units of 23 Armoured Brigade, detached from 8th Armoured Division, 40, 46 and 50 RTR, equipped with 2-pounder Valentines in the cruiser role. Watching the Valentines go forth to battle one New Zealand battalion commander, Ralf Harding, described their advance as 'a real Balaclava charge'. It was to have consequences all too similar to those of the Crimean War. That charge:

may have looked splendid and was the epitome of courage, but it proved a terrible waste when conducted within the framework of a defective plan. Against unshaken anti-tank guns, in one narrow sector, the destruction of 30 Valentines, unaccompanied by infantry, in ten minutes was appalling. On a day when 140 tanks were lost (116 from 23 Armoured Brigade) the result could only be rated disastrous and, in fact, wrecked Auchinleck's bid to throw the Axis back.

Kippenberger described how 23 Armoured Brigade's Valentines 'had come under crushing fire from several directions, had pressed on and run on to a minefield, had still pressed on and very, very few had come back. It was reported that some had pressed through as far as a Corps Headquarters'.

In Kippenberger's words 'One of the two eagerly awaited armoured brigades had been thrown away.' Later in the morning the armoured brigade assigned to support 6 New Zealand Brigade was deployed in no man's land and the New Zealanders' forward area. After several tanks were hit the brigade 'realized they were doing no good and departed'. One angry commanding officer apologized to Kippenberger about this, saying that he felt 'bitterly humiliated'. The New Zealander noted that he 'did not answer very graciously'.

Eighth Army made one final attempt to smash Rommel in this first battle of El Alamein. Operation MANHOOD on 26 July involved 9th Australian Division with 69 Brigade of 50th (Northumbrian) Division, supported by 2 and 4 Armoured Brigades, the latter still in the 'light' role with armoured cars, Stuarts and lorried infantry. This was an ambitious operation, with a feint attack in XIII Corps' area, while XXX Corps made the real attack to seize Miteiriya Ridge in the northern sector. But confusion was present almost from the start with some elements of the artillery fireplan cancelled as 69 Brigade's commander felt that they posed an unacceptable risk to South African troops covering his men.

Once the Australians and 69 Brigade had taken their objectives, 2 Armoured Brigade was to pass through minefield gaps created by South African sappers to provide support against a dawn counter-attack by Axis forces. But the plan went awry. By noon 69 Brigade was isolated in its forward positions with no armour support as 6 RTR had been stopped by anti-tank guns an hour earlier, after passing through the minefield gap. Then the Grants were attacked by eleven panzers and a tank battle ensued, a static engagement that raged for most of the day. Ordered to retire at dusk the British tanks fought off another panzer attack before withdrawing. Although the battalion lost only three of its forty-one Grants Rommel claimed 1,000 prisoners and thirty-two tanks knocked out. Von Mellenthin considered that the Panzerarmee had won 'important defensive victories and the balance of losses was highly favourable to us', but Rommel wrote that 'the one thing that had mattered to [Auchinleck] was to halt our advance, and that, unfortunately, he had done'.

This was the point at which Auchinleck decided to stand on the defensive while building up Eighth Army and the support organization within Middle East Command for a fresh offensive. He and the redoubtable Dorman-Smith had already begun the planning for such an offensive. Dorman-Smith proposed a re-organization, which Auchinleck approved, to ensure that infantry and armour would always fight under one commander. All-arms training would be improved while tank strengths would be increased, ammunition stockpiled, transport levels increased and the positions from El Alamein southwards would be strengthened.

While Eighth Army prepared to take the fight to the enemy again, it also prepared for a defensive battle in the El Alamein-Hamman area, inducing Rommel to make a premature strike in mid-August. Reinforced by two armoured divisions and two infantry divisions, Dorman-Smith's assessment was that Eighth Army could attack in late-September, smashing through the enemy positions around El Alamein. This was an almost accurate prediction of what did happen, although the breakthrough was a month later. Neither Dorman-Smith nor his chief would be present for that breakthrough as both were sacked by Churchill in mid-August; but they had ensured that Eighth Army held the initiative and that co-operation between armour and infantry was to improve immeasurably.

On the other side Rommel had lost two valuable sources of information. What he termed *die gute Quelle* (the good source) had been uncovered by British Intelligence. This was the US Military Attaché in Cairo, Major Bonner Fellers, whose signals to Washington were intercepted and deciphered by German Intelligence. Fellers had been ordered to use the State Department's diplomatic 'Black Code', details of which were stolen from the US Embassy in Rome by Italian spies in September 1941 while German cryptanalysts also broke the code, allowing Fellers' informative messages to be passed to Rommel. Fellers' unintended role was uncovered by British Intelligence through Ultra intercepts in June and his last messages, telling of panic in Cairo, were transmitted on the 29th.[8] Then, on 10 July, Rommel's 621st Radio Intercept Company, under the brilliant Captain Alfred Seebohm, was captured by Eighth Army troops. 'Seebohm had been able, on occasion, to place his vehicle next to Rommel's and to pass to him translated versions of British radio messages even before these were formally acknowledged.'[9] The almost simultaneous loss of two such valuable intelligence assets represented a major blow to Rommel.

Both sides were exhausted and in need of respite. Von Mellenthin noted the 'tremendous reaction by the Anglo-American war machine' that the presence of Panzerarmee at El Alamein prompted. 'It was clear that our enemies were gaining a decisive lead in the race to build up supplies.' In that race the Axis were at a disadvantage as a result of the failure to knock out Malta, which was recovering and providing a base for British interdiction of supply convoys to Libya; the arrival of the PEDESTAL convoy on 15 August marked the turning-point for Malta. Moreover, British bombers in the Middle East were also striking at the Cyrenaican ports. Rommel had no option but to remain at El Alamein rather than withdrawing to Cyrenaica since Hitler would never accept any solution involving giving up ground 'and so the only alternative was to try and go forward to the Nile, while we still had the strength to make the attempt'. The Desert Fox was the victim of his own earlier success. And so preparations were made for another attack.

Kesselring guaranteed that the Luftwaffe would fly in 90,000 gallons of fuel daily while a large tanker was due in Tobruk at the end of August, giving Rommel confidence to proceed with his plans.

Kesselring did in fact fulfil his promise but most of the gasoline was consumed on the long journey to the front, while the sinking of the precious tanker by a submarine off Tobruk harbour put an end to any hope of a victorious battle. We were compelled to launch our attack on the night of 30/31 August to take advantage of the full moon. Any further delay would have meant a postponement of three weeks, which ... was out of the question.

However, Eighth Army was waiting. Rommel was expected, his attack predicted by Dorman-Smith who, with Auchinleck, had left the desert, following their dismissal in mid-August. Succeeding Auchinleck as commander-in-chief was General Sir Harold Alexander while Eighth Army was commanded by Lieutenant General Bernard Montgomery. The latter had inherited plans for a fresh offensive and to meet a renewed Axis attack, expected to strike at the Alam el Halfa ridge in Eighth Army's rear. The ridge had been garrisoned by Auchinleck and Montgomery had reinforced that garrison. But many of Auchinleck's efforts to improve inter-arms co-operation and the tactical deployment of armour were taking effect. Rommel would find his forces facing a re-invigorated Eighth Army in which the handling of armour was improving.

Rommel's plan was relatively simple. While the Italian infantry, the German 164th Infantry Division and other German elements held the line from the coast to a point ten miles south of Ruweisat Ridge, a force would strike around the British left flank before wheeling north to advance on Alam el Halfa ridge. Capturing the ridge was critical to Axis success and would provide the jumping-off point for 21st Panzer to advance on Alexandria while 15th Panzer and 90th Light made for Cairo. The last-named formation was to form the Axis left flank in the attack with XX Italian Armoured Corps (Ariete and Littorio Divisions) and Afrika Korps in the centre and right flank respectively. There would also be diversionary operations to mislead the British about the true objectives.

Montgomery expected that Rommel's attack would be directed on XIII Corps' sector. Commanded by Lieutenant General Brian Horrocks, XIII Corps included 2nd New Zealand Division (one brigade of which was re-forming; its place was taken by 132 Brigade), two brigades of 44th (Home Counties) Division (132 Brigade was detached to the New Zealanders), 7th and 10th Armoured Divisions. While 7th Armoured was still weak, 10th deployed two armoured brigades: 22 Armoured Brigade, commanded by Pip Roberts, was dug in on the western end of Alam el Halfa ridge with 8 Armoured 'placed to the east, on the flank of the enemy's expected line of advance'. The motor battalion of 22 Armoured Brigade (1st Rifle Brigade) deployed 6-pounder anti-tank guns to support the tanks and their fire could be combined with that of the artillery in a defensive fireplan. The Desert Air Force was poised to play an important role.

As the attackers moved forward they were spotted from the air and attacked by bombers. The diversionary attacks in XXX Corps' area were rebuffed and the main effort concentrated on the attack force which 'made desperately slow progress' due to having to negotiate minefields, air attacks and confusion amongst units that became mixed up Afrika Korps' commander, Nehring, was wounded in an air attack, Colonel Bayerlein, his chief of staff, taking his place. Rommel arrived at Afrika Korps HQ at about 9am prepared to call off the operation but was persuaded by Bayerlein to continue the attack on Alam el Halfa. This was to begin at noon, although originally scheduled for six hours earlier, and the arc of the wheeling manoeuvre was reduced, placing Afrika Korps against the western sector of the ridge, the position allocated initially to XX Italian Corps. Afrika Korps would face the full fury of the defences.

The attack was delayed further by a sandstorm that hindered forming up. That storm also saved Afrika Korps from a pummelling by the Desert Air Force since it restricted flying for much of the day. An hour after noon 15th Panzer moved off but it was another hour before 21st Panzer made a start. Concentration was not the order of the day. Meanwhile, Eighth Army had taken a leaf from the German manual on tactical handling of armour. Two Crusader squadrons were deployed about two miles south of 22 Armoured Brigade's positions, their role, according to the *Official History*, to decoy the panzers into pursuing them and running on to the guns of 22 Armoured Brigade's Grants, the 6-pounders of 1st Rifle Brigade and a supporting Royal Artillery anti-tank battery at Point 102. However, Roberts wrote that he had deployed these squadrons to 'go up to five miles south and south-west of our positions and, without getting involved, to report on any enemy movement'. Reports that the enemy were 'coming straight towards us' began coming in from the two squadrons at about 3.30pm.

However, 15th Panzer then headed east without taking the bait of the Crusaders, if they in fact were bait. Forty-five minutes later, 21st Panzer followed. Although the *Official History* avers that the panzers did not engage the Crusaders, Roberts contradicts this, writing that there was 'some firing by their leading tanks, presumably at our light squadrons' which he ordered to return, but without betraying the brigade's position. As it looked as if the enemy was moving east and about 1,200 yards from his positions, Roberts ordered two units to prepare to quit their defensive positions. But then 21st Panzer turned left, facing 22 Armoured's positions and advanced slowly, heading for the centre and 3 CLY.

The leading panzers were Mark IVs with a new long-barrelled 75mm gun, the effectiveness of which was soon demonstrated, as Roberts recalled:

> Once one is in the middle of a battle, time is difficult to judge, but it seems only a few minutes before nearly all the tanks of the Grant squadron of the CLY were on fire. The new German 75mm is taking a heavy toll. The enemy tanks have halted and they have had their own casualties, but the situation is serious; there is a complete hole in our defence.

To close that hole, Roberts ordered the Royal Scots Greys, positioned over the crest from Point 102, to move 'at all speed' to join the CLY. As the Greys made for the seat of battle the panzers advanced again, but more slowly, making for the gap in the British line. They had not spotted the Rifle Brigade's 6-pounders, concealed in broken ground, and had closed to within 300 yards when the guns opened fire. Several panzers were struck and crippled but the Germans came on. Over the radio Roberts was exhorting the Greys to 'get the whips out' as the Germans came under fire from the British artillery. Then the Greys appeared over the crest from the north, moving swiftly into the gap. Light was fading as the battlefront was stabilized. But there was still some difficulty on the left flank with a force of about thirty German tanks threatening 133 Brigade. However, the guns of B Battery 1 RHA and the threat of the CLY Crusaders brought the Germans to a halt.

The action at Point 102 was the fulcrum of the battle at Alam el Halfa, the second battle of El Alamein. British casualties were light with only one man killed in the CLY (although the regiment lost twelve Grants and a Crusader) and two in 1st Rifle Brigade; fifteen CLY personnel were wounded. German tank losses came to just over twenty, although 22 Armoured Brigade claimed almost seventy. However, 21st Panzer had lost its inspiring commander, Major General Georg von Bismarck, killed by a British mortar round. That night the German and Italian tanks went into laager, but British aircraft and artillery bombarded their positions during the night.

Little action took place on 1 September although 21st Panzer tried to slip around Roberts' flank early in the morning, a move stopped by 22 Armoured Brigade's tanks while tanks of 8 Armoured Brigade's Sherwood Rangers and Staffordshire Yeomanry, both in action for the first time since being mechanized, threatened the German right flank. When a heavy artillery bombardment forced 21st Panzer to withdraw, 8 Armoured Brigade advanced. There was little fighting that day: 8 Armoured lost sixteen tanks while Afrika Korps lost thirteen. The Desert Air Force continued making life difficult for the Panzerarmee with an attack on Afrika Korps HQ killing seven officers.

Rommel considered cancelling his offensive but deferred his decision until the 2nd. By then his men had suffered another night of intense bombardment and his fuel situation was even more precarious. That night he signalled his intention to withdraw to OKH. Panzerarmee did not fall back to its starting positions as the British minefields codenamed 'January' and 'February' and some high ground were incorporated into the Axis lines.

When the battle ended, losses were almost evenly balanced with Eighth Army having lost about 2,000 men and Panzerarmee about 3,000. Tank losses were under forty on either side. Psychologically the battle was a significant success for Eighth Army as Rommel had failed in his breakthrough attempt. The British armour had fought well and in harmony with its artillery and infantry. Even so, retraining needed to continue to eliminate as far as possible the friction still existing between the arms. That became one of Montgomery's priorities, but he was able to build on Auchinleck's solid foundation, although giving Auchinleck no credit for that.

A principal feature of the final battle of El Alamein was the presence of vast minefields. We have already seen how Panzerarmee incorporated the British 'January' and 'February' minefields into their defences after Alam el Halfa; by 21 October Rommel's chief engineer, Colonel Hecker, estimated that more than 445,000 mines had been laid along the front. Some three per cent of these, about 14,000, were anti-personnel devices but the majority were anti-tank. Hecker had hoped to seed mines in the ratio of two anti-tank to one anti-personnel but never achieved this, although the footfall of a running infantryman could detonate the anti-tank Teller mines. For the same reason the leading infantry could not carry heavy weapons. The minefields were not the sole obstacle; well dug-in outposts, manned in company strength and with machine guns and even war dogs in some cases, also threatened advancing infantry.

Creating paths through these minefields presented a major problem for Eighth Army but one that would be resolved.

Eighth Army's tank strength was being increased and, on 3 September, the first of Roosevelt's promised 300 Sherman tanks arrived from the United States. Even though one ship was sunk en route the loss was made good and, by 11 September, there were 318 Shermans in the Middle East. The Sherman, the standard Allied tank in the second half of the war, was produced in greater numbers than any other American tank, before or since. It bore a resemblance to the Grant, having a high profile, but mounted a 75mm gun in a fully traversing turret. That gun was superior to anything then in British service, including the Grant's 75, which was a shorter weapon. The 6-pounder-armed Crusader was also arriving with units and by the opening of the final battle there would be 1,300 tanks in Eighth Army, with 1,136 in the forward area, including a clutch of the new Churchill I-tanks.

Also of benefit to the armoured divisions were the first self-propelled field guns, of which there were two: the British Bishop, a 25-pounder in a barbette on the hull of a Valentine; and the American M7 Priest, a 105mm howitzer on the hull of an M3. Bishop was strictly a stopgap due to the limitations on its 25-pounder (see page 64) while Priest (so called in British service because its anti-aircraft machine-gun mount resembled a pulpit) used a weapon that required retraining in gunnery techniques; it was to be replaced by Sexton, a 25-pounder on the hull of a Canadian Ram tank. In the meantime, Bishop and Priest would provide greater flexibility to the artillery of the armoured divisions. With 849 of the new 6-pounder anti-tank guns, plus 554 2-pounders, Eighth Army would be better able to deal with enemy armour; the Desert Air Force was also strengthened.

On paper Eighth Army had four armoured divisions: 1st, 7th, 8th and 10th. However, no infantry brigade was available for 8th Armoured Division (8 Support Group had included field, anti-tank and light anti-aircraft regiments, plus 14th Sherwood Foresters but was disbanded on 23 July) causing the division to be broken up, 23 Armoured Brigade being assigned to XXX Corps while 24 Armoured Brigade went to 10th Armoured Division and, later, 1st Armoured. Eighth Armoured Division was disbanded on 1 January 1943 and 24 Armoured Brigade followed two months later. Although the order of battle of an armoured division had been amended to include one armoured brigade and an infantry brigade, both 7th and 10th Armoured Divisions continued with two armoured brigades, but one of 7th Armoured's brigades was 4 Light Armoured Brigade which included mostly armoured cars with a regiment of Stuarts.

Montgomery, having fended off pressure from Churchill for a September offensive, planned to launch Operation LIGHTFOOT on 23 October. His ambitious, if simple, plan relied heavily on the armoured divisions, which were likely to suffer serious casualties. Concerned that there was insufficient time to train the replacement and reinforcement troops who had joined Eighth Army, he decided to modify his plan of attack. There would be 'crumbling' attacks on the Axis infantry, intended to draw Panzerarmee's armour out into battle against the British armour in position. He described this concept:

I aimed to get my armour beyond the area of the 'crumbling' operations. I would then turn the enemy minefields to our advantage by using them to prevent the enemy armour from interfering with our operations; this would be done by closing the approaches through the minefields with our tanks, and we would then be able to proceed relentlessly.

This bore little resemblance to what actually happened. The pivotal element of Montgomery's plan was breaking into the enemy lines and creating the minefield gaps, or corridors. This task was assigned to XXX Corps while the armour was under X Corps, which Montgomery described as a *corps de chasse*, considering it Eighth Army's Afrika Korps, an indicator that he did not understand how Afrika Korps functioned. To Lumsden, commanding X Corps, and his divisional commanders, this was not a viable plan, a view supported by the Dominions infantry division commanders, Freyberg, Morshead and Pienaar, who told Sir Olive Leese, commanding XXX Corps, that they did not believe that the armour could break out as quickly as Montgomery suggested.

The fears of those infantry commanders must have been due, at least in part, to the distrust between armour and infantry. There appear to have been no similar comments from the GOCs of 44th (Home Counties), 50th (Northumbrian) and 51st (Highland) Divisions, although only the Northumbrians had experienced battle in the desert before the summer of 1942. It is also possible that, as British Army officers, they felt unable to complain to Montgomery. In any case, the Dominions triumvirate were concerned that the plan for the armoured breakout would lead to disaster for the armour, followed by disaster for the infantry. They suggested that XXX Corps should continue its attack for longer before X Corps was launched into the breakout phase. Lord Carver has suggested that XXX Corps 'soon came to suspect that [X] Corps were not even seriously intending to try to break out'. If that were true it indicates deep lack of trust between armour and infantry. It made no difference to Montgomery who, when Leese reported the concerns of Freyberg, Morshead and Pienaar, simply restated his order that X Corps would have to pass through XXX Corps at dawn on the first day of LIGHTFOOT.

What Montgomery was planning was a Great War battle with modern weapons. This calls into question his understanding of the role of armour since his plan echoed the concept of using tanks as a screen for infantry. At the time, and in later writings and broadcasts, Montgomery criticized his armoured commanders, blaming them 'for their lack of drive at Alamein, where at least part of the blame should have been directed inwards, at his own failure to comprehend what tanks can and cannot reasonably be made to do'.[10]

Only days before D Day Montgomery revised his plan. Perhaps the doubts of the Dominions commanders had influenced him but, whatever the reasons, he explained his revised plan to conferences of officers from all three corps of Eighth Army on 19 and 20 October. The change was to affect the armoured divisions. Instead of breaking out and engaging and destroying Rommel's armour the British armour, as soon as they cleared the minefields, would form a screen between Axis infantry and Axis armour behind which the infantry battle would be fought. Thus Montgomery was forcing Rommel to counter-attack with his armour, something that should work to the advantage of the British armour.

As already noted, 24 Armoured Brigade was assigned to 10th Armoured Division while 23 was attached to XXX Corps. Another re-assignment was that of 9 Armoured Brigade, originally part of 10th Armoured, which was placed under command of 2nd New Zealand Division, thereby making the New Zealand Division a 'mixed' division of two infantry brigades and one armoured. (The division had suffered heavily in the recent fighting and its third infantry brigade was re-organizing as an armoured brigade.) In general the armoured personnel would get to know the infantry as they trained closely with the units they would support in battle.

The minefield problem was tackled in a number of ways: the introduction of Polish hand-held mine-detectors, the development of modified Matilda tanks to sweep with steel flails and detonate mines, and training Royal Engineers to search for mines and make them safe. The modified Matildas, known as Scorpions, pointed the way to the later use of such tanks in large numbers in north-west Europe.

With 8th Armoured Division broken up, Eighth Army disposed three armoured divisions, 1st and 10th in X Corps and 7th in XIII Corps. (However, those elements of 8th Armoured not assigned to 10th Armoured formed Hammerforce which joined 1st Armoured.) By 23 October, D Day for LIGHTFOOT, the armour included 1,348 tanks of all types (421 Crusaders; 285 Shermans; 246 Grants; 223 Valentines; 167 Stuarts and six Matildas), of which 1,136 were fit for action. In addition, there were 500 armoured cars, 382 of them with seven armoured car regiments and fifty-three with formation HQs. Of 25-pounders the Royal Artillery had no fewer than 832, of which 144 were in six RHA regiments (there were twenty-four M7 Priests mounting 105mm howitzers, also with an RHA regiment). The remainder were in field regiments of the Royal Artillery, Dominions artillery, and Greek and Free French brigades. Three medium artillery regiments and a single troop (with the Free French) deployed fifty-two medium – 4.5- and 5.5-inch guns – regiments while 849 of the new 6-pounder anti-tank guns and 554 2-pounders were in service; armoured division anti-tank regiments each deployed sixty-four 6-pounders while motor battalions typically had sixteen such weapons and infantry battalions deployed eight 2-pounders. (The average anti-tank regiment in an infantry division had sixteen 2-pounders and forty-eight 6-pounders.)[11]

Major General Raymond Briggs' 1st Armoured Division had the most modern equipment with ninety-two Shermans in the 161 tanks of 2 Armoured Brigade while his artillery included the M7 Priests of 11th (HAC) Regiment RHA and Deacons of ZZ Battery 76th Anti-Tank Regiment. Also included were six of the new Churchill I-tanks in a composite squadron, known as Kingforce, commanded by Major Norris King. Commanding 2 Armoured Brigade was Brigadier Frank Fisher who, on 18 October, outlined to officers down to squadron leaders the general plan for LIGHTFOOT. On the night of 20/21 October the brigade was in its assembly area near

El Imayid where Fisher discussed the final plans with the commanding officers of his three armoured regiments (Bays, 9th Lancers and 10th Hussars) and motor battalion (Yorkshire Dragoons). Early on the 23rd he visited his units 'to explain the general plan to all ranks and to stress the necessity of success in the forthcoming operations' and read Montgomery's special order of the day to the officers and NCOs.

Jack Merewood, a tank gunner in the Bays, wrote of the period before the battle:

> The days in October were spent driving the new Shermans and firing the guns. Because of the sand it was essential to be constantly stripping down, cleaning and oiling the guns ... When we stopped for any length of time camouflage nets were spread over the tanks to eliminate the shadow cast by the sun, thus making it more difficult to be spotted by enemy aircraft.[12]

The chances of being spotted by enemy aircraft were quite low since the Desert Air Force enjoyed complete air superiority while the Hurricanes of No. 208 Squadron provided tactical reconnaissance that produced a mass of valuable information on enemy dispositions and strength. Even had the Luftwaffe and Regia Aeronautica been able to fly over Eighth Army's rear areas there was little to see and much to deceive, such was the extent of the deception schemes that had been implemented. Although Rommel knew that Eighth Army outnumbered him, without *die gute Quelle* and Seebohm's radio intelligence he did not have an accurate picture of British strength.

For his part Rommel commanded a force at the end of a very long logistical support system. German and Italian armoured formations had 496 tanks, less than half Eighth Army's strength, and 192 armoured cars, also less than half the numbers deployed by their foes. In artillery the figures were again unbalanced: at most Panzerarmee Afrika had 500 artillery pieces (200 German and between 260 and 300 Italian, with eighteen German heavy howitzers) against 908 in Eighth Army; 850 anti-tank weapons, including eighty-six 88mm guns, against almost 1,500, of which 849 were 6-pounders, in Eighth Army. A contemporary British report estimated Axis anti-tank strength at 1,063 pieces. The level of anti-tank weapons in the Panzerarmee was to be significant as the battle developed, since those guns took a heavy toll of Eighth Army's tanks. (British tank crews also feared the German 76mm PAK36, a weapon captured in some numbers from the Russians and deployed in German service. However, when a captured PAK36 was examined by British artillery officers it was found that it was not Russian in origin, but British, the obsolete British 3-inch anti-aircraft gun, hundreds of which had been given to the Red Army which had adapted it to other uses. In turn the Germans had produced a new carriage for their captured examples which proved second only to the 88 in effectiveness as anti-tank guns. An opportunity to provide the British Army with an excellent anti-tank gun – and tank gun – had been given away when those guns were sent to Russia.)

Eighth Army also had greater manpower, deploying 174,000 men on the morning of 23 October against a maximum 108,000 in Panzerarmee, of whom 60,000 were

German. However, the advantage was not as great as Montgomery would have liked for the dogfight into which he was about to pitch his army.

Contrary to German practice, the armour, although held behind the line, was dispersed. Why had Rommel done this, since he so often criticized the British for this very failing? It may have been a result of the precarious Axis fuel situation, but it may also have been due to Rommel trying to predict what Montgomery might do. He thought that his rival would make several powerful attacks at various points before deciding which was most likely to succeed. Once that decision had been made that particular attack would be reinforced, leading to a redeployment that, in normal British fashion, would be ponderous, giving Rommel time to move his armour to where it was needed most. Since there was only enough fuel to move the armour once, Rommel had to be certain of the main British thrust. As a result 15th Panzer and Littorio (the second Italian armoured division) were behind the northern sector of Panzerarmee's line with 21st Panzer and Ariete behind the southern; the armoured HQs were so close that they might have been combined commands. Two divisions were held in reserve: 90th Light and Trieste deployed along the coast from Sidi Abd el Rahman to Ras el Kinayis.

Rommel's intelligence picture was such that he thought Montgomery would not attack until November and the Desert Fox was at home in Germany convalescing from illness when Eighth Army opened Operation LIGHTFOOT. General Georg Stumme was in command on that fateful night.

Operation LIGHTFOOT opened with aerial bombing followed by an artillery bombardment that became the yardstick by which subsequent heavy bombardments were measured. The initial fireplan was directed on Axis artillery and hammered Panzerarmee's gun lines for fifteen minutes, subjecting every enemy battery to a storm of fire. Then the guns fell silent for five minutes before beginning a fresh bombardment, this time on Axis infantry positions. This was the signal for the infantry to advance. Meanwhile, both armoured divisions of X Corps were moving to their start lines; their leading units were scheduled to reach Springbok track thirty minutes after midnight. Further advance depended on the progress made by the infantry and the mine-clearing teams.

Mine-clearing had been delayed due to unexpected soft ground on one lane, casualties among the sappers, and clouds of dust, sand and smoke, raised by the artillery fire, that obscured the full moon's light. Needless to say, the Scorpions, clanking along at a snail's pace, created even more clouds of dust and sand as they flailed the ground to clear mines.

Peter Ross, commanding Recce Troop of 3 RTR, left a vivid image of some of his experiences that night:

Wireless silence was now ended and word came from the leading tank that there were still fifty yards of gap to be cleared; the sappers were being mown down and couldn't work any faster. Two vehicles blew up on mines in the column to our left. Then I saw a ball of white light appear over the ridge, coming our way very slowly; then it accelerated beyond imaginable speed, passing over the [scout] car with an ear-splitting crack. There was a clank behind us and a Crusader tank appeared to have jumped to one side like a sleeping animal suddenly awakened. Its track was hanging loose and it had ... shifted about a foot.[13]

That round was almost certainly from an 88. Ross was fortunate that it missed his Daimler scout car.

Since the mine-clearing took longer than anticipated the infantry advance was delayed, as was the move of the armour. Confusion had been created by Montgomery's plan, which entailed a full armoured corps crossing the tail of the infantry corps. Even before moving off the armoured formations had suffered from traffic congestion. When 24 Armoured Brigade tried to cross what had been no man's land the area was already filled with artillery and New Zealand and South African transport, while the tail of 8 Armoured Brigade was just leaving. Carver wrote:

Dispersion, as far as it was possible at all, was a hazardous business, as mines were by no means confined to regular fields and slit trenches abounded. The congestion was appalling and the confusion was considerable. The whole area looked like a badly organized car park at an immense race meeting held in a dust-bowl.

The brigade was not to move off until the morning of the 25th. In the meantime, on the previous morning, when the infantry ought to have been on their objectives and the armour deployed for its intended task, the attacking divisions were not in line with each other and the armour was not through the minefields. For this delay Montgomery blamed the armoured commanders, suggesting that they were:

pursuing a policy of inactivity. There was not that eagerness on the part of senior commanders to push on and there was a fear of tank casualties; every enemy gun was reported as an 88-mm ... The Corps Commander was not displaying the drive and determination so necessary when things begin to go wrong and there was a general lack of offensive eagerness in the armoured divisions ... This was not the sort of battle they were used to.

Throughout the 24th Montgomery badgered Lumsden to force his armour through the minefields. He even threatened to sack the divisional commanders, failing to see that the responsibility was his for not being aware of the limits of armour. Subsequently 24 Armoured Brigade produced a report on AFVs in operations between 23 and 29 October, which pointed out that there had been little scope in those opening days to use the formations and tactics practised prior to the battle. However, when feasible, even within the restrictions imposed by the minefields, such tactics proved effective.

Holding ridges hull-down we found effectively done with tanks 50 yards apart, 100–150 yards between troops, with 1 tank per troop observing till all were called up for fire action. This function also avoided casualties from spells of heavy artillery concentrations on the ridge. FOOs with forward squadrons secured quick and accurate support from a battery or, using the artillery regimental FOO net, all the regiment.[14]

Montgomery maintained his crumbling operations against Axis infantry, including attempting to engage units that had not been involved hitherto; both the New Zealanders and South Africans were pressing on the defenders at Miteiriya. Then, at 6pm on the evening of 24 October, 1st Armoured Division's leading tanks debouched from the northern corridor to be counter-attacked by 15th Panzer, a riposte that fitted Montgomery's battle plan.

(Montgomery did not know that Panzerarmee had lost its commander: Stumme had gone forward to see what was happening and suffered a fatal heart attack. When this news reached Berlin, Hitler asked the recuperating Rommel if he would go back to the desert and, on the 25th, the Desert Fox had returned.)

By the morning of 25 October, also, all X Corps' armour had passed through the minefields to take up the positions Montgomery had intended to be held the previous day. Those first two days saw much confused fighting:

> Made even worse when a further minefield was encountered as 3 RTR and the Staffordshire Yeomanry attempted to push on from the Miteiriya Ridge. This had apparently not been charted and the sappers received many casualties before eventually being able to clear it. Once again, the enemy anti-tank guns were able to take full advantage of the tanks' difficulty in getting clear of the minefield and being able to disperse, and we had many casualties.[15]

Close goes on to note that fighting was 'very fluid' and that 'practically no progress was made during the next few days' although his brigade – 8 Armoured – had a number of small skirmishes with enemy armour in which they suffered casualties. Twenty-three Armoured Brigade, which had its three original RTR battalions reinforced by 8 RTR, was engaged in the northern sector for twelve days. On the first day of battle, 50 RTR lost twenty-five of forty-four tanks while 40 RTR lost fifty tanks over those dozen days. Such figures were 'fairly representative of those in most Valentine units'. (This brigade, from 8th Armoured Division, had been attached to XXX Corps to support the infantry.) 'Losses in tanks and men were steadily replaced from reserves, but many crews who were several times knocked out, simply got another tank and carried on.'

Tankmen continued to suffer from exhaustion. Peter Ross found this affecting him on the first day of battle, when he began to 'feel tired and sleepy'. His head ached from the sunshine and the strain of using binoculars for long periods and things began to seem unreal, as if he was not part of what was happening. When he spotted a 'dozen small black objects' through his binoculars he continued to stare at them and wonder why these cairns were growing in size. 'I went on staring stupidly, thinking that cairns should not be moving' until the realization dawned finally, and 'almost too late', that these were enemy tanks. He reported their presence quickly, cursed himself for not having done so earlier and hoped that his inefficiency had not been spotted.[16]

On his return to the front Rommel's principal concern was a possible breakout by Eighth Army's armour, to forestall which he ordered counter-attacks against the Australian west flank and the Kidney feature. The latter attack led to a battle in which the British defenders accounted for many Axis tanks. Rommel also ordered 21st Panzer and Ariete to move up to the northern sector which, in turn, allowed Montgomery to redeploy 7th Armoured, less 4 Light Armoured Brigade, from the southern sector, where it had fulfilled a diversionary role.

As fighting continued Montgomery realized that his original plan would not produce the victory he sought and began preparing for a renewed effort. By reducing operations on XIII Corps' front he was able to pull formations into reserve in readiness for the final stroke. Eighth Army's reserve was created under X Corps command and by 28 October included 7th and 10th Armoured and 2nd New Zealand Divisions. With strong enemy forces facing the northern corridor, Montgomery also decided to go over to the defensive in that sector and drew 1st Armoured Division into reserve as well.

Montgomery planned to launch his renewed assault in the coastal sector on 30 October with Freyberg's New Zealanders leading. As a prelude to a breakout on the axis of the coast road, 9th Australian Division was to intensify operations towards the coast. Eighth Army's new operation, SUPERCHARGE, would be launched on the original XXX Corps' front, north of Kidney, aimed at the junction of German and Italian troops with the main weight hitting the Italians.

However, during the 29th, it was realized that Rommel was changing his dispositions and that most German formations, except the Ramcke Parachute Brigade, were being moved into the northern sector where Rommel expected the main British attack. Montgomery modified his plan at the suggestion of Major General Richard McCreery, who 'as an experienced armoured commander ... [recommended] that [the attack] should go in just north of the existing northern corridor'.[17] Although he did not accept the suggestion from McCreery when it was made, Freddie de Guingand persuaded him of its wisdom, especially in the light of the new enemy dispositions.[18] Needless to say, Montgomery claimed the credit for himself: 'What ... I proposed to do was to deliver a hard blow with the right, and follow it the next night with a knock-out blow with the left.'

Although the renewed offensive was led by 2nd New Zealand Division, Freyberg's command included two British infantry brigades and 9 Armoured Brigade. The axis of attack was across the north-south Rahman track, the enemy front line, towards Tel el Aqqaqir and thence into the open desert. Since Montgomery expected Rommel to launch his armour against Freyberg's attack, 1st Armoured Division was to follow the New Zealanders to deal with the Axis armour.

D Day for SUPERCHARGE was set for the night of 31 October/1 November but was delayed by twenty-four hours to ensure that all units were in place, with those not involved out of the area. The initial assault at 1.05am on 2 November, Montgomery's 'hard blow with the right', surprised the enemy. Montgomery recorded how the attack, along a 4,000-yard front, penetrated to a depth of 6,000 yards and 'was a success and we were all but out into the open desert'. It was not quite so simple. That curt summary disguises much effort, suffering and destruction.

RAF bombing destroyed Panzerarmee telephone communications and wounded General von Thoma, Afrika Korps' commander. Rommel was led to believe that the attack was coming from the Australian positions and striking westward to south-east of Sidi Abd el Rahman and counter-attacks were not launched as soon as they might have been. Not until first light was the true situation recognized.

Montgomery intended X Corps' armour to pass through XXX Corps' salient and into the open to secure ground around Tel el Aqqaqir and Point 46 before developing operations to destroy Rommel's armour, thus bringing about 'the complete disintegration of the enemy's rear areas'. While X Corps was to secure its first objective before daylight, after which it could develop its operations, 9 Armoured Brigade was to throw the first armoured punch and breach the enemy gun line along the Rahman track, opening the way for 1st Armoured Division to pass through.

Brigadier John Currie commanded 9 Armoured Brigade. His men were in good spirits but might not have been had they been aware that Montgomery had decreed that he was prepared to accept the loss of the entire brigade to achieve its objective. Currie had informed his regimental commanders who had told most of their squadron leaders, but the message did not reach the ordinary troopers. Currie's command included a regular RAC regiment, 3rd Hussars, and two yeomanry regiments, the Royal Wiltshire Yeomanry and the Warwickshire Yeomanry. Their tanks included almost eighty Shermans and Grants and over fifty Crusaders, although most were war-weary with the Wiltshires' Crusaders needing much maintenance. Their journey to the start line was difficult with the Warwicks delayed, prompting Currie to ask for a delay in his H Hour, which Freyberg granted.

At 6.15am the artillery resumed fire, the tank drivers heard the order 'driver advance' and 9 Armoured Brigade lurched forward to battle. Thus began one of the most courageous actions fought by British tankmen in the Second World War. Their losses tell a story to match that of the Light Brigade at Balaklava. Of the 400 of Currie's command who rode into battle, about 230 were killed or wounded while seventy-five of ninety-four tanks were lost. Although the initial advance went well, the half hour lost in reaching the start line proved critical: it meant that darkness was changing into light before the brigade had achieved its objectives.

The initial clash with the enemy had been with tanks that had attacked 5th Cameron Highlanders, but the brigade then concentrated on reaching the Rahman track. Resistance was fierce with enemy tanks and anti-tank guns opposing the British tanks. The Hussars were reduced to seven tanks by the time they reached the track while the Warwicks and Wiltshires also met heavy anti-tank fire and were ordered to fight it out until 1st Armoured Division arrived. Once again the greatest punishment was coming from the anti-tank guns, as one British officer acknowledged.

Most of the longer range tank casualties, in my opinion, were from 76.2mm guns on a MkII chassis (in one case on wheels), or 88s, chiefly the former. This gun appears a more dangerous enemy than the 88, being less conspicuous and very powerful. I wish we could acquire some.[19]

He would probably have been outraged to learn that the guns he considered most dangerous had been British, and had been given away.

As 9 Armoured Brigade fought their slugging match with the anti-tank guns, both Currie and Freyberg were exasperated at the delay in Brigadier Fisher's 2 Armoured Brigade reaching the battlefront. By the time the Bays, Fisher's leading unit, had caught up with 3rd Hussars the latter had reached the Rahman track but was a shadow of its former self. At about 10.40am 2 Armoured Brigade passed through what was left of 9 Armoured to come up against the enemy's anti-tank screen. By then the losses in Currie's brigade meant that the formation had ceased to be an effective force: only seventeen tanks were capable of movement with the Wiltshires reduced to two runners. Carver wrote that:

Currie and Freyberg both said that a vigorous push would carry Fisher through the anti-tank screen beyond the track. But in fact the position was now much stronger than it had been four hours earlier when Currie had tried just that, failed and lost heavily in the process.

Perhaps aware that he had thrown his armour into a heavyweight slugging match, Montgomery turned his attention to the southern flank where, it was reported, two armoured car squadrons of The Royals had penetrated the enemy lines to reach open desert. They were aided by the fact that most enemy troops they encountered assumed them to be 'friendly' forces, Germans taking them for Italians and vice versa. To exploit this weakness Montgomery ordered a redeployment that sent Brigadier Neville Custance's 8 Armoured Brigade south-westwards around the flank of 2 Armoured. Meanwhile, XXX Corps was to attack Point 38, known as Skinflint, and 7th Armoured Division, under John Harding, was to push forward with all speed through the southern flank of the salient, its probable role being to advance on Ghazal station, about eight miles west of Sidi Abd el Rahman.

Although 8 Armoured Brigade was diverted, and its planned role of following through after 2 Armoured was cancelled, the latter was still engaged heavily around Tel el Aqqaqir; 8 Armoured was also engaged for a time around Tel el Aqqaqir against 15th Panzer. The scrap between 2 Armoured Brigade and the remnants of Afrika Korps proved the longest and toughest encounter between tanks of the final El Alamein battle. At 11am Afrika Korps counter-attacked but were fought to a standstill by the British tanks, which were all but stationary throughout the two hours of this engagement; supporting 2 Armoured were aircraft of the Desert Air Force and the British artillery. Rommel had taken personal charge of the attack, described by Correlli Barnett as 'one of the best actions of his career, in order to gain time for the organization of the retreat that must soon begin'. Rommel had even denuded his anti-aircraft defences of their 88s, deploying twenty-four to counter the British armour. The 88s soon became targets for the Desert Air Force and Eighth Army's artillery and their numbers were reduced steadily. At the same time Littorio Division's tanks were taking massive punishment, so much so that their commanders could keep them in action no longer.

When 8 Armoured Brigade was pulled out of the action around Tel el Aqqaqir it was noon. However, as Custance's tanks made their flanking move they hit the enemy anti-tank screen and could move no farther that day. His units lost eight Crusaders but claimed to have destroyed eleven panzers. At 2pm Rommel ordered another attack, at the same time moving most of what remained of Ariete north, together with the bulk of the artillery from the southern flank, which was then left with almost no reserves. In the coastal area Rommel also shortened his front by drawing back to Sidi Abd el Rahman.

Von Thoma ordered Afrika Korps to counter-attack again at last light but this does not appear to have happened, at least in any strength. By the end of the day's fighting Afrika Korps had no more than thirty-five tanks capable of action while ammunition stocks were desperately low. The Panzerarmee's total tank strength was no more than fifty-five. Rommel planned to withdraw to Fuka, some sixty miles west, to save what he could of Panzerarmee Afrika. Although Hitler ordered him to make a last stand, he later relented, allowing the Desert Fox to use his initiative. While the dispute between Rommel and Hitler was going on, Eighth Army at last cracked through Panzerarmee's positions into open desert.

The final battle of El Alamein was over, but Montgomery failed to prevent Rommel escaping. Although Ariete Division had been all but wiped out and Littorio savaged severely, the Afrika Korps' armour had not been cut off as 1st Armoured Division had failed to get behind it. Even so, most of Afrika Korps had been destroyed through the combined efforts of tankmen, field and anti-tank gunners and airmen. The great breakout promised for SUPERCHARGE had not happened but Montgomery still felt that he had succeeded.

In his *Principles of War* Clausewitz's 'fourth rule' was to follow up success with the utmost energy. His firm opinion was that the fruits of victory were to be obtained in the pursuit of the beaten enemy. With Panzerarmee now beaten beyond doubt, one would have expected Montgomery to have launched an energetic pursuit so that Rommel's command could be destroyed. Was this not, after all, the purpose of his *corps de chasse*, Lumsden's X Corps? Instead of seizing the opportunity to seal victory with the total destruction of the Axis forces, Montgomery failed to use his armour as he should.

In the confused situation as the fighting died down there were plans to follow up the enemy with X Corps' 'main task [being] to operate northwards and clear up the coastal sector' with 1st Armoured Division pivoting on Tel el Aqqaqir to occupy an area three miles south-south-east of Ghazal station while 7th Armoured was to pass around the southern flank, advance on Ghazal station and cut the coast road. At the same time HQ 8th Armoured was to initiate Operation GRAPESHOT with a small armoured force assembling south of Ghazal station and striking out for Tobruk, which it was to seize before the enemy could organize its defence.

Since X Corps had been worn down by the battle a new *corps de chasse* was created under Lumsden's HQ, including 7th Armoured and 2nd New Zealand Divisions, with the latter including 4 and 9 Armoured Brigades. Directed on Fuka, the New Zealanders became enmeshed so badly with supply columns that their advance ground to a halt. Not until 5 November did the pursuit truly get under way. Next day the skies opened and torrential rain lashed down all day and into the 7th giving Rommel an unexpected but welcome ally. Another, unwitting, ally was Montgomery who dispersed his armoured pursuit forces. While this was not entirely his fault, since there was such congestion in Eighth Army's salient that it was difficult for units to break out into the desert, it was a predictable problem.

Montgomery sent elements of X Corps on a short thrust to the coast to trap Rommel's forces but only Custance's 8 Armoured Brigade achieved any measure of success as it reached Galal and blocked the coast road and railway. Not long after a column of enemy transport, tanks and artillery was taken unawares by the British tanks, which knocked out over fifty tanks, both German and Italian. (Carver suggested that this column was the remnants of General de Stefanis' Italian XX Corps.) But this was an isolated success. The desert veterans had advised against Montgomery's short stabs to the coast, recommending instead that the pursuing force should strike deep into the desert, on an axis parallel to that of the retreating Panzerarmee, before swinging to the coast, perhaps as far west as Tobruk, to cut Rommel's retreat. Ignoring this advice, Montgomery planned his main trap east of Mersa Matruh at Ma'aten Baggush. This was sprung on 6 November but caught no enemy forces, which had left the area, although 22 Armoured Brigade engaged elements of 21st Panzer, halted by lack of fuel. However, the Germans held off the British armour until nightfall when fuel arrived and the panzers slipped away.

In spite of all that he said and wrote about using divisions as divisions Montgomery was employing brigade-sized groups and committing an error of which he was to accuse Eisenhower after the battle of Normandy when he argued that a single axis of advance should have been used. Thus Clausewitz's dictum was ignored and the fruits of victory slipped away. Montgomery had demonstrated a lack of appreciation of armour but laid the blame for all that went wrong on the armoured commanders. He had fought a Great War-style battle, throwing both infantry and armour into tactical situations that cost them heavily in men and machines. Even in Eighth Army's westward advance he showed no flair, arguing that his great caution was to ensure that he was not pushed back into Egypt 'like the others'.

Montgomery seemed to be in thrall to Rommel, especially when Eighth Army reached El Agheila. Twice before British troops had reached that point and twice before Rommel had pushed them back. For all his superiority, and intelligence on his enemy's strength, Montgomery still held Rommel in awe. In his *Memoirs* he claimed that he 'sensed a feeling of anxiety in the ranks of Eighth Army ... and therefore decided that I must get possession of the Agheila position quickly ... It was a difficult position to attack.' What followed has about it more than a hint of farce.

For all his alleged concerns about Rommel counter-attacking, Montgomery spent three weeks preparing to attack the El Agheila position. The attack was planned for 15 December before which the army commander took some leave, met with Alexander and got 'some more clothes'. With 7th Armoured and 51st (Highland) Divisions preparing a frontal assault and the New Zealanders a south-flanking move, Montgomery must have been taken off balance when, in a very obvious demonstration, Rommel withdrew his Italian formations with as much noise and light as possible. Montgomery decided to bring his attack forward to 13 December. But Rommel had planned to quit his positions completely on the night of 12/13 December, and did so. Eighth Army's attack went in after an intensive air and artillery bombardment. It met only thin air. The Desert Fox had slipped away, without losing a single soldier. His foe claimed that all had gone to plan and 'the enemy began to withdraw the moment our frontal attack developed'.

In spite of this, or perhaps because of Montgomery's fatuous claim, five British and thirteen New Zealand regiments were awarded the battle honour 'El Agheila', a battle that never happened. As Panzerarmee continued towards Tripoli, those and other units were engaged in some sharp battles with 7th Armoured Division encountering Afrika Korps, now with fifty-four tanks, at Mugta on the coast road on the 15th. In spite of the opportunity offered on this occasion, with the BBC announcing that Rommel was in a bottle into which Montgomery was about the insert the cork, Afrika Korps fought its way out in small battlegroups. The Axis retreat continued with further brief armoured clashes, including one at Tarhuna in which John Harding was wounded severely, command of 7th Armoured Division passing temporarily to Pip Roberts.

Tripoli fell on 23 January 1943 and Rommel's retreat continued towards the Tunisian frontier. The war had taken on a different complexion. Another Allied army had landed in French North-West Africa and Italo-German forces were now faced with foes on two fronts.

Notes

This chapter is based on Playfair et al, *The Mediterranean and the Middle East. Vols III and IV* from the Official History series, Liddell Hart, *The Tanks (Vol II)* and *The Rommel Papers*, Macksey, *A History of the Royal Armoured Corps*, Carver, *El Alamein*, Farrar-Hockley, *The War in the Desert*, Montgomery, *Memoirs*, Roberts, *From the Desert to the Baltic*, von Mellenthin *Panzer Battles*, and the war diaries of Eighth Army, X Corps, XIII Corps, XXX Corps, including those of their RA commanders, 1st, 7th, 8th and 10th Armoured Divisions, as well as those of their constituent brigades and reports drawn up after the final battle of El Alamein. I have also drawn on the research for my own book *The Sound of History* for the El Alamein battle. Information on artillery and tanks is taken from Hogg, *British and American Artillery of World War 2* and Hogg and Weeks, *Illustrated Encyclopaedia of Military Vehicles* and other sources are as follows:

1. NA Kew, CAB44/97, p.1
2. Barnett, *The Desert Generals*, p.197
3. Quoted in ibid, p.198

4. NA Kew, CAB97, p.82
5. NA Kew, WO169/4481
6. Ibid & CAB44/97, p.98n
7. NA Kew, WO169/4481
8. Fraser, *Knight's Cross*, pp.298–9
9. Ibid, p.345
10. Fraser, *And We Shall Shock Them*, pp.242-4
11. Joslen, *Orders of Battle*, pp.575–6
12. Merewood, *To War With The Bays*, p.66
13. Ross, *All Valiant Dust*, pp.66–7
14. NA Kew, WO201/545, Notes on AFVs in Operations 23–29 Oct'42
15. Close, *View from the Turret*, p.83
16. Ross, op cit, p.68
17. Alexander, *Memoirs*, p.28
18. Hamilton, *Monty: The Making of a General*, p.828
19. NA Kew, WO202/545

Chapter Six

The End in Africa

A s Panzerarmee Afrika reeled back from El Alamein, Allied troops landed far to the west in Morocco and Algeria and advanced into Tunisia. This was Operation TORCH which brought the British First Army, commanded by Lieutenant General Kenneth Anderson, into the final phase of the North African war and introduced another armoured division to that war. Such was the threat posed by Allied intervention at the western end of North Africa that Axis commanders chose to give up Libya completely and concentrate in Tunisia, which was reinforced heavily. Thus Italy's 'Fourth Shore' was abandoned and its African empire became history.

The new armoured formation in North Africa was the fourth British armoured division to be formed, although designated 6th Armoured (it was preceded by 1st, 7th and 2nd, in that order). Raised in September 1940 under Major General John Crocker, it passed to Major General Charles Gairdner, who later commanded 8th Armoured Division, and then, in May 1942, to Major General Charles Keightley, who took it to war in Tunisia.

Originally formed with two armoured brigades, a support group and an armoured car regiment, by the time of Operation TORCH, 6th Armoured conformed to the most recent organization with a single armoured brigade, an infantry brigade, an armoured reconnaissance regiment with armoured cars, and the former elements of the support group, now under command of divisional HQ, reinforced to include two field artillery regiments and Royal Engineer elements. Initially the division had included 20 and 26 Armoured Brigades, but the former left in April 1942 and a lorried infantry brigade, 38 (Irish), joined. The armoured units of 26 Armoured Brigade were 16th/5th Lancers, 17th/21st Lancers and 2nd Lothians and Border Horse, and there was also a motorized infantry battalion, 10th Rifle Brigade. The Irish Brigade included 1st Royal Irish Fusiliers, 6th Royal Inniskilling Fusiliers and 2nd London Irish Rifles.[1]

When, in September 1942, Keightley was ordered to prepare his division for deployment overseas he was also told to create an independent battlegroup, based on an armoured regiment. Codenamed Blade Force, the battlegroup would embark with the leading elements of First Army, ready for a special duty on disembarkation. The core of Blade Force was 17th/21st Lancers, the 'Death or Glory Boys', whose CO, Lieutenant Colonel Richard Hull, would command the battlegroup. Also included were a squadron of armoured cars of 1st Derbyshire Yeomanry, the divisional reconnaissance regiment, a battery of 12th (HAC) Regiment RHA with towed 25-pounders, a 6-pounder battery of 72nd Anti-Tank Regiment, a troop of 51st LAA Regiment, a company of 10th Rifle Brigade, an engineer troop and other elements from the divisional troops. Hull was promoted to colonel. The main force of 6th Armoured was to sail to Algeria in slow convoys joining First Army in the follow-up phase of the landings.

When First Army landed in North Africa, it included only elements of 6th Armoured and 78th Infantry Divisions and was not even at corps strength. Nonetheless, those elements were soon sent into action as 78th Division, with Blade Force under command, took the road for Tunisia. Hull's battlegroup was led by the Derbyshire Yeomanry armoured cars; the tanks of C Squadron 17th/21st Lancers travelled on railway flat cars. The objective was Tunis but, quick as Blade Force and 78th Division were, German reaction was such that First Army was denied the prize of Tunis. Blade Force was reinforced by US Army Stuarts and infantry from the British 1 Parachute Brigade and, as Macksey commented:

> For one wild moment on 26 November it looked almost possible that Blade Force might break through and seize Tunis. The Germans, who were desperately short of forces, were thrown into panic when the Stuarts charged across Djedida airfield and destroyed twenty dive-bombers on the ground for the loss of only one tank. Hull was of the opinion that this crucial airfield might have been secured if he had more infantry. But infantry was something he lacked and German confidence was restored.

Not only did the Germans bring in troops and aircraft but the weather was also on their side as heavy rain lashed down, turning the earth into thick cloying mud. Allied aircraft, on temporary airstrips, were grounded while the Luftwaffe had the use of all-weather airfields and dominated both air and ground. The swift thrust for Tunis, a well-planned use of armour in concert with other arms, had been a daring concept that, with a little better luck, and better weather, might have succeeded. Now, however, First Army was committed to a brutal campaign reminiscent of the Western Front of the Great War.

By the time 6th Armoured Division was complete in Tunisia it was late December and the division, together with 78th Division, was assigned to V Corps under Lieutenant General Charles Allfrey. With a full armoured division available the attack on Tunis was to be renewed and Allfrey was ordered to strike from the area of Medjez. The operation opened with 78th Division, supported by American troops, striking up the Medjerda valley. This was to be followed by 6th Armoured attacking from east of Medjez towards Tunis via Massicault but, although the first element went ahead in heavy rain, the ground had been turned into mud on which armour could not operate. Nor could infantry for that matter, and so the attack was called off. The Allies were thus committed to a defensive operation as a major offensive using armour could not be launched until spring. Stalemate reigned in Tunisia and the operational situation called more for infantry than for armour. 'In the days to come, amid mountainous country criss-crossed by streams and dotted with olive and orange groves, armour found itself thrown back on the defensive and often playing a minor role. In this difficult terrain, made for defence, the RAC also met for the first time the formidable new German Tiger tank.' (Macksey)

The Axis launched major armoured offensive operations in Tunisia in late January and February 1943, falling on American and French forces in the south where semi-desert conditions were more favourable for such operations. And the guiding hand behind those operations was that of Erwin Rommel. On 14 February Rommel launched a major offensive that caught the raw Americans unawares and dispersed widely between passes at Gafsa, Faid and Fondouk. Tactics that had succeeded against British forces in Libya and Egypt were implemented successfully at Sidi bou Zid where American tanks dashed into battle against German tanks which appeared to withdraw, prompting an American pursuit. The Americans then found themselves being savaged by anti-tank guns with over a hundred tanks destroyed. On 14 February, at Kasserine Pass, Rommel dealt a heavy blow to US armour and advanced north towards Thala.

But 6th Armoured Division had been sent to support the American troops and 26 Armoured Brigade, under Brigadier Charles Dunphie, went to aid Task Force Stark. The German advance lost its momentum on 19 February at Thala when engaged by 17th/21st Lancers with infantry and artillery support; 16th/5th Lancers were in action at Sbiba. Although a force drawn from 15th Panzer and Centauro Divisions defeated French and American troops at Gafsa and 26 Armoured Brigade was forced to withdraw at Thala, a counter-attack by Lothians' tanks had a surprise effect on the foe. Major General von Broich, commanding 10th Panzer Division, which the Lothians had attacked, believed their 'bold but futile charge' signalled that the enemy had been reinforced sufficiently to move over to the offensive. As the historian of 6th Armoured Division comments, that charge:

> had sent a ripple up [10th Panzer's] chain of command. Coming so soon after the repulse of the night before, it showed great fortitude and an aggressive spirit by the British ... Artillery fire against [10th Panzer] had increased dramatically overnight and [von Broich] was not sure that he could now halt a determined move against his division. He was low on ammunition and his stocks of fuel and rations could only last for four more days. Resupply was proving difficult. Von Broich telephoned Rommel and expressed his misgivings, explaining that the planned attack for that morning had been delayed because of heavy Allied artillery concentrations ...

With the Afrika Korps Assault Group also experiencing problems, Rommel went forward to meet both commanders. Later in the morning he met Kesselring, the supreme commander, and told him that the offensive had reached its limit since the Allies were gathering strength enough to repulse his attacks. Kesselring disagreed, as he believed the Axis still held the initiative, he had no respect for the Americans and considered that the British were not strong enough to withstand another determined onslaught. One more push and he believed that the Axis could smash through Thala and advance to le Kef and western Tunisia. He and Rommel argued for an hour but the Desert Fox prevailed. The attack was called off and Axis forces would withdraw. But Rommel had another problem on his mind as Montgomery's Eighth Army approaching the Mareth Line in eastern Tunisia represented a much greater threat.

On 23 February it appeared to the Allies that Rommel's forces were pulling back. Dunphie's brigade was complete as 16th/5th Lancers had re-joined and the British-American defences had been reinforced. Two squadrons of 16th/5th went forward but met no enemy: 10th Panzer had withdrawn. Further reconnaissances on the 24th found both Kasserine Pass and Kasserine village clear of enemy troops, although there were booby-traps and mines aplenty. By the end of the day it was clear the enemy had gone. Dunphie's defence had given Rommel pause for thought and, although Kesselring may have been right about the British ability to withstand another push, the Desert Fox had appreciated that a thrust into western Tunisia was of less strategic and operational importance than holding Eighth Army on the Mareth Line.

The Mareth Line had been built by the French to prevent an Italian invasion of Tunisia from Libya. Based on a strong natural position, it stretched roughly westward about a dozen miles inland from the coast into the Matmata Hills and even had a natural anti-tank ditch, the Wadi Zigzaou, fronting it. German engineers strengthened the line with concrete blockhouses, steel gun cupolas and minefields. Montgomery recognized that the main defences were so strong and that there was so little space for a flanking move on the coastal sector that a left-flanking move was necessary. The French maintained that a sand sea west of the Matmata Hills made such a move impossible but two French officers had studied the area in 1938 and reported that it was passable. With greater use of four-wheel-drive vehicles, the sand sea was even less of an obstacle and a Long Range Desert Group reconnaissance produced a suitable route. Montgomery's plan began taking shape. It would involve a flanking movement by 1st Armoured Division around the Matmatas and on to El Hamma: Operation PUGILIST was scheduled for 19 March. Before that, however, Ultra intelligence confirmed that Rommel planned to attack Eighth Army, a move Montgomery thought might 'upset the preparations for our own attack against the Mareth Line'.[2] Rommel's strike was made on 6 March at Medenine. This was a heavy armoured attack, employing 160 tanks from three panzer divisions, supported by about 200 artillery pieces and four battlegroups, each at two-battalion strength. However, Rommel was not in command. The attacking force was directed by General Messe, an Italian officer, who sent his forces in at first light under cover of fog. But they were expected and met the fate that so many British tank attacks had met previously. Eighth Army had assembled a screen of field and anti-tank guns, the latter including some of the new 17-pounders, 3.7-inch heavy anti-aircraft guns and even a troop of captured 88s manned by British gunners. The first advance by the panzers ran into the anti-tank guns as soon as the fog burned away. The tanks were forced to withdraw but came back on three more occasions before finally admitting defeat. Panzerarmee Afrika, restyled First Italian Army since 20 February but still including Afrika Korps, had lost over fifty tanks, all but seven to anti-tank guns, manned by Royal Artillery and infantry personnel. Only one Sherman squadron was engaged and no British tanks were lost. After this remarkable victory for Eighth Army, Montgomery could continue with his plans for PUGILIST.

Rommel, now commanding Heeresgruppe (Army Group) Afrika (which also included Fifth Panzer Army), believed that the defence of Tunisia should be based on Wadi Akarit rather than the Mareth Line and, on 9 March, left to try to persuade Hitler and Mussolini of this. Although Hitler agreed to a partial withdrawal to Wadi Akarit, the Mareth Line was not to be abandoned, since Wadi Akarit could be outflanked. The Desert Fox was ordered to take sick leave and General Jürgen von Arnim succeeded him as Heeresgruppe Commander. The Mareth Line was held in strength with three panzer divisions behind it: 15th, although weak, was closest, with 21st covering the Gabes Gap on the coast and 10th farther back, behind Wadi Akarit. The line itself was held by four Italian and two German infantry divisions.

PUGILIST was launched on 20 March, although there was fighting on the 19th at Wadi Medfid, on the left flank, involving 8 Armoured Brigade. Montgomery planned an assault by XXX Corps at the northern end of the line while the New Zealand Corps (Freyberg's division reinforced by 8 Armoured Brigade and the French L Force) would flank around the Matmata Hills, establish themselves on the Gabes–Matmata road and cut off the enemy. Behind XXX Corps, X Corps – 1st and 7th Armoured Divisions – would await the opportunity to exploit success and strike for the port of Sfax. That was the plan. The execution was somewhat different.

On the right flank Montgomery launched the infantry of XXX Corps, with support from Valentine I-tanks and strong artillery and aircraft but the defences were so strong that, by the early hours of 23 March, it was clear that Eighth Army could not break through. Montgomery, awakened from his sleep, decided to reinforce the left hook while two infantry divisions, supported by 7th Armoured, masked the enemy near the coast. X Corps, less the Desert Rats, would join the New Zealand Corps' outflanking move, Operation BOOTLEG. Montgomery also asked Alexander, now commanding 18 Army Group, to deploy General Patton's II US Corps to support him, asking that the Americans should strike south-east towards Wadi Akarit, but the proposal was rejected by Alexander as too ambitious. Paradoxically, Montgomery had previously demanded that the Americans should support his attack but keep out of his way.

It was not until the night of the 25th that the first phase of the reinforced left hook took place when New Zealand infantry secured Djebel Melab, allowing 8 Armoured Brigade to push into the Tebaga Gap the next afternoon, accompanied by New Zealand infantry. The plan was that 8 Armoured (which had lost its deputy commander, Colonel Edward 'Flash' Kellett, killed in action on the 22nd) should secure its first objectives to clear the way for 1st Armoured Division to pass through the Gap and make a night advance to El Hamma. Horrocks, who had relieved Lumsden as commander of X Corps, was to command the left hook and described the opening phase:

> The New Zealand Division and 8 Armoured Brigade supported by every gun we had were to attack at 1600 hours with the sun behind them, a most important

factor in desert fighting … The air support was on a scale never attempted before by either side during the war. The continuous low-flying attacks organized by Harry Broadhurst, the new commander of the Desert Air Force, were to form the pattern of army/air co-operation for future battles in Europe.

Although Freyberg asked Horrocks if the tanks really would go through 'if we punch the hole', an indication that old concerns about armour had not disappeared, the latter was confident and told Freyberg that he (Horrocks) would be going with them.

The New Zealand infantry and the tanks of 8 Armoured Brigade played their part to perfection with infantry taking high ground that the tanks could not ascend, including Point 209 which was captured by 28th (Maori) Battalion against stiff opposition. This allowed the Sherwood Rangers' tanks to move on; they had lost three tanks to fire from Point 209 before the Maoris seized it. On the left of the brigade advance when 3 RTR ran into mines and hidden 88s it was infantry who winkled the enemy from their positions and secured the passage of the tanks.

Horrocks later wrote that the 'battle went like clockwork' with the infantry and 8 Armoured Brigade working in close harmony. Then it was time for 1st Armoured Division to be unleashed.

This was the sort of attack which the Germans themselves always tried to carry out, the real *Schwerpunkt*, everything concentrated in great depth on a comparatively narrow front. There was some very hard fighting, particularly by the Maoris on Hill 209, which was too steep for the tanks, but nothing could withstand this punch – air, artillery, tanks, infantry – in fact everything we had got.

It was the most exciting and worrying night of my life. As my small tactical HQ, consisting of three tanks, took up its position in the armoured mass, I realized very well that if this attack went wrong, there was no doubt as to whose head would be on the block. I could hear the armchair strategists in their clubs in London saying 'Heavens! The man must be mad. Fancy trying to pass one armoured division through an enemy armoured division. And in the dark too.' Because that was what we were trying to do.

The deployment of armour in a night attack was novel, but the tactic was chosen as the valley through which 1st Armoured had to pass would have made a perfect ambush site in daylight; the hills overlooked the tanks and provided wide fields of fire for the defenders. But the Germans were taken off balance by this move, especially as they had not expected the British to make a nocturnal armoured attack. And the massive air support provided was extremely unsettling, even to seasoned troops.

There was a halt between dusk and the rising of the moon, during which Horrocks got down into his tank to see how the crew were. He need not have worried as the gunner-operator and driver 'were cheerful and completely unimpressed by the fact that they were taking part in a unique military operation: they might … have been driving up the long valley at Aldershot. In moments of crisis the phlegm of the British soldier is very reassuring'.

When the advance resumed Horrocks' chief worry was getting through the valley in the dark. If they failed to do so, they would be surrounded by enemy troops on high ground to either side. At times the advance was restricted to a one-tank front but:

> we rumbled on and this difficult night advance was brilliantly carried out by 1st Armoured Division. As the night wore on the noise of the firing came more and more from the rear, and suddenly I realized that we were through – the impossible manoeuvre had come off. It was an unforgettable moment.

Such had been the success of the advance that 1st Armoured Division faced a last-ditch defence around El Hamma while what was left of 21st Panzer and 164th Light Divisions was caught between the armour and the New Zealanders, who were fighting hard to mop up pockets of resistance. Needless to say 21st Panzer was snapping at the tail of 1st Armoured but this had been foreseen and a strong anti-tank screen was deployed by 76th Anti-Tank Regiment. Including some of the new 17-pounders, the screen proved most effective and Horrocks considered the new anti-tank gun, codenamed Pheasant, 'the answer to the German 88'.

With the forces facing XXX Corps now in danger of being encircled, a withdrawal began and, once again, the weather intervened to assist the Germans and Italians. Sandstorms delayed 1st Armoured Division's attack at El Hamma and Axis forces slipped away by the coast road. But they had lost heavily, with about 7,000 prisoners being taken, and 15th and 21st Panzer Divisions had been mauled so severely that they never recovered. On the morning of 28 March 1st Armoured Division found El Hamma abandoned. By noon 1st King's Dragoon Guards were at Gabes. The battle for the Mareth Line was over. The attack had been 'pushed so vigorously that the enemy could only hold Gabes just long enough to allow the withdrawal of their forces … to the Wadi Akarit.'

The victory at Mareth was very much an armoured victory and the first really impressive use of armour in the offensive by British forces of the war. Strangely, in his history of the RAC, Macksey refers not to the success of this operation but only to the fact that, at El Hamma, 'a mere trio of staunchly manned 88mm and four 50mm guns … prevented [1st Armoured Division] crossing a wadi, giving the rest of the Axis forces time to escape envelopment'. Liddell Hart also gives little attention to the operation, summing it up in only five paragraphs, one of which notes that 'A warm tribute to the gallant fighting of the armoured units in this brilliant attack was paid by General Freyberg'.

Describing Montgomery's decision to switch to the left-flanking operation and deploying so much armour and air support with the New Zealanders, Alan Moorehead calls this 'possibly the boldest thing Montgomery ever did'.[3] But at Mareth, as at Alam el Halfa and El Alamein, Montgomery was the beneficiary of a legacy bequeathed him by Auchinleck, Dorman-Smith, Lumsden and others, including the unfortunate Pope. It is hard to see Montgomery being the guiding hand behind the armoured operation in PUGILIST as, until the end of the war, he continued to demonstrate a less than complete appreciation of the use of armour.

Axis forces withdrew the forty miles to Wadi Akarit and prepared for the inevitable Eighth Army assault. Since an attack was expected Montgomery decided to wrong-foot the enemy by launching his operation before the full moon. D Day was 6 April and, once again, XXX Corps was to make a frontal assault on the enemy positions with the armour of X Corps exploiting the infantry's success. The plan, Operation SCIPIO, suffered from Montgomery's seeing X Corps as a *corps de chasse* and superimposing one command upon another.

Before the main infantry attack was launched, 4th Indian Division attacked and penetrated the mountainous Fatnassa complex. With Indian, Gurkha and British soldiers infiltrating through the mountains, the main assault was launched by five battalions from 50th (Northumbrian) and 51st (Highland) Divisions with massive artillery support. The Northumbrians' attack was directed on a major anti-tank ditch to the right of Djebel Roumana. When Northumbrian soldiers, supported by tanks of 4 CLY, made a flanking attack towards Roumana and began to loosen the enemy's grip on the feature, a battalion from 4th Indian Division broke into the anti-tank ditch on its left. With Tuker, the Indian GOC, convinced that the defence was splitting apart, Horrocks sought Montgomery's permission for X Corps' armour to advance. But it was another four hours before 8 Armoured Brigade's tanks began threading their way through breaches in the anti-tank ditch, a delay attributable to Montgomery's command system.

The enemy were waiting for the armour, and mines and anti-tank guns brought their advance to a snail's pace. Before long it was obvious that an armoured breakthrough was not going to happen that day. This was emphasized when the enemy counter-attacked with armour and infantry. That night the Axis forces withdrew. Eighth Army had fought and won its last battle in North Africa. However, some of its armour would fight with First Army. During the afternoon of the 7th American troops of II Corps met soldiers of Eighth Army. Although Eighth Army advanced quickly along the coast to take Sfax and Sousse by 12 April, the bulk of the fighting in Tunisia was now to fall on First Army.

John Crocker, who had commanded IX Corps in First Army, had been wounded and Montgomery suggested that Horrocks might take his place. The suggestion was accepted and Horrocks left X Corps for IX Corps, taking with him 7th Armoured Division; 1st had made the transfer two weeks earlier. For the closing weeks of the Tunisian campaign, therefore, First Army had a greatly strengthened armoured component.

We left 6th Armoured Division at Kasserine in late February. Since then it had said goodbye to the Irish Brigade and welcomed 1 Guards Brigade as its lorried infantry, while 26 Armoured Brigade's regiments had replaced their Valentines with Shermans. One soldier described the Shermans as 'Great, snorting, roaring things … churning the earth up and crushing stalwart young trees absentmindedly in their stride'. And 26 Armoured had a new commander. Charles Dunphie had gone to act as an adviser to the Americans and Pip Roberts assumed command. Thus it was that the three armoured regiments were kept busy throughout March receiving, and training with, the Shermans.

> Various programmes were implemented to allow the crews to become familiar with their new mounts and new weapons. Morale was high as they at last felt that they were no longer outgunned by their opponents. While its armour perfected their new techniques, 6th Armoured Division fulfilled a role as First Army's reserve in the newly raised British IX Corps ...

As a result of converting to the Sherman it was April before 6th Armoured again took to the field. Its first deployment was interwoven with Eighth Army's actions at Mareth and Wadi Akarit. Defeat for First Italian Army at Wadi Akarit would mean a northward withdrawal along the coastal plain, leaving the retreating army's inland flank vulnerable to attack by First Army. To take advantage of this opportunity, Alexander ordered Anderson to prepare IX Corps to interdict Messe's army's withdrawal through Kairouan.

To position itself on the coastal plain before Kairouan, Crocker's IX Corps had to fight through the Fondouk Pass in the Eastern Dorsal and time its arrival to catch the enemy at their most vulnerable. Arriving at Kairouan too soon would place 6th Armoured Division in the path of the retreating First Italian Army, including two panzer divisions, but arriving too late would be to hit thin air as the enemy would have passed through. Since 6th Armoured was based around Sbiba, about sixty miles from Kairouan, there was every possibility of getting the timing just right. Meanwhile IX Corps was reinforced with 34th US Division, a brigade from the British 46th Division, a regiment of Churchill I-tanks, medium artillery and sappers.

The nature of the terrain made it essential that the infantry secure the high ground before the armour passed through Fondouk Pass. The official historian summed up the country as:

> not easy. Near Fondouk the dry Wadi Marguellil narrows to a width of about two miles and is flanked on either side by high rocky ridges, Djebel ech Cherichira to the north, Djebel Haoureb to the south. On the north the high, rocky outcrop of Djebel Rhorab is, tactically, unpleasingly dominant.

Moreover, two battalions from 46th Division's 128 (Hampshire) Brigade were not considered battleworthy by HQ 18 Army Group and the infantry of 34th US Division were short of training, having spent much time on LoC duties. In spite of this, the Hampshires crossed Wadi Marguellil and made for Djebel Rhorab, supported by a Churchill squadron and a full divisional artillery, plus sixteen medium guns. It was a different story with 34th Division which had two regiments (equivalent to British brigades) in the attack that fell behind their timetable quite early on, lost their supporting artillery fire and came under enfilading fire that forced them to go to ground. It was then, as the Hampshires moved towards Djebel Rhorab, that

Crocker ordered 6th Armoured to 'reconnoitre vigorously to discover the nature of the opposition in the Fondouk area and to help 34th Division'.

Crocker had underestimated the German defenders of the area, 991st Infantry Regiment, a penal unit, whose men he thought would be eager to desert. Instead this formation of military criminals proved resolute. Under pressure from Alexander to send 6th Armoured Division through Fondouk Pass, irrespective of 34th Division's situation on the morning of 8 April, Crocker ordered 26 Armoured Brigade to do just that. The infantry, including 1 Guards Brigade, continued their struggle in the hills and the Germans were still active on the infantry's final objectives and so it was clear that the armour would suffer heavily. Roberts had already sent 17th/21st Lancers forward 'to advance cautiously to the gap in the pass and it was soon obvious that it was well covered by enemy fire; particularly from the southern side'. The Lothians were sent to check the state of the wadi bed but found it unsuitable. As both regiments were about these tasks Crocker appeared on the scene and ordered Roberts to 'Attack now'.

> I was left holding a very unpleasant baby. If there were not mines in the gap, then an advance by the 17th/21st covered by 12 RHA might very likely see us through. If there were mines in the gap, it would be a disaster. To try to confirm this and their extent would take ages. Clearly, to carry out the corps commander's order to the letter and in the spirit, we must make an effort and take a risk now.

Roberts called the commanding officers of 17th/21st Lancers and 12 RHA to an O Group and explained the situation. His orders were for 12 RHA to put down a concentration of fire on the far side of the gap and behind a small hill to the right, under cover of which the Lancers would advance. Once the tanks were through the gap the artillery fire would continue under control from a Forward Observation Officer.

The CO of the Lancers called his squadron leaders to a regimental O Group to tell them that the regiment was to force the gap by speed and weight of numbers. Of course those officers were aware that their predecessors of the 17th Lancers had received a similar order at Balaklava in October 1854. Once again they would charge into a 'valley of death'. As they left the O Group Major Charles Nix said farewell to Major Maxwell with the words 'Goodbye – I shall never see you again. We shall all be killed.' His words were prophetic. Nix was killed that day, struck in the head by a bullet.

Under cover of smoke and fire the Shermans of the Lancers moved forward, as the regimental history describes.

> After ... a few hundred yards B Squadron ran into the edge of the minefield. Immediately tanks began to blow up on the mines, though some got through, only to be knocked out by anti-tank guns beyond. As the crews baled out they were met by an inferno of mortar bombs and machine-gun bullets from the

high ground, and accurate sniping by infantry close to the tanks and well camouflaged.[4]

Ahead lay more mines through which Captain Gilbert Micholls led his troop to reach the plain beyond. But their purgatory was not yet over. At the base of the feature dubbed the 'Pimple' the Shermans were in plain sight of enemy anti-tank guns that wasted no time in turning their full fury on them. Without cover the Lancers could only stand and return the enemy fire but, one after another, the Shermans fell to the German guns. Gilbert Micholls was among the dead.

As Major Nix led the remainder of his squadron through the mine belt, more tanks fell victim to the concealed devices. As he urged his men on from his open turret hatch, Nix was shot by an enemy soldier. When only two tanks were left a radio message was received, calling them back. Maxwell's C Squadron had followed Nix's B, although it was echeloned to the right. Within minutes every tank of the two leading troops had struck mines and been blown up. Maxwell requested and received permission to withdraw. The surviving Shermans reversed out of the minefields, following their own tracks.

It was A Squadron's turn to go forward, using a different route and trying to take advantage of the wadi bed, but they ran into anti-tank guns and found entry to the bed impossible. But then the anti-tank fire diminished, since many guns had been knocked out by B and C Squadrons or by field artillery while the infantry were making steady progress as the defence crumbled. Thirty minutes before noon sufficient progress had been made in spite of casualties to persuade Roberts to follow up with his other regiments. And so 16th/5th Lancers advanced with a company of 10th Rifle Brigade in support. Teamwork between armour and infantry led to success with only one tank lost. Anti-tank guns were knocked out by the Shermans, Green Jackets dealt with stubborn enemy posts, 75s and infantry automatic weapons punished the enemy positions and the German infantry suffered many casualties. Then the Shermans were through and chasing the enemy defenders from the area of the Pimple. Within hours the leading tanks were more than a mile east of Fondouk.

It had not been a clean battle. Hustled into action the armour had suffered, and yet when 16th/5th and the riflemen of 10th Rifle Brigade went forward together they demonstrated yet again what tanks and infantry in concert could achieve. The Fondouk Pass could have been breached at much lower cost had more time been given to preparing a combined arms attack. There followed a pursuit of the withdrawing enemy during which the holy city of Kairouan was bypassed, 26 Armoured had a brisk engagement with the tail of 10th Panzer and, finally, a successful attack on enemy positions north of the Kairouan plain. Following this the brigade was withdrawn to re-organize for further operations.

On 11 April, while 6th Armoured pursued the retreating enemy, General Alexander was casting his plans for the final destruction of Axis forces in North Africa. The main effort was to be made by First Army although Eighth Army would play a part through operations north-west of Enfidaville to tie up enemy forces that might otherwise be deployed against Anderson's army. Since the terrain over which Eighth Army was now fighting was not conducive to armour, the final armoured warfare of the campaign would be conducted by First Army.

Anderson was to make his main thrust for Tunis from the south-west with V Corps on the axis of the Medjez–Massicault road. X Corps was to support that attack and lock some of the Axis armour into battle by an attack in the area of the Pont du Fahs–Goubellat plain. This attack, preceding that by V Corps, would involve both 1st and 6th Armoured Divisions as well as 46th Infantry Division. The US II Corps was also to have a part in the final drive while the French XIX Corps held the Eastern Dorsal between IX Corps and Eighth Army. IX Corps was to open its advance on 22 April with an attack by 46th Division to secure the jumping-off area for 6th Armoured to smash through to the Goubellat plain, whence it would swing north towards Massicault. At the same time 1st Armoured was to drive northwards on IX Corps' western flank. The opposition was well-known to 6th Armoured and included 10th Panzer and the Hermann Göring Divisions, the latter having opposed 6th Armoured earlier in the year.

For this operation 6th Armoured welcomed a new unit transferred on loan from Eighth Army (and 1st Armoured Division): 11 (HAC) RHA, equipped with M7 Priests, the American self-propelled 105mm howitzers on M3 hulls. The Priests added greater flexibility to the divisional artillery than was possible with towed 25-pounders since they could keep up with the tanks and thus came closer to achieving the ideal balance of an armoured division.

As planned 46th Division opened IX Corps' operation in the small hours of 22 April with attacks by two brigades supported by Churchills. In the afternoon Major General Keightley was ordered to pass his tanks through a gap that 138 Brigade had forced during the morning, even though the infantry were still heavily engaged. Roberts led 26 Armoured Brigade forward against little opposition although mines claimed some casualties; he noted that this was when he saw his first Tiger tank – a knocked out specimen 'but I didn't have time to inspect it'. Meanwhile 1st Armoured Division was also advancing: farther north 2 Armoured Brigade was moving northwards to evict the enemy from the south-east of the plain below Goubellat.

As the afternoon wore on 26 Armoured Brigade met increasing enemy activity. When anti-tank guns were encountered north of Two Tree Hill, C Squadron 17th/21st Lancers, travelling behind the two leading regiments, deployed to protect the divisional flank. Then 10th Panzer moved south to meet the British threat and, as darkness approached, 6th Armoured was ordered to laager for all-round defence on the ground it had taken. The division was to be ready to resume the advance on the morrow and to engage the German armoured reserves.

The next day, St George's Day, the advance resumed. Since the enemy had identified the previous day's advance by 6th Armoured as 'a deep penetration of the Hermann Göring Division's positions which had been checked by [German] armour' opposition was certain to stiffen. And so it proved with 7th Panzer Regiment and 501 Panzer Company being particularly difficult. German tanks firing from hull-down positions knocked out three 17th/21st Lancer Shermans and a subsequent flanking move ran into a small force of eight Panzer IVs and a Tiger. In the tank-on-tank battle that followed three Shermans were lost but the Tiger and five Mark IVs were knocked out. As the battle developed another seven Marks IVs became casualties before the Germans withdrew. Although the ground also proved difficult, restricting manoeuvre and slowing progress, day's end saw a gain of ten miles. Meanwhile 1st Armoured's advance was affected by mines spread liberally in standing crops but the division was west of Djebel es Srassif that evening. When the advance resumed next day 6th Armoured pushed hard against the defence presented by 10th Panzer Division but Crocker decided to change his plan, believing that the opportunity to push deep into enemy territory had gone. On the night of 24/25 April he switched 1st Armoured to come behind 6th and, on the 25th, passed it through its sister division.

Keightley's division then swung towards Djebel Kournine to the north, Crocker now intending to press ahead on a narrower front with both divisions and accelerate the advance. But the two German divisions continued fighting grimly and the ground favoured them. It required the full co-operation of the Guards Brigade but Roberts wrote that, although 1 Guards Brigade was to make a night attack and he had 10th Rifle Brigade 'form a small party to get up to the top of Djebel Kournine', the brigade was pulled out next day, handing over their front to some of 46th Division.

The withdrawal of 6th Armoured was General Anderson's decision. He ordered the division into Army Reserve so that it might help exploit V Corps' advance, which was slowing down. Meanwhile 1st Armoured and 46th Divisions continued their advance. In the final operation Crocker was to play no part. Injured while watching a demonstration of a PIAT he was succeeded by Brian Horrocks from Eighth Army. From Anderson, Horrocks received the simple order 'Capture Tunis'. Under his command he would have:

> two infantry divisions, the 4th British and 4th Indian, with 160 Churchill tanks and two armoured divisions, the 6th and 7th, supported by the whole tactical air force commanded by 'Mary' Coningham, and an immense weight of artillery. My spirits soared. If I failed to break through with this immensely powerful force under command, then I deserved to be shot.

The Allied plan for the final defeat of Axis forces in Tunisia was codenamed Operation STRIKE and Horrocks' IX Corps had the key role: break into the enemy's lines on a narrow front with two infantry divisions, allowing 6th and 7th Armoured Divisions 'to dash through and break into the inner defences of Tunis – the high ground some six miles west of the city – before the enemy had time to man them'. V Corps was to capture Djebel Bou Aoukaz before this so that IX Corps' flank would be protected while II US Corps was to take the high ground east and west of Chouigui as well as river crossings at Tebourba and Djedeida before seizing Bizerta; XIX French Corps was to take Zaghouan. First Army's third armoured formation, 1st Armoured, had lost many tanks in the fighting during which it captured Djebel Bou Aoukaz and was understrength, as a result of which it was placed in Army Reserve. But the capture of Djebel Bou Aoukaz paved the way for the advance on Tunis.

Early on 6 May over 600 guns unleashed their shells on the area in front of IX Corps, continuing their fireplan over the next twenty-four hours, with an average of 368 rounds per gun. At 3am the infantry advanced, overrunning the anti-tank guns in the dark, and in less than four hours the armour was pushing through the gap in the enemy line in readiness for its race to Tunis. Although the going was slow at first, Horrocks wrote:

By midday we were through the crust and the tanks were grinding their way forward down the valley towards Tunis. It was a most inspiring sight to see these two well-trained and experienced armoured divisions being used in a role for which armoured divisions were specifically designed – to exploit a breakthrough deep into the enemy's heart. They worked like efficient machines, aircraft, guns, tanks, infantry and vehicles each fitting into the jig-saw of battle in its proper place.

In Roberts' words:

As far as 26 Armoured Brigade was concerned, having passed through 4th Indian Division, who had done their job admirably, there were no real problems. Odd tanks, even one Tiger, and a few anti-tank guns with small pockets of infantry, had to be dealt with. Nevertheless we were halted early in the afternoon. Many prisoners had been taken, but I never discovered why we were not allowed to continue the race into Tunis. Next morning, however, we were ordered to continue our advance to Tunis. ... However, as we were nearing Tunis, we were halted and instructed to swing south-east and to cut off the enemy from entering the Cap Bon Peninsula and establishing a 'fortress' there which might be expensive to reduce. So, we swung right-handed, away from the route to Tunis and in the direction of Hammamet, some fifty miles away.

The Desert Rats, who had fought in North Africa from the beginning of the campaign, were also successful and, in spite of enemy resistance, 22 Armoured Brigade's advance 'was steady and relentless'. Their first objective was taken but, since 'time did not permit of the Queen's Brigade being moved up and taking over the position thoroughly' the GOC, Major General Erskine, decided to keep each brigade in 'the firm positions they both held rather than to loosen the hold of each and complicate the long task of replenishment'. He also thought that it would give his soldiers some rest. Both 22 Armoured and 131 (Queen's) Brigade were prepared fully for whatever the morrow might bring.

Dawn on 7 May saw 22 Armoured Brigade move off for its second objective. Opposition along the way was overcome 'by good minor tactics in which the Light Squadrons played an important part'. Meanwhile 131 Brigade followed up with the divisional artillery and took over the positions the armoured brigade had taken, repeating the performance on the next objective. As the divisional historian recorded:

By now it was time for the armour to begin its task of dominating all roads leading into Tunis from the west and the armoured cars began to carry out close reconnaissance of the city itself. At a quarter past three in the afternoon General Erskine gave the order for 22 Brigade to go into Tunis.

Tunis was in Allied hands and the armoured divisions were sent on mopping-up operations: 1st Armoured Division came out of reserve and headed for Creteville on the 8th; 6th Armoured found the remains of Afrika Korps at Hammam Lif where the division fought its last significant battle in Africa with the Lothians' B Squadron making a spectacular flanking race along the beach; 7th Armoured went north into the bulge above Tunis and cleared la Marsa and Carthage, their last battles on African soil. On 11 May Hammamet was taken by 17th/21st Lancers, sealing the peninsula, and the presence of 26 Armoured Brigade on the peninsula persuaded most Axis soldiers there to surrender. Two days later all Axis forces in Tunisia had surrendered and General Alexander signalled to Churchill: 'Sir, it is my duty to report that the Tunisian campaign is over. All enemy resistance has ceased. We are masters of the North African shores.'

The armoured divisions had played a major part in that final victory, not least in the race for Tunis of which Horrocks wrote, 'I never felt so confident about any battle before or after. Everything went like clockwork.' That final race had seen armour used as it was intended to, demonstrating that, with good leadership and good equipment, British armour could achieve decisive victory. Even so, Macksey noted that some considered that the armoured divisions could have been in Tunis on 6 May and points out that the reason they stopped when less than halfway there

> was the action of a single Tiger tank at one point backed up by a few Mark IIIs and IVs which, in fact, were the only firm rocks amid a sea of the German Army in flight. Correctly assuming that they would comfortably reach Tunis next day, IX Corps sat down to establish a firm base when all the signs pointed to an enemy in rout.

Thus there were still reasons to believe that the British Army had not yet absorbed and applied fully all the lessons of armoured warfare, even though the basic doctrines of such warfare had been born in that army.

Notes

This chapter is based on Playfair et al, *The Mediterranean and the Middle East. Vol IV* from the Official History series, Liddell Hart, *The Tanks (Vol II)* and *The Rommel Papers*, Ford, *Mailed Fist*, Blaxland, *The Plain Cook and the Great Showman*, Horrocks, *A Full Life*, Macksey, *A History of the Royal Armoured Corps*, Montgomery, *Memoirs*, Roberts, *From the Desert to the Baltic*, Verney, *The Desert Rats*, and the war diaries of Eighth Army, First Army, X Corps, IX Corps, XIII Corps, XXX Corps, including those of their RA commanders, 1st, 6th and 7th Armoured Divisions, as well as those of their constituent brigades. Information on artillery and tanks is taken from Hogg, *British and American Artillery of World War 2* and Hogg and Weeks, *Illustrated Encyclopaedia of Military Vehicles*. Other sources are:

1. Doherty, *Clear The Way!*, p.7
2. Montgomery, *Memoirs*, p.158
3. Moorehead, *The Desert War*, p.219
4. ffrench-Blake, *A History of the 17th/21st Lancers*, p.133

Chapter Seven

Lessons to be Learned

Following victory in Tunisia there was a pause in British ground operations for two months until the invasion of Sicily on 10 July. This gave the opportunity for re-organization of formations and units, for training and for re-equipment where necessary. It also allowed for rest and recuperation as well as reflection on how the campaign in North Africa had been handled, and how its lessons might be applied to future campaigns in Europe. Of course there had been a steady flow of information back to the UK on the campaign as it progressed, on the quality – or otherwise – of equipment, on tactical thinking and co-operation between arms. All this was shaping the doctrine that would be applied by the Army, including its armoured divisions, in the remainder of the war.

Allied grand strategy was also being discussed, with the Americans eager to invade north-west Europe as soon as possible and the Soviets calling for the western Allies to open a second front. British thinking was that the forces in North Africa should be committed to further operations in the Mediterranean to knock Italy out of the war and 'tighten the ring' on Germany. It had already been agreed that British and American forces would invade Sicily, but the Americans had yet to agree that this should be followed up with landings on mainland Italy. As a result, preparations were under way for operations in both the Mediterranean and north-west Europe. Many formations that had taken part in operations in North Africa were designated for the invasion of France and would be shipped back to the UK as soon as possible, although some would fight in Sicily and the early phase of the Italian campaign. These included 7th Armoured Division and 4 and 8 Armoured Brigades.

This pause in armoured operations permits an opportunity to look at how British armour had developed, in terms of doctrine, operations and equipment, since 1939. The crucible of operational experience had led to the distilling to its essence of all the doctrinal theory that abounded in military circles, as may be seen in the July to December 1942 progress report of the RAC, which noted that:

> The tactical distinction between the employment of Armoured Brigades and Tank Brigades is becoming increasingly nebulous … This trend is naturally reflected in the … American Sherman tank – accepted by the troops as the best tank they have yet been given … the concept of the heavy slow powerful 'Infantry' or 'Assault' tank has definitely receded.[1]

The basic divisional order of battle had had a major change in May 1942 with the second armoured brigade replaced by an infantry brigade, as had happened in the

Middle East at the end of February. Further modifications in August 1942, April 1943, March 1944 and May 1945 retained that combination of one armoured and one infantry brigade. The Middle East orbat of February 1942 made the brigade group the basic battle formation with the support groups being broken up and their artillery units added to the brigade groups. While the May 1942 orbat for a division in the UK reflected this basic outline artillery units remained under divisional command. With Montgomery's arrival in Eighth Army the division again became the basic battle formation, with artillery returning to divisional command. In the April 1943 re-organization the divisional reconnaissance regiment, until then an armoured car regiment, became an armoured regiment; and there were various other modifications. Military Training Pamphlet No. 41 of July 1943 (MTP 41/1943) included the 'Normal organization of an armoured division' which it noted 'may alter as a result of evolution'. On a working basis the document noted that the division included:

An armoured divisional headquarters.
An armoured brigade.
An infantry brigade.
Divisional troops:
  One armoured reconnaissance regiment.
  Two field artillery regiments, one of which will normally be self-propelled.
  One anti-tank regiment RA, of which one battery will be self-propelled.
  One light anti-aircraft regiment RA.
  Two field squadrons and one field park squadron RE.
  Armoured divisional signals.
  Services.

The pamphlet noted that an armoured division was organized for employment as a single fighting entity, was well balanced for that purpose, and would normally fight as a whole under command of its own GOC. It went on to point out that:

It is a mounted, hard-hitting formation primarily constituted for use against hastily prepared enemy defences, for exploitation of initial success gained by other formations and for pursuit.

It is designed for use in rapid thrusts against the enemy's vitals, rather than in hammer blows against his organized defences. It is the rapier in the hands of the higher commander, rather than the bludgeon.

Its full power will only be exerted by the employment of its armour concentrated, and supported by all the other components of the division.

And that its normal roles were:

Co-operation with the main army and the Air Forces in effecting the complete destruction of the enemy, usually by envelopment, or by deep penetration through his defences after a gap has been made in his main position by other formations.

Pursuit.
Co-operation with other arms in the defence, usually by counter-attack.
To threaten the enemy and so force him to alter or disclose his dispositions.

With the armoured division operating as intended:

the enemy will be forced to react, and his armour will normally be constantly encountered. Only when the bulk of the hostile tanks have been destroyed will armoured formations attain such a measure of freedom and mobility as will enable them to exploit to the full their ability to inflict a decisive blow against the enemy's main forces.

The division's armoured brigade was intended to strike the decisive blow, with the remainder of the division's resources, 'together with all available aircraft', deploying to:

* fight any preliminary action necessary to enable the armoured brigade to be launched against a vital objective over suitable country.
* support the attack of the armoured brigade.
* consolidate and mop up after such an attack.

MTP 41/1943 compared the operation of an armoured division to the work of a rugby scrum with the armoured brigade as the wing forward. 'The vast majority of the players at first employ all their strength and energy to hold and push back their opponents' but when this is done the wing forward may 'break away ... to penetrate the defence, and the remainder of the forwards will back up his attempt to score'. The success of the armoured brigade depended on the initial efforts of the remainder of the division, or other formations, and their continuing support when the breakaway had been made.

By the time MTP 41/1943 was issued the armoured brigade included a brigade HQ, three armoured regiments and a motor battalion. Each regiment deployed sixty-nine tanks (fifty-five gun tanks, six close support – CS – and eight anti-aircraft – AA – tanks) while the armoured reconnaissance regiment had fifty-one tanks (thirty-one gun tanks, twelve CS and eight AA tanks), the armoured brigade HQ had a further ten gun tanks and divisional HQ employed eight gun and two AA tanks, giving the division an overall total of 278 tanks. (The term 'cruiser' was still being used to describe the Grant and the Sherman although 'gun tank' or 'battle tank' are more appropriate.) In addition to this substantial armoured force, there were armoured cars, scout cars, carriers, two field artillery regiments – a total of forty-eight weapons – an anti-tank regiment with both 6- and 17-pounders, and a light AA regiment with Bofors 40mm guns, as well as the lorries to carry the armoured brigade's motor battalion and the three infantry battalions of the lorried infantry brigade. In all the division had over 3,000 vehicles, including its tanks, and almost 15,000 personnel.

The infantry brigade in an armoured division included a brigade HQ, three battalions and a support group. Unlike other infantry, those attached to an armoured division were usually carried in lorries and were therefore mounted infantry, with tactics resembling 'those of mounted infantry in the past', trained especially for their role. 'When mounted their speed on roads is greater than that of the armoured brigade. When dismounted it is essential that they should be trained to move for considerable periods at a really rapid pace.'

How did the lorried infantry differ from the motor battalion of the armoured brigade? The principal difference was that the motor battalion was tactically mounted, i.e. carried as far forward as possible (the provision of half-tracks was to assist in this). Other differences included the fact that the motor battalion had greater firepower, although weaker in manpower, and had many more vehicles, including carriers and scout cars, and also possessed anti-tank guns. Each motor battalion company had integral reconnaissance and administrative elements, making it flexible enough to operate as a self-contained sub-unit. By contrast the infantry brigade units had greater manpower but less firepower. Their role was described thus:

If the 'rugger' analogy is maintained, infantry brigades may be considered as the 'front row forwards' since their first object is to get the better of their opponents in the 'tight' and to push them so as to produce an opportunity for penetration, and then to back up the battle.

Since tanks by themselves cannot win battles, it is the function of the infantry brigade, as of the remainder of the division, firstly to enable the armoured brigade to come into action on favourable ground, secondly to support its attack, and thirdly to mop up and consolidate the ground it has gained.

The artillery element of the armoured division was now stabilized at two regiments, one of towed 25-pounders and one of self-propelled 25-pounders, or M7 Priests with 105mm howitzers, with the SP regiment normally with the armoured brigade. However, both regiments came under command of the divisional Commander Royal Artillery (CRA), a centralized command which meant that the fire of both could be concentrated 'for the achievement of the divisional commander's object'. Although not intended to fire in the anti-tank role, the 25-pounders were to be sited 'with adequate anti-tank fields of fire'. However, it was also emphasized that the SP guns were *artillery* 'and that any attempt to employ them improperly as *tanks* will result in most serious casualties, without the attainment of any compensating advantage'.

Defence against enemy armour was the role of the divisional anti-tank regiment, now evolving into a four-battery unit, deploying forty-eight guns, of which two were towed batteries each with twelve 6-pounders and the other two were self-propelled with American M10 tank destroyers, armed with 3-inch guns (later replaced by 17-pounders in M10s and Achilles). This regiment was usually used 'with a view to furthering the achievement of the general plan of the divisional commander';

it also provided protection during long halts while the division was on the move, replenishing, recovering or in harbour. It was emphasized that:

> The skill, determination, and resource of every member of an anti-tank regiment must, therefore, be of the very highest order, especially in the armoured division where, because of the circumstances of its employment, the anti-tank personnel will be confronted with situations demanding the highest qualities of courage, self-reliance, and initiative.

As with the SP field guns, there was an injunction against becoming engaged in an armoured mêlée, although the SPGs' light armour and good performance across country made them 'suitable for employment in support of the attacking brigade, especially for consolidation, and as a mobile reserve'. It may be noted that US Army doctrine saw the tank as the main weapon of exploitation but envisaged SP anti-tank guns dealing with enemy tanks; those SP weapons were dubbed tank destroyers, a doctrine found to be flawed deeply.

Diminishing enemy air strength in the Mediterranean meant that the divisional light AA regiment may not have been as important as before but continued to be included in the orbat to protect the field artillery positions, defiles, and troops and transport while forming up. It also had a secondary role against enemy tanks although this was considered 'exceptional' by July 1943.

The overall number of armoured formations in the Army had reduced from its peak in 1942. Two of the three youngest armoured divisions – 42nd and 79th – were to be disbanded although the latter was reprieved by being chosen in early 1943 as the parent formation for all British specialized armour; 42nd ceased to exist in October 1943. A month after the invasion of Europe 9th Armoured Division was also disbanded in the UK; neither 9th nor 42nd Divisions ever saw action. As we have already noted 8th Armoured Division was broken up shortly after landing in Egypt and disbanded on 1 January 1943; although 23 Armoured Brigade survived as an independent brigade, 24 Armoured Brigade was also disbanded, its only action having been at El Alamein. Tenth Armoured Division saw no further action after El Alamein and deployed to Palestine and Syria, eventually being disbanded in Egypt in June 1944.

Concerns felt by crewmen about the reliability of the Crusader had also been reported back to Whitehall where the Director of Armoured Fighting Vehicles (DAFV) expressed serious concern at the poor state of reliability, as did the Deputy Chief of the Imperial General Staff, Lieutenant General Ronnie Weeks. In Weeks' view 'reliability must be considered more important than numbers', a theme that now permeated official thinking in Whitehall where an emphasis was placed on producing better tanks. Six design requirements were set: reliability; gun; speed; endurance; armour; fighting compartment. The Sherman, then being delivered in increasing numbers, was reliable with a satisfactory gun, but was outgunned by the latest German tanks. In fact, it was felt by the General Staff that the American 75mm, as fitted in the Sherman, was 'the best dual-purpose tank weapon yet produced' and, at the earliest opportunity, should be adopted as the standard gun in British tanks. In a sense this was a return to the mistake made, for different reasons, with the 2-pounder. Fortunately, there was another view. 'A first-class anti-tank weapon of the six-pounder or heavier type modernized to its highest performance' had been called for. Work was in hand to lengthen the 6-pounder and provide it with armour-piercing Capped Ballistic Capped Ammunition (APCBC) with greater penetrative power. This was overtaken by a War Office request that a quarter of tanks in British service should be fitted with the 17-pounder to engage more heavily-armoured tanks. As a result it was decided to adapt Cromwell, then under development, to mount the 17-pounder. However, the changes to the basic design, involving a lengthened hull, stronger suspension and a very high turret, led to another tank, A30 or Challenger, which proved a disappointment and certainly did not live up to its name.

Nonetheless, the idea of mounting the 17-pounder in a quarter of British tanks did come to fruition with the adaptation of the Sherman to carry the new weapon. This British version, dubbed Firefly, was issued on a one-in-four basis to all British armoured units in the armoured divisions, including those later equipped with Cromwells; the Firefly in a Cromwell troop was even more obvious than its counterpart in a Sherman troop. (The arrival of Firefly brought about a troop- and squadron-level re-organization, with a Firefly added to the existing three tanks of a troop but the number of troops in a squadron reduced from five to four.)

Cromwell had begun life in 1941 as a requirement for a heavy cruiser, weighing about 25 tons, with a 6-pounder gun and 75mm frontal armour. The General Staff, realizing that the earlier concept of light cruisers 'swirling around the battlefield like a naval fleet' did not match the reality of warfare, wrote this requirement. The resultant tank, Cavalier, was not a success but Leyland Motors suggested modifying the design using a de-rated Rolls Royce Merlin aero-engine with mechanical reliability of a level not yet seen with British tanks. With insufficient Merlins available, Leyland had to make do with the Nuffield Liberty engine and the result was given the name Centaur. As an interim design it saw limited service. Leyland continued pursuing the Merlin alternative and when de-rated Merlins, re-named Meteors, became available the design was changed once more. The end result was Cromwell, a 25-ton tank capable of 40mph and carrying a 6-pounder in its turret with a 7.92mm Besa co-axial machine gun. Cromwell's distinctive large, flat-sided turret was spacious enough for its armament to be improved to a 75mm while a support version mounted a 95mm howitzer. Cromwell also met the reliability criterion, although there were early worries on that point. Its performance and cross-country agility were welcomed by crews.

Tanks were growing bigger as demonstrated by the appearance of the Panzer Mk VI, or Tiger, in Russia and Tunisia. The United States had begun developing a 50-ton heavy tank, M6, armed with a 3-inch gun, but the US Army's Armored Force decided that mobility came before either armour or gun power and cancelled the project. (In addition, as already noted, the Americans remained fixated on the tank-destroyer concept, a belief that self-propelled anti-tank guns on lightly-armoured hulls would fight other tanks, allowing US tanks to execute the exploitation role.) A British heavy tank, TOG, was also abandoned, but this had been a throwback to the Great War whereas the American M6, although beset by problems, had potential. Cancellation of M6 was followed by another programme, T20, which was also killed off by the Armored Force, which preferred to up-gun and up-armour Sherman; it had been expected that T20s would also enter British service. Eventually the US Army did get a heavier tank, the M26 Pershing with a 90mm gun, but only towards the end of the war. None were supplied to the British Army which was waiting for the A41 universal tank, which became Centurion, the finest tank of its generation. The mid-war period was one of flux in the development of armour with many new theories being promoted about weapon performance and armour protection. The American cancellation of M6 may be seen as short-sighted in light of the appearance of the Tiger but DAFV made a similar decision in Britain; the DRAC even described the 88mm–armed Tiger as 'a clumsy fighting vehicle'. Macksey commented:

> The evidence concerning anticipated enemy equipment and techniques was inevitably incomplete and therefore subject to a measure of guesswork. It was not entirely unreasonable that, at a moment when DAFV was rejecting heavy assault tanks, the defensive potential of the Tiger tank ... was for some time underrated, although DAFV's expectation that the Germans would mount heavy anti-tank guns on self-propelled mountings, in the same way as the British and Americans intended to do, was entirely justified.

The Defence Committee, prompted by the Ministry of Supply, made clear that it preferred not to rely on American production for Britain's tank needs in the remainder of the war 'on the grounds that it was undesirable to let it appear that the war had been won by American tanks. A preference to continue with Churchill and Cromwell was stated'.

As well as Tiger the Germans had developed another new tank, Panzer Mark V, or Panther. A medium tank weighing 45 tons – half as heavy again as demanded in the original specification – it carried a 75mm gun twice as long as that of the improved Panzer Mark IV. On Hitler's orders the gun was made even longer. Having overcome teething problems, Panther proved an excellent tank; a powerful gun, thick armour and speed all contributed to it being the best German tank of the war. It was developed to combat the Russian T-34 and was superior to it in most respects, except that Germany could not match Soviet production levels: only 5,500 Panthers were built between 1942 and 1945 whereas 11,000 T-34s rolled off the production lines in 1944 alone. Although there are no doubts about the technical qualities of the Panther, it was over-engineered which meant longer time in production and more complicated maintenance in the field. Had the Germans been willing, a captured T-34, which provided the specification for Panther, could have been used to reverse engineer a German version, of which many more could have been built; but German engineering hubris ensured that this simpler Panzer Mark V did not develop beyond a thought.

It is worth considering the T-34 briefly. The best all-round tank of the war, it was also built in the greatest numbers, with over 57,000 produced by 1945 (the USA produced over 50,000 Shermans). Design work started in 1936, based on the BT-7. With a high-velocity 76.2mm gun, low turret, sloped armour, powerful engine and Christie suspension, T-34 was a shock to German panzer crews. It was later fitted with an enlarged turret and the 85mm anti-aircraft gun to become T-34/85. Wide tracks and excellent suspension allowed it to operate effectively, even on ground covered in snow or mud, giving it a tactical as well as numerical superiority over its adversaries. Not surprisingly, T-34 remained in service and production after the war and its production totals have been exceeded only by its successor, the T-54.

Also under discussion at this time were armoured warfare tactics since it was not clear whether those that had worked in the desert would translate to Europe. However, it was appreciated that the conditions experienced in Tunisia approximated more closely to those of Europe and that the armoured division as deployed in Tunisia, with its armoured brigade and lorried infantry brigade, was well balanced. Its only apparent defect lay in having only an armoured car regiment for reconnaissance and so it was decided to use an armoured regiment instead.

The revised organization was not viewed as definitive since emphasis was laid on the fact that the division had to be flexible with its organization adjustable to circumstances. In the next phase of the war, as British armoured divisions fought in Italy and north-west Europe, that flexibility was demonstrated by the adoption of the battlegroup within the divisions, and the addition of a second infantry brigade to cope with the problems created by Italy's terrain.

By this stage of the war the British armoured division was a much more professional formation. Training of new soldiers, many posted as casualty replacements, had been improved so that new crews reporting to units for the first time were better prepared for combat. This contrasted sharply with the earlier days of the war when the arrival of inadequately trained replacements had added to the existing burden on fighting men. There had been a Royal Armoured Corps Depot in Egypt, at Abbassia, north-east of Cairo, since pre-war days that fed men into the armoured units in the Middle East. As the war progressed the lessons learned in action had been taught to new arrivals whilst specialist courses for all ranks in skills such as gunnery, signals and maintenance were also provided. By early 1943 the system of assimilating reinforcements and preparing them for their units had been refined to such an extent that an Armoured Replacement Group had been created, consisting of armoured delivery regiments and, closer to the fighting front, armoured delivery squadrons to feed both battle-ready men and machines to their new units. This scheme mirrored that established in the UK.

Among changes that began in the Middle East were some affecting gunnery. Initiated in the summer of 1942, these were soon being taught at the Gunnery School at Lulworth in England. Macksey notes that these changes inspired the commandant of the Gunnery School, Colonel R. A. H. Walker, to start 'a crusade to develop long range fire (up to 2,000 yards) and indirect shooting'. At that time tank guns were generally free elevating and controlled by the gunner's shoulder. Walker averred that the free elevating gun 'had to be replaced by an elevating wheel; that elevating and traversing gears must be tightened up; and that telescopes with improved magnification must be introduced'. Walker's comments were supported by Major General Raymond Briggs who became Director RAC in early August 1943. However, as Macksey states:

> the indirect fire requirement was already shown to be less important than the enthusiasts believed. Rarely was it undertaken above troop level, but longer range shooting had already been demonstrated in action both in Tunisia and Sicily. Early in 1944 the new techniques were adopted and, as the seat of war moved to Europe, the centre of activity in the development of better gunnery shifted to the UK, at the AFV Schools and in the experimental establishments.

The AFV Schools were making a major contribution to the development of armour as the 'whole of the British-orientated armoured forces, including elements from certain foreign nations, looked to Bovington and Lulworth'. Officers were being instructed at the Tactical School where lessons from the front were passed on but it also served as a 'brains trust' to discuss and argue over ideas. Elsewhere, the Military College of Science had a Fighting Vehicles Wing where suitably qualified officers could qualify as instructors in the more rarefied aspects of tank technology. This Wing developed, first, into the RAC School of Tank Technology and then the Armour School. By mid-1943 new recruits for RAC units – and there were about 2,000 each month – were receiving training based on battlefield experience, as were new officers. Nor was there any shortage of AFVs for training. The days of scarcity had gone: at the end of 1943 the RAC had 15,732 AFVs across the world.

The experience of Operation JUBILEE, the Dieppe raid of 20 August 1942, knowledge of the German work on coast defences – the so-called Atlantic Wall – and the problems created by the enemy use of minefields in North Africa all led to the decision to employ specialized armour in the invasion of Europe. By July 1943 a range of specialized armour was being developed, including updated Sherman-based flail tanks to supersede the early rudimentary mine-clearing tanks. Assault engineer tanks, based on the Churchill, were also in development as was a range of other 'Funnies', as they were known. General Sir Alan Brooke, CIGS and a former GOC Mobile Division, believed that all such specialized armour should be grouped under a single commander. This decision led to the reprieve from disbandment for the most junior British armoured division, 79th, which was re-roled to assume the specialized armour task. Command was given to Major General Percy Hobart, who had already raised 11th Armoured Division.

As well as operating the specialized armour 79th Armoured Division was to train British, Canadian and American armoured units in the use of amphibious tanks, Shermans fitted with flotation screens and Duplex Drive (DD), allowing them to travel through water. The DD Shermans were intended to play a major role in the landings in Normandy, although sea conditions restricted their use. They were also used later in the campaign. The conversion and deployment of 79th Armoured Division illustrates the most enlightened and innovative use of armour by the British Army in the Second World War. It was unmatched by any other combatant, especially in the method of employment, with Hobart acting as specialized armour adviser to the commander 21 Army Group, General, later Field Marshal, Sir Bernard Montgomery, and with a similar command and oversight system at formation, unit and sub-unit levels so that the special skills and equipment of the division were not misused.

At much the same time each field army HQ received a new element of staff with the introduction of a Brigadier RAC (BRAC) and staff. Brigadier George Richards, who had commanded 4 and 23 Armoured Brigades, was appointed BRAC to HQ Eighth Army in time for the invasion of Italy while Brigadier Harry Watkins became BRAC at Allied Forces HQ with the special remit of protecting RAC interests there, as well as setting up the RAC structure in southern Europe. No BRAC was appointed to First Army which was allowed to fade away as preparations continued to invade Sicily.

There were other changes at higher levels that indicate maturing attitudes towards armour. In late 1941 three armoured groups had been created, commanded by Crocker, McCreery and Creagh, the most experienced armoured commanders. These had been intended as operational formations and to co-ordinate training at formation level but were short-lived; they were armoured corps in all but name. As well as the abolition of the armoured groups, the post of Commander RAC was replaced by a post of Major General RAC at Home Forces HQ while, in February 1943, DAFV had been retitled DRAC; the AFV branches in the War Office also became RAC branches.

Perhaps the most important change that had come about was not one that could be quantified. It was the recognition that armour was not something *different* but an integral and essential part of any field army. An armoured division was seen as a 'formation consisting of all arms' to work with all arms and the air forces to destroy the enemy's forces. The 'them and us' attitude of the past was dying out and its disappearance ensured that much more effective use would be made of armoured divisions in the future and that those divisions would work more closely with other arms.

As training and preparations were being finalized for the invasion of Sicily, armoured divisions in the UK were training for another invasion that would take place in 1944 and put British troops back on French soil for the first time since 1940. However, only three of the five armoured divisions in Britain would fight in north-west Europe, where they would be joined by 7th Armoured, the Desert Rats. Those were Guards, 11th and 79th Armoured Divisions, all of which we shall meet in subsequent pages.

Note

This chapter is based on Liddell Hart, *The Tanks (Vol II)*, Macksey, *A History of the Royal Armoured Corps*, and Military Training Pamphlet 41/1943, Part 1, The Tactical Handling of Armoured Divisions and Part 2, The Armoured Regiment. Information on artillery and tanks is taken from Hogg, *British and American Artillery of World War 2* and Hogg and Weeks, *Illustrated Encyclopaedia of Military Vehicles*. Joslen's *Orders of Battle* provided the information on the various armoured divisions while that on 79th Armoured Division is drawn from my own book, *Hobart's 79th Armoured Division at War*.

1. Quoted in Macksey, p.139

A Vickers Mk VI Light Tank of 3rd The King's Own Hussars in pre-war days. The tank commander's forage cap would have been an unlikely choice of headgear on active service, as well as being unsuitable.

Vickers light tanks of an unknown unit during the brief campaign in France in 1940.(*Courtesy Mr Frank Small whose uncle, the Revd Richard Talbot MC, may have taken the original*)

Cruisers of 1st Royal Tank Regiment in action at Beda Fomm in February 1941 at the conclusion of Western Desert Force's successful offensive that began with Operation COMPASS in December 1940. (*Courtesy of the artist, David Rowlands*)

The early opposition in North Africa, Italian M13/40 light tanks, derived from a Vickers design. Although lightly armoured they carried a 47mm main gun that was more than a match for the British 2-pounder of the period.

The Panzer III (PzKw III) was armed with either a 37mm or 50mm main gun but was not superior to British tanks. Intended to fight other tanks it was superseded in this role by the Panzer IV which had been intended for an infantry support role but was upgunned with a 75mm main gun to suit it for the medium role and to fight other tanks.

Two Crusader Cruiser tanks in the desert. While elegant and speedy the Crusader was under-gunned until fitted with the 6-pounder; even then it remained a mechanically unreliable vehicle.

America's first contribution to Britain's armoured forces was the M3 Stuart light tank, known as the Honey to British tankmen. Although fast it was lightly armed, with a 37mm gun, and lightly armoured and thus best suited to the reconnaissance role. This example has been knocked out in the desert. (*Bundesarchiv*)

Perhaps the worst example of British tank design, Covenanter (Cruiser Mk 5) was regulated quickly to training duties and never saw active service. This example belonged to HQ Squadron 2nd (Armoured) Bn Irish Guards and bears the name 'Ulster', one of Ireland's four provinces.

The American M3 Lee/Grant Medium Tank was an interim design pending the production of the M4 Sherman. The Grant's main 75mm gun was housed in a sponson on the hull, limiting the tank's tactical versatility; its turret gun was only 37mm. The M3 on the left is a Grant, distinguishable from the Lee by its turret, modified to carry the radio British-fashion, and the absence of the raised commander's hatch.

American M7 Priest self-propelled 105mm howitzers provided the armoured divisions with highly mobile artillery support. They replaced the Bishop SP 25-pounder, a marriage of a Valentine hull and 25-pounder gun, but were later superseded by Sexton, a 25-pounder SPG based on the Canadian Ram tank hull. (*IWM E 18869*)

Before the final battle of El Alamein, British armoured divisions received the latest American medium tank, the M4 Sherman, which was to be the principal Allied medium tank for the rest of the war. The dust raised by this group of Shermans gives some idea of the difficulties faced by tank crews in the desert.

Normandy 1944: an M5 Stuart of 7th Armoured Division in the reconnaissance role. Later in the war many Stuarts were stripped of their turrets.

The first major armoured clash between British and German tanks occurred at Villers Bocage in June 1944 when Tigers and Panzer IVs knocked out most of a squadron/company group of 7th Armoured Division. This photograph shows a Tiger I of Michael Wittmann's battalion en route to Villers Bocage.

A Sherman passes an infantry section on a dusty Norman road. The tank is camouflaged heavily, making it impossible to identify its parent formation.

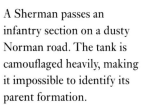

Guards Armoured Division Shermans move up to the front.

Tanks of 11th Armoured Division advance in Operation EPSOM. A Sherman Crab flail of 79th Armoured Division is visible in the left foreground.

Sherman crews ready for Operation GOODWOOD, an attack by all three armoured divisions. The Firefly's 17-pounder is obvious by its length while another Sherman Crab is in the background.

Shermans of 3rd Royal Tank Regiment in 11th Armoured Division advance into battle in Operation GOODWOOD. (*Courtesy of the artist, David Rowlands*)

Canadian armour made two remarkable advances in the closing stages of the battle for Normandy. Here ground troops watch as heavy bombers help clear the way for the advance. (*Library and Archives Canada: PA 154826*)

Cromwells of 7th Armoured Division fight their way through the city of Lisieux with the famous basilica in the background. (*Courtesy of the artist, David Rowlands*)

A 17-pounder-armed Challenger leads Cromwells of 7th Armoured divisions in Normandy. In spite of its clumsy appearance the Challenger was lower overall than either a Sherman or Tiger.

On 3 September 1944, Guards Armoured division liberated the Belgian capital, Brussels. Major General Sir Allan Adair salutes the ecstatic crowds in the city.

A Sherman Firefly showing its 17-pounder to advantage in the Belgian town of Namur. (*US Army official photograph*)

A Sherman troop of 23rd Hussars (11th Armoured Division) moving through Deurne on the outskirts of Antwerp.

The best British tank of the war, Comet, shows off its elegant lines and 77mm gun. Comet entered service with 11th Armoured division in March 1945. What a difference its availability a year earlier would have made. (*Tank Museum*)

A Sherman of 1st (Armoured) Bn Coldstream Guards crosses the bridge at Lingen after Captain Ian Liddell's VC-earning clearing of it. Welded to the right side of the turret is a rocket-launching tube 'liberated' by the Coldstream from an RAF aircraft. Other tanks had rocket-launching rails fitted to their turrets. (*Courtesy, Steve Snelling*)

Eighth Army's final operation in Italy, Operation BUCKLAND, saw infantry carried in improvised armoured personnel carriers, including this Kangaroo with men of 2nd London Irish Rifles. The Kangaroos were either de-gunned Ram tanks or 'defrocked' M7 Priest SPGs.

A Cromwell and a Challenger of 7th Armoured Division in Hamburg in May 1945. This Challenger was one of the few remaining in service.

Saluting the end: Shermans of Guards Armoured Division in parade with Fireflies in the majority.

Saluting the end: the Desert Rats in the Victory Parade in Berlin. Challengers are still in evidence while the American M24 Chaffee light tank had assumed the reconnaissance role.

Commanders: Major Generals Sir Percy Hobart of 79th Armoured Division (left) and Pip Roberts of 11th Armoured Division with Field Marshal Montgomery, Commander 21st Army Group. Hobart was one of the prophets of armoured warfare while Roberts, who commanded at regimental, brigade and divisional levels, was the best British operational practitioner of the art. Montgomery never grasped the art of armoured warfare. (*Tank Museum*)

Lieutenant General Sir Herbert Lumsden. GOC of 1st Armoured Division and Commander X Corps, Lumsden suffered the loss of his command as a result of Montgomery's failure to understand armour. Sent to act as Churchill's personal liaison with General MacArthur's US forces in the Pacific he was killed on the bridge of the battleship USS *New Mexico* when it was struck by a Japanese kamikaze bomber on 6 January 1945. Herbert Lumsden was the most senior British combat casualty of the war.

Major General Sir Allan Adair, GOC Guards Armoured Division. A capable and extremely popular commander, he was later appointed Colonel of the Grenadier Guards. Although Montgomery disliked him he could find no excuse to sack him.

Air Chief Marshal Tedder, later Lord Tedder, who, with Auchinleck, defined and refined the art of tactical air support in the desert. He was Eisenhower's air commander in the European campaign and understood thoroughly the need for close co-operation between tactical aircraft and armoured forces.

Lieutenant General Sir Richard McCreery, Commander Eighth Army. (This photograph was taken when he was commanding X Corps.) The best British practitioner of armoured warfare, he understood better than any other British field army commander what tanks could do and how armoured forces could best be deployed. Operation BUCKLAND was a classic use of armoured forces.

Chapter Eight

Across the Med

Operation HUSKY, the invasion of Sicily, took place on 10 July 1943. The initial landings were made by infantry and airborne troops supported by naval gunfire and air attack. Once the infantry were ashore, however, waterproofed tanks landed from LCTs, or landing craft tanks, which had been under development since 1940, but echoed a concept dating back to the Great War.

The invading formations were from both British and American sources, with Canadians joining the British element. In the planning stages the Allied forces were codenamed Force 545, or Eastern Task Force, under Montgomery, and Force 343, or Western Task Force, under General George S. Patton. The overall command was Force 141 under General Sir Harold Alexander. These forces became Eighth Army, Seventh (US) Army and 15 Army Group respectively. Although it had been intended that the British element would be Twelfth Army the title Eighth Army was retained at the behest of Montgomery who argued that it would be good for morale.[1]

Sicily was not a country for armoured divisions, especially not in the eastern area where Eighth Army was to operate. However, American armour had more room to manoeuvre in the west where it clashed with German armour, including Tigers. The British armoured commitment to the campaign was two armoured brigades, 4 and 23, each less a regiment, and a Sherman-equipped Canadian tank brigade. (On 14 July Major General Erskine, GOC 7th Armoured Division, arrived in Sicily with a small tactical HQ to act as armoured adviser to Eighth Army.)[2] All three brigades performed an infantry support role in a difficult campaign. Then, and even now, Sicily favoured the defender. Narrow roads, at times enclosed by lava-stone walls, climbing tortuously through hill country presaged the Normandy bocage. To begin with, the armoured brigades were able to create ad hoc columns to leap ahead of the infantry and seize objectives inland but, once clear of the island's south-eastern corner, the terrain closed in and such movement became difficult, if not impossible. Then it was a different story. In Macksey's words:

> it was to be a campaign of tortuous crawling along narrow lanes set amidst hills, villages and orange groves. This, at first, was war of the ambuscade, the point crews of each column grimly aware of the threat from concealed tanks and guns which often reserved their fire to point-blank range. Firepower, protection and mobility took second place to caution and luck in dealing with a skilled enemy who held ground of his own choosing. The four RAC units … initially held the upper hand against Italian troops who tended to surrender after a sharp dose of shell from 75mm guns. Small, improvised Sherman tank columns were able to

dash ahead of the infantry and seize objectives inland. But gradually the close country thwarted movement – and then they encountered the Germans.

The Germans were determined and took a heavy toll of the armour. As well as anti-tank guns – always well-sited and concealed – they used handheld anti-tank weapons and snipers, some of whom were so accurate that 'they shot men clean between the eyes, and tank commanders were shot through the hands when only these were exposed on the edge of the cupola'. The Sharpshooters (3 CLY) in 4 Armoured Brigade lost their CO, Lieutenant Colonel Geoffrey Willis, early in the campaign during the battle for the Primosole bridge; two squadron leaders were also lost, either dead or wounded, during that battle.

As the fighting moved into the hill country around Monte Etna the advancing elements of Eighth Army's 50th (Northumbrian) Division were formed into columns, the advance guard of which included a reconnaissance troop, a section of sappers and armour from the Sharpshooters.

> These improvised columns may well have been the best available solution to the problem of how to make use of armour, and it was no fault of the Sharpshooters if Nature had designed the terrain for infantry rather than tanks.
>
> The Germans, taking every advantage of the country and their knowledge of it, made skilful use of very small units – single tanks on some occasions – with which to fight rearguard actions. All that the Sharpshooters could do was to support the infantry, and then only on the narrowest front.
>
> Enemy tactics soon became clear. As usual they showed masterly skill in the siting of their anti-tank guns and … made good use of mines and harassing mortar fire.
>
> One favourite and effective trick was to use a single Tiger tank to cover a road approach. This would then knock out the leading armoured car and, having done so, slip back to another well-sited position. To counter this it became necessary to make a whole series of small plans of attack, each one with a co-ordinated artillery fire-plan, sappers to deal with mines and craters, and so on.[3]

The Sharpshooters' experience encapsulated the campaign for the armoured units. In the closing phase, as the Germans pulled back to Messina, and with Patton's Seventh Army converging on the town, 23 Armoured Brigade was pulled out to make room for the Americans. Few were sorry. As the historian of 23 Armoured commented, 'Sicily was the hardest, the bloodiest, and above all, the most disillusioning campaign in which the brigade had served during the war.'[4]

While Sicily had been difficult and disillusioning for tankmen who had become used to the manoeuvre space available in North Africa for most of the campaign there, Italy was to provide further disillusionment. Eighth Army deployed three British armoured divisions during the Italian campaign – 7th, 1st and 6th – as well as Canadian and South African divisions, and a Polish brigade, but none had a happy experience. Opportunities for manoeuvre warfare were rare in a peninsula where mountains and rivers shaped the battleground and, as in Sicily, much of the armour's work was supporting the infantry. Not until the very end of the campaign was there an opportunity for armoured manoeuvre as the visionaries of the interwar years had imagined it, but it proved an opportunity for one of the best examples of such warfare from the western Allies of the entire war.

The Italian campaign began on 3 September 1943 with Eighth Army's XIII Corps landing in Calabria in Operation BAYTOWN. No British armour was involved in the early operations in Calabria but 1 Canadian Armoured Brigade (as 1 Canadian Tank Brigade had been re-designated on 23 August[5] provided support to both 1st Canadian and 5th British Divisions. Six days after the Reggio landings, Fifth US Army landed at Salerno, south-east of Naples, in Operation AVALANCHE. Those landings were made by two corps, II US and X British, with 23 Armoured Brigade providing two regiments, the Royal Scots Greys and 40 RTR, with waterproofed tanks to support X Corps. The tanks had a difficult time – the Greys lost some even before touching down as an LCT was hit by fire from 88s. Even when ashore and stripped of their waterproofing they were impeded by soft ground just as a German counter-attack with armour hit the lodgement area. Both regiments were involved immediately in an infantry maul. Even though the tanks were committed individually, as they were freed from the soft ground, they helped stabilize the front and accounted for several enemy tanks; one Sherman knocked out four Mark IIIs and IVs in minutes.

That first encounter set the tone of the battle for the beachhead. X Corps' follow-up division was 7th Armoured, which began to land on the 15th, although a small advance party had arrived with the assault troops. First ashore from 22 Armoured Brigade was 5 RTR – and two squadrons were quickly placed under command of 23 Armoured Brigade – but a last-minute change by the movements staff in North Africa meant that the infantry brigade was left behind and infantry battalions had hastily to be created from AA gunners who landed at much the same time; these men (including the author's father) were 131 (Queen's) Brigade for the next three days.[6] As the build-up continued, it became clear to Kesselring that the invaders were not to be thrown back into the sea and the Germans began withdrawing.

At the end of September the division, with 23 Armoured under command, moved up towards Naples which was entered on 1 October. With many demolitions along the way the tankmen had cause to be grateful for the sappers with their Bailey bridges, which were to be a feature of the Italian campaign, and for another new invention, the Scissors bridge 'a prefabricated construction spanning 30 feet … carried on the chassis of a tank; it could be lowered into position by the crew without their having to expose themselves. The Scissors Bridge proved its value time and again during the next eighteen months.'

Advancing from Naples, Erskine sent 22 Armoured Brigade into the lead on 2 October but, although there was initial good progress, before long another problem of fighting in Europe was met: towns and villages reduced to rubble. There were to be no smooth runs through such areas as by-passes had to be found or created. The historian of 11th Hussars wrote that 'Gone for ever were the days of free manoeuvre in the Desert, of fast movement from one flank to another.' Fighting their way forward against stubborn delaying opposition, similar to that experienced in Sicily, X Corps' divisions approached the Volturno river where 7th Armoured faced its first major river crossing in Europe.

The crossing operation, made more difficult by a shortage of bridging equipment, was made between 12 and 16 October by 46th and 56th Divisions supported by the Desert Rats whose orders were to make diversionary attacks 'mainly with artillery and patrols, but to lose no opportunity of making a crossing if it were possible'. The divisional engineers bridged the river at the site of a demolished bridge and a raft was also put into use. Meanwhile 4 CLY found a ford upstream of the bridge and tanks were waterproofed rapidly to allow them to cross. Workshop personnel even followed the Shermans into action to finish waterproofing while the tanks fired at the enemy. One squadron crossed and by the night of the 16th there was a firm bridgehead across the Volturno. The other divisions of X Corps and VI (US) Corps were also across and ready to move on.

The Desert Rats were involved in some patchy fighting as Fifth Army's advance continued, with a squadron of 5 RTR capturing the village of Mondragone on 1 November. But orders had already been received for the division to return to the UK to prepare for the invasion of France and the units were pulled out of the line and vehicles handed over, mostly to 5th Canadian Armoured Division, which was arriving in Italy. By January 1944 almost all of 7th Armoured Division was in Britain.

Eighth Army had advanced through Calabria into Puglia and then swung northwards to Foggia. Although strengthened to two corps by the arrival of further divisions, the only armour was 4 Armoured and 1 Canadian Armoured Brigades. The first major obstacle was presented by the Germans at Termoli on the Adriatic coast. But first the Biferno river had to be crossed; Montgomery had also launched a seaborne attack on Termoli with a Special Service Brigade under command of 78th Division, two brigades of which were also to sail to Termoli.

While Italy's terrain placed obstacles aplenty in the way of the Allied advances, the weather also created problems. Earlier than usual rains caused rivers to swell and rise and the Biferno became a much greater barrier than it had been only a week earlier. In a difficult battle to stem a German counter-attack by 16th Panzer Division, British infantry held out even though deprived by the weather of their customary artillery and air support. Some tanks of 4 Armoured Brigade got through to support the defence, reinforcements landed from the sea and, with improving weather, air support became available. When the German pressure had eased, an attack by 38 (Irish) Brigade supported by Canadian tanks proved successful in securing the town and nearby high ground. Although Eighth Army was able to advance further, Montgomery's dream of liberating Rome by Christmas proved elusive and the German Winter Line was a barrier that held the Allies as winter deepened its grip. At the end of December Montgomery left Italy to take command of 21 Army Group for the invasion of France and Sir Oliver Leese became Eighth Army's commander.

During December the Canadians fought a battle that was 'the first example in the Mediterranean war of a large pitched battle in a town'. The town was Ortona, dubbed 'the Stalingrad of the Abruzzi'. Although it had neither strategic nor tactical significance the Germans decided to defend it in strength, even while Kesselring accused the British of endowing it with an importance equal to that of Rome. After more than two weeks of constant fighting the Canadians met the German defences of Ortona, three battalions of Fallschirmjäger determined to resist as long as possible.

The first Canadian contact with the defenders of Ortona occurred on 21 December when the Edmonton Regiment, supported by Shermans of the Three Rivers Regiment, entered the town. At first the Canadians pushed along the line of the central streets on a narrow front of 500 yards. Against the opposition mounted by the Germans this front proved too much for one battalion and the commander of 2 Canadian Brigade, Brigadier Hoffmeister, deployed a company of the Seaforth Highlanders of Canada and then the entire Seaforth battalion; this latter reinforcement was made on the 23rd. The British *Official History* summarizes what followed:

Thereafter the Edmontons on the right, and the Seaforth on the left, with tanks and detachments of anti-tank guns, fought house by house until on the 28th December they emerged victorious at the town's northern end, leaving behind them mounds of rubble.

The Canadian *Official History* quotes a German report from LXXVI Panzer Corps about the fighting on Christmas Day:

In Ortona the enemy attacked all day long with about one brigade supported by ten tanks. In very hard house-to-house fighting and at the cost of heavy casualties to his own troops [he] advanced to the market square in the south part of the town. The battle there is especially violent. Our own troops are using flamethrowers, hand grenades and the new *Ofenrohre* [shoulder-launched 88mm anti-tank rocket launcher].[7]

The Germans made very skilful use of the town's layout. With side streets too narrow to be negotiated by a Sherman, most fighting was funnelled into the much wider south-north streets where the Germans created killing zones by demolishing buildings or allowing the Canadians to advance into the piazzas before engaging them. Groups of buildings were fortified while the front walls of those facing them were demolished to deny the attackers their cover. The Canadians brought their anti-tank guns, both 6- and 17-pounders, into action against the buildings; these were much more effective than field guns in this role. Infantry with pioneer support 'mouse-holed' their way from one building to its neighbour by using 'beehive' charges to breach top-storey dividing walls, allowing the infantry to fight their way down to the ground floor. This allowed infantry to advance without using the streets where they would have been exposed to enemy fire.

The tanks also acted as artillery while infantrymen offered close protection to the Shermans in turn to ward off the attentions of Germans with *Ofenrohre* or other weapons. The Canadians suffered 650 casualties, the Edmontons alone suffering 172 of those, of whom sixty-three were killed. Much had depended on junior officers and NCOs, and close co-operation between infantry, armour and artillery. The gallantry awards for the Ortona battle make that clear with five DSOs, three MCs and seven MMs to members of the two infantry battalions, the Three Rivers Regiment and 90 Anti-Tank Battery, Royal Canadian Artillery. In addition, the Canadians had virtually written the manual for fighting in a built-up area, the lessons of which would be put to good use in later battles in Italy and north-west Europe.

At the turn of the year, as Montgomery bade farewell to Eighth Army, the advance on the eastern sector had been only fourteen miles in a direct line since 28 November. Progress was down to half a mile per day with very high infantry casualties: in December Eighth Army had sustained 6,453 casualties and had no opportunity to bring to bear Montgomery's superiority in armour. Nor would such an opportunity present itself in the immediate future as German resistance, terrain and worsening weather combined to bring an end to major fighting on Eighth Army's front. With Montgomery's departure it would fall to his successor, Oliver Leese, to seek an opportunity to unleash Eighth Army's armour.

In the early months of Leese's tenure as Eighth Army commander neither terrain nor weather permitted employment of armour in its intended role. The most famous of British armoured divisions, 7th, was sent back to Britain to prepare for Operation OVERLORD but 5th (Canadian) Armoured Division arrived in Italy to join 1st Canadian Division in Eighth Army and form I Canadian Corps. The army group commander, General Alexander, felt that he already had enough armour available for the conditions that faced his two armies in Italy but was overruled by General Brooke, the CIGS. In spite of this reinforcement, and the arrival of II Polish Corps (which included an armoured brigade), Eighth Army was playing a defensive role and it would be May 1944 before it moved over to the offensive. By then it had been joined by two further armoured divisions, 6th British and 6th South African, while 1st Armoured Division was preparing to leave North Africa for Italy.

While Eighth Army had been virtually static, Fifth Army had been battling to break through the Gustav Line, the major German defensive line across Italy that included the formidable heights dominating the Liri valley, the obvious route to Rome since the coastal route was constricted by high mountains that left only a narrow strip of land that was vulnerable to ambush. US forces gained some ground in the Gustav Line in January but it was mostly given up freely by the Germans. In contrast efforts to cross the Rapido river resulted in huge casualties while an attempt to outflank the Gustav Line by landing an American corps (half of it British) at Anzio resulted in that corps coming under siege in the Anzio beachhead. Further breakthrough attempts were also frustrated while the bombing of the Benedictine Abbey on Monte Cassino and the town of Cassino made matters worse for the attackers; it was impossible for tanks to support infantry in the rubble of Cassino and an attempt to outflank the Monte

Cassino position by a small armoured force, using what was dubbed Cavendish Road, came to naught.

A new plan was formulated that involved sidestepping Eighth Army across the Apennines, Operation DIADEM, of which Eighth Army's part was Operation HONKER. Initially, Eighth Army's break-in to the enemy positions would depend on infantry supported by artillery and engineers with substantial air support. II Polish Corps was to attack the high ground while 4th British and 8th Indian Divisions of XIII Corps created a bridgehead over the Gari river, through which 78th Division would pass and advance, with 6th Armoured Division supporting it in its efforts to reinforce and expand the bridgehead. In fact the role assigned to 6th Armoured was quite complex. Each armoured regiment of 26 Armoured Brigade supported an attacking formation: 17th/21st Lancers with 10 and 28 Brigades of 4th Division, the Lothians and Border Horse with 12 Brigade of the same division and 16th/5th Lancers with 78th Division. A battlegroup from 6th Armoured, dubbed the Divisional Armoured Reconnaissance Group, was to be ready to exploit the disintegration of enemy defences in the Liri valley. The battlegroup included 1st Derbyshire Yeomanry, the recce regiment, 10th Rifle Brigade, 72nd Anti-Tank Regiment, a self-propelled battery of 51st LAA Regiment, and 625 and 627 Field Squadrons Royal Engineers. Since 26 Armoured Brigade was supporting infantry formations it would fall on the Divisional Armoured Reconnaissance Group to provide the impetus for the attacking XIII Corps until the armoured regiments could be recalled from their duties with the infantry and re-organize for the pursuit.

The work of supporting the infantry cost the armoured units many casualties in men and tanks. Advancing towards the report line *Grafton* with 5th Northamptons, C Squadron 17th/21st Lancers lost four tanks with two men killed and six wounded. Major George Ponsonby was awarded a Bar to the MC he had earned in Tunisia when he led his squadron across Amazon bridge and into action with the Hampshires. At the Piopetto he found two bridge-laying tanks knocked out and his way apparently blocked by the water course but 'with great initiative and dash he got his squadron around an obstacle over an improvised ford, the construction of which he supervised, and so continued to give the infantry battalion much needed support'.[8] Ponsonby continued his exemplary leadership over the following four days and contributed much to the success of several operations.

As 38 (Irish) Brigade prepared for their phase of the attack, 16th/5th Lancers, supporting the Irish formation, lost their commanding officer, John Loveday, wounded fatally when an enemy shell dropped close to the O Group he was conducting with Lieutenant Colonel Ion Goff of 2nd London Irish Rifles. Goff also died of his wounds. In the subsequent attack the Lancers' Shermans supporting H Company of the Irish Rifles were brought to a standstill by an anti-tank gun, probably an 88, which knocked out the leading tanks. The impasse was ended when a young NCO of the Rifles, Corporal Jimmy Barnes, led what was left of his platoon in an attack on the gun emplacement. Most of his men were killed by machine-gun fire and Barnes was the last to die but not before he had hurled a grenade into the German position, causing the gun team to abandon their weapon. Although Barnes was recommended for a posthumous VC, this was never awarded.

On 17 May Major Robert Gill, commanding B Squadron 16th/5th Lancers, was killed while supporting 1st Royal Irish Fusiliers as they advanced into a storm of artillery, mortar and machine-gun fire. Also killed was one of the Fusiliers' company commanders and his runner, although these were the sole fatalities in the company which took its objectives with the Lancers' support.

Perhaps the best summary of the effectiveness of 26 Armoured Brigade's support for the infantry of XIII Corps came from John Horsfall who took command of 2nd London Irish Rifles after the death of Ion Goff:

> The initial ordeal of the forward companies was brief enough as they raced over the battlefield. To begin with our opponents in open trenches were easily collared, as our men were in to them while they were still taking cover. However, the buildings were a different matter, and wherever we saw our men held up the supporting 16th/5th tanks worked up to them and literally pulverized the opposition by direct fire at very close range.
>
> I must say that the tanks' 75 was a marvellous gun, and a single shell from it was sufficient to bring down a large part of the front wall of a house. ... Also the tactical co-ordination of the tank troops was very impressive with one of their number hull down and shooting as the others crept forward in the smoke. In a number of instances the enemy were trapped in their basements and cellars before they knew what was happening. In other cases I noticed the garrison ran for it after a few direct hits – those of them who were still in a position to do so. Some may have got out unseen, but our men were too close to them in most cases and here they had the first glimpse of triumph – the sight of a flying enemy, and knew then, and forever, who had the mastery.
>
> While this stage lasted I think a good many of our opponents were shot down under the fire of the tanks' besas. The Lancers were often waiting for them, and were on to them in a flash when they ran in small parties or gruppes.[9]

By the time 78th Division was nearing the last of its objectives the Poles were again assaulting the heights which they had taken but been forced to abandon earlier in the battle. On the morning of 18 May it was clear that the Gustav Line had been broken but another barrier lay ahead – the Hitler Line, stretching from Aquino along the Melfa river through Pontecorvo and over the Aurunci mountains. The Death or Glory Boys, first of 26 Armoured Brigade's regiments to encounter the defences of the Hitler Line, found that the opposition had vanished, as did the Derbyshire Yeomanry at Aquino airfield. Although one Derbys' Sherman was knocked out in Aquino the yeomanry were able to report the bridge across the Melfa still intact. This led to the Divisional Armoured Reconnaissance Group being launched into action in the hope of bouncing the Hitler Line.

With 36 Brigade and 17th/21st Lancers, the Group approached Aquino but the Germans, now aware of this chink in their defences, had moved more troops into the little town. Enemy retaliation prompted a withdrawal from Aquino and a fresh attack next day by two battalions, supported by Canadian Shermans. Over several hours the Germans gave a master class in defence, their anti-tank guns hitting every Sherman of the two leading Canadian troops and knocking out a baker's dozen. A probe by 11 Brigade with six Shermans of 17th/21st Lancers fared no better with four tanks knocked out. Leese saw that the Hitler Line was not to be bounced and a major attack by I Canadian Corps was ordered. Twenty-six Armoured Brigade returned to the bosom of 6th Armoured Division, which was to prepare to advance in exploitation as soon as the Hitler Line was broken.

On 24 May the Canadians broke through the Hitler Line, 5th Canadian Armoured Division deploying in its intended role for the first time. The Germans continued fighting tenaciously and, although the Canadian tanks took their foes off balance at first, the German tanks, including Panthers, exacted retribution: Lord Strathcona's Horse lost seventeen Shermans that afternoon. But the enemy was withdrawing and 6th Armoured Division was to join in the pursuit.

This was to be the first opportunity for 6th Armoured to operate in its true role in Italy. The division also had a new GOC, Major General Vyvyan Evelegh, formerly GOC 78th (Battleaxe) Division. Evelegh and his soldiers may have wondered at the definition of the word 'pursuit' after their experiences of the next few days. Initially the plan was to advance through the Liri valley, following Highway 6, along the right side of the valley as 5th Canadian Armoured was advancing on the left. Problems began when it was found that 78th Division was still fighting for Aquino and there was no crossing over the Melfa. Leese's HQ ordered Evelegh to break out through the Canadian Corps' sector. As the division's historian notes:

> This produced another problem for Evelegh. In the Liri valley were four infantry divisions and three armoured divisions. The amount of transport supporting those divisions ... was enormous. Each of the infantry divisions used nearly 3,400 vehicles, and an armoured division about 3,000. In addition there were two corps headquarters together with their artillery, engineer and support vehicles. To complicate matters, 6th Armoured Division was now being asked to move from its assigned roads on to those of an adjacent corps and division. Not unexpectedly, there was some confusion and delay, and some very large traffic jams.

It would seem that Leese was imitating Montgomery by creating traffic congestion.

The Derbyshire Yeomanry, with 10th Rifle Brigade, led the way along the new route. At the Melfa an intact wooden bridge was discovered but attempts to secure it resulted in its destruction, stranding four Derby Shermans on the enemy side. Efforts to relieve the tanks were frustrated, partly due to the traffic congestion, and the crews were ordered to withdraw as close as possible to the riverbank, abandon their tanks and cross the river on foot under cover of darkness. This was but a taste of what was to follow.

Evelegh was keen to reach Arce where the road split, Highway 6 continuing on its way to the Eternal City with another road branching off northwards. That junction at Arce assumed critical importance. But the division was held up less than four miles from there, near the village of Coldragone. What seemed initially to be an obstacle caused by a blown bridge and heavy machine-gun fire proved even more difficult as the road passed through a narrow valley with hills to either side. The leading infantry of 1 Guards Brigade – 3rd Grenadiers – were pinned down and Evelegh ordered 3rd Welsh Guards to advance through the Grenadiers to seize and hold the high ground so that the armour could move on and capture Arce.

But the Welsh Guards were far back in the divisional column and had to be brought forward on the tanks of the Lothians, a journey of many hours that saw the guardsmen left without their own transport and, more immediately, without food, although the Lothians ensured that some, at least, had a hot meal before going into action. Both Grenadiers and Welsh were to suffer considerably over the next several hours. They were joined by the other battalion of their brigade, 2nd Coldstream, as they fought for the heights of Monte Grande, Monte Orio and Monte Piccolo. The fighting was a cold-blooded infantry battle since the opposing sides on Grande were too close for artillery fire to be called down. As ever the Germans, paratroopers in this case, were resolute in defence and, at one stage, forced two companies of Grenadiers to abandon hard-won positions. With Monte Grande back in German hands pressure was increased on the Coldstream on Piccolo but with the artillery now able to provide support, as were some tanks of 26 Armoured Brigade, the defenders were eventually forced to withdraw, in part due to a threat to their flank from 8th Indian Division. 'Eventually' in this case meant three days. The Guards had suffered 254 casualties.

Accompanied by Gurkhas the Lothians entered Arce on 29 May. On 2 June XIII Corps' commander, Lieutenant General Kirkman, 'decided to put 78th Division into reserve and to put 6th Armoured Division once more into the lead to carry out a long, fast pursuit'. Evelegh's men were to pass through his former command at Alatri on the 3rd and advance along the line Trivigliano–Genazzano. The advance was led by the latest addition to 6th Armoured Division, Brigadier Adrian Gore's 61 (Rifle) Brigade, which entered Trivigliano early on the 4th, having knocked aside some stubborn rearguards en route. On that same day the Allies liberated Rome.

On 6 June the eyes of the world turned to France with Operation OVERLORD, the liberation of Europe, beginning. That task involved three British armoured divisions, to which we shall now turn our attention.

Notes

This chapter is based on Molony et al, *The Mediterranean and Middle East*, Vols V and VI from the Official History, Liddell Hart, *The Tanks (Vol II)*, Macksey, *A History of the Royal Armoured Corps*, Ford, *Mailed Fist*, Verney, *The Desert Rats*, my own *Eighth Army in Italy 1943–45*, and the war diaries of 18 Army Group, Eighth Army, X Corps, V Corps, 6th and 7th Armoured Divisions and their constituent brigades. Information on artillery and tanks is from Hogg, *British and American Artillery of World War 2* and Hogg and Weeks, *Illustrated Encyclopaedia of Military Vehicles* and other sources as follows:

1. NA Kew, WO201/1812 shows that the British contribution to the Sicilian campaign was to be Twelfth Army.
2. Nicholson, *The Canadians in Italy*, p.166
3. Graham, *Sharpshooters at War*, p.125
4. Quoted in Liddell Hart, *The Tanks*, p.267
5. Nicholson, op cit, p.276
6. Doherty, 'Salerno 1943 A Different View: The Gunner/Infanteers' in *Britain At War*, August 2008, pp.19–25
7. Quoted in Nicholson, op cit, p.329
8. NA Kew, WO393/10
9. Horsfall, *Fling Our Banner to the Wind*, pp.56–7

Chapter Nine

Preparing for OVERLORD

In Chapter Seven we considered some changes that had occurred in the early years of the war, as a result of which the shape and mission of an armoured division evolved as did the development of tanks. By the time of the invasion of north-west Europe in June 1944 there had been further changes and further developments in tanks and the other AFVs that would work alongside them.

In the United Kingdom the expansion of the Army had led to the creation of new armoured divisions, including 9th, 11th, 42nd and 79th, each formed in conventional fashion from units of the Royal Armoured Corps. Less conventional was the formation of an armoured division from the regiments of the Brigade of Guards, which required the conversion of infantrymen to tankmen. Not just any infantrymen but guardsmen, the elite of Britain's Army and those charged with the personal safety of the sovereign. The divisional history records the background to its formation, noting that in spring 1941 General Sir Alan Brooke, then C-in-C, Home Forces, appreciating that a sizeable armoured component would be needed to counter any German invasion of Britain, decided that two infantry divisions should be converted to armour. One was 42nd (East Lancashire) Division, a TA formation which was redesignated as 42nd Armoured Division on 1 November 1941. The other was formed from the Brigade of Guards which had thus far not created an infantry division, as in the Great War.

> Although the Brigade of Guards was traditionally infantry, and believed by many to be the best in the world, there were certain advantages in forming a Guards Armoured Division. The Regiments of Foot Guards had the officers and men of the right type available, they could be converted probably more quickly than other units, and a large number of officers in the Brigade, holding the general view that armour rather than infantry was becoming the predominant arm, were keen to embark on the venture.[1]

King George VI expressed agreement with the proposal which was welcomed by the senior officers of the Brigade. Guards Armoured Division came into being on 17 June 1941 with Major General Sir Oliver Leese, a Coldstreamer, as its GOC and its headquarters at Leconfield House. The division included two armoured brigades – 5 and 6 Guards – a support group and ancillary units, with engineers arriving in August. In September 2nd Household Cavalry Regiment (2 HCR) joined as the reconnaissance unit and field, anti-tank and light AA artillery followed in June 1942. By that date it was recognized that the original orbat was outdated and the support group was disbanded and replaced by 32 Guards Infantry Brigade. Six months later the two-brigade organization of an infantry and an armoured brigade was adopted with 6 Guards Armoured Brigade departing the fold.

A detailed programme of training in maintenance, gunnery and wireless was soon under way. Some training was carried out on Covenanters, which had been relegated to this role. One Irish Guards officer, Lieutenant John Gorman, recalled that he knocked down a courtyard wall and crushed a light van at Warminster railway station while attempting to entrain for an exercise. The incident resulted in Gorman gaining the nickname 'Blockhead'. However, he would earn the Military Cross in a remarkable action on his first day in battle in Normandy. Gorman recounted how a great sense of camaraderie developed. His own troop:

had the highest level of comradeship of any men I had ever met. They looked after each other, and me, in a most generous way. We always seemed to have time for a quick 'brew-up' of tea (not the later slang for a burning tank) ... One of the Desert War lessons was that a tank crew had a much better chance of survival from night attacks by shelling, or bombing from the air, if it dug a large hole capable of holding five men packed together like sardines in a tin and had the tank drive over it. We practised this on our exercises and it gave me a whole new understanding of the values and attitudes of these good men.[2]

Forming Guards Armoured were armoured battalions of Grenadier, Coldstream and Irish Guards and a lorried Grenadier battalion in 5 Guards Armoured Brigade while 32 Guards Infantry Brigade initially included battalions of Grenadier, Coldstream and Scots Guards but later changed to Coldstream, Irish and Welsh; a Scots' battalion joined in the final months of war.

In September 1942 Sir Allan Adair, an Irishman and a Grenadier, succeeded Leese as GOC. He would command the division when it landed in Normandy and remain in command until after the war, when it converted to the infantry role.

Formed some three months before Guards Armoured 11th Armoured Division had the redoubtable Percy Hobart as GOC and also included two armoured brigades with a support group. This gave way in June 1942 to the new organization of an armoured and an infantry brigade; 30 Armoured Brigade departed, leaving 29 Armoured, while 159 Infantry Brigade joined. The re-raised 27th Lancers served in the reconnaissance role until 2nd Northamptonshire Yeomanry succeeded it in late March 1943. The divisional historian described the training regime under Hobart:

All the General's relentless energy and determination were concentrated on the task. Up hill and down dale, both literally and figuratively, he chased his men, from Brigadiers downwards; yet all respected his remarkable talents and the single-mindedness with which he used them. General Hobart was a hard taskmaster, but he left a stamp both outward and inward upon the division which no observer could disregard. The outward stamp is the divisional emblem, the bull ... ; of the inward stamp one can only say tritely that the subsequent preparedness of the division for battle was due in large measure to the lessons taught it so forcibly by General Hobart.[3]

The division's most strenuous training period was in May-July 1942 when there was continuous armoured training with an emphasis on all-arms co-operation. Exercise followed exercise including the two-week-long Exercise TIGER, run by Montgomery, as a result of which many lessons were learned. However, TIGER also had its frictions, the worst of which was resolved by the Canadian umpires. Participants were not permitted to buy any food or drink but this did not apply to the umpires who went off each morning 'ostensibly to a conference, and return[ed] later with eggs and beer and sundry other of life's necessities' which then became available to the participants.[4]

   With an Allied invasion of French North Africa planned for November 1942 the division was warned to prepare for overseas service. The necessary work was done and first-line reinforcements had embarked for the Mediterranean when the order to join First Army was rescinded: Tunisia demanded more infantry rather than more armour, such was the nature of the country. One result of the planned deployment was the relief of Hobart as GOC. He was considered too old for such service and failed to satisfy a medical board of his fitness.

   Hobart's successor, Major General Montagu Brocas Burrows, an Inniskilling Dragoon, had already commanded 9th Armoured Division. He in turn was succeeded by Pip Roberts in December 1943. With his experience in action, including command at divisional level, Roberts was the ideal GOC for 11th Armoured as it prepared for OVERLORD.

   Hobart had not disappeared from the scene completely and came back, at Brooke's request, to command 79th Armoured when that formation was re-organized to command all British specialized armour. His hard training ethic ensured that the division was ready for D Day, even though some equipment was not delivered until just before embarkation.

   Neither 9th nor 42nd Armoured Division saw active service with the latter disbanding in October 1943. Raised in 1941, with Major General Miles Dempsey, later to command Second Army, as GOC, the division was a standard formation of two armoured brigades and a support group, later converting to the one armoured and one infantry brigade establishment. Dempsey was succeeded as GOC by Major General John Aizlewood.

   In March 1942 Brian Horrocks succeeded Burrows as GOC 9th Armoured Division which the latter had commanded since formation in December 1940. In his memoirs Horrocks praised Burrows for his 'most meticulous basic training for all ranks' and noted that he learned 'a great deal myself about the control of armour in mobile warfare where all orders are given by wireless from a command tank', which he believed stood him 'in good stead later on'. Promotion to command a corps in North Africa took Horrocks away from 9th Armoured but his knowledge of armour was demonstrated clearly in Tunisia. Succeeding him as GOC was Major General

John D'Arcy, son of an Archbishop of Armagh, who continued Horrocks' good work with his division only to see it broken up and disbanded in July 1944.

The development of tanks continued apace with Cromwell entering service. Fastest of all the wartime British tanks, Cromwell could reach 40mph (64km/h) but, as this was too much for the Christie suspension, the Meteor engine was governed to 32mph (51.2km/h). Initially fitted with a 6-pounder gun that could fire both HE and AP, it was later equipped with a 75mm firing the same ammunition as the American 75 fitted to the Sherman. Well armoured, with up to 102mm of protection, Cromwell was agile and could outmanoeuvre German tanks but its armament was still its weakest point; it came into its own after the breakout from Normandy. In the European campaign 7th Armoured Division's units were all equipped with Cromwells, making the Desert Rats the only Cromwell-equipped formation. However, as with the Sherman troops of the other divisions, each troop had a Sherman Firefly with a 17-pounder gun. Of course, the Firefly was much more conspicuous in a Cromwell troop. (Those 17 pounder-equipped Challengers that served with 7th Armoured were every bit as conspicuous as a Firefly.)

A close support version of Cromwell, fitted with a 95mm howitzer was produced, as was a Liberty-engined version, Centaur, also equipped with the 95mm howitzer. Centaur saw limited specialized service in Normandy but the CS Cromwell was used more extensively.

As British armour fought its way through Normandy production of the best British tank of the war was about to begin. This was Comet, a development of Cromwell, fitted with a 77mm gun that was a de-tuned version of the 17-pounder anti-tank gun.

The main tank in the inventory of the British armoured divisions – and independent armoured brigades – was the American M4 Sherman. Since this was also the principal tank of the American armoured formations, and those of the other western Allies, it was produced in greater numbers than any other American tank, a distinction it still holds. However, as the war progressed, Sherman fell behind the standards set by German tanks, especially in the quality of the gun fitted to it. Although several variants were produced these did no more than keep Sherman battleworthy and, with Panthers, Tigers and King Tigers appearing, it became more vulnerable and less of a match for enemy armour. No urgency had been given to a successor and the M6 heavy tank project was shelved by the US Army in June 1942, although it was a design that 'would probably have become one of the most useful tanks in the Allied inventory'. The T20 project evolved through the T23, T25 and T26 to become, eventually, the M26 Pershing medium tank with a 90mm gun, which reached US Army units in Europe in the closing stages of the war. The flawed armoured doctrine that saw tank destroyers as fighting enemy tanks while US tanks exploited was largely responsible for the decision to concentrate on Sherman production – along with tank destroyers such as M10 and M18 – and prevent production of heavy tanks. Since Sherman was seen as a proven and reliable design this would also have influenced decisions on production.

With no sign of a Sherman replacement coming along, and no British equivalent nearing production, the British Army was concerned about Sherman's continuing effectiveness. Proposals were tabled to improve it so that it could fight on a more equal basis with Panthers and Tigers. This resulted in the fitting of a 17-pounder anti-tank gun. British designers had already been working on a 17-pounder-armed variant of Cromwell, which became the A30 Challenger, but this had many problems, not least a reduction in armour thickness to save weight. Moreover, the A30 concept was basically that of a tank to fight tanks, rather than a multi-purpose tank. Major George Brighty of the Royal Tank Regiment was the man behind fitting the 17-pounder to the Sherman, supported and assisted by a fellow RTR major, George Witheridge, who had commanded C Squadron 3 RTR in North Africa, one of the first recipients of the M3 Grant – in fact Witheridge was blown out of his Grant at Gazala in 1942. In spite of many difficulties their determination brought about the 17-pounder-armed Sherman. Of course, both gun and turret had to be re-designed with the gun 'shoehorned' into a modified turret. In January 1944 the improved Sherman was ordered into production with a War Office requirement for 2,100. Seeing their first action on 6 June 1944 in Operation OVERLORD, thereafter Sherman Fireflies provided sterling service for the British armoured divisions until the end of the war with one Firefly being issued to each Sherman troop. Although the Firefly was ordered in considerable numbers, some 200 Challengers were also ordered, the intention being to equip each Cromwell troop with a Challenger but, as Challenger production fell well behind schedule, the Cromwell regiments also received Sherman Fireflies.[5]

Another change in the armoured divisions' order of battle was implemented from March 1944, increasing divisional strength to 343 tanks from the 278 of the previous organization. The single biggest increase was in the armoured reconnaissance regiment to which were added an additional nine cruisers and thirty lights, while six CS cruisers, and three AA tanks were removed; this brought the overall complement to eighty-one tanks: forty cruisers, thirty lights, six CS cruisers and five AA tanks. The armoured regiments were each strengthened by the addition of eleven light tanks, although two AA tanks were removed, leaving a typical regiment with seventy-eight tanks, of which fifty-five were cruisers, six CS cruisers, six AA tanks and eleven lights; the complement of cruisers and CS cruisers was therefore unchanged. As a result an armoured brigade disposed 234 tanks: 165 cruisers, thirty-three lights, eighteen CS cruisers and eighteen AA tanks. In addition, the armoured brigade HQ had ten cruisers, as before, and eight observation post (OP) tanks. At divisional HQ were another eight cruisers and two AA tanks.

Also added to the establishment of an armoured division, as part of the divisional troops, was an independent machine-gun company, replacing the support company previously attached to the infantry brigade. The divisional artillery included a self-propelled Royal Horse Artillery regiment and a towed Royal Artillery field regiment, plus an anti-tank regiment, one battery of which was usually self-propelled, and a light AA regiment. While both field regiments had a complement of twenty-four weapons, the anti-tank regiment deployed forty-eight 6- or 17-pounder guns and the light AA regiment fifty-four Bofors 40mm guns.

By June 1944 British armoured commanders had absorbed many lessons from earlier campaigns. While the division between cruiser and infantry tanks had all but disappeared in operations, the two types still existed with Sherman classed as a cruiser in British service alongside Cromwell and the earlier cruisers. By now the main I-tank was Churchill (Valentines were still in limited use, some converted as self-propelled anti-tank guns) which equipped tank brigades. Each assaulting division on D Day was assigned an armoured brigade rather than a tank brigade and throughout the campaign infantry divisions would usually have the support of one of the independent armoured brigades or tank brigades. Thus there was a clearer appreciation of the need for closer co-operation between arms but the standard British armoured division still had a fairly rigid distinction between armoured and infantry brigades. The German example of an armoured division that was an integrated and flexible all-arms formation had still not been adopted. However, the US Army was using the German model, having replaced the brigade HQs within its armoured divisions by two combat commands, usually designated Combat Command A and Combat Command B. The combat commands were not of fixed size or composition but could be adjusted as operational tasks demanded, being infantry-heavy, armour-heavy or equally-balanced as required. (American armour doctrine had been based on French practice until 1940 when the US Army adopted the German model.)

It would not be long before British divisions in north-west Europe adopted a system similar to those used by their Allies and their foes. In the light of the criticism later made of 7th Armoured Division by Montgomery and others it is interesting to note that the Desert Rats were using the more flexible system of command almost from the day they landed in Normandy; it was not adopted by Guards or 11th Armoured Divisions until after Operation GOODWOOD.

Notes

This chapter is based on Liddell Hart, *The Tanks (Vol II)*, Macksey, *A History of the Royal Armoured Corps*, and the war diaries of Guards, 7th, 9th, 11th, 42nd and 79th Armoured Divisions and the constituent brigades of the first three named. Information on the development of artillery and tanks is from Hogg, *British and American Artillery of World War 2* and Hogg and Weeks, *Illustrated Encyclopaedia of Military Vehicles* and other sources are:

1. Rosse and Hill, *Guards Armoured Division*, p.17
2. Gorman, *The Times of My Life*, p.25
3. *Taurus Pursuant*, p.4
4. Ibid, p.5
5. Fletcher, *Sherman Firefly*, passim

Chapter Ten

Tanks into Europe

When Allied forces landed in Normandy in the dawn light of 6 June 1944, armour was critical. British and Canadian divisions in Assault Forces Gold, Juno and Sword had each been strengthened by the addition of an armoured brigade while their US counterparts in Assault Forces Utah and Omaha enjoyed similar support. Operation OVERLORD, the liberation of Europe, had begun. A long process of planning, preparation and innovation lay behind OVERLORD, a process begun not long after British forces had been evicted from the mainland in June 1940.

That process included the development of armoured forces to work in concert with the other arms as well as with tactical air elements. It had involved raising and training those armoured formations, familiarizing them with the formations with which they would work, and providing them with the equipment needed to fight effectively. Such equipment included the means of transporting tanks across the sea and landing them on defended beaches. Tank landing craft, first experimented with in the First World War, had been developed while even larger tank landing ships had become available. Both LCTs (landing craft, tanks) and LSTs (landing ships, tank) could discharge their cargoes straight on to a beach and provided the means by which Allied armour could play its part in the opening phase of Operation OVERLORD.

New armoured divisions had been created: Guards, 2nd, 8th, 9th, 11th, 42nd and 79th had all been formed, although 2nd and 8th had been despatched to the Middle East. Manpower problems caused the disbandment of 9th and 42nd, leaving Guards and 11th to provide the armoured muscle for Second British Army. However, as we have already noted, Britain's most famous armoured formation, 7th Armoured, the Desert Rats, had been brought to the UK in early 1944 to add their experience to the armour deploying in France. And the Desert Rats were the first of the British armoured divisions to arrive in France, with a reconnaissance party of 22 Armoured Brigade coming ashore with HQ 50th (Northumbrian) Division on D Day. Next day the tanks of 22 Armoured Brigade (1 RTR, 5 RTR and 4 CLY) came ashore at Arromanches. However, it took a week before the infantry brigade, 131 (Queen's), joined due to the unseasonal storm that caused havoc in the Channel, swept the beaches and damaged both Mulberry artificial harbours that had been built to obviate the need to seize a harbour. (While disembarking in a fast tide, 5 RTR had lost two tanks by 'drowning' a week earlier.)

The experienced 7th Armoured Division was equipped with Cromwells and commanded by Major General George 'Bobby' Erskine. Its brigades included battle-hardened units and personnel and Montgomery had been insistent that this famous formation would join him in the British Liberation Army. Hardly were the Cromwells of A Squadron 5 RTR ashore than they deployed for action, supporting 56 Brigade in the bocage close to the coast. In this close country of small fields, high banks and hedges, and deep, narrow lanes, it was difficult for tanks to operate. The advantage lay with the infantry. Nothing could have been further from the wide open sweeps of the desert and:

> One officer, Lieutenant Garnett, had the unnerving experience of having enemy infantry actually leaping onto his tank from the high banks at the side of the road, not an experience encountered in the desert. He and the wireless operator had to drive them off with revolvers, a small but significant indication of the close, sometimes hand-to-hand bocage fighting that was to mark the weeks that followed.[1]

(Garnett's experience led to the adoption of close co-operation between tanks and infantry in battlegroups, a practice not adopted by the other two divisions until many weeks later.) B Squadron deployed to support Commandos; in the course of the day the regiment lost two tanks but captured six enemy guns. Meanwhile 1 RTR worked with 69 Brigade but 22 Armoured Brigade's motor battalion had lost their carrier crews, whose ship had been diverted. The first divisional action occurred on 10 June when the Desert Rats advanced, through 50th Division, on Tilly. Without the infantry brigade this was a difficult operation; although 56 Brigade came under command there were still only the three armoured regiments, some of 8th King's Royal Irish Hussars, the divisional reconnaissance regiment, 5 RHA and two companies of 1st Rifle Brigade; there was also a dearth of transport. Opposing them were units of the elite Panzer Lehr Division who, although trained as a highly mobile formation, adapted quickly and effectively to defensive operations. Michael Reynolds sums this transformation up by noting that Panzer Lehr made:

> the individual tank the hub of their defence. Each semi-independent Panzer-Grenadier group was based on a single tank which became their armoured anti-tank gun and armoured machine gun; and the tank invariably led local counter-attacks against Allied penetrations. In fairness it has to be said that it was much easier to adapt to the defence in the 'bocage' than it was to the attack, although the Germans were always worried that their positions would be infiltrated, particularly at night.[2]

The engagement that followed was a scrappy battle in which the shortage of infantry handicapped the British armoured units – 4 CLY (Sharpshooters) and 5 RTR. Although 4 CLY entered the little village of Jerusalem their tanks were unable to prevail until infantry of 2nd South Wales Borderers joined them. A Squadron 5 RTR made it to Verrières by outflanking enemy blocks but lost sixteen dead and five tanks. Next day a further attempt to advance came to a stop against thick woodland while 131 Brigade joined, along with 1 RTR, on the 12th. Even so only a limited advance was possible. The ground precluded any breakthrough by armour. Worse was to follow over the next few days.

The setback at Tilly prompted the commander of XXX Corps, Lieutenant General Gerard Bucknall, to seek an alternative axis of advance for 7th Armoured. That alternative was around the right flank; the US 1st Division had reported light opposition on the advance to Caumont. As a result Erskine was to advance on Villers Bocage via St Paul du Vernay, Livry and Briquessard in Operation PERCH. Since some of the division was still engaged with the enemy, the advance was spearheaded by 22 Armoured Brigade with the Irish Hussars, less a squadron, reconnoitring to front and on both flanks, and 5 RHA; 1 RTR was still in action as were two battalions of 131 Brigade, leaving only 1/7th Queen's and 1st Rifle Brigade as the division's infantry element.

After an early delay at Livry the advance resumed. By morning the bulk of 131 Brigade had joined the division with orders to occupy Livry, now in British hands. On 13 June the armoured brigade was to move beyond Villers Bocage with 4 CLY ordered to occupy high ground about a mile north-east of the town while 5 RTR took high ground a mile south of the town; 1/7th Queen's was to hold the town and a battery of 65th Anti-Tank Regiment (Norfolk Yeomanry) was charged with covering the ground twixt the CLY and 5 RTR. The brigade advance began at 5.30am and by 9am there had been no contact with the enemy, save by patrols from the Irish and 11th Hussars (XXX Corps' reconnaissance regiment) and then only with small parties.

The leading group of 22 Armoured Brigade – A Squadron CLY and A Company 1st Rifle Brigade – made good progress to Villers Bocage where they received an enthusiastic liberators' welcome. (It will be noted that this was a squadron/company group, the first indication that British armoured commanders were using the same flexible compositions as their American allies and German opponents.) Through the town raced the Yeomanry tanks and Green Jackets. Soon they were climbing the high ground beyond to Point 213, which they were to hold. Verney wrote:

When the tanks turned off the road the latter halted and their officers went forward as usual to receive their orders from the tank squadron leader. The Commanding Officer of the 4th CLY, Viscount Cranley, also went up to the front in his scout car. Suddenly several Tigers appeared just to the south of the Caen road and immediately opened fire. In a matter of moments the Company's vehicles and the two nearest tanks were blazing. Sergeant Bray of the Rifle Brigade got one 6-pounder into action and claimed three German vehicles before a direct hit destroyed his gun. Thus, in a few minutes, the leading Squadron and Company of the Brigade were cut off, the Riflemen dismounted and separated from their officers, and a very nasty situation looked like developing.

The leading group had been bounced by a group of Tiger and Panzer IV tanks, led by Germany's leading tank 'ace', Michael Wittmann. The *Official History* claims that 2nd Panzer Division opposed 7th Armoured but, as Michael Reynolds argues in *Steel Inferno*, the enemy was Wittmann's group of tanks, as only minor elements of 2nd Panzer had reached Villers Bocage.[3] Indeed Reynolds goes on to state that 'Wittmann in a single Tiger I, supported only marginally by his other four tanks, brought the 7th Armoured Division to a complete halt'.[4] Wittmann first knocked out A Squadron's rear tank and then motored down the infantry column, at a range of no more than eighty yards, destroying the Green Jackets' trucks and half-tracks. All this while the British were preparing to enjoy a brew.

This first clash led to a battle that raged in and around Villers Bocage until nightfall. A Tiger that appeared through the smoke of battle seemed impervious to the 75mm round that Major Carr, second-in-command of the CLY, fired at it but the Tiger's response brewed up Carr's tank, killing most of the crew and wounding Carr grievously. And the battle had only begun. In a town filled with the smoke and confusion of battle, Lieutenant Cotton and Sergeant Brammall of the CLY, with the support of anti-tank guns of 1/7th Queen's, had the satisfaction of extracting some revenge and claimed hits on six Tigers. Reynolds records that one Tiger and a Mark IV, at least, fell victim to PIATs and sticky bombs, the latter hurled from first-floor windows. German records indicate that three tanks of one company were knocked out by 'close-range weapons'; six Tigers and two Mark IVs were found abandoned in Villers Bocage after the battle; the Mark IVs were from Panzer Lehr. German dead from the two Tiger companies engaged included ten dead and twelve wounded.

Although fighting died down with darkness the battle of Villers Bocage was not over. The town was evacuated by British troops who established a new defensive perimeter. The little enemy activity during the night included some shelling and minor patrolling. Thus an opportunity for assessing the tactical situation and losses prevailed. Since the commander of the Queen's Brigade had been cut off near Amaye, Erskine had assigned Lieutenant Colonel Michael Carver, CO of 1 RTR, to take over. Carver noted that his 'brigade' included only a Queen's battalion, his own regiment, supporting field and anti-tank artillery and a squadron of 11th Hussars (actually a squadron of Irish Hussars).[5]

My orders were to make sure that the village of Briquessard and the two crossroads north of it were securely held. Briquessard was where the minor road, by which we had moved south, joined the main road from Caumont to Villers Bocage. I sent 1/6th Queen's to Briquessard and looked after the other crossroads myself, sending the reconnaissance troop to make contact with the Americans on our right. We were all well established by the end of the day.[6]

Losses in 22 Armoured Brigade had been severe: 4 CLY had lost RHQ, including their CO, and A Squadron with most personnel dead, wounded or missing; casualties in 1st Rifle Brigade included almost all of A Company, from which only a few men had escaped. No fewer than twenty-seven tanks had been lost, plus all the soft-skinned vehicles of the leading group. But the enemy had failed to break through 7th Armoured's front and strong artillery support was available; in addition to 5 RHA,

Erskine could call on 5 Army Group Royal Artillery, with two medium and one heavy regiments, as well as 1st US Division's artillery.

Carver's orders for the next day were to open at first light and keep open the road to 22 Armoured. Thus he deployed two squadrons of 1 RTR with a company of 1/6th Queen's and reached his objective against some opposition. En route two Panthers, a Tiger and several Panzer IVs were knocked out and the enemy driven back. Also at daylight, 5 RTR moved towards Tracy Bocage ridge while the remainder of 22 Armoured Brigade held a box east of Amaye. With insufficient infantry to clear Tracy Bocage and secure the ridge, Bucknall ordered Erskine to adjust his line to keep his right flank in 'the closest possible touch with the Americans'. That meant pulling back from the Villers Bocage sector, a withdrawal that was to be carried out that night. Verney commented that:

> It was a sad disappointment that the brilliant thrust conceived by General Bucknall which had carried the Division to Villers Bocage, far behind the enemy's lines to a deeper penetration than was to be made for many weeks to come, could not be supported. It was a remarkable gain at a time when expansion of the beachhead was badly needed, but there were just not the additional infantry available to give the Division the backing required in close country of this type – nor was there that element of good fortune which might have made just the difference.

However, that argument is disputed by Michael Reynolds who notes that most of 1st Rifle Brigade and two battalions of the Queen's:

> remained uncommitted on the critical day and that one complete infantry brigade (151) was in Corps reserve; in fact two infantry brigades of 49th Infantry Division were also unemployed – they were released to 50th Division on the night of 13 June. Any of these three brigades could have been allotted to Erskine before his Division set off on its epic task, and the blame for this failure to concentrate sufficient forces at the right place at the right time must be laid at the door of Bucknall.[7]

Carver expressed disappointment at the withdrawal as he considered 'that we had seen off the enemy'.[8] In this he was right, as was demonstrated when the Germans counter-attacked at 7.00pm, before the withdrawal began. A determined attack by two infantry battalions supported by thirty tanks was shattered by Allied artillery fire, leaving the British perimeter ringed by blazing tanks. About a dozen panzers were knocked out, anti-tank gunners claiming eight of them. The German infantry also lost heavily: the overall effect was no interference with the withdrawal, which was covered by RAF heavy bombers striking at Villers Bocage.

Seventh Armoured Division re-formed along a line from east of Caumont, and the junction with 1st US Division, through Briquessard and Torteval. On the right was 50th Division, but a three-mile gap separated the formations which 8th

Hussars covered until 50th Division advanced to fill it. Following a German attack at Briquessard on 17 June, in which 8th Hussars had eight men killed and lost five tanks, the line was adjusted to behind Briquessard ridge, positions the division held until the end of June when 2nd US Armored Division relieved them. Since the armour was held back, the main front-line burden fell on the infantry, the pressure on whom was exacerbated by the long hours of daylight. With Stand-to at 4.15am and evening Stand-to at 10.15pm there was little chance for adequate rest. Fatigue was increased by life in slit trenches, regular patrolling in difficult terrain where 'it was possible only to see to the next hedge' and aggressive opposition. The front-line positions attracted considerable mortar and artillery fire and 7th Armoured's infantry were not sorry to say goodbye to them and move to the vicinity of Jerusalem to rest and refit. In three weeks of action in Normandy the division sustained 1,149 casualties, a harsh price to pay but one exemplifying the suffering of the Allied armies in the battle for Normandy.

A further casualty of that early fighting was the reputation of 7th Armoured Division and its commander, Bobby Erskine, which would have repercussions after Operation GOODWOOD with Erskine being relieved following eighteen months in command. More than a hundred officers of the division were to be sent back to Britain or posted elsewhere. Bucknall also paid the price of failure, being relieved of command of XXX Corps with Brian Horrocks, recovered from his wounds in Tunisia, succeeding him.

And so 7th Armoured Division had its unpleasant introduction to war in north-west Europe. It would see further action, and take further punishment, in Operation GOODWOOD but would fight to the final defeat of Germany in May 1945. By the time of GOODWOOD it would be joined by Guards Armoured and 11th Armoured Divisions. The latter was commanded in north-west Europe by Major General Pip Roberts who had served in 7th Armoured in North Africa, but its first commander, and the man who brought it to fighting efficiency, had been the man who had also performed the same role with 7th Armoured as the Mobile Division, Egypt: Percy Hobart, who was now in France commanding Britain's youngest armoured division, 79th.

Hobart had been given command of 79th Armoured Division by the CIGS, General Sir Alan Brooke, when he decided to reprieve the formation from disbandment. Both the Army's most junior armoured divisions had been destined for this fate due to Britain's acute manpower shortage. Brooke's reprieve followed his decision to place all Second Army's specialized armour under a single command. And so 79th said goodbye to its original brigades – 27 Armoured and 185 Infantry – to welcome several armoured brigades and an assault engineer brigade. Not only was 79th Armoured to command all specialized armour, it was also to oversee training for such, including those which would not come under divisional command, the DD, or swimming, tanks used by British, Canadian and American armoured units on D Day. Hobart was also given the role of specialized armour adviser to Montgomery's 21 Army Group. The two men knew each other well as they were brothers-in-law, Montgomery being the widower of Hobart's favourite sister, Betty.

Hobart's division had a critical role in Operation OVERLORD. With the building of the Atlantic Wall it was clear that an invasion of Europe at any point within range of air cover from Britain would meet not only opposition from German soldiers but also a host of physical obstacles designed to prevent landing. Since landing at a port was out of the question, as proved by Operation JUBILEE at Dieppe in August 1942, there was no choice but to land across defended beaches. The Atlantic Wall was a modern variation on an ancient theme, siege warfare. And as with siege warfare in yesteryear the role of engineers and specialized siege machines was critical. Hobart, an engineer by training, commissioned in the Corps of Royal Engineers, and a convert to the new order of armoured fighting vehicles, was the ideal man to command machines and a formation combining the assets and skills of engineers and tank warfare specialists.

Under his command was what was described as a menagerie of funnies, AFVs designed or adapted for special tasks. These included specially-adapted Churchills, known as AVREs (Armoured, or Assault, Vehicles, Royal Engineers), fitted with devices that included bridge-laying equipment, fascines to ease passage over anti-tank ditches and streams, carpet-laying AVREs that unrolled a 'bobbin' of carpet across soft sand to allow vehicles easier passage, petards that could hurl explosive devices, dubbed 'flying dustbins', at concrete obstacles or reinforced strongpoints. The AVREs could also place explosive charges directly against such targets, or allow sappers to use the tank's side hatches to place charges under cover of the tank itself. There were also Crabs to flail paths through minefields for other armour and infantry to pass in relative safety. These adapted Shermans retained their 75mm main armament which they could use if necessary. In time these would be joined by flamethrowers, or Crocodiles, also based on the Churchill, Buffaloes, or LVTs (landing vehicles, tracked), Kangaroos, armoured personnel carriers (APCs), adapted from Canadian Ram tanks with turrets removed, or de-gunned M7 Priest self-propelled howitzers. There were also various lesser-known 'funnies', including armoured bulldozers.

The DD (Duplex Drive) or swimming tank had been developed through a series of British tanks fitted with the duplex drive developed by Hungarian engineer Nicholas Straussler; the tanks used in this role on D Day and later were M4 Shermans. The plan was for DD Shermans to be the first vehicles ashore on D Day to support the assaulting infantry, but tide and weather conditions prevented this in most cases, most tragically in Assault Force Omaha, with the result that it was often the 'funnies' of 79th Armoured Division that were first ashore. That they were successful is shown by a comment in General Eisenhower's report on the campaign in Europe.

Apart from the factor of tactical surprise, the comparatively light casualties which we sustained on all beaches, except OMAHA, were in large measure due to the success of the novel mechanical contrivances which we employed and to the staggering moral and material effect of the mass of armour landed in the leading waves of the assault. The use of large numbers of amphibious tanks to afford fire support in the initial stages of the operation had been an essential feature of our plans, and, despite the losses they suffered on account of the heavy seas, on the beaches where they were used they proved conspicuously effective. It is doubtful if the assault forces could have firmly established themselves without the assistance of these weapons. Other valuable novelties included the British AVRE ... and the 'flail' tank which did excellent work in clearing paths through the minefields at the beach exits.[9]

The number of gallantry awards to personnel of 79th Armoured Division and the operational flexibility demonstrated by crews on D Day is further proof of their contribution to the success of the Allied landings.

However, the American assault forces lacked the support of Hobart's unique armoured division, although they had been offered 'funnies'. Since the Churchill was not part of the US Army's equipment it was unlikely that the Americans would adopt the AVREs and no American tank was suitable for conversion to the role. But the Crab mine-clearing tank was based on the American Sherman and this argument cannot hold for American failure to use Crabs. One account of operations of 79th Armoured Division on D Day, written by an American military analyst, answers the question of what difference 'funnies' might have made on Omaha Beach,

given that one of the primary tasks assigned the AVREs and Crabs was gapping, it may be fairly asked what their actual effect on D Day was. They did provide additional armoured support to the assault infantry, which might actually have been their critical role. Indeed, it may in some cases have been better to eschew the complex and marginally useful 'devices' and simply employ the AVRE as a tank. In the final analysis, it seems clear that that was the critical shortfall on Omaha – a simple lack of armoured vehicles of any kind rather than a lack of armoured engineer vehicles. And yet it also seems to be an inescapable conclusion that some form of armoured engineer vehicle may have been a critical missing ingredient on the western end of Omaha Beach, where a mass of armour was impotent for so long simply because they were unable to get inland. However, that would have been no true guarantee of earlier success or of fewer casualties given the immense boost the unique combination of terrain, obstacles, fortifications and firepower gave the Germans.[10]

One is tempted to conclude that these arguments, somewhat circular and almost contradictory, owe more to chauvinism than balanced analysis, especially when compared not only with Eisenhower's comments, but also with the views of a modern US Army officer, Major M. J. Daniels, who wrote of how Hobart continued to innovate throughout the European campaign:

Hobart alludes to the urgency and challenges faced by the division in the run-up to the Scheldt campaign in a letter dated 3 October when he wrote, 'Am getting some new units and things: and hectically engaged in complicated movements and inspections, and the inevitable race against time. NOT in the case of my old units: they are all right.' His concern lay in integrating new troops and equipment while in the middle of a campaign. These soldiers had not benefited from the intensive training and rehearsals conducted back in Britain, and much of this new equipment was as yet untested in the European theatre. As such, Hobart gave Brigadier Duncan the mission to establish training and instructional wings that would ensure the division could effectively and efficiently incorporate these new capabilities on future operations.[11]

American forces made use of Hobart's 'funnies' as the campaign progressed and developed specialist AFVs of their own but never with the co-ordination provided in 21 Army Group by 79th Armoured Division. Anderson also wrote that Brooke's decision to centralize 'the development, organization and use of specialized vehicles and equipment under a single command … was much wiser than the decentralized approach of the Americans'.

Hobart's division remained a valuable asset to the Allied forces as they fought their way into Germany with his command burgeoning to become the largest armoured formation in the Allied armies with over 20,000 personnel and more than 1,500 armoured vehicles.

Hobart had created 11th Armoured Division and trained it to battle-readiness. However, he had been relieved of command on health grounds while the division continued preparing for action, which finally came in Normandy. General Sir Miles Dempsey, who commanded Second Army, wrote that 11th Armoured 'proved itself throughout the campaign in North-Western Europe an outstandingly fine division. I have never met a better'.

Commanded by Major General Pip Roberts, 11th Armoured Division began landing near Bény-sur-Mer on 13 and 14 June, just as the Desert Rats were fighting the battle of Villers Bocage. Composed of 29 Armoured and 159 Infantry Brigades, it was to join VIII Corps, commanded by Lieutenant General Sir Richard O'Connor, commander of Western Desert Force in its successful offensive against Tenth Italian Army in Egypt and Libya.

Almost two weeks passed before the division saw action. As units moved inland through peaceful and comparatively undamaged countryside, many were surprised at the inhabitants' reaction which was described as 'guarded, as though half … still believed the Germans' parting threat that they would return'. The air of those early days was likened to an exercise in England, 'an unsolicited testimonial to the nature of the training at home'.

The Normandy campaign was a succession of difficult operations against a determined enemy ever defiant in defence who ensured that his defensive tactics would inflict maximum damage on any attacker. Roberts' command had its battle inoculation in one such operation, EPSOM, VIII Corps' plan to break out of the bridgehead, attack southwards and cross the Odon river. O'Connor intended 15th (Scottish) Division to attack under cover of fire from over 700 guns, including those of I and XXX Corps: two brigades of 15th Division were to seize St Mauvieu and

Cheux, after which 11th Armoured would pass through the infantry, exploit to the Odon and, if possible, cross the river, an advance of up to four miles. If it proved impossible to cross the Odon, the third brigade of 15th (Scottish) would secure the bridgehead, leaving 11th Armoured to advance to the Orne river, another six miles away, to clear the way to the high ground south of Caen. On VIII Corps' right flank the high ground around Rauray was to be secured by XXX Corps in Operation DAUNTLESS, the day before EPSOM was launched.

For its part in EPSOM 11th Armoured was strengthened with a second armoured brigade, John Currie's 4 Armoured, of which Michael Carver assumed command when John Currie was killed by a shell. VIII Corps also included 43rd (Wessex) Division which had a consolidation role in EPSOM, taking over ground won by 15th (Scottish).

Weather played a critical part: most of the aircraft intended to support the attackers were grounded across the Channel in England, leaving only the Normandy-based No. 83 Group. Heavy overnight rain made the going difficult and mist shrouded the ground when 44 (Lowland) and 46 (Highland) Brigades, with armour of 31 Tank Brigade, left their start line at 7.30am to cross the soft ground separating them from their objectives. The Scots had a difficult time but by noon the way was open for 11th Armoured Division to advance towards Tourmauville, Gavrus and the Odon bridges. Moving off at 12.50pm, hardly had 29 Armoured Brigade cleared the ruined village of Cheux than it met opposition so stiff that the race to the Odon was stalled. Instead the brigade became involved in several hours of hard fighting for no gain. Once more the infantry of 15th (Scottish) were called into action, this time the men of 227 (Highland) Brigade who met equally tough opposition, including accurate artillery fire, and so bad was the rain that there were now no aircraft to support the ground troops. Nature had come to the aid of the Germans. By the end of the day German troops still held VIII Corps' objective and had claimed the destruction of fifty British tanks.[12] Eleventh Armoured Division's introduction to action was proving every bit as unpleasant as that of 7th Armoured.

The divisional history noted that:

> To clear the woods and villages just north of the Odon it was found necessary to commit the remaining Scottish brigade the same evening; but very little progress was made with the attack and it was discontinued, to be resumed on the morrow with the support of 29 Armoured Brigade; for the situation which, it had been hoped, would warrant the separate employment of the two divisions in alternate stages of the battle, now clearly demanded their close co-operation if either was to get through.

Nor had XXX Corps secured its objectives. The Germans still held the high ground at Rauray from which they could enfilade VIII Corps' right at le Haut du Bosq where a squadron of 11th Armoured's reconnaissance regiment, 2nd Northamptonshire Yeomanry, suffered grievously before it was pulled out, its place taken by 4 Armoured Brigade. However, that threat from the right 'remained constant throughout the operation and was largely responsible for its eventual abandonment'. The first day of EPSOM was a 'complete defensive success' for the Germans but achieved only by I SS Panzer Corps deploying its last reserves; 21st Panzer and 12th SS Panzer Divisions were 'taxed to the utmost'.

O'Connor pressed on next day, making some progress in spite of continuing doughty opposition and lack of air support from other than No. 83 Group due to weather conditions; a rare Luftwaffe appearance was seen off by 83 Group fighters. While the Jocks of 15th (Scottish) advanced, the Wessexmen who had taken over St Mauvieu and Cheux were attacked by enemy armour. A number of attacks were fought off with the Germans losing six tanks. Meanwhile the Scottish infantry and Roberts' tanks probed forward but the enclosed nature of the terrain and the presence of enemy troops to the flanks, and even the rear, made it difficult to maintain contact between armour and infantry. By midday 29 Armoured Brigade reported that they were ahead of the infantry along the entire front. Doubtful though this was, it was decided to 'push on boldly' to the Odon where crossings could be forced even without infantry support.

In fact it was the Argylls of 227 Brigade who captured intact the bridge at Tourmauville, thereby establishing a small lodgement on the Odon's south bank. The leading armour reached there at 5.30pm and, within an hour, two further squadrons of 23rd Hussars were over the river to be followed, later in the evening, by 4th King's Shropshire LI (4 KSLI) and 1st Herefords of 159 Brigade who moved into the lodgement under persistent shell- and mortar-fire from the Germans. The brigade's third battalion, 3rd Monmouths, remained north of the Odon but still lost a platoon, most of them killed or captured.

On the 28th the infantry consolidated their positions while 29 Armoured Brigade began probing forward from the bridgehead, which was about 1,000 yards long. To their front the ground rose sharply to a plateau beyond which lay Esquay village. That plateau was Hill 112, a feature not to be forgotten by British soldiers in Normandy:

> Like many battlefield features, this protuberance was neither impressive nor well defined, though the whole ridge of which it formed a part dominated the Odon valley and the country to the north. It was not, however, the highest point in the neighbourhood; a mile to the southwest stood its companion, Hill 113, guarding the little town of Évrecy. Yet 112 was invested at the time with a peculiar negative quality; it was untenable. Death stalked the rider who attempted to mount its broad saddle. All the fighting for 112 was cruel, and the memory of the place is bitter. Possibly bitter for the enemy too; for, while the two combatants were more or less evenly matched, neither could hold the place, and each could deny it to the other. But maybe the Germans knew this and suffered less in consequence.

During that morning of 28 June two squadrons of 23rd Hussars and a company of 8th Rifle Brigade attacked the northern slopes of Hill 112 and, in sharp fighting, seized the crest. But they came under counter-attack from German troops on the southern slopes. A small number of Tigers, no more than six, were so well concealed in prepared positions that they could move quickly from one position to another to meet any attack. As the fighting continued during the afternoon those Tigers moved frequently, thereby creating the impression of greater numbers, and the British suffered accordingly. Late in the day 23rd Hussars were relieved by 3 RTR while the third armoured regiment, 2nd Fife and Forfar Yeomanry, was positioned north of 112; 8th Rifle Brigade remained dug in on the crest. From those positions the Green Jackets and 3 RTR fought off a fierce counter-attack supported by tanks and intensive mortar fire. Thus ended the third day of EPSOM with VIII Corps much better placed to meet the expected major counter-attack.

Dempsey and O'Connor knew from Ultra reports that a further two panzer divisions, 9th and 10th SS, were en route to the front. Since the shape of VIII Corps' salient – over five miles deep but less than two wide – invited an attack aimed at cutting off and destroying the corps, it was essential to strengthen the bridgehead before allowing 11th Armoured Division to advance the six miles to the Orne. For this reason the divisional advance had been restricted as we have seen. Now, on 29 June, the fourth day of the battle, a major counter-attack was expected.

The morning of the 29th passed without any attack. Allied aircraft and artillery harassed enemy troop movements, actions which, subsequent examination of Seventh German Army's telephone log and interrogation of its commander indicated, had stopped the planned counter-attack before it began. But there were some German attacks which were beaten off, including one at brigade strength on the axis of the Noyers–Cheux road. Before darkness fell 4 Armoured Brigade deployed a regiment to sweep the ground between Grainville and the Noyers road, clearing up pockets of enemy troops. And on Hill 112 the Green Jackets, supported by 3 RTR, wrested a small wood on the southern slope from the Germans while the Fife and Forfar Yeomanry moved out on the eastern shoulder giving VIII Corps effective ownership of the hill.

However, that brigade-strength attack, believed to be the planned major attack, led to an unexpected order for 29 Armoured Brigade to withdraw into positions back across the Odon, an order that also brought back 4 Armoured's regiment from its sweeping task. Needless to say, the order was resented in 29 Armoured Brigade but the bridgehead over the river was held by 15th (Scottish) Division, reinforced by elements of 43rd (Wessex). Withdrawing the armour from Hill 112 allowed the Germans to re-occupy it.

The withdrawal of the armour was probably a mistake, though understandable. Neither Dempsey nor O'Connor realized that the attacks on 29 June composed the major German counter-attack, which dwindled somewhat on the following day, although still inflicting serious damage to the British. Expecting even more furious assaults on 30 June, O'Connor's view was that '… the area around Point 112 and Point 113 – though excellent for an armoured offensive, if it could have gone through with a bang – was no place for 11th Armoured Division, with its insecure communications across the Odon to "wait about" in'.[13]

Much British blood was to be expended before Hill 112 was again in Allied hands, thus making the premature withdrawal of the armour a tragedy. That withdrawal also rankled in 11th Armoured Division whose historian was to write a year later:

> but the general feeling that, in spite of tank losses, a further sweep southwards from Hill 112 coupled with the continued repulse of enemy attacks on the flanks, was well within its powers, was indicative of the high state of the division's morale. And upon reflection, the several results of the action seemed far from discouraging. 29 Armoured Brigade had driven a wedge into the enemy's country and held it for two days against its best troops. 2 N Yeo had withstood the fiercest counter-attacks of the operation and repelled them, though sustaining heavy losses, especially on the first day and during the big German attack on the evening of the 29th. 159 Infantry Brigade had established, and held firm, a bridgehead in difficult wooded country under persistent artillery and mortar fire and, with the aid of the gunners' excellent shooting, had broken up numerous threatened attacks upon it. Finally, the system of communications based on personal radio contact between commanders and subordinate commanders had been demonstrated to any not already convinced of its necessity as one of the essentials for the functioning of an armoured formation.

One might cavil with some of the assumptions of the writer but his comments make clear the morale that existed in his division and the confidence felt by its men.

As 11th Armoured Division moved into reserve at the end of the abortive Operation EPSOM it left the battalions of 159 Brigade behind to defend the bridgehead, at first under command of 15th (Scottish) and then 43rd (Wessex) Divisions. Not until 6 July did 159 Brigade join the division in reserve south of Bercy. In their defensive role in the bridgehead the infantrymen had needed a huge portion of the morale and confidence of which the divisional historian was so proud. Under their new commander, Brigadier J. B. Churcher, they performed outstandingly in repelling attack after attack. Carver's 4 Armoured Brigade left the division on 3 July.

The divisional historian, clearly selected for his literary bent, wrote that 11th Armoured, restored to its original form, 'rested behind the lines, cogitated upon the lessons of the Odon battle and prepared for a yet more ambitious undertaking'. That undertaking was to bring all the British armoured divisions in Normandy together, with Guards Armoured Division entering the fray for the first time.

The last of the three standard armoured divisions to land in Normandy, Guards, did not have such a speedy introduction to action. Nonetheless, they soon gained some idea of what lay ahead of them as they 'swanned' behind the lines inspecting the detritus of earlier battles. Some Irish Guards, of the 2nd (Armoured) Battalion, were awed at the sight of Tigers and Panthers with guns that stretched 'from here to Sunday week' and by the holes in Shermans caused by those guns.[14] Nonetheless, the Micks were not discouraged from stripping wrecked Shermans of anything that might be useful with their Technical Quartermaster Sergeant, WO II Coppen, commenting that their 'job is to collect spares and you'll thank us yet.' And so bogies, sprockets, tracks and other items from Shermans were removed to be stored in Coppen's little kingdom.

The Micks were not impressed by the well-fed *paysans* of Normandy and Captain Terence O'Neill, later Prime Minister of Northern Ireland, was less than pleased when told by a shopkeeper, 'Vraiment, on n'a pas apercu l'occupation allemande'.[15] And O'Neill was a Francophile. Irrespective of what Norman shopkeepers felt about the German occupation, the Guards were preparing to evict those Germans from Normandy as soon as possible. As part of the Allied plan to break out of the duchy, Montgomery planned a major armoured offensive, preceded by Operation GREENLINE, to pin down four fresh enemy infantry divisions and prevent their relieving panzer divisions for operations against the Americans. The latter, in turn, were working up to a 'heavy attack with six divisions about five miles west of St Lô' in preparation for Operation COBRA, the US element of the first truly strategic 21 Army Group offensive and the beginning of the end for the German armies in Normandy. Before that, however, GREENLINE would also precede Montgomery's major armoured attack, Operation GOODWOOD, in which all three British armoured divisions would participate.

On 14 July Montgomery wrote to Brooke, explaining the rationale for using all three armoured divisions in concert. Casualties had affected the fighting ability of the infantry divisions in terrain that suited the defender. Pointing out that he believed British losses in infantry to be about three men to every German, he added:

> But Second Army has three armoured divisions, 7, 11 and Gds. These are quite fresh and have been practically untouched. A fourth armoured division will be complete ... by 27 July, i.e. the Canadian Armd Div.
>
> Having got Caen, my left flank is now firm; my whole lodgement area is very secure and is held by infantry divisions. And available to work with the infantry I have eight independent armoured Bdes ... with a tank strength of over 1,000 tanks.
>
> And so I have decided that the time has come to have a real 'showdown' on the Eastern flank, and to loose a corps of three armoured divisions in to the open country about the Caen-Falaise road.[16]

Dempsey, Second Army's commander, was prepared to lose tanks to save infantry lives, seemingly believing that tanks could be lost without significant loss of life. It appeared that Dempsey was 'prepared to accept heavy losses in [tanks], providing the losses in men were low'.[17]

While Operation GREENLINE was generally successful, and helped maintain the strategic deception of a landing in the Pas de Calais, it cost 3,500 casualties – mostly infantry – and seems to contradict both Montgomery's and Dempsey's assertions that they wanted to save infantry lives. Be that as it may, planning continued for GOODWOOD.

O'Connor's VIII Corps was to control the three armoured divisions in GOODWOOD. At the same time, II Canadian Corps was to launch Operation ATLANTIC, capturing the southern part of Caen, bridging the Orne and preparing for a further advance. In Montgomery's view this was essential if GOODWOOD was to succeed. I Corps, meanwhile, was to secure the left flank of the Orne bridgehead against possible attacks from east or south-east. In all, VIII Corps deployed some 750 tanks which were held well west of the Orne so as not to give the enemy advance warning of Second Army's intentions. This meant that the tanks would have to move eastward with as much stealth as possible to launch their attack from, for the Germans, an unexpected quarter. That unexpected quarter was the 'shallow and congested bridgehead east of the Orne', protected by 3rd British Infantry Division of I Corps. Moving through that bridgehead meant that the first three miles of VIII Corps' advance would be along a corridor less than two miles wide with both flanks still in enemy hands. The Desert Rats' history notes that the bridgehead:

> consisted of a strip of orchards and villages along the river valley, about ten thousand yards long, and between one thousand and three thousand yards in depth. It was served by one bridge that [6th] Airborne Division had captured intact, and three Bailey bridges which were later built. The southern sector was held by 51st (Highland) Division, whose task was to clear the east bank of the Orne, particularly the factory area around Giberville. The three armoured divisions concentrated for this operation, the Guards, 7th and 11th, were then to pass through, the 11th leading ...

Deploying VIII Corps' armour to the attack was fraught with problems, not least the need to travel along roads registered by German artillery to cross the Orne river and canal between Ranville and the sea over three double bridges. It was impossible for the corps to advance to battle as a solid mass; divisions would have to play follow my leader to reach their start lines with armoured brigades preceding the infantry brigades. O'Connor's suggestion that the infantry be given greater mobility, and some measure of protection, by converting redundant M7 Priest SPGs to armoured personnel carriers was given short shrift by Dempsey.[18] GOODWOOD was to suffer as a result of Dempsey's decision. The army commander seemed not to consider O'Connor's achievement in Operation COMPASS in 1940 when, with a small mobile armoured force, he had destroyed an army many times larger than his own command. Although only enough SPGs were available for conversion to carry two battalions their presence would have been invaluable.

D Day for GOODWOOD was 18 July and RAF Bomber Command was to provide support to counter the enemy's strongly-held positions. Much of the enemy defensive plan was the work of Field Marshal Erwin Rommel, now *hors de combat* with wounds, and never to return. The defensive area, under command of General Eberbach, was almost eight miles in depth – a detail not appreciated by Second Army's intelligence – and held by three infantry and two panzer divisions. Although German tank strength in the area was estimated at about 230, according to the *Official History*, Reynolds has shown that it was much stronger – 377 tanks, StuGs and SPGs were available.[19] The Germans had not laid anti-tank minefields, thus giving their armour considerable freedom of manoeuvre, whereas British armour had to negotiate a belt of British minefields that could not be breached until the operation began as they were under observation from, among other points, the smokestacks of the Colombelles factories which overlooked the entire British bridgehead.

There were further problems with the basic plan, as we shall see, while, on 17 July, Dempsey had issued an order setting definite objectives for each armoured division, thereby reducing the scope of the objectives that Montgomery had outlined in a personal note to O'Connor on the 15th. Those were:

> To engage the German armour in battle and write it down to such an extent that it is of no further value ... as the basis of the battle. To gain a good bridgehead over the Orne through Caen and thus improve our positions on the eastern flank. Generally to destroy German equipment and personnel, as a preliminary to a possible wide exploitation of success ... The three armoured divisions will be required to dominate the area Bourguébus–Vimont–Bretteville, and to fight and destroy the enemy.[20]

Although he often failed to show that he understood the strengths and weaknesses of armour, this note indicates that Montgomery realized that, on this occasion, the enemy's armour had to be destroyed and his suggestion that there might be an exploitation of success shows strategic vision. Whether he appreciated the mechanics of destroying the German armour is another question, especially in view of the fact that the armour could only be released from the bridgehead a division at a time, so long and narrow was the front from which they were to start.

VIII Corps was committed to advancing over ground favouring the enemy as it rose gently to the Bourguébus ridge (the name used by British sources; it was also known as the Verrières ridge), described by the Corps' historian as providing the defenders with 'complete observation over almost the entire area ... whilst [they] also had the benefit of long fields of fire and facilities for concealed movement in the woods and villages, of which they did not fail to take advantage'.[21] O'Connor's staff could do nothing about the topography of the bridgehead, which also created a problem for artillery support by necessitating holding the artillery west of the Orne from where its range was so limited that it would be unable to support the armour in assaulting the ridge. Thus air support was essential but the air forces depended on weather conditions; low cloud or heavy rain would keep the planes on the ground. Nor did the list of headaches for VIII Corps' staff end there:

> Since VIII Corps' activities were so controlled by the orders of Montgomery and Dempsey, and restricted by the nature of the area in which it had to operate, O'Connor and his staff were perhaps more concerned with the mechanics of GOODWOOD than the philosophy of it. The amount of detailed staff work to be undertaken in the short time available before 18 July was enormous: although

the Second Army staff did a lot of it, everything had to be co-ordinated between the two headquarters, and then instructions had to be passed down the long chain of command to the men on the ground. Every slip, every delay, might mean a loss of life when the battle started.[22]

Even getting the armoured divisions to their start lines required a mass of staff work. With the Orne river and canal running close together in parallel, a double water obstacle had to be bridged and bridging was limited by space and the time and materials available to the engineers. A restricted number of crossing points also meant a limit on the routes forward and very complex movement tables.

Air support for GOODWOOD was described by the Corps' history as being on 'a larger scale than anything hitherto staged in direct support of ground forces' and something on which the success of the operation was 'entirely dependent'.[23] In all, 1,056 RAF heavies, 539 USAAF heavies and 482 USAAF mediums were assigned while fighter-bombers of 83 Group, 2nd Tactical Air Force, would fly close air support sorties. Although O'Connor asked for a second strike by the heavies at about 3.00pm on the first day, when the armour would be positioned to move on the final objectives, this could not be provided. And it was at this juncture also that the armour would move ahead of the maximum range of the medium artillery.

The corps plan put Roberts' 11th Armoured Division in the van, thus giving the lead to 29 Armoured Brigade. Guards Armoured would follow, leaving the Desert Rats as last onto the field. Roberts, however, was unhappy with his orders which required him to take Cuverville and Démouville, villages two and three miles respectively from the start line and on his right flank, as well as Cagny, five miles away and to his left. His concern was that he would have to deploy his infantry, 159 Brigade, for these tasks but he wanted his infantry as close as possible to his armour to deal with defended positions that could be cleared only by foot soldiers. Although O'Connor removed the need to take Cagny, he was unable to relieve Roberts of the other tasks, which had been imposed on him by Montgomery who would not permit 51st (Highland) Division, through whose lines the armour would advance, to leave their positions in case of German counter-attacks.

Roberts was unhappy about his predicament but:

I really had no alternative but to accept that situation and replied accordingly, but still think it was a stupid arrangement. And particularly so, when I realized that on the right of VIII Corps, the Canadians were attacking with their right on the River Orne, and on our left, 3rd Division … under I Corps were harassing the enemy and protecting the left flank. Thus, I could not and cannot see that there was any chance of the Germans making a counter-attack during this period.

It was only on the night of the 17th that 29 Armoured Brigade, plus a squadron of Sherman Crab flail tanks from the Westminster Dragoons, and divisional HQ got across the Orne, although 159 Brigade was already over. To assist 159 Brigade in taking the villages, Roberts deployed 2nd Northamptonshire Yeomanry, the divisional reconnaissance regiment, under 159 Brigade's command. He was confident that the villages would have been hit so badly by air strikes and artillery fire that they would create little delay (which seems to contradict the rationale of his earlier protest to O'Connor).

At 5.45am Bomber Command Lancasters and Halifaxes began their attack, which lasted forty-five minutes, after which the American medium bombers dropped fragmentation bombs and, as they completed their mission, the artillery opened fire and 29 Armoured Brigade rolled forward. As the tanks advanced, the American heavies – 539 B-17 Flying Fortresses – bombed German gun positions in the Troarn and Bourguébus areas. The aerial bombardment was enough to make men mad and many suffered that very condition while others were deafened or in shock.

That German military genius Graf von Moltke declared that 'no plan of operations extends with certainty beyond the first encounter with the enemy's main strength' or, put simply, 'no plan survives first contact'. As Macksey notes, the proof of that axiom was soon hammered home to 11th Armoured Division.

> Preceded by a massive air bombardment and endeavouring … to keep up with a creeping barrage, the 11th Armoured Division entered what was to become a killing ground. Harassed by anti-tank guns and SP guns, and then picked off at longer range by tanks moving into fire positions on the Bourguébus Ridge, the 11th was brought to a halt. The Guards became telescoped in trying to get round them and [were] also hit by fire from front and flanks. Therefore, 7th Armoured Division … only managed to get a single squadron of 5 RTR into the fray amidst a choked mass of burning or damaged vehicles. The ratio of British AFV losses to those of the Germans was of the order of 3 to 1 – the majority suffered by the 11th (some 130 all told), although neither the Guards nor the flanking armoured brigades got off scot free.

As already noted the brain behind the German defences against which VIII Corps flung itself was that of Erwin Rommel. The Desert Fox knew the mind of his opponent and this, in a sense their final encounter, must have brought Rommel, when he learned of it from his sickbed, some satisfaction.

> Rommel had created roughly five defence lines supported by mobile reserves and Pzkw IV, Panther and Tiger battalions. The German armour could counter-attack but, more dangerously, it could redeploy rapidly to block any British penetration with long-range fire.[24]

In spite of the fury of the Allied air strikes many German commanders survived and reacted quickly to the armoured thrust. Many 'sat tight and fought from the fortified villages that stood like rocks in an armoured British sea' while others, such as Hans von Luck of 21st Panzer Division, were soon on the battlefield organizing anti-tank defences. 'Soon British armour was being shot up from the flanks and rear. Disorder began to emerge.'[25]

With the departure of the heavy bombers the Germans regained their equilibrium. The second heavy strike requested by O'Connor at 3.00pm might have provided them with a salutary lesson and reduced the toll on the British armour but that strike did not happen and the Germans took the tactical advantage. Reserve panzer battalions were inserted into the battle, including Mark IVs and Panthers from 1st (Leibstandarte Adolf Hitler) and 12th (Hitlerjugend) SS Divisions (I SS Panzer Corps) and Tigers from 101st SS and 503rd Heavy Battalions. These increased the pressure on the British and the deadly fire of Panthers and Tigers, combined with anti-tank guns, wrought destruction on Shermans and Cromwells.

Reynolds notes that:

> The movement of 1st SS Panzer Regiment to the battle area went undetected by Allied aircraft and its arrival on the Bourguébus ridge at about 1245 hours coincided with that of the already depleted Fife and Forfar Yeomanry [29 Armoured Brigade], whose two remaining squadrons were advancing past Four towards Soliers and the ridge running from Bourguébus to la Hogue. Within minutes they lost twenty-nine tanks, including their commanding officer's. The situation was so bad that at 1258 hours the 23H, in reserve in the Grentheville area, were ordered not to advance south of Soliers.[26]

The historian of 11th Armoured Division wrote that:

> At 1445 the expected counter-attack came in. It was launched from the Four-Frénouville area by Panther tanks. Six of these were knocked out, but the armoured regiment in the area, 2 FF Yeo, was also badly mauled. Shortly afterwards, continued enemy pressure on the left flank forced a withdrawal to the area of Grentheville, which had been cleared by 8 RB. Later in the afternoon 5 Guards Armoured Brigade made a most welcome appearance on the left flank, and having occupied Cagny they pushed east towards Vimont. [29 Armoured Brigade] were now ordered to get firm on the line Bras-Hubert Folie-Bourguébus, but progress towards the last named place proved impossible and the brigade eventually held a line overlooking Bras, Hubert Folie and Soliers, although the idea of occupying even these villages was abandoned. Behind them 159 Brigade settled down for the night a thousand yards north of Grentheville, which was occupied by 8 RB.

Guards Armoured had also suffered. Among its casualties was the artist Rex Whistler, an officer in 2nd Welsh Guards, the divisional reconnaissance regiment which, with its Cromwells, was protecting the flanks. As he climbed down from his tank to speak to another tank commander Lieutenant Whistler was caught in the blast of a mortar bomb and killed.

Meanwhile, an officer of 2nd Irish Guards had not only survived what ought to have been a very one-sided encounter with the first King Tiger met by Second Army but had knocked out the brute and one of its companions, earning the MC on his first day in action. Lieutenant John Gorman, whom we have met already, was a troop leader in 2nd (Armoured) Irish Guards whose Sherman bogged and had to be rescued while en route to battle. As a result, Gorman subsequently took a wrong turning and 'charged up a cornfield, towards a hedge at the top of the rise, and turned the corner into a lane which ran along the hedge'.[27] It was there that he saw the King Tiger, 300 yards ahead of him. Behind the behemoth and to Gorman's right were three other tanks. At that stage the German tank was engaging other Guards' tanks in the valley below where, had he not taken the wrong turning, Lieutenant Gorman's tank, *Ballyragget*, ought to have been. With their attention on their targets the Germans did not spot the two Irish Guards' Shermans.

John Gorman and his driver, Corporal Baron, had discussed what to do if confronted by a King Tiger and had decided that the only viable course of action was to ram it, using the Sherman's speed to take advantage of the slow traverse of the Tiger's turret. And so he ordered 'Driver, Ram!' As the Sherman raced across the intervening ground Guardsman Scholes, the gunner, loosed off an HE round at the King Tiger's turret. It prompted the commander to put his head out of the turret hatch to see what had happened. He was too late in ordering his turret to be traversed as *Ballyragget* smashed into the King Tiger. After the collision the Tiger's 88mm gun was protruding about two feet beyond the Sherman. Gorman, aware that the other German tanks would now engage his Sherman – and he considered the Sherman to have 'the softest armour known to man' – ordered his crew to bale out. Meanwhile, Sergeant Harbinson, who had towed *Ballyragget* out earlier, had followed his troop leader and appeared on the scene, only to be engaged by the other German tanks. His Sherman brewed quickly, two crewmen dying in the flames. Harbinson, although rescued, was burned so badly that he died ten days later.

To ensure that the King Tiger remained out of the battle – its crew had also baled out – Gorman went in search of his Firefly, the commander of which, Sergeant Workman, had been decapitated by a round from the King Tiger. Removing the corpse of the unfortunate NCO from the turret, Gorman took the Firefly and another Sherman back to the scene of his encounter where he destroyed both the King Tiger and another German tank, as well as *Ballyragget*.[28]

The war diary of 2nd Irish Guards[29] identified all the German tanks as Panthers but the tank that Gorman engaged was later identified positively as a Tiger II, or King Tiger, the first example encountered in Normandy. Although he considered his actions as foolhardy and his survival as a matter of luck, John Gorman's courage, decisiveness and leadership had saved several lives, all of which was recognized by the award of the Military Cross for this action. Corporal Baron received the Military Medal.

During the afternoon there had been indications of German reinforcements arriving and there were one or two attempts by Panthers to break through our front east of the embankment from Soliers to Grentheville. The 23rd Hussars were covering the front east of the embankment and 3rd Royal Tanks held the front west of the embankment. Fife and Forfar Yeomanry had to be withdrawn to re-organize. It will be remembered that they had lost the whole of one squadron just west of Cagny and had then suffered heavy casualties from Four. After the war, during the Staff College battlefield tour, it was discovered that during the late morning the left hand squadron of 23rd Hussars, in trying to relieve 2nd Fife and Forfar Yeomanry, had themselves had casualties, but retained sufficient strength to resist an attack from the east end of the Bourguébus ridge and when this had been repulsed took up a position along a hedgerow a few hundred yards SW of Frénouville (… about one mile SE of Cagny).

The Desert Rats' historian recorded that 5 RTR:

were behind the last regiment of 11th Armoured, and, as this enormous mass of tanks moved slowly out of the gap, they were at first opposed only by an isolated Mark IV on the left, which, after knocking out two tanks, was destroyed by the concentrated fire of eight of our guns. While the Guards got into Cagny, Grentheville was cleared by 5th Royal Tanks after a short action against a few infantry, and small groups of prisoners came in all the while … The occupation of Grentheville provoked a small counter-attack from the south-east by six tanks, which withdrew after two had been knocked out.

By the time 7th Armoured Division deployed its role had been changed to that of supporting 11th Armoured; this was a direct result of the refusal to lay on another saturation bombing attack on Bourguébus ridge. (O'Connor was never given a reason for that refusal.) However, 7th Armoured had been delayed so badly by traffic congestion that only a squadron of 5 RTR entered the battle.

While 5 RTR and the Rifle Brigade pressed on next day their progress met with stubborn opposition that 'showed no signs of weakening'. Although three Tigers and a Panther were claimed as destroyed, and two Panthers were captured intact, the attack had reached stalemate.

Soon the plain before Bourguébus was covered with nearly 500 burning British tanks.[30] 'There were dozens, indeed hundreds, of tanks, Cromwells (the British fast tank), Churchills (the heavier armoured but slower British tank), and the ubiquitous Shermans all over the battlefield, some still burning, others blackened hulks. The great naval-type sweep across the only flat plain in Normandy had failed in its object of piercing a possibly mortal salient in the German front. It was now an infantry battle, in our case, to secure Cagny, and this our 3rd Battalion did that night.'[31]

For all practical purposes, GOODWOOD was at an end. However, Montgomery did not call off the offensive until three days later when the heavens opened, turned the battleground into a morass, grounded tactical aircraft and brought the battle to a close. Before that there had been further casualties in the armoured divisions. Roberts noted that 11th Armoured Division had suffered 191 tank casualties in the two days of fighting, with fifty-five of those sustained on the second day. The division had lost 735 officers and men, losses that could not be made good as easily as those of tanks. Total tank losses in VIII Corps were 399: thirty-three in Guards Armoured and sixty-seven in 7th Armoured in addition to those of 11th Armoured. British tank losses were three times those of the Germans.

Reynolds discusses the relative losses, pointing out that the figure of over 400 British tanks lost is 'much exaggerated' and that the true figure was 253, many of them repairable, while German losses were also exaggerated. The British *Official History* claim that 1st SS Panzer and 21st Panzer Divisions lost 109 tanks on 18 July is inaccurate and Roberts' figure, given in an interview at the Staff College in 1979, of seventy-five German tanks and assault guns lost 'can be accepted as accurate'. Thus Reynolds considers that GOODWOOD had not achieved three of its four aims: of Dempsey's four geographical objectives, Vimont, Garcelles, Hubert-Folie and Verrières, only Hubert-Folie had been taken while Bretteville-sur-Laize, an objective laid down by Montgomery, was over five miles away; 'Montgomery's aim of writing down German armour had not been achieved', as shown in the figures above; the cost for 21 Army Group had been high with British casualties in VIII and I Corps totalling 3,474 while Canadians had also suffered 1,965 casualties. However, Montgomery's fourth aim – to hold the greater part of German armour on the eastern flank, thereby preventing its deployment against the planned American breakout on the western flank, was achieved.[32]

GOODWOOD was seen as a failure by many[33] but others considered that it had achieved its aim. Roberts, a Montgomery supporter, wrote:

But the real achievements of the operation are seldom mentioned. Apart from advancing six miles against strong opposition in forty-eight hours, by the end of the operation there were opposite Second Army front seven Panzer divisions, four heavy tank battalions (Tigers); opposite First American Army, there were two Panzer divisions, one PanzerGrenadier division (with no tanks), no heavy tanks (Tigers). Surely this must have played a significant part in achieving the American breakout? This, I always thought, and still do, was Monty's plan, and GOODWOOD contributed a good deal towards it. Exploitation to Falaise was just a nice idea if the miraculous happened.

That assessment ties in with Montgomery's own and with that of Dempsey who, in 1951, claimed that the 'plans were efficient and well carried out ... with the possible exception of 7 Armd Div which he regarded as lacking in drive on this occasion' and largely responsible for the failure to gain the 'geographical objectives'.[34] Dempsey seems to have been influenced by hindsight and by loyalty to Montgomery, a comment that may also be made about Roberts' assessment. There had been a rigidity about the planning and execution of GOODWOOD that can be attributed only to Montgomery. D'Este writes that neither he nor Dempsey:

seemed to have grasped the conflicting position in which they had placed O'Connor: on the one hand, security was overemphasized and on the other

O'Connor was told to get his armour forward quickly. Perhaps too much was expected from the bombardment, but O'Connor was forced to employ unsound tactics in an effort to accomplish a Herculean task. How different the outcome might have been had Dempsey ordered a combined tank-infantry thrust down the corridor to Bourguébus, where there would have been sufficient infantry available to deal with problems such as Cagny. What the British Army terms 'thrustfulness' had been absolutely essential on 18 July, and the spearhead of 11th Armoured Division under the command of the most battle-experienced divisional commander in 21 Army Group was the perfect instrument to accomplish this, provided that the tanks and infantry were permitted to work in unison instead of being forced to accomplish entirely separate tasks.[35]

As Reynolds points out, three of the four aims of GOODWOOD were not achieved. Macksey's summary is accurate, especially when he wrote that GOODWOOD:

had not lived up to its intentions nor the effort applied, but it taught valuable lessons, not least … the importance of adapting the system of command and control in relation to the need to vary the tank and infantry mix to the circumstances.

The *Official History* comments that, with armour of both Guards and 11th involved at Cagny,

the momentum of the advance was soon lost and the enemy was allowed to focus forces for defence and counter-attack. While tanks of several regiments were milling about round the Cagny area, thousands of vehicles … were crossing the river and canal and moving forward in the bridgehead. Descriptions of the resulting confusion provide unedifying reading and show that the carefully prepared traffic control plan was unable to ensure that approaches to the corridor were kept open.

Macksey commented that the armoured divisions had maintained rigid command structures. In 11th Armoured Division this had left 159 Brigade with no tanks, other than those of 2nd Northamptonshire Yeomanry, the divisional reconnaissance regiment, when it had been deployed to assault and capture fortified villages. It had also left 29 Armoured Brigade with only the motor rifle companies of 8th Rifle Brigade as it advanced towards the Bourguébus ridge. In spite of the lessons of North Africa, the armoured and infantry brigades were still not being seen as a flexible team. But this was about to change with the immediate agent of that change being Richard O'Connor.

Roberts felt that the Northamptonshire Yeomanry, which he had deployed to support 159 Brigade, would not be used as a reconnaissance regiment but should be used as an additional armoured regiment. This would require the Northamptons undergoing training in working with infantry and Roberts discussed the regiment's shortcomings in the battle for Cuverville and Démouville and how to overcome them. When, some days later, Roberts met O'Connor, the corps commander:

> told me that we were going to operate on the right flank of Second Army, right in the middle of the bocage country. He said, and this was very relevant, that, 'You must be prepared for the very closest of tank/infantry co-operation on a troop/platoon basis.' I agreed entirely and so set to work at once to get this organized. Quite simple for the armoured regiments and infantry battalions, as they had done it on a squadron/company basis, but the Northamptonshire Yeomanry would need special attention. It was my intention to have two brigades each containing two armoured regiments and two infantry battalions. Who commanded each group must be decided by the brigade commander and would, to some extent, depend on the type of operation. This organization was not to be anything permanent; it must be entirely flexible and any armoured regiment must be prepared to work with any infantry battalion, and the brigadiers themselves must be prepared to operate as armoured brigadiers or infantry brigadiers. In fact, this flexible arrangement remained until the end of hostilities and was highly satisfactory.

The re-arrangement was implemented in both Guards and 11th Armoured but 7th had already been operating on similar lines. Treating the armoured reconnaissance regiment as a fourth unit of the armoured brigade made sense, as did treating the motor battalion of that brigade as a fourth member of the infantry brigade since it allowed armoured regiments to be paired with infantry battalions. This was easiest of all in Guards Armoured where close 'family' pairings were achieved, although the initial marriages were arranged on the simple basis of who happened to be laagered next to whom. Thus the first pairings mixed Coldstream and Irish in two battlegroups but this was soon modified to create Coldstream and Irish Groups; both Grenadiers and Welsh had 'family' groups from the start.

Operation GOODWOOD had not been launched in isolation as British and Canadian formations had been deployed and on 20 July the emphasis shifted to the Canadian front where II Canadian Corps prepared to attack the Verrières ridge, the British Bourguébus ridge. The Canadian Operation ATLANTIC met a fierce German counter-attack, composed of battlegroups from 2nd Panzer, 1st SS Panzer and 2nd Divisions, and the Canadian infantry units were shattered. Although tank support had been provided it was not only insufficient – at about a squadron of tanks per brigade – but was not integrated with the infantry effort. This was good tank country but the armoured commanders held their tanks behind the infantry and used their guns to fire in front of them, reducing the Shermans to mobile artillery pieces. Needless to say, this fostered ill feeling between infantry and tankmen. Rather than an increased level of trust and co-operation, a return to distrust threatened.

Nor did the Canadians hit back with an armoured counter-attack, even though 2 Canadian Armoured Brigade held about a hundred tanks in reserve – one in four of them Fireflies – these were deployed by squadrons ready to support an infantry brigade should they be called upon, as was the contemporary doctrine for independent armoured brigades. It is unlikely that the brigade commander considered forming a battlegroup to meet the panzers. As Jarymowycz argues, such a contingency 'was simply not required in the prevailing tactical thought'.[36] Since Canadian armour was modelled on the British pattern, the same doctrine also applied. Thus 4th Canadian Armoured Division was a mirror of a British formation, as was 1st Polish Armoured Division, then also arriving in Normandy.

A few days later, on 25 July, the town of St Lô and the surrounding area was bombed by more than 2,000 aircraft to soften up German defences as the Americans began the operations that would lead to the eventual breakout from Normandy. Operation COBRA encountered tough resistance but, by the 30th, Avranches, forty miles south, had fallen and Patton's Third Army was ready for its attack into Brittany. While the Germans had counter-attacked the Americans, 21 Army Group was about to make its first truly strategic offensive with Dempsey launching Operation BLUECOAT towards Caumont on the day Avranches fell. Guards Armoured Division played a part in BLUECOAT, following through on the initial success of 6 Guards Tank Brigade, whose Churchills were arguably more suited to the bocage than the Shermans. After confused and exhausting fighting with many casualties in the armoured units Guards Armoured was eventually 'pinched out' of the advance as the flanking formations moved forward and the Germans retreated.

During its subsequent spell out of the line No. 2 Squadron 2nd (Armoured) Irish Guards had a visit from the Army Group Commander, accompanied by the Secretary of State for War. Montgomery delivered one of his morale-boosting speeches to the assembled guardsmen. With the burnt-out hulks of Shermans in the background he expressed the confident opinion that:

> Even though the Germans might escape through the Falaise gap, he hoped to destroy them west of the River Seine. After that, he said, they would 'roll up the Buzz Bomb bases and see the cliffs of Dover from Calais. In the fighting to date we have defeated the Germans in battle; we have had no difficulty in dealing with the German armour, once we had grasped the problems ... We have nothing to fear from the Tiger and the Panther tanks; they are unreliable mechanically, and the Panther is very vulnerable from the flanks. Our 17-pounder will go right through them. Provided our tactics are good, we can defeat them without difficulty.'[37]

Many must have wondered if Montgomery was talking about the fighting in which they had been engaged. Did he really believe what he was saying? The experience of those guardsmen was that they faced a 'basic and ineluctable problem': all main German tanks – Panzer IVs, Panthers, Tigers and King Tigers – could destroy the Sherman while only one in four Shermans – the Fireflies with their 17-pounders – could meet German tanks on anything approaching equal terms. Montgomery repeated this misplaced confidence in Allied tanks after the Ardennes offensive when he suggested that the Germans might have achieved their aims had they been equipped with Allied tanks while the Allies might never have broken out of Normandy had they been equipped with panzers.

The GOODWOOD/ATLANTIC offensive was followed on 25 July by Operation SPRING, launched by II Canadian Corps reinforced by Guards and 7th Armoured Divisions. But the attack had been anticipated and the German commander, General Hans Eberbach, deployed forces to counter it; these included 9th SS Panzer which was situated so that it could strike the flank of any Allied southward move. In addition, 2nd Panzer moved close to 9th SS while 116th Panzer Division, detached from Fifteenth Army, concentrated near St Sylvain. Eberbach's armoured punch could also be strengthened by 10th SS Panzer Division which, although it was still in action, he intended to move to Bretteville as soon as possible.

II Corps moved off before dawn on 25 July. Before the sun had burned away the last traces of darkness the Germans had launched their counter-attack. The resultant battle lasted all day with the Canadians suffering heavy losses. Although there were some local successes an attempt to advance beyond Verrières was stopped by anti-tank defences on the rise beyond the village. This phase of SPRING had been conducted by infantry with the tanks of 2 Canadian Armoured Brigade in support while Guards and 7th Armoured waited for the opportunity to push forward once a gap had been pierced in the German line. But that never happened. The Desert Rats, with 2 Armoured Brigade, helped stem some German counter-attacks and had fierce encounters with SS panzers. Those battles led to the loss of fifty-six British and Canadian tanks, the equivalent of a regiment, but the Germans also sustained serious losses. (Guards Armoured remained in reserve.) Total Canadian casualties on the day were about 1,500. Dempsey considered that SPRING had helped the American offensive to the west where progress was being made, although some of their worst casualties were caused by American planes bombing their own ground troops. Among the victims of the attack was the highest-ranking US Army officer to die in Europe, Lieutenant General Lesley J. McNair, father of the tank-destroyer doctrine.

Montgomery now appreciated that First US Army had landed 'the main blow of the whole Allied plan', 'was making excellent progress' and determined to do whatever he could to further their operations.[38] That included Second Army attacking east of Noyers 'where there was no armour at all'. Thus was born Operation BLUECOAT, Dempsey's attack from the Caumont area. Montgomery had intended this to be a six-division effort but Eisenhower asked for it to be brought forward, writing that 'I feel very strongly that a three-division attack now on Second Army's right flank will be worth more than a six-division attack in five days' time'.[39] With First Canadian Army now operational there was a major re-organization in the British-Canadian sector with the armies shifting towards the Allied centre. Almost every formation in Second British and First Canadian Armies had to change position with some elements of VIII Corps not even receiving their movement orders until shortly before noon on 28 July, and then having to drive up to fifty miles to be in position for D Day on 30 July.

The enemy front, south and east of Caumont, where the attack was to be made had been held by only two weak German infantry divisions until 2nd Panzer had moved in recently and had changed little since mid-June. This had given the Germans time to sow extensive minefields and construct strong defences. The ground also favoured the defenders, being the densest form of bocage with tree-shrouded hills and valleys, few metalled roads and only one road capable of handling two-way traffic. Other than that road, which led south from Caumont, there were only narrow by-roads and farm tracks with the inevitable high banks topped by thick hedges. Many small streams cut across the land in all directions and the bridges over them could not support tanks or other heavy vehicles, while the banks were usually marshy. Two larger waterways, the rivers Vire, on the west flank of the advance, and the Souleuvre, about ten miles south of Caumont, presented major obstacles, especially for armour, as they had cut deep valleys into the landscape.

So that the attack might be launched with the full advantage of surprise there was to be neither preliminary artillery bombardment nor air attack. However, once the attack began the gunners would provide support with counter-battery fire on all known German positions, following this up with concentrations of fire or bombardments as required. An hour after H Hour British and American heavy bombers would lay carpets of bombs ahead of the attackers. Tactical air support was also planned. But, as had happened so often since 6 June, the weather failed to co-operate with the planners and morning fighter and fighter-bomber sorties were cancelled. Even the heavies were affected with more than half the 700 British bombers due to bomb in front of XXX Corps being recalled because their targets were obscured completely. Others had to bomb from low level while American medium bombers supporting VIII Corps attacked through dense cloud. In spite of these problems, according to German prisoners, 'the bombing as a whole was devastating in its effect'.

The attack was held up by minefields and heavy fire, although Sherman Crabs of 79th Armoured Division deployed to beat paths through the minefields, which proved to be greater obstacles than expected. By the end of the day the maximum advance achieved was six miles south of Caumont by VIII Corps. O'Connor's advance was led by 15th (Scottish) Division on the left, supported by 6 Guards Tank Brigade, and 11th Armoured on the right, organized in two balanced battlegroups.

The lessons of GOODWOOD had been taken to heart; and not before time for this battle was being fought in tight bocage where the advantage lay with the defending infantryman with his Panzerfaust, the anti-tank gunners with their skilfully concealed weapons, or the machine gunners with their devastating weapons. And thus 11th Armoured Division advanced in two columns with 29 Armoured Brigade commanding the left column, of two armoured regiments, the motor battalion and an infantry battalion, while 159 Brigade commanded the right column with an armoured regiment and two infantry battalions; 2nd Northamptonshire Yeomanry ... followed up under divisional command.[40]

Although Liddell Hart was to attribute the inception of the mixed brigade battlegroup to Roberts, the divisional war diary indicates otherwise, noting that:

> For the advance fresh brigade groupings were adopted. Experience of US and 7th Armoured Division in the bocage had demonstrated the necessity for the closest co-operation of tanks and infantry … Under these, reasonable progress could only be assured by infantry moving with tanks on all routes and often actually riding on them.[41]

That first day Roberts' division made steady progress in spite of some sharp skirmishes. At the end of the day the 29 Brigade column had passed Dampierre and the 159 Brigade column was about two miles short of St Martin, having taken St Jean des Essartiers. However, there was to be no stop for the night, during which it was discovered that a southward path was free of enemy surveillance; 4 KSLI moved down it to the main road where they were reinforced by tanks. Next day further progress was made, helped by the sappers having cleared or breached the minefields, allowing more troops to move forward.

By 11am on 31 July the village of St Martin had been taken by 11th Armoured. Then, from 2 HCR, assigned as an armoured car regiment from corps HQ, came news of another clear track, through l'Evêque forest. Even better, the report also stated that a bridge over the Souleuvre was intact and clear of the enemy, even though it was about five miles behind his front line. Another troop of armoured cars and some tanks set off to secure the bridge. Although the cars were destroyed in an ambush en route, the tanks completed the job and the bridge was secure. That night troops of 11th Armoured crossed the Souleuvre to the high ground west of le Bény-Bocage where a bridgehead was established and Point 205 occupied. In addition, contact was made with US troops and arrangements made to defend the right flank.

Having learned of the capture of the bridge O'Connor ordered Guards Armoured to move up on 11th Armoured's left to secure additional crossings near le Tourneur. Against strong opposition from 21st Panzer the Guards fought their way to le Tourneur while 11th Armoured captured le Bény-Bocage and HCR armoured cars probed to within two miles of Vire. However, since Vire was an American objective, Second Army was instructed to wheel to its right, taking VIII Corps towards Condé sur Noireau and Flers while XXX Corps made for the Orne. The Germans were left in control of Vire, no one at Montgomery's HQ seeming to realize that the town was ripe for falling into British hands. That led to unnecessary and bloody fighting for Vire. However, both Guards and 11th Armoured made good inroads on 2 August with the former on the high ground overlooking Estry and the latter reaching the Périers ridge and occupying Etouvy. Since both divisions had pushed hard into the enemy lines, by-passing elements of 21st Panzer, there was considerable mopping up to be done and the arrival of the first wave of 9th SS Panzer added to the fighting. But the Germans were trying to turn a tide that was not to be turned and the area was soon secured.

Meanwhile 7th Armoured had been ordered to take Aunay sur Audon from the west on the 31st as 50th (Northumbrian) Division's advance had been delayed. However, the Desert Rats had to move through 43rd (Wessex) Division and were caught in traffic congestion, including the tail of the Wessex division, as they negotiated Caumont's outskirts. Such was the slow pace of the advance that their leading tanks were only at Breuil, five miles from Aunay, at nightfall. Traffic congestion had caused more delays than the Germans. In spite of their best efforts 7th Armoured's attacks on Aunay on 2 and 3 August were pushed back by 10th SS Panzer. The Desert Rats were forced back almost to Breuil, a rebuff that led to the relief of their GOC, Major General Erskine, by Major General Verney, formerly commander of 6 Guards Tank Brigade, on the 4th. (And Horrocks relieved Bucknall at the head of XXX Corps.)

Field Marshal Gunther von Kluge, the German commander, now conducting a tactical withdrawal, was withdrawing elements of Fifteenth Army from defensive positions in the Pas de Calais to reinforce the exhausted soldiers of Seventh Army and Fifth Panzer Army, the renamed Panzer Group West. To von Kluge the developing BLUECOAT offensive threatened to crack his line near Vire, where Seventh and Fifth Panzer Armies hinged and he was determined to reinforce the sector. At the same time he had to meet a threat on the eastern flank while the Americans were thrusting forward. But his plans were stymied by Hitler intervening to order an armoured counter-attack by at least four armoured divisions while infantry divisions held the line between the Orne and Vire. Thus was set in motion the Mortain counter-attack, Operation LÜTTICH.

As von Kluge made his plans for LÜTTICH First Canadian Army was planning its first major operation, TOTALIZE. On the night of 7/8 August, as von Kluge's panzers were trying to break through to Avranches, Simonds' II Canadian Corps was ready to move. Crerar, commanding First Canadian Army, had told Simonds to begin planning for TOTALIZE 'several days before Montgomery issued his Directive' and the extra days thus granted allowed Simonds to build up his attack force and implement some fresh ideas. Those ideas included deploying seventy-six M7 Priest SPGs converted, or 'defrocked', to become armoured personnel carriers (APCs), a concept turned down by Dempsey when O'Connor proposed it for GOODWOOD. The APCs were dubbed 'Kangaroos', from the eponymous marsupial's method of carrying its young in a pouch.

TOTALIZE included two armoured divisions, neither British but formed on the British pattern. These were 4th (Canadian) and 1st (Polish) Armoured Divisions, recently arrived in France, and they were to fight alongside two Canadian infantry divisions, a British infantry division and a British tank brigade. Lewin wrote of Simonds' plans that they represented something

> Patton might well have studied … for in daring and ingenuity they surpassed anything so far attempted by the British army – or the Americans. Simonds' difficulty was this: he had to thrust down the Caen-Falaise road amid open country which, as several preliminary probes revealed, gave ample scope to the 88s, the mortars and the machine guns in the strong enemy line. This hard crust he had

to crack with his armour: but until his armour had reached the crust he had to keep the heads of the enemy down without providing the conventional warning of an artillery preparation. He therefore adopted the wholly unconventional plan of using heavy bombers, in a tactical role at night, to carpet the flanks of his line of advance; meanwhile his assault troops moved to the centre, the forward infantry being transported in [APCs] ... Ingenious devices were also evolved for the maintenance of direction in this unprecedented attack: radio–directional beams for the tanks, target-indicator shells with coloured bursts, tracer from Bofors firing on fixed lines, and searchlights to illuminate the sky as the moon failed.[42]

Hobart's 79th Armoured Division was also to make its contribution to the attack. Simonds formed his force in separate columns, each on a four-tank front, with vehicles 'packed nose to tail'[43] in what was almost a phalanx formation. Each column was preceded by 'Funnies' from 79th Armoured, Sherman Crabs to clear mines, Churchill AVREs to provide assault engineer support and Churchill Crocodile flamethrowers. Although over 1,000 heavy bombers were to support the attack, only 660 dropped their bombs, the remainder being unable to identify their targets. The Canadian official historian noted that not a single bomb fell on Allied troops.

Poor visibility also led to problems on the ground with crashes among the advancing AFVs although the attack continued nonetheless. Initial objectives were taken and the usual enemy counter-attacks during the morning of the 8th were beaten off. As the armoured divisions took up the baton from the infantry formations German resistance hardened with the arrival of elements of 12th SS Hitlerjugend to bolster the relatively new 89th Infantry Division which had relieved 1st SS Leibstandarte. In particular Kampfgruppe Meyer, under command of Kurt Meyer, CO of 25th SS PanzerGrenadier Regiment provided doughty opposition although Meyer's launch of a counter-attack against the infantry of the first phase of TOTALIZE failed and resulted in heavy losses in men and AFVs.

Meyer's counter-attack did not affect the armoured phase of the operation but the armoured divisions had their own, home-grown, problems, resulting from poor co-ordination at II Corps HQ[44] and the failings of a brigade commander. These caused delays that contributed to II Corps not achieving its objectives. Although Falaise was not taken the attack had broken through the German defences astride the Caen-Falaise road and a lodgement had been secured behind the enemy anti-tank screen anchored on Tilly-la-Campagne. In addition, the leading infantry held Point 122 on the right and the villages of Cramesnil and St Aignan on the left. Although the Canadians broke off TOTALIZE on the 10th the advance continued while plans were being laid for the follow through, Operation TRACTABLE.

TRACTABLE was launched on 14 August, the day before Allied forces landed in southern France in Operation DRAGOON. Between the end of TOTALIZE and the opening of TRACTABLE Patton's Third Army took Alençon, south-south-east of Falaise, threatening von Kluge's forces with encirclement. But the American thrust was also risky and the fresh Canadian attack would take some pressure off their north American neighbours and set up 21 Army Group and 12 US Army Group (now operational under General Omar Bradley) for the final defeat of the German forces in Normandy. By this stage von Kluge had lost the ability to re-organize as he saw fit, an important element of command. Allied pressure continued to dictate German operations.

Unlike its predecessor, TRACTABLE was launched in daylight, H Hour being noon on the 14th. Lessons had been taken from TOTALIZE and once again mechanized infantry accompanied the armour while smoke obscured the enemy's view of the attackers. General Stanislaw Maczek's Polish 1st Armoured Division remained under Canadian command; Simonds' forces also included 4th Canadian Armoured. Heavy bombers once again pounded the enemy's positions and medium bombers also contributed. However, there were problems. The Germans knew the plan since a Canadian officer, travelling between the HQs of divisions had become lost and driven into German lines the night before. He had been killed by the Germans who found Simonds' orders on his body and swiftly deployed tanks, troops and anti-tank guns along the expected line of the Canadian advance. Another problem was that many heavy bombers bombed Allied troops instead of their targets, causing some 400 casualties amongst Canadian and Polish personnel.

Since von Kluge's Operation LÜTTICH had been defeated soundly by Allied air and ground forces the German forces were being enveloped as the Allied advance continued. TRACTABLE was intended to further that envelopment by taking Falaise, Trun and Chambois and linking up with US forces, thereby sealing the Germans in what was dubbed the 'Falaise Pocket'. To prevent their escape through the 'Falaise Gap' Montgomery intended to seal that gap with 21 Army Group thrusting 'southwards and eastwards to secure Falaise and Argentan' and 12 Army Group swinging 'its right wing northwards from le Mans up to Alençon and then on to the general line from Carrouges to Sées', about twelve miles south of Argentan.

Operation TRACTABLE began on time, its smokescreen cover thickened by dust raised by AFVs. The leading troops were soon on the Laison river, where fascine-carrying AVREs of 79th Armoured Division improvised crossings, allowing most of the armour to be across by 3 o'clock. Aware of the Canadian axes of advance the Germans reacted quickly and sharply and losses were heavy in the Canadian armoured units, although infantry were soon on hand to aid their comrades. In spite of the difficulties Canadian and Polish armour was closing on Falaise as night fell. The Canadians were then ordered to take Falaise while continuing their advance on Trun. Fighting for Falaise continued until the 17th when the last SS soldiers were rounded up. By then von Kluge had issued the retreat order to his armies, his last act as C-in-C West. On the 16th the Canadian and Polish armoured divisions had begun their final drive for Trun and Chambois. Next day the Poles outflanked 12th SS Panzer Division, expanding the bridgehead north-west of Trun while taking some of 4th Canadian Armoured's objectives. Maczek deployed a battlegroup to the south-west, isolating Trun, where it took the high ground overlooking the town and the Dives valley. This allowed 4th Canadian to take Trun during the morning of the 18th. Another Polish battlegroup moved south-east, captured les Champeaux and prepared to attack Chambois. The front held by this battlegroup was about four miles from the US V Corps and by the end of the day Maczek's battlegroups were directly north of Chambois with reinforcements on their way from 4th Canadian.

Canadian and Polish armour continued their close co-operation next day when Simonds laid his plans for closing the Falaise Gap. The Canadian division was to strike towards Chambois on the western flank of two of Maczek's battlegroups while the other two Polish battlegroups struck eastward to secure Hill 262 and cover the eastern flank. Meanwhile Canadian infantry divisions, supported by armoured units, continued their offensives. While one Polish battlegroup made for Chambois, the Canadian Taskforce Currie covering their advance, two other battlegroups attacked Hill 262 with Battlegroup Zgorzelski capturing Point 137, due west of Hill 262, and Battlegroup Stefanowicz taking the latter. Late the following afternoon Canadian and Polish troops linked up with US troops to close the Falaise Gap. On that day also, Major David Currie, of Taskforce Currie, had taken his battlegroup into St Lambert and held his positions against a series of determined German counter-attacks before continuing his attack, capturing the entire village and cutting off an escape route for many of the Germans trapped in the 'pocket'. Currie was awarded the Victoria Cross for his great gallantry and leadership, the first such award to the Canadian army in Normandy.

The fighting was far from over as the Germans made a determined effort to break out of the 'pocket', and tanks of II SS Panzer Corps, which had been idle due to lack of petrol, received fuel and entered the fray. German blows fell hardest on the Poles who held on grimly to their gains fighting off every attack even though all but cut off. As the British official historian wrote:

> Isolated for three days, and short of supplies until a small quantity was dropped to them by parachute early on the 21st, the Polish Armoured Division had fought with the greatest gallantry and stood its ground to a man.

Second British Army had not been idle during this time. Both 7th and 11th Armoured Divisions had been involved in supporting operations; Guards Armoured was in reserve. Deployed under command of I Corps, the Desert Rats were 'to exploit First Canadian Army's success to the Seine, a distance of sixty-five miles, advancing due east along the general axis of St Pierre-sur-Dives, Livarot and Lisieux'. Eleventh Armoured Division, meanwhile, had come under command of XXX Corps to act as its spearhead: as First Canadian Army advanced from the Caen-Troarn line, Second British Army would advance east and south-east with XXX Corps on the right and XII Corps on the left.

On 17 August 131 Brigade of 7th Armoured led off through St Pierre-sur-Dives, climbing to the 800-foot-high plateau above the river valley. The villages in the valley were cleared against light opposition, mostly mortars and machine-gun fire, but the main German defensive positions were on the high ground where 'every bend concealed a Tiger, Panther or anti-tank gun, and every village had its quota of infantry'. Against such opposition the infantry and Irish Hussars' Cromwells pushed forward to reach Livarot, which was entered by patrols of 1st Rifle Brigade, the Hussars having found an 'intact and unguarded' bridge. Another bridge was built at Livarot while 1/5th Queen's secured a second bridgehead on the Lisieux road where the sappers built a further bridge, allowing the divisional advance to Lisieux to proceed.

Good co-ordination of armour, infantry, artillery and engineers was demonstrated as the divisions advanced, especially in fighting off spirited enemy counter-attacks, even one supported by six Tigers. The divisional historian described Livarot as:

Our first real experience of 'liberation'. Tricolour flags were out before our troops arrived; the apothecary was arrested as a collaborator, and, for those who got in early, excellent wine, as a change from Calvados or watery cider, was produced by the proprietress of the principal local café. The welcome was restrained but sincere, and here for the first time we met the Resistance movement, which provided us with good information and also handed over a number of Allied airmen ...

The battle for Livarot had been tough and that for Lisieux proved tougher, but the city was taken after two days of fighting. Approaches to Lisieux had been covered by infantry with machine guns and *panzerfäuste*, the latter weapon underlining the need for infantry to be in close support of the tanks. Once Lisieux was in British hands the advance resumed:

From Livarot onwards, although limited by a narrow frontage, the Division had at last operated as an armoured formation, if only to a small extent. Nothing particularly dramatic had occurred and for most of the way, except for the twenty miles between Livarot and St Georges, the advance had been continuously contested. Moreover, casualties had not been light, and the time had not yet come when we should be fighting against a completely beaten and demoralized enemy as was the case in the advance to Ghent. At the time it was hard to believe that the Battle for France was now virtually over, for the enemy still appeared to have plenty of fight left in him, but the final move to complete a decisive victory was now drawing near. On 29 August we were transferred to XII Corps, a happy association which was to continue almost uninterrupted till we entered Hamburg eight months later.

Meanwhile 11th Armoured had been fighting its way out of bocage country and, led by the Inns of Court Regiment, in armoured cars, took Flers 'and it was at this stage, I think, that we first began to speak of "liberating" places rather than "capturing" them'. In fact, Flers had been abandoned, setting a pattern for the days that followed:

The lack of opposition in the morning of each day appeared to demonstrate that the enemy was now conducting a planned withdrawal to the east, blowing bridges and planting mines wherever he could, but leaving behind organized rearguards which we were overtaking during the afternoon. This course was being forced upon him by the increasing threat to his flanks from north and south.

As the advance continued the division moved into the Falaise 'pocket' where German troops 'were fighting with a tenacity born of desperation' and it was there that 11th Armoured captured its first general, Kurt Badinski, GOC of 276th Infantry Division, and his staff, who were among over 900 prisoners taken on 20 August. And so the brigade groups pushed on, Argentan was taken and the division crossed the Orne for the second and last time. Opposition remained tough with many mines and demolitions in addition to determined soldiery. By 23 August it was all but over in the Falaise 'pocket' and 11th Armoured settled down to a spell of re-organization.

On 28 August 11th Armoured set off for the Seine, led by 2 HCR, now acting as the divisional reconnaissance unit. Also under command was 8 Armoured Brigade which met tough opposition that was overcome eventually. Further progress was made next day, at the end of which 8 Armoured Brigade ceased to be under command of the division; it had been protecting the right flank until Guards Armoured could come up, after which both armoured formations were to continue leading the advance. When the Guards arrived, the Household Cavalry reverted to Major General Adair's command and the Inns of Court re-joined Roberts'. There had been other changes in both 7th and 11th Armoured Divisions. The former now included 5th Royal Inniskilling Dragoon Guards – the Skins – in 22 Armoured Brigade, replacing 4 CLY (the Sharpshooters had been amalgamated with 3 CLY in 4 Armoured Brigade due to battle losses) while 15th/19th King's Royal Hussars replaced 2nd Northamptonshire Yeomanry in 11th Armoured (the Northamptonshire Yeomanry regiments were also amalgamated due to losses).

Roberts' division moved on to Amiens, driving through the night in lashing rain in a move that surprised the Germans. Next morning – 31 August – some enemy infantry were brushed aside as the division entered Amiens where 'both columns were joined by German parties under the misapprehension that they were their own'. Even better followed. At dawn divisional HQ found itself alongside a German field bakery defended by a Mark IV which was destroyed before it could open fire. Then General Eberbach, newly-appointed commander of Seventh Army, was captured with some members of his HQ staff. A large map showing all German dispositions in the west was also taken. Divisional HQ thought to show off their prisoner – the highest-ranking German taken to date – to their corps commander but Horrocks had his mind only on the pursuit:

What the hell, he wished to know, were all those Germans doing there, and would we please get them out of the way as soon as possible? So General Eberbach and his staff were evacuated through the usual channels. Or rather the official channels; for prisoners are a most irritating encumbrance on a big advance and it was becoming usual at this time to hand them over to the Maquis, who invariably proved most willing to co-operate in this respect.

Subsequently 23rd Hussars and a company of 8th Rifle Brigade captured the main bridge across the Somme while the Fife and Forfar Yeomanry added another bridge soon afterwards. The bridgehead was extended and 159 Brigade was relieved by a brigade of 50th Division and became available for further pursuit.

Thus ended a most memorable day, about which it remains only to say that besides our other notable captures over 800 were added to the already impressive total of enemy prisoners, and a large quantity of German equipment also fell into our hands.

As 11th Armoured moved into Amiens, Guards Armoured was setting out to join them, having been instructed by Horrocks that 'You will come on as quickly as you can, moving by night if necessary, and pass through 8 Armoured Brigade to seize the crossings over the Somme at Corbie'. The divisional history records:

The resultant orders that reached the division were quite short but they were in dramatic contrast to any that had been previously given. It was an exciting moment, as everybody realized that we should ... for the first time be carrying out the mobile operations for which we had been training for three years. Curiously enough, though, experience gained in the preceding weeks led us to adopt a different organization from any that we had ever practised; during the years of training we had found increasingly that under European conditions, as opposed to those of the desert, tanks and infantry needed to work in close co-operation down to the lowest level if the best results were to be achieved ... for the forthcoming operations it was considered best that each brigade should control an equal proportion of infantry and armour. Under the old organization this would have been impossible to arrange, but the decision to give once more an armoured car regiment to each armoured division, which in our case involved the reversion of 2nd Household Cavalry Regiment to divisional command after some two years' absence as Corps troops, provided the solution – the 2nd Welsh Guards was no longer needed for specific reconnaissance purposes, and each brigade could be provided with two armoured and two infantry battalions. As each regiment other than the Scots Guards ... had one battalion of each type, four regimental battlegroups were formed ...

By the time 11th Armoured had re-organized in Amiens, Guards Armoured had come up through Beauvais on the right and both prepared to advance. On 1 September Horrocks told Roberts that his next objective was Brussels, but this was subsequently changed to Antwerp and the Guards were directed on the Belgian capital. Both armoured divisions thrust forward, their armoured car regiments reconnoitring in front, although 2nd Welsh Guards with their speedy Cromwells were also to the fore.

Opposition was encountered but none that delayed the advances. In fact, Roberts was delayed more by Allied changes of plan than by the enemy as his units sat about through much of 2 September waiting for an airborne operation that never happened; it was then that Roberts was assigned Antwerp as his next objective.

> I asked General Horrocks what my main task was at Antwerp and he told me to go for the docks and prevent their destruction. This also confirmed my view that we would finally be going east towards Germany. All the Germans in the Channel ports would be looked after by the Canadians and the Poles and XII Corps on our immediate left, albeit a little behind us.

As 11th Armoured set off for Antwerp early on the 3rd the Guards were en route to Brussels. The previous day their GOC, Major General Adair, had told his officers that 'My intention is to advance and liberate Brussels. That is a grand intention'.

> His manner was inspiring to the extent that all ... left with the certain knowledge that they could pass on the same spirit to their own order groups. Speed was essential and any serious opposition was to be by-passed, while we were to move on two centre-lines ... this was only the first of many times when we advanced thus in brigade groups on more or less parallel routes ...

On their way to join 11th Armoured the Guards had captured another German general, the commander of Corps HQ Somme and discovered that the enemy had intended to fight his usual style of withdrawal and hold the British on the Somme. The Germans had identified the American threat farther east to be the greater and had expected to pin the British along the Somme. They had miscalculated badly and a British breakthrough had been achieved – almost unnoticed by the British on the ground who were inclined to describe this period as 'the great swan' – and the German command structure had lost cohesion. At least some of the credit for that must be given to the Guards and 11th Armoured Divisions, as well as to Horrocks who understood armoured warfare better than either his army or army group commanders.

And so, on 3 September, four years to the day since the UK had declared war on Hitler's Germany, Brussels was liberated by Guards Armoured Division. Their run to Brussels had met with some pockets of opposition, most of them dealt with speedily by the HCR armoured cars while others were by-passed to be cleared by the tanks and infantry. One major obstacle close to Brussels needed the combined efforts of armoured cars, Grenadier tanks and infantry to overcome the anti-tank guns sited there. At the same time 2nd Welsh Guards were racing up another route, determined to be first into Brussels. It was suggested that some of their Cromwells had touched 60mph on the main road. In the event the Grenadiers entered the city at much the same time.

So both brigades reached the city as darkness was falling to be greeted … in a manner which can surely never have been equalled. As we approached our pace gradually slackened until it was literally reduced to a crawl. But this time there was no need to worry; it was no enemy opposing our entry, only hordes of Belgians careering madly about in such a frenzy of joy that movement was almost impossible.

The brigades of 11th Armoured also met some opposition en route to Antwerp. Driving forward through the 3rd they set off at first light next day with Roberts determined to be in Antwerp before dark. Moving on two centre lines the divisional advance continued, knocking aside any opposition, and leading elements of 29 Armoured Brigade had reached the docks by 2pm, finding them virtually undamaged. Roberts noted:

Now, the 'docks' were no little harbour; they stretched almost as far as the eye could see. At first glance they seemed to be in good shape and the fact that they were was confirmed by the locals. However, it also emerged that a vital point was the main lock-gates much farther north-west and leading into the Scheldt.

There was fierce fighting in Antwerp and 159 Brigade captured the German HQ, the commander, General von Stolberg-Stolberg, and some 6,000 prisoners. But fighting continued throughout the night and Roberts was concerned to learn next morning that the main bridge over the canal had been blown. He felt that if he had had more detailed maps of the city beforehand he might have realized better the significance of the canal, which divided the city from the suburb of Merxem. Nonetheless:

If there is any one exploit for which 11th Armoured Division is to be remembered, this will probably be the pursuit to Antwerp and the capture of that city. The reasons for this selection will be the speed of the advance and the importance of the prize.

The division had covered 340 miles in six days since crossing the Seine and 580 since Caumont. All had been covered on the tanks' own tracks, some of which – as with some SPGs – had exceeded their mileage lives. And five of those six days had also involved some fighting. It may not have been on a large scale but it meant stopping, issuing orders, deploying into fighting order and then re-organizing, all of which affected the advance.

During this same period 7th Armoured Division made for Ghent.

For the first time since the African campaign, the Division was once more to be used in its most successful role, the break-through, unhampered by pockets which could not be by-passed. Certain aspects of the campaign we had already glimpsed – the cheering crowds, the proffered drinks, the flowers, kisses, and energetic if sometimes trying partisans, but in front of us had always been enemy forces, usually comparatively well equipped, who were acting in obedience to an organized command.

Although there was opposition on the roads to Ghent it could be overcome by firepower and manoeuvre; within a week the Desert Rats had taken their objective, having covered a direct route of a hundred miles and taken 9,000 prisoners.

All three armoured divisions had shown their true worth, advancing and fighting as armoured formations should, using speed, manoeuvre and firepower to disrupt and overcome the enemy.

The drive by the 11th Armoured and Guards Armoured ... is celebrated, representing as it does a classic example of exploitation by armour. The night drive on 30 August of forty miles to seize the bridges over the Somme at Amiens (and the capture by 2 FF YEO of the German Seventh Army commander at breakfast) set the standard for events to come. Across the old First World War battlefields, into Belgium, through Brussels and on to the north where 3 RTR arrived to capture the docks, intact ... theirs was a progress through cheering crowds of liberated people to wipe out the memory of a past defeat – a progress made possible by the reliability of the Cromwells and Shermans, and one which, appropriately enough, was shared by many of the RAC units which had done their best to stem the rot in 1940.

But there was still much work to be done as autumn approached and the Germans tried to regain their equilibrium.

On 1 September Montgomery had been promoted to field marshal but was no longer overall Allied commander on the mainland as Eisenhower opened his HQ in France on that date. Tensions between Eisenhower, Montgomery and other commanders, both British and American, were to have their effects, some of them adverse, on the campaign ahead. And it was a Montgomery plan, sanctioned by Eisenhower, that led to the next major action for British armoured divisions. Montgomery believed that he could thrust into northern Germany, thereby avoiding the northern reaches of the Siegfried Line, by seizing the crossings of the Maas, Waal and Lower Rhine rivers and encircling the Ruhr, Germany's industrial heart, from the north. His plan was for airborne forces to seize the river crossings while armour led the thrust into Germany. The Allies' only strategic reserve was First Allied Airborne Army, which Eisenhower committed to the plan, which he approved. Montgomery's staff gave the names Operations MARKET and GARDEN to the airborne and ground elements, although the combined title MARKET GARDEN is more familiar. Eisenhower's support was due to his desire to maintain pressure on the retreating Germans and the pressure he was feeling from the United States to commit the Airborne Army to action. (This included three American and two British airborne divisions, a British airportable division and a Polish airborne brigade.)

The ground forces consisted mainly of Horrocks' XXX Corps, with Guards Armoured in the van; two infantry divisions were held in reserve. Two American airborne divisions, 101st and 82nd, were to take the bridges between Eindhoven and Nijmegen while British 1st Airborne Division would seize the bridge at Arnhem. It was anticipated that XXX Corps would reach the south end of 101st Airborne's area on the first day, link up with 82nd on the second and with 1st British on the fourth at the latest. At that point the airborne divisions and XXX Corps would combine to smash their way out of the Arnhem bridgehead.

But the intelligence behind the planning was flawed deeply. It was believed that the German will to resist had been broken and that XXX Corps would face only limited resistance on the advance along Highway 69 since the enemy would be spread out over a sixty-mile-plus front trying to contain the airborne pockets – or carpets, as Montgomery called them – between Second Army and Arnhem. Airborne forces were not intended to fight without support for long periods – and the four days anticipated for the advance to Arnhem was close to their limit. That was especially so as the airborne troops had insufficient anti-tank weaponry. Moreover, the road to Arnhem presented its own problems. Highway 69, a single-carriageway, two-lane road, crossed the flat polder land on an embankment. Off road the ground was frequently too soft for vehicles, especially tanks, and was cut across by dykes and drainage ditches, further restricting tactical movement by vehicles, while trees and bushes atop the dykes and lining roads and paths restricted observation, especially as autumn was only beginning.

Of course there were many other problems, including Montgomery's failure to cut off the Scheldt estuary which allowed thousands of Germans from Fifteenth Army to escape. Over 200 artillery pieces were also saved while Hitler had recalled Gerd von Rundstedt to command in the west. Von Rundstedt had immediately begun planning a defensive strategy and a screen began taking shape with artillery, tanks and ad hoc formations and units. Among the defensive formations was First Parachute Army, created almost from scratch under General Kurt Student in early September. As Horrocks commented, the Germans had made an 'astonishing recovery ... after their crippling defeat in Normandy'. In the Arnhem area II SS Panzer Corps (9th SS Panzer Division Hohenstaufen and 10th SS Panzer Division Frundsberg), commanded by General Wilhelm Bittrich, was in an assembly and re-fitting area north and east of the town.[45] The Allies knew the two SS armoured divisions were in the area as Montgomery admitted in his *Memoirs*:

The 2nd SS Panzer Corps was refitting in the Arnhem area, having limped up there after its mauling in Normandy. We knew it was there. But we were wrong in supposing that it could not fight effectively; *its battle state was far beyond our expectation* [author's italics]. It was quickly brought into action against 1st Airborne Division.[46]

Since Montgomery and his planners underestimated completely the ability of the Germans to rebuild effective fighting formations the threat posed by II SS Panzer Corps was not appreciated. Thus Guards Armoured was sent forward into an exceptionally difficult situation. Even their initial move from the Escaut canal was fraught with danger as John Gorman recorded (see page 1). And yet, as Macksey comments:

> it is ironic that the failure of the gallant episode at Arnhem is better remembered than the heroic attempts by Guards Armoured Division and the infantry supported by 8 Armoured Brigade to reach the embattled airborne division across the saturated ground leading northward out of Eindhoven.

And heroic is an apt description of the efforts made by the Guards to reach the beleaguered airborne soldiers. The Guards themselves heaped praise on the Typhoon pilots who provided excellent close support and were on hand to answer calls to deal with dug-in enemy positions, especially anti-tank guns, and knowing 'just where our own tanks and men were … shot up everything else in all directions; many targets were engaged within a hundred yards of our own troops, but nevertheless no casualties as a result were reported'.

The Grenadier Group passed through the Irish Group when the latter reached Nijmegen but the US airborne were still about 300 yards short of Nijmegen bridge. Even with the Grenadiers supporting the American infantry the Germans still held the route to the bridge. It was decided to send a US regimental combat team across the river in folding canvas assault boats while every available Guards tank lined up along the riverbank to bombard enemy positions on the Waal's far bank. Eventually the Nijmegen road bridge was taken and the Germans abandoned the town, but the Grenadiers had suffered so many casualties that the Irish Group was again ordered into the lead.

The Irish led off on the morning of the 21st. However, their only route was along a road on a high embankment where tanks became sitting ducks for German anti-tank gunners on a day that RAF Typhoons were not available for support. (General Lewis G. Brereton, the American commander of first Allied Airborne Army, banned No.83 Groups from operating in the Arnhem area.)[47] Nor could the artillery help as the advance had outranged all but one regiment. The Irish advance came to an exhausted and frustrated halt eight miles from Arnhem.

> The official report on the last Irish Group battle had said that the tanks had lacked vital support at a critical moment of the battle; but the truth of the matter was that the German resistance had been badly underestimated and the difficulties of the route for armour never truly appreciated. A Guardsman summed it up, 'We all felt pretty terrible about the unfortunate Airborne. Everything combined to stop us reaching them, but we tried so hard and got so near'.[48]

While the main body of Adair's division had been stopped before reaching Arnhem, a patrol of Household Cavalry under David Corbett found its way to Arnhem along byroads and lanes. The route they reconnoitred played an important part in the evacuation of some of 1st Airborne Division.[49]

The division deployed to blunt German counter-attacks, including some supported by Bittrich's panzers. Meanwhile the Desert Rats protected XXX Corps' left flank, 'the long left flank of the Guards and 43rd Divisions who so nearly succeeded in relieving the 1st Airborne Division at Arnhem'. However, its principal task was to clear the road between Eindhoven and Veghel, the centre line of XXX Corps, of enemy troops. The road 'was not a good one, narrow and embanked most of the way, and running through flat sandy fields, interspersed by considerable stretches of birch and pine forests', all providing cover for the enemy and restricting the manoeuvre of tanks.

Needless to say the cutting of the road had created 'appalling' traffic congestion north of Eindhoven with long queues of Guards echelon vehicles waiting to get through. On the 25th the Inniskilling Dragoon Guards:

reached St Oedenrode, three and three-quarter miles south of Veghel, against considerable opposition from enemy bazookas, who were still across the road, supported by a Panther, and in the woods to the east of it, but patrols of the 101st United States Airborne Division were contacted coming down from Veghel. The following afternoon the centre line was once more cut by a small raiding party supported by a Panther. This was eventually driven off, although the enemy still remained in some strength within a few thousand yards of the road, around Olland and north-west of Veghel, and the centre line was subjected to a considerable amount of harassing fire between Veghel and St Oedenrode. Armoured patrols had, however, reached five thousand yards to the north-west to the railway line at Schijndel.

Seventh Armoured remained in this general area until the line was stabilized, patrolling, beating off enemy counter-attacks and building up a picture of enemy dispositions. There were many casualties, including two Honeys (Stuarts) and a Cromwell of 1 RTR 'lost to bazookas in a very few minutes' close to Nulands Vinkel and, in general, 'it was a monotonous and depressing period'.

Eleventh Armoured was also drawn into the operations, if only on the periphery; it seemed that Arnhem was exercising a magnetic attraction on Montgomery's forces. Roberts' division's advance was part of VIII Corps' operations to protect XXX Corps' right flank and involved actions against enemy infantry and armour. On 21 September 23rd Hussars, pushing beyond Nunen, engaged seven Panthers and a Tiger. Two Panthers were knocked out and the others withdrew under a storm of British artillery fire. By the 25th the division had achieved its objectives, cut the Venlo-Helmond railway, pushed beyond Deurne towards Bakel, and taken Helmond. Tragically, at this point, while Brigadier Harvey of 29 Brigade, was holding an O Group with the COs of his two leading units, Lieutenant Colonels Silvertop (3 RTR) and Orr (3rd Monmouths), they were caught up in a minor scrap between a pair of German halftracks and 15th/19th Hussars in which Harvey was wounded, although only slightly, Silvertop and Orr were killed and 29 Brigade's brigade major was wounded seriously.

There followed a period of hard fighting and relatively slow progress. The Germans were trying to win time until winter made operations all but impossible, thereby preventing Allied intrusion into Germany. Enemy forces were defending Walcheren, Beveland and South Zeeland in the west. It would take a major operation by First Canadian Army to eject them and open the Scheldt estuary to shipping. In the centre of the line the Germans were happy to withdraw across the Maas, which allowed them to economize on troops, but they wanted to hold western Holland with the launch sites for V-weapons targeted on Antwerp and Britain and bases for fast attack boats to intercept Allied shipping in the Scheldt estuary.

During October First Canadian Army supported by 79th Armoured Division cleared the Breskens pocket, South Beveland and Walcheren island. Elsewhere in the Low Countries Guards and 11th Armoured Divisions helped widen the Allied salient along the Maas and from Nijmegen to Geertruidenberg. As usual the Germans defended with determination, retreating only when under great pressure. Nonetheless 2nd Fife and Forfar Yeomanry could claim the distinction of firing the first rounds onto German soil when five 17-pounder shots were discharged across the frontier.

Fighting in flat lands, where villages and copses provided ready-made strongpoints and a myriad of waterways a network of obstacles, strung together by minefields, there was little hope of rapid progress. Tanks and infantry, closely supported by artillery, carefully probed ahead, blasting each potential ambush position, warily scanning for the lurking tank or self-propelled gun which might loose off to kill the leading tank prior to retiring to its next delaying position.

In spite of the difficulties it was clear that the British armoured divisions were working like well-oiled machines, and the same was true of the independent armoured brigades and tank brigades. By this stage infantry divisions could depend on having an armoured brigade under command while the specialized armour of Hobart's 79th Armoured Division was available as necessary and played a critical part in most operations. Even regiments from one of the armoured divisions might be detached to work alongside units from an infantry division, as when the Inniskillings of 7th Armoured Division were detached to support 53rd (Welsh) Division in the successful attack on s'Hertogenbosch. This operation also included other elements of 7th Armoured and 'Funnies' from 79th. It was clear that the British Army had come a long way since the beginning of the war and had now achieved the levels of flexibility shown by the German army. Co-operation between armour, artillery, infantry, other arms and the tactical air forces had reached a level that the Germans could only dream of. But the German army remained a formidable opponent as 11th Armoured Division found when it took over part of the Maas sector north of Venlo and attacked a German outpost at Brockheizen: 3rd Monmouths suffered heavily, losing ten officers and 130 men including, among the fatalities, their new CO.

The Desert Rats ended October with further operations alongside infantry formations north of Tilburg. This was hard fighting conducted as 'an infantry battle at an infantry pace'. For ten days the division fought in Western Brabant 'with its dykes, embanked roads and frequent woods, [and] swift armoured movement was only possible when virtually unopposed'. For the loss of 'twenty-two tanks and a considerable number in killed and wounded' 7th Armoured accounted for eight SPGs, twelve anti-tank guns of varying calibres and about 800 casualties. But it was not country in which the Cromwells were at their best since they could not manoeuvre and use their considerable speed. Thus the division was happy to learn that it was being withdrawn from the line. On 10 November it moved to concentrate in the Bree area, although 22 Armoured Brigade was left behind temporarily. Twelve days later the division said goodbye to Major General Verney, who was succeeded by Major General Lewis Lyne. D'Este comments that Verney was removed by Dempsey because he could not cure the division's bad habits;[50] the Desert Rats were still seen as being too careful.

Guards Armoured remained in the Nijmegen area for over a month, resting, refitting and training for further operations. Although units had operational responsibilities, calls on them were few. The Irish Group had two tasks: 2nd (Armoured) Battalion came under command of 82nd (US) Airborne in Nijmegen while the 3rd Battalion guarded Nijmegen's bridges against attack by land, air or water. It was an unusual and interesting role with a certain degree of risk from shellfire or bombing; in one raid a German jet dropped a stick of bombs outside Battalion HQ, killing Lieutenant P. G. E. Sarsfield Hall. The Grenadiers also deployed on bridge-guarding duties, their task being to watch over the six bridges across the Maas and the Maas-Waal canal, which were vital for the logistic support of the troops in the Nijmegen area.

In mid-November XXX Corps moved to relieve the northernmost elements of Ninth US Army and the Guards assumed responsibility for the area from Geilenkirchen to the Maas with Sittard as the hub of operations. The division spent over five weeks at Sittard. Involved in patrolling they saw no action other than occasional enemy shelling. Casualties were light, although the Coldstream lost two men to mines and the Irish Guards two to an enemy shell that struck 3rd Battalion HQ. Then preparations began for Operation SHEARS, for which 7th Armoured was to relieve the Guards in the line; the Guards would then attack through the Desert Rats. However, SHEARS was not to take place. In a preparatory exercise every tank of a Grenadier squadron bogged in soft ground and the operation was postponed. Later it was postponed again and, finally, cancelled. By then it was almost Christmas.

Until now both Guards and 11th Armoured Divisions had been equipped with the Sherman, with Cromwells in their reconnaissance regiments. In October 11th Armoured had been advised that the division would re-equip with the new Comet. An area of northern Belgium, between Ypres and Ostend, had been assigned to 29 Armoured Brigade to receive and train on the Comet. Re-equipment was to begin on 1 December while 15th/19th Hussars, the divisional reconnaissance regiment, would re-equip with Comets in February 1945. By 12 December the Shermans had been handed in at Helmond and Deurne and the brigade moved to Belgium to receive the Comet. Hardly had the programme begun than the Germans launched their Ardennes offensive, leading to what has been dubbed the battle of the Bulge. As a result 29 Armoured Brigade was ordered to reclaim the Shermans and prepare for action again; 4 Armoured Brigade was placed under temporary command of 11th Armoured in its place. Twenty-nine Brigade had a limited role in the subsequent fighting but Roberts wrote that he 'heard that ... [it] had done very well'.

Elements of Guards Armoured also deployed to meet the German threat and were stationed close to 29 Armoured Brigade. When the Germans engaged 29 Armoured, 32 Guards Brigade Group was despatched to assist and held part of the line until relieved by 5 Parachute Brigade of 6th Airborne Division. Although 7th Armoured Division was on full alert, the Desert Rats were not in action, except against German aircraft, although, due to the Germans using English-speaking soldiers disguised as Americans, they arrested 'a number of innocent American officers and soldiers who had decided that Christmas was as good a time as any for visits to their girlfriends in our area'. On Christmas night the Desert Rats heard German soldiers singing 'Stilige Nacht' across no man's land and responded in kind; the divisional choir had taken part in a BBC Christmas broadcast from 21st Army Group (British army groups adopted the ordinal designation in December 1944).

Neither Guards nor 11th Armoured Divisions would return to the offensive until February 1945 but the Desert Rats were involved in January's Operation BLACKCOCK. Postponed since December the intention was to bring the Allied line up to the Roer river on a front of about twelve miles, clearing the Roer triangle, and 7th Armoured was given a major role plus an additional armoured brigade – 8 Armoured – and 155 Infantry Brigade from 52nd (Lowland) Division for the first phase. Frosty weather ensuring hard ground allowed tanks to operate effectively and, over more than a week, the Desert Rats and their comrades, assisted by Funnies from 79th Armoured Division – including Kangaroos transporting infantry – fought their way forward against stiff opposition and achieved their objectives in spite of many difficulties. The operation was:

> remarkable in two particulars, first, for the successful employment of an armoured division in mid-winter, over snow, and, secondly, as the first occasion that the Division had ever operated with Commando troops.

A very well planned system of traffic control had allowed the division to deploy its brigades and units. All forward movement took place over a single one-way road, relying on liaison officers with radios posted at every junction, who kept watch for four days and nights. The Commando co-operation was marked by the posthumous award of the Victoria Cross to a Royal Army Medical Corps soldier, Lance Corporal Henry Harden (the sole RAMC VC of the war) on 23 January. Although co-operating with tanks for the first time, the men of 45 (RM) Commando 'fell into the drill at once'.

The Desert Rats remained along the Maas until 21 February, a 'period of little activity', although the division was briefly under command of XVI US Corps, the only time it served under American command; it had been part of every British and Canadian corps in 21st Army Group. In the meantime Operation VERITABLE, the battle of the Reichswald, opened on 8 February to clear the area between the Maas and Rhine rivers. VERITABLE was a 21st Army Group operation involving three armies, as Ninth US Army was still under Montgomery's command; Ninth Army's element, codenamed GRENADE, was the southernmost part of the advance. First Canadian Army was to carry out the northernmost thrust while Second British Army advanced through the Reichswald. That British thrust was entrusted to Horrocks' XXX Corps, reinforced for the purpose. Initially largely an infantry operation, both Guards and 11th Armoured were committed as it progressed.

Horrocks described VERITABLE as 'the biggest operation I had ever handled in war'. XXX Corps was 200,000 strong on 8 February and the attack was made by nine divisions supported by 1,400 guns. Had the operation been launched when originally intended, it might have had the advantage of hard frozen ground but a thaw had begun and the chief memory for those who fought in the Reichswald was mud. According to Horrocks 'It was so bad that after the first hour every tank going across country was bogged down, and the infantry had to struggle forward on their own.' The tanks to which he referred were the Churchills and Shermans of the tank and independent armoured brigades, and those of 79th Armoured Division.

At first Guards Armoured Division was employed in an infantry role: 32 Guards Brigade reverted to its infantry order of battle. Not until later in the battle did the division operate in its true role and the armoured battalions entered the picture. Before that Roberts' 11th Armoured Division was committed, together with 4th Canadian Armoured. The plan for VERITABLE had envisaged three phases, the first being clearing the Reichswald and securing the Gennerp-Asperden-Kleve line. Phase two was breaching the second German defensive system east and south-east of the Reichswald, capturing the Weeze-Üdem-Kalcar-Emmerich area and its communications, and the final phase was the breakthrough of the Hochwald 'layback' defence lines and the advance to secure the Geldern-Xanten line. Phase two, known to the Canadians as Operation BLOCKBUSTER, had as its principal aim the smashing of the Germans' Schlieffen Position, the last defensive line west of the Rhine. For this phase II Canadian Corps included two Canadian infantry divisions – 2nd and 3rd – and 4th Canadian Armoured Division, as well as 11th Armoured and 43rd (Wessex) Divisions from XXX Corps.

Since 29 Armoured Brigade had departed to re-equip, and then been diverted to the Ardennes fighting, its place in 11th Armoured had been taken by 4 Armoured Brigade. The BLOCKBUSTER action was 'the first and only ... undertaken without 29 Armoured Brigade' and was also an action the nature of which demanded that the infantry take the lead. Moreover, the fighting was to be done at night as well as in daylight over a battlefield 'more systematically laid waste than any over which we fought before or after'. In many respects the battle resembled one from the Great War, with advances in small stages. Since the front was so narrow and there were few roads, the plan was to leapfrog groups of armour and infantry through each other.

The first group into action was the Royal Scots Greys with 4 KSLI who fought a night action under real and artificial moonlight that took them, after much hard fighting, to the railway line south-west of Üdem, having captured 350 Germans, four SPGs and two tanks. The Canadians had occupied Üdem but, with the locus of enemy opposition south of the railway and east of the Greys' position, it was decided to amend the plan by mopping up these defenders at the same time as taking the Gochfortzberg feature, the next element of the original plan. And so 159 Brigade Group tackled the Gochfortzberg while 4 Armoured Brigade Group dealt with the Germans ensconced south of the railway. The latter attack went in first, on the last morning of February, with 44 RTR and 2nd King's Royal Rifle Corps (2 KRRC) advancing over difficult ground with few tracks against determined opposition and many *panzerfauste* parties. At 2.30pm 3/4 CLY and the Herefords launched their attack on Gochfortzberg with strong artillery support and, within two hours, took the feature and 120 prisoners. Although attempts to advance over the crest eastward brought down heavy enemy fire, the German line was weakening and the Canadians made good progress, having taken the high ground east of Üdem, and were testing the Hochwald defences. As a result 159 Brigade's orders were to make a nocturnal advance towards the Schlieffen Line and Sonsbeck.

That advance was not easy, the ground being treacherous enough for several tanks of 15th/19th Hussars to bog. A small stream required a bridge but the approaches were not firm enough to support a 'scissors' bridging tank and a bridgehead had to be established before dawn. A crossing for tanks was ready by noon the next day, created by bulldozers and AVREs dropping fascines; once more Hobart's Funnies came into their own. Advancing was still difficult, especially as tanks had to stay on the roads, and enemy artillery fire was heavy, but 3rd Canadian Division had relieved the Herefords and Green Jackets and, later that evening, the 15th/19th Hussars/Herefords were able to pass through the Monmouths' forward positions to meet the first positions of the Schlieffen defences a mile farther on.

More hard fighting followed over waterlogged ground and, although one arm of the division's advance was stopped by tanks bogging and the infantry meeting heavy machine-gun fire, another road was found that allowed the advance to move on. Next day further progress was achieved and by 3 March the division was within a mile of Sonsbeck where they were relieved by Canadian troops, withdrawn from the advance and bade farewell to 4 Armoured Brigade on the 7th before moving into a rest area in Belgium where 29 Armoured Brigade, now equipped with Comets, re-joined.

Guards Armoured had put the full divisional strength into VERITABLE after the armoured brigade joined the infantry at Nijmegen on 21 February. Two days later the tanks juddered to the front along the railway track between Gennep and Goch. For the first and only time in the campaign the division fought alongside 6 Guards Armoured Brigade, originally its second brigade (it had been 6 Guards Tank Brigade until 2 February). But the Guards were in almost a spectators' role to begin with as 11th Armoured and 3rd Canadian Divisions fulfilled their phase of the operation. In fact it was not until 2 March that the division was ordered to prepare to fight in its usual regimental groups. Once more the Irish Group was to lead.

Opposition was strong and a revised plan became necessary as the Irish Group made for the wooded ridge between Kapellen and Bonninghardt. Consolidating on the village of Hamb, less than a mile below, one troop deployed to the ridge. All four tanks were hit by anti-tank-gun fire but only one had to be abandoned; the others occupied the high ground until reinforcements arrived. An infantry platoon joined them before dawn and the little group seized a nearby feature, although two tanks bogged. Then followed a morning of sharp fighting in which six tanks were knocked out but the Germans were driven off. With the Irish Group through to Kapellen it was the turn of the Grenadier Group which met yet more doughty opposition but took an important road junction and two dozen prisoners; two enemy SPGs were knocked out.

Fighting continued in this vein. Bonninghardt fell to a 32 Brigade attack with the Welsh Group supported by 2nd Scots Guards in their first action in the campaign (the Scots were to replace 1st Welsh Guards who had suffered heavy losses). Resistance had been strong in the village where the defenders were Fallschirmjäger, from General Schlemm's First Parachute Army. One German CO asked 'Have I the honour to be with First Guards Panzer Division?' and when told that he was 'stated that he was satisfied and added that he was very impressed with the good treatment he had received at the hands of his captors'. He was one of 243 prisoners.

Ninth US Army had also made good progress and the Rhineland battle was nearing its end. As American and British fronts came into increasing contact, XXX Corps had swung to the north-east and Guards Armoured had passed through 3rd British Division en route for Kapellen. By night-time on 6 March the Americans were reaching Rheinberg, 53rd (Welsh) Division was south of Alpen and Adair's division had taken Bonninghardt and the high ground. But the Germans were still fighting hard and shelling the forward slopes of the Kapellen-Bonninghardt ridge, inflicting casualties on the Guards. Thirty-two Brigade was ordered to act as a pivot between 52nd (Lowland) Division on the right and 4th Canadian Armoured on the left as the final advance to take the Wesel bridge was launched. And so the final act of VERITABLE began.

Attacks began on the 6th but not until the 9th did 4th Canadian Armoured, 2nd Canadian Infantry, 43rd (Wessex) and 52nd (Lowland) Divisions accomplish their tasks. So, too, had Guards Armoured. Theirs had been to cut the main road following the Rhine's left bank. That road lay some two miles forward of the ridge with, halfway between the two, a railway line that, like the road, connected Rheinberg and Xanten. To add to the Guards' problems the line was embanked, as was another that crossed it at right angles. A Scots/Welsh group was ordered to secure the railway crossover point on the afternoon of 7 March with the Coldstream Group, if needed, passing through to cut the road. The Coldstream Group awaited the order to advance to the main road but first a German strongpoint on the right flank, known as Haus Loo, had to be knocked out or its fire suppressed. Nonetheless, the Coldstream went forward in two well-balanced groups – a half-squadron of tanks with each of two companies.

No. 2 Company soon reported heavy firing at close range both from the front and from Haus Loo on the right and was told to slow down until Captain Watkins could find another way to bring his tanks up. This he soon did and together they doggedly fought their way forward to the objective, with No. 3 Company following close behind. As they reached the main road, however, where there were numerous houses affording good cover, the opposition became very stiff and the shelling even heavier ... While consolidating Lieutenant Malcolm Lock's tank received a direct hit in the turret; all the crew were badly wounded and he himself, who had done brilliantly, in the battle, died shortly afterwards.

The divisional historians described VERITABLE 'as one of the stiffest battles ever fought by troops of the division, and the steady and resolute way in which the attack was pressed home under particularly adverse conditions was beyond all praise'. The Coldstream felt very proud: 'Guards Armoured Division had broken Schlemm's lateral near Menzelen after a very stiff fight'. That forced the Germans to withdraw across the Rhine, blowing the remaining bridges in the process.

Operation PLUNDER, the Rhine crossing, was the next major operation for 21st Army Group. Second British Army was to cross at three main points: Rees (XXX Corps) and Xanten and Wesel (XII Corps) with airborne landings (Operation VARSITY) on the XII Corps front to capture bridges beyond the Rhine. About seven miles upstream Ninth US Army was to cross at Dinslaken. PLUNDER was to be launched on the night of 23/24 March with no armoured divisions involved immediately, other than 79th with its Funnies. The Desert Rats were the first armoured division to cross the Rhine, beginning on the morning of the 27th, followed by Guards the next day while 11th Armoured was to move up from Belgium, also on the 28th.

On 27 March 11th Hussars led 7th Armoured across the great river and forward to link up with 6th Airborne Division at Hamminkeln. The Inniskillings followed and were engaged by some enemy soldiers at a blown bridge between Brunen and Raesfeld. Over the next two days 22 Armoured Brigade led the advance on a three-regimental front with 5 RTR on the left, Inniskillings in the centre and 1 RTR on the right. Initially the heaviest opposition faced 5 RTR who reached Borken on the night of the 28th, having seen much fighting, taken some ninety prisoners and killed another fifty Germans, to find the Skins and 9th Durhams there already; opposition along their route had been light. Although it was early spring tanks were confined generally to the roads as the fields were very wet and many that ventured off road became bogged. Other impediments to progress included huge craters from Allied bombing while small groups of Germans held out in many places, some occupying strongpoints such as fortified houses, others using natural cover, and frequently with their handheld anti-tank weapons.

Meanwhile the Guards were also across the Rhine as the spearhead of XXX Corps. Directed on Groenlo and Enschede, en route to Bremen and Hamburg, the division set off in the early hours of the morning of Good Friday, 30 March, the Grenadier Group leading. Having crossed the Rhine the head of the column passed through

Anholt and Dinxperlo and then east almost to Bocholt, which was still held by the Germans and where the King's Company/No. 2 Squadron Group 'had its first taste of unpleasantness in the shape of a road block of felled trees and mines'. Craters and road blocks, covered by fire, reduced the speed of the advance but by midday the Grenadiers were in Aalten where opposition was much fiercer and the Irish Group was deployed to the left to attack Aalten from the west. In spite of bridging problems the Guards were in Aalten that afternoon and had a firm grip on the town by nightfall. The speed of the advance from the Rhine may not have been news-making but it represented the best advance to date on XXX Corps' front. When the advance was resumed at dawn next day a squadron of Household Cavalry passed through the Grenadiers who were still leading.

The divisional advance continued as a litany of small towns and small actions, with battlegroups working in harmony to overcome enemy defences and the artillery and tactical air playing their parts to good effect. Both brigade groups made good progress on their diverging axes with the Coldstream Group able to move fast on secondary roads, although they met strong opposition at Borculo on the Berkel river. The Household Cavalry demonstrated their finely honed reconnoitring skills again and again, finding intact bridges that facilitated good progress or routes to outflank strongpoints. Most were aware that the war was almost over but equally aware that the German soldier, defending his homeland, was as tenacious as ever, although the cohesion of German units and formations was not comparable to what it had been in the past.

On 3 April the Coldstream Group was in the lead when the Household Cavalry reported a bridge still intact across the Ems river leading to the small town of Altenlingen. However, it was covered by a determined force of infantry with three anti-tank guns, identified as 88s, and was prepared for demolition. Although the Coldstream Group was ordered to seize the bridge it seemed that this could not be done before the enemy destroyed it due to a strong roadblock that prevented tanks rushing the bridge. However, Captain Ian Liddell, commanding a company of 5th Coldstream, having deployed his two forward platoons to the near bank, sprinted forward alone to the bridge, scaled the ten-foot high roadblock in front of it and neutralized the charges, which were clearly visible.

> [H]e had to cross the whole length of the bridge … under intense enemy fire, which increased as his object became apparent to the Germans. Having disconnected the charges on the far side, he re-crossed … and cut the wires on the near side. It was necessary for him to kneel, forming an easy target whilst he successively cut the wires.
>
> He then discovered that there were also charges underneath the bridge and completely undeterred he also disconnected these. His task completed he then climbed up on to the road block in full view of the enemy and signalled his leading platoon to advance.
>
> Thus alone and unprotected, without cover and under heavy enemy fire, he achieved his object. The bridge was captured intact and the way cleared for the advance across the river Ems.[51]

And so the advance continued. Horrocks commented that this had been 'a magnificently planned, perfectly timed and bravely executed action'.[52] It earned the Victoria Cross for Captain Liddell who did not live to know that. He was killed in action on 21 April, the very day another member of Guards Armoured earned a posthumous VC.

That posthumous VC went to Guardsman Edward Charlton of the Irish Guards. Horrocks commented that 'Slowly – too slowly for my liking – we penetrated deeper into Germany. The Guards Armoured, 3rd Division, 43rd (Wessex) and 51st (Highland) Divisions all took a hand.'[53] Soon it became clear to Horrocks that XXX Corps would have to take the city of Bremen, a task for which he felt the corps was 'not properly balanced'. However, a plan was worked out with Montgomery and XXX Corps continued towards Bremen with 52nd (Lowland) Division under command and Guards Armoured shifting temporarily to XII Corps to advance on the left of 7th Armoured. This helped isolate the Germans in Bremen by eliminating the garrison in the Zeven area and taking Stade in the Cuxhaven peninsula.

On 18 April one Guards group encountered strong resistance south of Visselhövede but the town was captured next day, although 2nd German Naval Division launched a counter-attack that penetrated to the group HQ before being beaten off in a two-hour battle. A German regimental commander and about 440 men were captured. The other attacking Guards group met much less opposition and advanced to within four miles of Zeven. Next day, the 20th, both Grenadier and Irish Groups made good progress, although there were still pockets of determined opposition and casualties resulted. The Irish Group captured the ordnance unit of a German marine division and its chief of staff at Elsdorf, the unit having driven up the road unaware of the presence of the Guards. The chief of staff's capture brought intelligence that the marine formation was not moving towards Bremen or Hamburg. However, the following morning a sharp German attack was launched on an Irish Guards troop/platoon group post at Wistedt.

The attack was made by a company-sized group led by two SPGs, one of whose first rounds hit the Sherman posted as sentry in that direction. As any Sherman crewman would have expected, the tank immediately burst into flames. The crew baled out, but the driver, Guardsman Edward Charlton, saw the German infantry running down the road and climbed back onto the Sherman, removed the Browning machine gun from the turret and leapt onto the road to confront them.

He faced them four-square, firing steadily. A bullet struck his left arm; he moved to a gate in the hedge and supported his arm on the top bar, still firing. His left arm was hit again, and he propped the Browning on the gate, firing and loading it with one hand. A final burst of fire shattered his right arm, and Charlton collapsed by the gate, the Browning on top of him. The Germans swept over him, but Charlton had ruined for them the effect of their sudden attack; the platoon and the other tanks had recovered themselves. The Germans carried Charlton away, but he was already dying, and there was nothing they could do for him except bury him with the honour he deserved.[54]

(Some time later a German officer who had taken part in the attack, and was then in a prisoner-of-war camp, was brought to the Irish Guards to show them Charlton's grave because he had talked so much about his bravery.[55] Charlton's posthumous Victoria Cross was the last VC of the European war and was unusual in that much of the information in the citation came from German officers and NCOs who had witnessed more of his valour than had his comrades.)

The German attack continued with two more Shermans, including the Firefly, hit and set on fire but reinforcements came down the autobahn from Sittensen, catching and beating off another five SPGs en route and helping persuade the Germans in Wistedt to depart for Zeven.

Such was the nature of the engagements in which Guards Armoured was involved and which proved the effectiveness of the group system, whether at battalion, squadron/company or troop/platoon level. The advance continued with Rotenburg falling after unsuccessful attempts to persuade the local commander to surrender peacefully; Zeven was taken by the Grenadiers and Coldstream on 24 April. Towns and villages were taken, a prisoner-of-war camp was liberated and still the tanks rumbled onwards. It was clear to all that the war was almost over but still there was determined opposition, not least from 15th PanzerGrenadier Division. Also facing the Guards were the SS guards of Sandbostel camp, which the division liberated only to discover the horror of the Nazis' 'final solution'. Horrocks wrote that until then he had felt no particular hatred for his enemy but he saw 'a ghastly picture' on entering Sandbostel with Sir Allan Adair.

> The floor of the first large hut was strewn with emaciated figures clad in most horrible striped pyjamas. Many of them were too weak to walk but they managed to heave themselves up and gave us a pathetic cheer. Most ... had some form of chronic dysentery and the stench was so frightful that I disgraced myself by being sick in a corner. It was difficult to believe that most of these hardly human creatures had once been educated, civilized people.[56]

So appalled was Horrocks at what he saw in the camp that he ordered the local burgomasters to supply a quota of German women to clean up the camp and care for the prisoners.

The next objective for Guards Armoured was Bremervörde and the nearby German naval experimental station which was handed over without a fight, although there had been delays reaching there due to cratered roads. As the advance to Bremervörde continued it met heavy fire but eventually the Irish Group overcame the German marine battalion defending the canal bridge there; however, an attempt to rush the bridge failed and the task of crossing the canal was assigned to 51st (Highland) Division.

Guards Armoured Division now had 1 HCR, recently transferred from Italy, as an armoured car regiment as well as 2 HCR and the unit soon proved itself as good as its sister regiment in the reconnaissance role while leading the division north to Stade to dominate the Elbe estuary. Stade fell to guardsmen who had already heard of the death of Hitler and knew that German resistance must soon collapse as enemy determination seemed to have waned considerably. On 2 May Horrocks informed Adair that the Germans on XXX Corps' front had offered to surrender unconditionally. No further advance was to be made unless specific orders were received. Local German officials were surrendering and 1 HCR took intact the bridge over the Oste near Burweg, even though demolition charges had been laid; the defenders, forty in number, surrendered happily. However, there was one final tragedy when a West Somerset Yeomanry OP tank was blown up on a sea mine over which an armoured car squadron and five tanks had already driven. The crew of the OP tank, including Captain Richard Wheaton, the FOO, were all killed. That evening the division learned that hostilities would end officially at 8am next day, 5 May.

Both 7th and 11th Armoured Divisions had experiences similar to those of the Guards as they advanced into Germany from the Rhine. The Desert Rats, with 22 Armoured Brigade commanding the leading troops, pushed up to the Ems and the airfields at Rheine, 'often fighting three separate actions at one time'. Almost every village was fought over and, like Guards Armoured, the story is one of co-operation at regiment/battalion, squadron/company and troop/platoon levels, of:

> road blocks stormed or by-passed, innumerable bridges built and miles of road opened up by the Royal Engineers, and all the time a few more casualties every day and a steadily mounting bag of prisoners. Sometimes the infantry would be carried in armoured troop-carriers, and these fully proved their worth. Always there were the wide and fruitful reconnaissances by the 11th Hussars out to the flanks and as far as it was possible to get ahead, with a never-ending stream of valuable information.

As the division developed an over-long left flank – progress was slower on the left – 155 Brigade of 52nd (Lowland) Division was placed under command to cover it. There, too, resistance was stronger with hand-held weapons the greatest menace. German infantry would lie concealed by the roadside or near a roadblock 'and with one discharge from their cheap single-shooters could immobilize or destroy a tank'. One tactic used to counter this threat was for advancing tanks to hose the roadsides with their machine guns. Otherwise, where possible, travelling fast reduced greatly the chances of a hit.

Seventh Armoured used the bridgehead developed by 11th Armoured to attack through the Teutoburger Wald, a wooded ridge, at Ibbenburen and advance to the Weser river south of Bremen. Ibbenburen proved a difficult town as it was garrisoned by officer cadets and NCOs from a nearby tactical school who fought with great skill and tenacity and made best use of the nearby woods' natural cover. Nonetheless, the town was taken but it was a hard-fought advance with individual houses being used as strongpoints and defenders fighting back from blazing ruins. The attack was made by a squadron of Inniskillings and a company of Durhams after the Devons had secured the high ground. It was reinforced by a flank attack launched by 155 Brigade and then by troops of 53rd (Welsh) Division. Only when the Welshmen arrived and entered the fray did the battle end. It had taken most of two days and cost many lives.

From Ibbenburen the division advanced to Diepholz via a bridge over the Weser-Ems canal that was captured by 5 RTR. Later 7th Armoured was directed on Bremen but not committed to what was an infantry task. Relieved by 3rd Division the Desert Rats moved north-east to Nienberg where the Welsh division had crossed the Weser but met fierce opposition from German marines on the Aller at Rethem. On 11 April 5 RTR deployed to support the Welsh and 'after destroying eight 88s and some other guns they and the infantry with them fought their way into the town'. Two nights later 53rd Division secured a crossing over the Aller and, on the 14th, 4 Armoured Brigade crossed; 2nd Devons went with them.

From the Rethem bridgehead 7th Armoured advanced via Walsrode to Soltau, their progress impeded by craters, roadblocks and booby-traps but 1 RTR were two miles from Soltau as night fell on 16 April. That day saw the liberation of a large prison camp at Fallingbostel where the inmates had already taken charge under command of RSM Lord of the Grenadiers who had been captured at Arnhem with 1st Airborne Division. Soltau was by-passed by 22 Armoured Brigade, leaving 155 Brigade, supported by the Inniskillings and Churchill Crocodile flamethrowers of 7 RTR, to deal with the town. The main advance continued in spite of bad going on very boggy roads. By the 19th Tostedt and Bucholz had been taken. From there the division was charged with cutting the Bremen-Hamburg autobahn and capturing Harburg, as well as clearing large numbers of enemy soldiers from the forests north of Soltau, 'a long and tedious task'.

A wide gap had opened between 7th and 11th Armoured Divisions and was covered by armoured-car patrols from 11th Hussars and the Inns of Court while the Desert Rats' left flank was completely open, although Guards Armoured was moving up on that flank en route to Bremervörde. The Irish Hussars and the Queen's, with support from Typhoons, cut the autobahn at Hollenstedt on 19 April and the advance continued in the face of continuous opposition. Harburg was reached on the 20th and a battle for the town began, although the blowing of the last bridge over the Elbe led to an investment of the town. Meanwhile, Buxtehude was taken where the prisoners included an admiral and 'several hundred of the German Navy's women's service' who were 'of forbidding appearance and of pronounced Nazi ideas'.

With VIII Corps over the Elbe and 11th Armoured and 6th Airborne Divisions on the shores of the Baltic, while the Red Army was approaching Berlin, the end of the war was near. Until the final German surrender 7th Armoured was clearing the country to the south and south-west of Harburg, maintaining the cordon around the town, fighting off occasional counter-attacks and, in the enemy pocket close to Soltau, 1 RTR and the Household Cavalry with 160 Brigade of 53rd (Welsh) Division carried out a sweep and took many prisoners. By then 'the air was filled with rumours of German surrender' and before long the first real signs of this were apparent in the divisional area. On 29 April a deputation approached the lines and was taken to 131 Brigade HQ, although the two staff officers involved (there was also a civilian) blew themselves up on a German minefield on their return journey. Three days later

General Wolz arrived at Divisional HQ and thus began the chain of events that led to a local surrender on 3 May.

Formal overall capitulation followed on 5 May and the long journey of the Desert Rats that had begun in Egypt's sands was over at last. The division's role was recognized officially when it took pride of place in the Victory Parade in Berlin on 21 July 1945. On that occasion Winston Churchill addressed them and said of their long journey from Egypt to the Baltic that it was 'a march unsurpassed through all the story of war so far as my reading of history leads me to believe'. He also said:

> May your glory ever shine! May your laurels never fade! May the memory of this pilgrimage never die! May the fathers long tell the children about this tale! May you all feel that in following your great ancestors you have accomplished something which has done good to the whole world; which has raised the honour of your own country and which every man has a right to be proud of.

Seventh Armoured's position in the parade that July day and Churchill's tribute provided the coda to the symphony of the Desert Rats' wartime service.

For 11th Armoured the European campaign ended on the shores of the Baltic. Their final lap had also begun on the Rhine before fighting their way through a myriad of small and nasty actions costing many lives. The division was once again in VIII Corps, now commanded by Lieutenant General 'Bubbles' Barker, with 6th Airborne Division as the other major component. Their Comets were 'a real morale booster' and inspired confidence in the crews that they could meet Panthers or Tigers on much better terms than with Shermans. Directed on Holtwick and then Osnabruck the division was on the left flank of VIII Corps. At first progress was good with more delays caused by the state of the roads than by enemy resistance as 'the enemy, though still capable of obstinate defence, was in no state to mount a counter-attack' even when opportunities for such were presented.

An unusual feature of the advance was an attack by Luftwaffe aircraft on 1 April during which four Focke Wulf 190s were shot down by the guns of 58th LAA Regiment. Roberts described this as 'about the best day our AA regiment had in the whole campaign'. Next day the advance continued over the Teutoburger Wald with the 3rd Monmouths/2nd Fife and Forfar Group clearing woods on high ground west of the axis of advance while 15th/19th Hussars advanced along the road skirting the southern edge of the escarpment to Brochterbeck.

> Anybody who feels queasy about the long-term effects of mechanization on the élan of cavalry regiments would have had his doubts notably allayed by the performance of 15th/19th Hussars on 2 April 1945. While one squadron was blasting its way into Brochterbeck, a village which showed no inclination to put out white flags, the remainder of the regiment turned northwards and proceeded to assault the pass. The road from Brochterbeck to Holthausen is flanked, but not bordered, by the woods. Some fifty yards intervenes in most places. There

are, however, numerous isolated trees by the roadside itself; behind any of these a determined man with a bazooka would have been well placed. And it was by infantry with bazookas that the pass was defended. But these defenders must have been completely nonplussed by the speed of the attack; for although the tanks were fired at all the way, not one was stopped. Making full use of the pace of their Comets, the Hussars charged up the long, winding hill. By 1130 they were firmly established at the top.

This success allowed 29 Armoured Brigade to press ahead and the 23rd Hussars/8th Rifle Brigade and 3 RTR/4 KSLI Groups advanced to Tecklenburg, which was defended stubbornly but fell to the Hussars/Rifle Brigade Group. But 159 Brigade Group had not achieved the same success in clearing the woods, which the Germans had reinforced with troops from an NCOs' training school at Hanover. Two separate attempts to dislodge them were beaten off with considerable losses in spite of the tremendous courage of Corporal Edward Chapman. When his section came under heavy machine-gun fire, causing many casualties:

He ordered his men to take cover and went forward alone with a Bren gun, mowing down the enemy at point-blank range [and] causing them to retire. His section isolated, Corporal Chapman again halted the enemy advances with his Bren gun, at one time firing it over his shoulder, to cover those bringing him ammunition. He then carried in his company commander who was lying wounded, but on the way back the officer was killed and Corporal Chapman wounded.[57]

Chapman was awarded the Victoria Cross for his gallantry and survived to receive his Cross. Although the Monmouths were relieved by a battalion from 7th Armoured Division, this was their last operation with 11th Armoured Division. The battalion had sustained so many casualties that it was amalgamated with 2nd Monmouths in 115 Brigade; 1st Cheshire Regiment took their place in 159 Brigade.

Operations continued with a night advance to Osnabruck with 3 RTR/4 KSLI in the lead under a brightly-shining moon and against German opposition that was as staunch under moonlight as in daylight. With a bridge seized intact at Eversheide, the 23rd Hussars/8th Rifle Brigade pushed on to the next objective, taking the bridge over the Ems-Weser canal at Herringhausen after which 3 RTR/4 KSLI leapfrogged forward towards the Weser. In the space of seventy-two hours three water barriers, a dominating feature and Osnabruck had fallen.

German resistance along the Weser was expected to be tough and so it proved. The divisional bridgehead over the river at Stolzenau came under heavy attack with the engineers' bridging site attacked by aircraft including Ju87s, the once-feared Stukas, Ju88s and Fw190s. Ground counter-attacks came from soldiers of 12th SS Panzer Division, among others, but the overwhelming firepower of the Royal Artillery, the support of the Typhoons and Tempests of the Tactical Air Forces and the courage of the soldiers of 159 Brigade and 1 Commando Brigade who joined the operation ground down the opposition and opened the way for the advance to continue. Interestingly, the divisional historian noted that 11th Armoured had not been attacked by enemy tanks since Antwerp although leading units had met and overcome tanks in ones and twos. With no apparent role for the divisional towed 17-pounder batteries, their detachments were re-roled as infantry; the self-propelled 17-pounder batteries were retained since they could fire HE shells and carried heavy machine guns, allowing them to be employed in an offensive role – almost as tanks. And so Todforce came into being, named for Lieutenant Colonel A. F. Todd, its CO, as a battlegroup of two SP 17-pounder batteries/squadrons with two 'de-horsed' batteries/companies, giving Roberts a useful tactical reserve. He commented that Todforce 'had a very high morale and were delighted with their new role'. Todforce was employed on a range of tasks on the left flank to relieve other units for the pursuit.

About this time Roberts and his staff first learned of the existence of Bergen-Belsen concentration camp. The news came from two German officers who approached under a white flag to negotiate a German withdrawal from the area around the camp. This was done and a medical team was sent to Belsen.

Of course it was absolutely ghastly and was the worst and most horrible thing I have ever seen in my life; there was no doubt that the Germans, or at any rate the majority of them, who had been transported in our lorries [on Roberts' orders] were quite genuinely astonished and horrified. Just imagine hundreds of nude bodies being taken out of huts and thrown into enormous mass graves made by bulldozers. I was glad to see the terrible German woman who had been in charge of the place being one of those carrying corpses to the grave.

By 19 April the division was at Lauenberg on the Elbe where the Germans blew the bridge as the leading battlegroup – 3 RTR/4KSLI once again – was approaching. Although local German commanders considered the possibility of laying down their arms and allowing the British free passage in view of the proximity of the Red Army, their senior commanders vetoed the idea.

In retrospect this was a great misfortune. It is now known that it was Eisenhower who ordered Montgomery not to go for Berlin, but this instruction was given after bridges were built over the River Elbe at Lauenberg and Artlenberg by 29 April. If we had crossed the Lauenberg railway bridge on 19 April, I feel sure that we could have had our leading troops twenty-five miles east within twenty-four hours, before Eisenhower was aware of the fact. Could he, or would he, have kept the British out of Berlin? And had we, and by 'we' I mean 21st Army Group, got to Berlin, what a much more suitable 'West' Germany could have developed after the war.

Roberts was wrong in assuming that British troops beating the Red Army – and that was very doubtful anyway – to Berlin would have resulted in a 'more suitable' post-war west Germany since the decision on zones of occupation had already been made by Churchill, Roosevelt and Stalin. No battlefield action was going to change that.

Thus it was that 11th Armoured continued its advance. Crossing the new bridge at Artlenberg on 30 April, two brigade groups set off against sporadic opposition.

... but in places mines had to be cleared, and small villages had to be captured as they were sometimes held by anti-tank guns and say 100 men. It was not difficult but time consuming. However, by the evening of 1 May we had Sandesneben on the right and Gronwold on the left.

Next morning ... we soon crossed the Hamburg-Lübeck autobahn, and by 1500 had occupied Bad Oldesloe and Reinfeld. On our right 2nd Fife and Forfar Yeomanry and 1st Cheshires occupied Sibenbaumen and Kastorf, liberating at the same time a PoW camp, mainly RAF.

But the direction of the divisional advance had been changed and it was directed on Lübeck, one of the Hansa, or Hanseatic League, ports, on the Baltic. At 3.30pm on 2 May the Fife and Forfar/Cheshire Group entered the town against only light opposition while the 23rd Hussars/8th Rifle Brigade Group made for Travemünde and Neustadt. By evening the latter battlegroup was reporting that the naval installations and airfields of the area were in good condition. On the 2nd, 3rd and 4th the division took about 70,000 prisoners, including no fewer than twenty-five generals and admirals, as well as liberating Allied prisoners of war. Not all German troops had given up the fight, however, and a strong SS force was ensconced in the Forst Segeberg with no intention of surrendering. Although the 3 RTR/4 KSLI Group was closest to the SS men, it was not asked to deal with them. Instead, the German 8th Fallschirmjäger Division, which had already surrendered, was ordered to round up the SS. This they did, the SS yielding to their former comrades, with no loss of British lives.

Next day came the official announcement that Montgomery had accepted the unconditional surrender of all German forces facing 21st Army Group. Two days later came news that all German forces had surrendered unconditionally. Meanwhile 11th Armoured was ordered to occupy the province of Schleswig as far as Flensburg on the Danish border. In going for Lübeck and then occupying Schleswig, 11th Armoured ensured that the Red Army would not overrun Schleswig-Holstein and enter Denmark. Thus Roberts' soldiers had made a critical contribution to the shape of the post-war Germany. The division had also achieved the distinction of being the first British troops to fight on the Baltic coast. Liddell Hart wrote of 11th Armoured that 'Within a few months it achieved a reputation in Europe matching that which the long-famous 7th Armoured Division had gained in Africa'. (However, he is incorrect in attributing the creation of mixed brigade groups to 11th Armoured, since that system had already been adopted by the Desert Rats as the war diary of 11th Armoured makes clear.)[58]

For the armoured divisions of 21st Army Group war was over and their task complete. While this chapter has concentrated on the three standard armoured divisions in the

British Army, reference has also been made to 4th Canadian and 1st Polish, which were formed and operated on the British model. An additional Canadian armoured division – 5th – joined the fray in early 1945 when the Canadian Corps that had fought in Italy was transferred to north-west Europe. There might have been one other division on the British model but General Leclerc's 2éme Division Blindée was equipped by the Americans and therefore followed the American template although Leclerc, with his experience of fighting alongside the British in North Africa, had expressed a desire to be incorporated in the British forces for the liberation of France.

Notes

This chapter is based on Ellis, *Victory in the West*, Vols I and II, from the Official History of the War, Liddell Hart, *The Tanks (Vol II)*, Macksey, *Armoured Crusader* and *A History of the Royal Armoured Corps*, Roberts, *From the Desert to the Baltic*, Verney, *The Desert Rats*, Rosse and Hill, *The Story of Guards Armoured Division*, the 1945 histories of 7th and 11th Armoured Divisions (*A Short History of 7th Armoured Division* and *Taurus Pursuant*) and the war diaries of Second Army, I, VIII, XII and XXX Corps, Guards, 7th, 11th and 79th Armoured Divisions, the constituent brigades of the first three named divisions and those of some individual units. Information on the development of artillery and tanks is from Hogg, *British and American Artillery of World War 2* and Hogg and Weeks, *Illustrated Encyclopaedia of Military Vehicles* and other sources are:

1. Neillands, *The Desert Rats*, pp.215–16
2. Reynolds, *Steel Inferno*, p.99
3. Ibid, pp.102–5
4. Ibid, p.102
5. Carver, *Out of Step*, p.183
6. Ibid
7. Reynolds, op cit, p.108
8. Carver, op cit, p.185
9. Eisenhower, *D Day to VE Day*, pp.85–6
10. Anderson, *Cracking Hitler's Atlantic Wall*, p.248
11. Daniels, *Innovation in the Face of Adversity*, p.67
12. Reynolds, *Sons of the Reich*, p.20
13. Baynes, *Forgotten Victor*, pp.192–3
14. Fitzgerald, *History of the Irish Guards in the Second World War*, p.366
15. Ibid
16. Quoted in Ellis, *Victory in the West* Vol I, p.328
17. NA Kew, CAB106/1061
18. Baynes, op cit, pp.204–5
19. Reynolds, *Steel Inferno*, p.172
20. Stacey, *The Victory Campaign*, p.168
21. Quoted in Baynes, op cit, p.206
22. Baynes, op cit, p.201
23. Quoted in ibid, p.202
24. Jarymowycz, *Tank Tactics*, p.115
25. Ibid, pp.115–16
26. Reynolds, *Steel Inferno*, p.176

27. Gorman, *The Times of My Life*, p.38
28. Ibid, pp.38–40
29. NA Kew, WO171/1256
30. Jarymowycz, op cit, p.116
31. Gorman, op cit, p.40
32. Reynolds, op cit, p.186
33. Jarymowycz, op cit, p.116
34. NA Kew, CAB106/1061
35. D'Este, *Decision in Normandy*, p.388
36. Jarymowycz, op cit, p.121
37. Fitzgerald, op cit, p.427
38. Montgomery, *Memoirs*, p.260
39. Quoted in Ellis, p.336
40. Doherty, *Normandy 1944*, pp.237–8
41. NA Kew, WO171/456
42. Lewin, *Montgomery as Military Commander*, pp.227–8
43. Ibid, p.228
44. Reid, *No Holding Back*, pp.362–3
45. Reynolds, *Sons of the Reich*, p.98
46. Montgomery, op cit, p.297
47. Graham and Bidwell, *Coalitions, Politicians and Generals*, p.241
48. Verney, *The Micks*, pp.187–8
49. Gorman, interview with author, Feb 1995
50. D'Este, op cit, pp.388–9
51. *London Gazette*, 7 June 1945
52. Horrocks, *A Full Life*, p.235
53. Ibid, p.262
54. Fitzgerald, op cit, pp.574–5
55. Ibid, p.575
56. Horrocks, op cit, pp.264–5
57. *London Gazette*, 13 July 1945
58. Liddell Hart, *The Tanks*, p.373; NA Kew, WO171/456, war diary 11 Armd Div Jul 1944

Chapter Eleven

Finale in Italy

We left 6th Armoured Division preparing to pursue the Germans along the Tiber valley. At first the advance was led by Adrian Gore's 61 Brigade, which had joined the division on 29 May, a reinforcement prompted by the realization that armoured divisions in Italy required more infantry than the standard lorried brigade and motor battalion. With a dearth of infantry in Italy the new brigade had been created by removing 26 Armoured Brigade's motor battalion, 10th Rifle Brigade, and transferring two other battalions of the Rifle Brigade – 2 and 7 – from their respective divisions, re-roling them as lorried infantry rather than motor battalions. Adrian Gore, who had commanded 10th Rifle Brigade in Tunisia, was appointed to command the new brigade, which was brought up to strength by an influx of former light anti-aircraft gunners whose regiments, now redundant, were disbanding. One such unit had been 117th LAA Regiment which became Green Jackets happily as it had originally been 8th Royal Ulster Rifles before conversion to the gunner role.[1] (There were two other armoured divisions in Eighth Army, 4th Canadian and 6th South African, which also received second infantry brigades. In the case of the South Africans this was 24 Guards Brigade.)

Sixth Armoured's advance took it along the left, or eastern, bank of the Tiber and General Alexander, commanding Allied Armies in Italy, was keen that the advance should be as speedy as possible to maintain pressure on the enemy. For his part the enemy was equally keen to slow the British pursuit. This was achieved by blowing bridges, cratering roads, booby-traps and ambushes, all carried out skilfully, together with delaying actions by 29th and 90th PanzerGrenadier Divisions. The first objectives for 6th Armoured were Narni and Terni, after which the division was to make for Perugia. That Narni and Terni were reached and taken owed much to close co-operation between the arms, including 8th Indian Division which captured Terni.

The division, now transferred to Lieutenant General McCreery's X Corps, advanced with each of its armoured regiments taking the lead in turn, sometimes with the Guards Brigade up with the forward tanks and other times accompanied by the Rifle Brigade. With the self-propelled guns of 12th RHA and the Ayrshire Yeomanry not far behind, it meant that there was always some artillery to hand to deal with any stubborn groups of the enemy. Narni was reached and passed without any more difficulty than had been met at all the other enemy 'pinch points'. The tail of the escaping Germans was not far ahead.

The main problem at Narni was not German opposition, for the enemy had slipped away, but the Nera river that flows through a deep gorge. However, the gorge was bridged by Royal Engineers who built, in twenty-four hours, a 180-foot-long bridge capable of taking Shermans, only one of the 856 Baileys that Allied engineers built that summer. Even the divisional LAA and anti-tank gunners, whose own roles had all but disappeared, worked with the sappers, as the 'Sheldrake Pioneers'. The debt owed to the engineers is illustrated by verses quoted in the history of 17th/21st Lancers:

> The Guards, with battle's chronic thirst,
> Stood waiting for the Sixty-first.
> The Sixty-first, with swords aglow,
> Stood waiting for the Guards to go.
>
> An awkward pause, and then the twain
> Agreed 'twas Armour's turn again.
> The Armour, harboured 'neath a ridge,
> Cried, 'Hi-de, Holdfasts! build that bridge.'[2]

It took the full effort of the armoured and infantry brigades to clear Perugia with every bound forward being met by counter-attack until, on the morning of 20 June, the Guards entered the city to find that the Germans had abandoned it during the night.

Such was the German pattern of withdrawal on both sides of the Tiber (6th South African Armoured Division was leading the advance on the river's far bank). Field Marshal Kesselring was determined to buy time for the Gothic Line to be completed and intermediate lines to be manned to slow the Allied advance. When Kesselring deployed 15th PanzerGrenadier Division on the eastern shore of Lake Trasimene, General Leese, Eighth Army's commander, moved 6th Armoured to XIII Corps on the other shore where 6th South African and 78th (Battleaxe) Divisions had cracked the German line; 78th Division had 9 Armoured Brigade operating under command. Sixth Armoured Division was to exploit the breakthrough and continue Eighth Army's advance past Cortona to the Arno river via Arezzo. The division moved to XIII Corps less 1 Guards Brigade which was left to meet any counter-attacks at Trasimene and thus 26 Armoured and 61 Brigades took over the advance from Cortona from 78th Division.

Along the Chiana valley on Highway 71 the advance moved quickly with the 16th/5th Lancers Battlegroup, which included 10th Rifle Brigade, C Battery of 12 RHA (HAC) and 111 Battery 72nd Anti-Tank Regiment, leading. But, some six miles before Arezzo, the road was dominated by high ground to the right, reaching to the 1,000-foot-high Monte Lignano. The ridge of high ground then descended to form a defile, the l'Olmo Gap, with another peak, Monte Castellare, on the other side. Holding the gap and the high ground either side were troops of 15th PanzerGrenadier Division. With the road deteriorating through cratering the advance slowed.

The first attempts to outflank the German positions by C and B Squadrons of the Lancers were checked by enemy fire and the battlegroup withdrew. Next day the advance was resumed, this time led by Derbyshire Yeomanry and 2nd Lothians with all three battalions of 61 Brigade, but this was also thwarted by effective fire from the high ground. Since the enemy dominated the valley and Highway 71 completely it was clear that progress would be possible only when the high ground was cleared. Major General Evelegh therefore deployed all three infantry battalions supported by a squadron of 17th/21st Lancers and a troop of Derbyshire Yeomanry on a sweep along the ridge to dislodge the Germans.

Although the Green Jackets could get onto the ridge they could not force the enemy off the top. Companies of 10th Rifle Brigade made the first attempts. Their footholds were consolidated and strengthened by the 2nd Battalion but further attempts to evict the occupants failed. Then 7th Rifle Brigade made a night attack and captured Monte Maggio and the enemy observation post there, but could not remove the Germans dug in near the summit on the reverse slope. While the situation had improved a little it seemed as if stalemate was setting in. Fighting continued with the enemy counter-attacks leading to hand-to-hand battle. Eventually, on the night of 9/10 July, 61 Brigade was relieved by a brigade of 8th Indian Division.

The Germans had strengthened their line considerably and the corps commander, deciding to assault in much greater strength, requested reinforcements. Second New Zealand Division was brought forward but took four days to arrive and prepare. Those four days were not wasted as the Germans were bombarded heavily by artillery, including six field, five medium, one heavy and two heavy anti-aircraft regiments – some 200 guns. The fresh attack was launched on 15 July with 6th Armoured's role to make for Arezzo with 26 Armoured Brigade once the high ground had been secured. (At the same time 4th British Infantry and 6th South African Armoured Divisions were to attack towards the Arno farther downstream.)

It took the might of 1 Guards and 6 New Zealand Brigades to force the Germans off the high ground in fighting that was difficult and costly in casualties. Even with the power of the artillery it was clear that two infantry brigades had been necessary. When l'Olmo Gap was found to be clear the tanks of 16th/5th Lancers led 26 Armoured Brigade through towards Arezzo. Opposition was only perfunctory and the town was soon in British hands, the Germans having withdrawn across the Arno towards the Gothic Line. The other two armoured regiments and 10th Rifle Brigade pushed on, taking Quarata and the bridge over the Arno at Ponte a Buriano before the Germans could destroy it. But Kesselring had achieved what he wanted: to delay the Allies sufficiently to allow his own forces to withdraw to the Gothic Line. Remaining with XIII Corps, 6th Armoured advanced along Highway 69 through the Arno valley towards Florence, acting as corps flank defence. However, the main effort during the advance fell on other divisions. Having been outflanked, Florence fell to the Allies on 11 August. All the city's bridges, except the Ponte Vecchio, had been destroyed.

Having been in action for three months – some elements had been committed since the beginning of the year – 6th Armoured Division, now a tired formation, was withdrawn from action so that its soldiers could rest and its vehicles and equipment undergo much-needed maintenance, or be replaced by new. On completion of this spell the division re-joined XIII Corps, which was to transfer to Fifth US Army. Major General Evelegh had said goodbye to the division at the end of July on being posted to the War Office. His successor was Major General Gerald Templer, once the Army's youngest corps commander but who had requested that he revert to major general to command a division on active service. Templer had already proved himself an outstanding infantry GOC with 56th (London) Division in the winter fighting of 1943–44 and the Anzio beachhead. He arrived at HQ 6th Armoured Division on 25 July. Clearly a dynamic commander, one 10th Rifle Brigade officer wrote of him that 'Gerald Templer was a new broom if ever there was one. We were just beginning to feel the impact of his very different style when he was wounded by a mine on the side of the road, set off by a Guards Brigade lorry.'[3]

Templer was wounded on 6 August while driving his jeep to visit some of his units.

> he met a truck coming in the opposite direction. Recognizing the general, the truck driver pulled over to allow the jeep to pass. However, the roadside was mined and the truck struck a mine just as the two vehicles passed. A rear wheel from the truck was blown through the air and struck Templer in the back, crushing him against the steering wheel. His back was broken – his war was over. Even such a serious injury could inspire Templer to humour and he joked that he had been hit by a piano, normal front-line impedimenta for a Guards' battalion. The lorry, which belonged to Headquarters, 1 Guards Brigade, had indeed been carrying a piano; ever afterwards, Templer insisted that the Grenadier Guards were responsible for his injury.[4]

And so 6th Armoured Division received another new GOC, Major General Horatius Murray, known as 'Nap', who came from commanding 153 Brigade of 51st (Highland) Division in north-west Europe and who 'brought with him a realistic outlook to the difficulties of fighting in Italy'. Murray was to command the division until after the war. His attributes were to be put to the test as his division deployed under American command. Fifth Army's commander, General Mark Clark, was an officer of considerable hubris with little respect for British soldiers, although they formed a significant part of his command. And the American operational system was strange to British soldiers. As one CO of a battalion of 38 (Irish) Brigade later wrote:

> The American fighting technique was unusual, and parts of the attack of the United States Army reminded me of scattered elements of a race course crowd surging to greet the winner. Our own men one scarcely saw in the course of an assault, but an American one was quite different. There appeared to be no planning other than the assigning of objectives, and the GIs merely advanced en masse spurning the usual precautions which our own infantry thought necessary. Their casualties from German shellfire were colossal and the overall scene hardly differed from some of their splendid Civil War paintings. 'Pickett's Charge at Gettysburg' had it all.[5]

Thus to all the other frictions of war was added the friction of working under the control of an ally whose approach to battle, and to armoured warfare, was markedly different.

The Allies were preparing for Operation OLIVE, the offensive to break through the Gothic Line and on to the Lombardy Plain where, it was believed, conditions would be much better suited to the deployment of armour. Eighth Army was to attack through the Gothic Line on the eastern side of the Apennines near to the Adriatic coast where there was ground more suited to manoeuvre and, therefore, armour but where defences were much stronger. Alexander's plan called for Eighth Army to deliver a right hook, supported by a hard jab on the left, delivered by Fifth Army straight through the central Apennines towards Bologna; Alexander would decide the timing of that straight left jab.

Both 6th Armoured and 6th South African Armoured Divisions were in XIII Corps under Clark's overall command. Clark also had one US armoured division – 1st, or 'Old Ironsides'. Fifth Army could advance along two main routes from Florence, the main road to Bologna, via the Futa Pass, and the road to Imola, via Il Giogo Pass. Needless to say, the Germans had fortified both routes. Anyone who has driven through the Apennines will appreciate that the terrain itself presented a formidable obstacle and the fortifications, including machine-gun nests, dug-in anti-tank guns and well-camouflaged infantry positions, made that obstacle even more formidable. In addition, every bridge, viaduct and culvert had been prepared for demolition while the many sharp bends and cuttings along the roads had received similar attention. As a result, 'the only way to unlock this combination was for infantry, supplied by mules and jeeps, to clear the heights, for engineers to bridge the obstacle and for tanks and infantry to regain contact at the next obstacle'.[6]

James Wilson's words provide a succinct description of 6th Armoured's experience in the assault on the Gothic Line. Even worse was the fact that it was almost impossible for tanks to operate off the roads as the tracks were frequently too narrow for a Sherman and, in most cases, were terraced into the hillsides and of insufficient strength to bear a Sherman's weight. Once again gunners from the LAA and anti-tank batteries were transferred to help the engineers whose work was critical in such conditions.

On 25 August the division set off along Highway 67, the road to Forlí, with the armoured regiments in turn supporting the move and 61 Brigade providing the infantry; 1 Guards Brigade was detached into the mountains to the east to maintain loose contact between XIII Corps and Eighth Army. Highway 67 ran from Dicomano in the Sieve valley up to the Muraglione Pass and thence to Forlí in the Po valley, hardly a route that any armoured commander would have chosen willingly, especially as aerial reconnaissance had shown it to be strewn with demolitions. Not surprisingly, 6th Armoured took a month to pass its leading units through Dicomano and the Muraglione Pass. Every road from Dicomano had been obstructed with, in the first ten miles north of the town towards the pass, twelve gaps blown, including two in corniche sections each over 300 feet long that made diversions impossible. The German engineers were using the country to impede the Allied advance with considerable success and progress became even slower when the fixed defences were met. XIII Corps was opposed by 715th Infantry Division, whose 1028th Grenadier Regiment faced 6th Armoured on Highway 67. A tantalizing fifteen miles from Forlí, with the Lombardy Plain in sight, the divisional advance came to a stop.

> The employment of an armoured division in such a mountainous region was impractical. The road to Forlí was never going to be opened, despite much wishful thinking by high command, without the sustained and strengthened commitment of an overwhelming infantry force. The offensives being undertaken by … Eighth Army on the Adriatic and, to a lesser extent, by the Americans through the mountains between Florence and Bologna, meant that there was nothing to be gained by a major offensive in 6th Armoured Division's sector. The division's role was therefore to threaten a move, hold the line and harass the enemy.

Of this phase of the campaign Murray wrote:

> I met Mark Clark soon after my arrival. He made the usual polite gestures, which are a feature of such occasions, and then went on to unfold his plan. It soon became clear that the attack was really designed as an all-American affair. It seemed to me that Mark Clark determined that it would be American soldiers who would break out onto the plain and capture Bologna; he had a weakness for that sort of thing. The 'eye-wiping' stage of the war was apparently still with us. The Americans fought a splendid battle but the ground, and later the weather, proved too much for them and they were finally halted some miles short of the plain. As the battle developed we got more and more involved and I was forced to employ the tank crews as infantry. We remained in the Apennines for six months and were only finally withdrawn in February 1945.[7]

In spite of the suffering of the soldiers of XIII Corps, including those of 6th Armoured, Clark showed no appreciation. His biographer noted that 'Kirkman's corps, helping to make the 'main wallop' over the mountains, Clark judged, had 'been of little value to me.'[8] Clark's xenophobic attitude to British soldiers and their commanders was to continue until the end of the campaign.

As 6th Armoured advanced along the Tiber valley from Rome another British armoured division was arriving in Italy. On 27 May HQ 1st Armoured Division flew into Italy; the division had not seen action since Tunisia and its constituent brigades and units took time to assemble at Altamura south-west of Bari. The only El Alamein veteran division to rejoin Eighth Army in Italy, it was to deploy under V Corps – to which it was assigned on 22 June – in Operation OLIVE, but the assembly process took so long that the division was barely worthy of the description by the time it was committed to action. This is no reflection on its GOC, Major General

Richard Hull, who had considerable combat experience, including commanding an armoured brigade in Tunisia, as well as Blade Force in the race for Tunis after the TORCH landings. Of Hull, one of the youngest divisional commanders of the war, Roberts wrote that some found him 'stuffy',[9] but this may have been because Hull was a rarity among interwar officers in that he had graduated from university before being commissioned in the 17th/21st Lancers. (He was to become a field marshal and CIGS.)

HQ, divisional troops and 2 Armoured Brigade assembled at Altamura in early June. The division's infantry brigade – 18, once 7 Motor Brigade – had been serving with 1st Infantry Division and was not immediately available. Instead the division was allocated 66 Brigade, forming from the Gibraltar and other garrisons in the Mediterranean area, and 43 Gurkha Lorried Infantry Brigade from the Middle East; the division was re-organizing on a two–infantry brigade basis in common with other armoured divisions in Italy on 21 July. The Gurkha brigade had only finished equipping on 15 August when 1st Armoured began moving to a concentration area at Porto Recanati in preparation for OLIVE. Three days later the move of 66 Brigade was cancelled and 18 Brigade returned, 66 Brigade taking its place in 1st Division. Not until 23 August was the division complete with the arrival of the two artillery regiments, 2 RHA and 23rd Field. It will be appreciated that there was no time for 1st Armoured to train as a division. No divisional exercise could be held and thus Hull sent his commanders a letter in which he wrote:

> There will be no time for a Div exercise so I am sending you these notes on certain points that I consider especially important. The end of the war with Germany is, I consider, in sight, but just as in a race, it is essential to keep going flat out till the very end …[10]

Hull's notes emphasized the importance of high standards in march discipline, traffic control, junior leadership, tank gunnery, speedy consolidation by the infantry, and the overall need for good teamwork. But it was no substitute for a divisional exercise that would have allowed the various units, especially those completely new to the division, to become better acquainted with those with whom they would have to work, and rely upon, in battle.

Not only was 1st Armoured at a loss for a divisional exercise but HQ V Corps was in a similar situation, not having been in a major offensive action for the best part of a year, and 46th and 56th Divisions, also in V Corps, had only just returned from the Middle East. As the official historian comments, none of the four HQs were 'run in'.

D Day for Operation OLIVE was 25 August but 1st Armoured Division was not to enter the fray until what Charles Keightley, commanding V Corps, described as Phase III: the first two phases included rushing and forcing the Gothic Line while the third phase was exploitation with 56th (London) Division making for Bologna with 1st Armoured, followed by 4th Division, thrusting for Ferrara on the Po plain. This was a role for which an armoured division was suited ideally. However, not only was 1st Armoured's teamwork rusty, the division suffered from the Eighth Army commander's decision to hold it back in readiness for the order to advance. Although 46th Division had secured a crossing of the Conca river suitable for armour, and the Canadians had created a bridgehead from which 1st Armoured could exploit, Leese had kept Hull's division too far back to be able speedily to join the battle. He had done so deliberately to avoid blocking the roads forward, perhaps mindful of the traffic chaos at El Alamein. Leese had also been taken by surprise by the speed with which the Canadian Corps had punched into the German lines. Had he committed 1st Armoured to Canadian command at that stage –there was sufficient space in the Canadian sector – Hull's armour might have been able to take a major exploitative role. However,

> Leese's mind worked at infantry pace. At Alamein he had commanded XXX Corps which had done most of the infantry work to crack the line, for the armour had at first refused [sic] to fight its way through the German positions, insisting that its task was to go through the 'gap' and 'pursue' the enemy. The 1st Armoured Division still held that outdated notion – shared, apparently, by Leese. It was looking for a gap.[11]

Thus the division was held back and it would be over a week before it was committed. By then Eighth Army had broken through what the Germans called Green I, the first line of fortifications on the Gothic Line, only to find that the enemy was reinforcing his troops and had stopped V Corps on the Coriano ridge, some ten miles from Rimini. By 5 September no fewer than six German divisions faced Eighth Army along the ridge, and of those divisions one was a panzer and another a panzergrenadier. To clear the ridge V Corps devised a new plan that included naval gunfire support in addition to artillery and air support. D Day for the renewed offensive, which saw 1st Armoured and 5th Canadian Armoured Divisions assault the ridge was 12 September, two days after Fifth Army's left jab.

First into action were the infantry brigades of the armoured formations. These met with significant success, the Germans being dazed and battered by the heavy bombardment, and about a thousand prisoners were taken while 18 Brigade's Yorkshire Dragoons (an infantry battalion in spite of its cavalry title; officially it was 9th King's Own Yorkshire LI) had captured San Savino. But there was no swift exploitation of this success: 9th Lancers of 2 Armoured Brigade were to advance from San Savino but found their way blocked by a deep ditch that concealed German tanks, including Panthers, that took their toll of the Lancers' Shermans.

First Armoured's tanks met many other difficulties. Leese had intended that Eighth Army would leap forward from the Coriano ridge to Ravenna, some thirty-five miles away, but the terrain still favoured the defenders and Eighth Army was approaching exhaustion. At no time had the Allies the desired three-to-one superiority over the enemy along the Gothic Line (overall, there was only marginal superiority) and the strain on the attackers was telling. There were many well-sited and camouflaged anti-tank guns that preyed on the Shermans, which also frequently found their way impeded by deep and muddy ditches. This was not ideal country for tanks. However,

43 Gurkha Brigade crossed the Marano in the evening of 15 September and 4th Division's 28 Brigade attacked across the front of 1st Armoured the following night, taking Cerasolo ridge. Hull then received orders to re-organize in anticipation of the next move.

As the advance progressed slowly the Yorkshire Dragoons took Monte Arboreta on the night of the 18th/19th but lost part of the feature to counter-attack. The lost ground was regained and 1st Armoured was due to break out of this sector and advance to Point 153, a mile north-east of 7 Armoured Brigade's most forward positions. But German resistance remained fierce and tragedy hit 2 Armoured Brigade on the 20th. As the Bays formed up to renew the attack they came under fire and a Sherman troop deployed to deal with enemy machine guns but ran into 88s; the Shermans were knocked out. The brigade commander, Brigadier Goodbody, then asked for the attack to be cancelled or postponed but was told that the Bays had to advance at 10.15am to support the Canadians to their right. The Bays complied with the order and suffered heavily. So vicious was the enemy opposition that two squadrons were all but destroyed in less than an hour; only three tanks remained battleworthy. Twenty-one men, including six officers, were killed. Another casualty of that day appears to have been the brigade commander: Goodbody was succeeded by Brigadier J. F. B. Combe on 22 September.[12]

And still the attack continued, even though torrential rain began falling on the 21st and further impeded the attackers, delaying the next phase of the advance, Operation CAVALCADE, a Canadian operation with 2nd New Zealand Division under command alongside 5th Canadian Armoured. But movement was at infantry pace, such was the nature of the countryside, the weather and the doughty defence, with the solid farmhouses and outbuildings of the area providing strongpoints that had to be dealt with.

As V Corps was to set off for Bologna 43 Brigade crossed the Marécchia and cut Highway 9, the main road to the city, although the latter task was not achieved until 24 September. First Armoured was to lead the corps advance to Bologna and preparations were under way when news was received that the division was to be disbanded, although 2 Armoured Brigade would survive as an independent formation. The Gurkhas were to transfer to 56th (London) Division but 18 Brigade was to disband and provide reinforcements for 46th Divisions; 1st Buffs were to reduce to cadre with both 14th Sherwood Foresters and the Yorkshire Dragoons disbanding.

The disbandment of 1st Armoured Division was not due to any failings in the division, although it had not been allowed to prepare adequately for operations in Italy. Instead the reason lay in Eighth Army's heavy infantry casualties, over 14,000 in the course of Operation OLIVE with 1,700 British infantry personnel killed.[13] With no infantry reinforcements available from the UK, which was providing replacements for north-west Europe, replacements for Eighth Army had to be found from the Mediterranean area with anti-aircraft gunners, many of whom were redundant due to the much reduced enemy air threat, re-roled, as were Royal Navy and Royal Air Force personnel.

It was a sad end for Britain's first armoured division. Perhaps if it had been given time to train properly before OLIVE it might have played a more influential role and helped reduce casualty figures amongst the infantry units. Perhaps.

The failure of Operation OLIVE to achieve a breakthrough on to the plain of Lombardy and a possible end to the war in Italy in 1944 meant that Allied soldiers suffered a second winter campaign. Such was the nature of this that armour had little part to play and it was spring 1945 before the surviving British armoured division in Italy – 6th – saw action again in its intended role. But that proved a remarkable action as part of what was arguably the best manoeuvre operation by the western Allies of the war. Before then, however, the division, with 78th Division, took part in an attack in the Santerno valley in mid-December that was essentially an infantry operation which failed to gain its objectives but cost 61 Brigade heavily with 220 casualties. Thereafter, until March, 6th Armoured was static and its soldiers saw dismounted action as infantry before being brought down to the low ground behind Eighth Army's lines to rest, re-organize and re-equip. Their old Shermans were handed in, to be replaced by newer models, mounting a superior 76mm gun while 17-pounder Sherman Fireflies were also issued as well as close support Shermans fitted with 105mm howitzers. While the 76mm gun was a great improvement on the earlier 75mm fitted to the Sherman, the 17-pounder of the Firefly was a huge boost to morale, since tankmen knew that the gun could take on the best of German armour and give the Firefly crew a real fighting chance.

There followed intense training to familiarize the crews with their new equipment and practise close co-operation with infantry. The battlegroup system was already in use with the division's groups formed from the units of 26 Armoured and 61 Brigades. Unlike the north-west Europe divisions, however, there were only three battlegroups; the divisional reconnaissance regiment, 1st Derbyshire Yeomanry, was held as an armoured reserve while 1 Guards Brigade was also held in reserve, ready, in Murray's words, 'to punch holes if required'.[14] Losses had brought changes in the orders of battle of both Guards and 61 Brigades: 10th Rifle Brigade was disbanded on 20 March 1945, its soldiers allocated to 2nd Rifle Brigade in 61 Brigade and its place taken by 1st King's Royal Rifle Corps (1 KRRC); in 1 Guards Brigade 2nd Coldstream left on 2 March to join 24 Guards Brigade in place of 5th Grenadiers, who were disbanded, while 1st Welch Regiment took 2nd Coldstream's place in 1 Guards Brigade.

Eighth Army was now commanded by Lieutenant General Sir Richard McCreery, who had succeeded Leese on 1 October 1944. McCreery had commanded X Corps and, briefly, V Corps and had been Alexander's chief of staff in the Middle East. Before that he had been sent as an armoured adviser to Middle East HQ but, sadly, he and Auchinleck did not get on and he was removed from his post. Before his appointment to Cairo he had commanded 8th Armoured Division and had seen action in France in 1940 commanding 2 Armoured Brigade. Commissioned in 12th (Prince of Wales's Royal) Lancers in 1915 he was:

one of the most knowledgeable and experienced armoured commanders in the war ... He was determined that the Division would be used in an armoured role, but only when the circumstances were favourable ... It presupposed breaking out through the infantry when the latter had softened up the opposition and the battle was on the verge of becoming fluid. Such situations are difficult to read and the conclusion we came to was that we would have to be prepared to fight our own way out if needs be. We knew also that there was little likelihood of breaking out on a broad front. It was essential to make our battlegroups as flexible as possible.[15]

Coincidentally, the new commander of Fifth Army, Lucian Truscott, was also a cavalryman and had brought cavalry 'thinking speed' to the US infantry, introducing the famous 'Truscott Trott' as a divisional commander; his division had the reputation of being the fastest moving in the US Army. Truscott did not share the anti-British bias of his predecessor, Clark, who now commanded 15th Army Group, and found a fellow spirit in McCreery. It was due largely to their co-operation and planning that the final campaign in Italy evolved as it did. Clark, who remained anti-British and, especially, anti-McCreery, although (or possibly because) the latter had served under him as a corps commander, had decided that Eighth Army was no longer an effective fighting formation and that Fifth Army would undertake the final assault. He reckoned without his two army commanders who presented him with a detailed plan that envisaged both formations co-operating in an attack to destroy the German forces in northern Italy. Clark gave his approval to the plan, Operation GRAPESHOT , in which the armies would carry out a double encirclement, a strategy the Germans described as *Kiel und Kessel*, or 'wedge and trap'. Eighth Army would launch Operation BUCKLAND on 9 April with the support of the entire Allied air effort until the 12th when Fifth Army would launch Operation CRAFTSMAN.

McCreery planned carefully for BUCKLAND and wrought great changes in Eighth Army while doing so. Although more formations, including I Canadian Corps, had been transferred to north-west Europe, he raised the army's morale to a high pitch and gave it the tools needed for success. A miniature 79th Armoured Division was created with specialized armoured vehicles: 25 Tank Brigade became B Assault Brigade RAC/RE and then 25 Armoured Engineer Brigade with flame-throwing Churchill Crocodiles, Flail tanks to clear paths through minefields, bridging tanks and tank-dozers (almost 200 specialized AFVs were produced in workshops in Italy) while 9 Armoured Brigade was re-roled to operate amphibious LVTs, or Buffaloes, codenamed Fantails, and Kangaroo APCs. These played critical parts in BUCKLAND.

Prior to the main offensive, commando operations secured the right flank of Eighth Army's advance by taking islands in Lake Comácchio and the spit of land separating the lake from the Adriatic. Then 167 Brigade of 56th (London) Division crossed Comácchio in Buffaloes to complete the operation by creating a wedge between the Reno river floodbank and the area west of the lake that the Germans had flooded. The Germans may have considered the expanse of water that was Lake Comácchio and the neighbouring inundation an impassable obstacle but McCreery thought otherwise.

He had flown over the area and identified a route for Eighth Army's advance via Argenta, which became known as the Argenta Gap, around which he built his plan. With the commandos and 167 Brigade having achieved their objectives, all was set for the main attack.

For Operation BUCKLAND McCreery had reinforced V Corps to a strength of five divisions, the Italian *Gruppo di Combattimento* Cremona and 2 Parachute Brigade with 6th Armoured held in reserve until the initial attack reached Argenta. The spearhead of that initial attack was 78th Division which was expanded to include 2 Armoured Brigade, and elements of 9 Armoured and 25 Armoured Engineer Brigades, with infantry riding in Kangaroo APCs manned by 4th Hussars. Leading the division into battle was a breakout force to clear the way for the mobile force, or Kangaroo Army; a reserve force was held for special roles.

On 9 April Eighth Army launched BUCKLAND with over 1,500 artillery pieces and more than 1,000 Allied aircraft hammering the Germans before V Corps crossed its start lines. Before long the Kangaroo Army was racing into action, the Reno was reached and Argenta was cleared by 18 April while Fifth US Army had launched Operation CRAFTSMAN on 14 April. It was time to unleash 6th Armoured Division. Initial progress was slow with the way through Argenta a mass of congestion and streets filled with rubble.

> Both 56th and 78th Divisions were using the route to supply their own units at the front and the resulting transport problems were a nightmare. By late afternoon on 19 April, however, the Lothians and 16th/5th Lancers were both passing through the leading infantry with their support groups and preparing to move from Consandolo, ten miles north of Argenta.

Murray had been told by McCreery that reports had been received that Argenta was in British hands but suggested that he confirm this with Keightley. Putting the division on six hours' notice to move, Murray went to see Keightley who thought the way was clear but Murray then went forward to see Major General Keith Arbuthnott, GOC 78th Division, to confirm this.

> Unfortunately the 'gap' was even less obvious than we had thought, but two factors decided me in accepting this challenge. In the first place the opposing troops must have had quite a hammering in the previous ten days since the operation commenced and might well be reasonably disorganized. Secondly, we were now within striking distance of the Po, and in this area 6th Armoured Division would have its last chance of fighting an armoured battle. We would never have forgiven ourselves if that fleeting chance had escaped us: it was now or never.[16]

And so the decision was made. Murray's orders from Keightley were straightforward: pass through 78th Division's left flank, swing north-eastward, advance to Bondeno, with the divisional left flank along the Reno, and link up with Fifth Army.[17] Once that junction was achieved the destruction of what remained of Tenth and Fourteenth Armies, 'caught in the noose of Bologna's defences',[18] would be complete. According to the CO of 17th/21st Lancers the 'gap' was 'literally only a few yards wide'[19] but enough to give an armoured division the chance to perform its role. The battlegroups rode to their final battle with enthusiasm.

Battered the Germans may have been but they were still determined to oppose the Allied advance. The first water obstacle met by the advancing armour was the Po morto di Primaro, along which were ensconced elements of 26th Panzer Division. At San Nicolo they showed the Lothians/2nd Rifle Brigade Group that they had lost none of their vigour and did likewise to 16th/5th Lancers/1 KRRC at Traghetto. This was only a temporary setback as the KRRC crossed the river that night to establish a bridgehead into which the Lancers crossed via a Bailey bridge next morning. While the Rifles secured the bridgehead the Lancers probed out to the right, with 17th/21st Lancers on their left. Although advancing over territory suited to anti-tank operations they pushed ahead some four miles beyond Traghetto. The 17th/21st found better going as they were closer to the Reno and by day's end had drawn ahead of 16th/5th, along whose path many ditches and thickets concealed *Panzerfauste* parties and some anti-tank guns. Five tanks were knocked out by enemy action. Val ffrench-Blake, CO of the 17th/21st Group, noted that an 'Air OP plane was ahead of us, and spotted a tank which was destroyed by the "cab-rank" of Rover David – a specially trained Mustang squadron'.[20]

No amount of opposition was to be allowed to slow the advance and McCreery kept close watch on developments, ensuring that the problems of the Gothic Line would not be repeated. Of the army commander, Keightley commented admiringly that McCreery was usually closer to the battle than he was himself. From McCreery 'pungent and pertinent criticism descended, based on his assessments of the grouping demanded by the terrain'.[21] Thus 1 Guards Brigade entered the battle through 16th/5th Lancers, and the 17th/21st Lancers/7th Rifle Brigade Group resumed their advance at 4.00am on 21 April. By daylight the group had covered another four miles and entered Segni to encounter stout opposition. Although German troops, with some tanks, held the Fossa Cembalina where it meets the Reno they were flushed out by air attacks, and a battlegroup attack allowed sappers to bridge the Fossa with an Ark. (Look at a map of the region and it appears to be flat, perfect country for tanks, but it is crossed by ancient drainage ditches that made excellent anti-tank obstacles. Many roads were raised above the level of the surrounding countryside, making tanks frighteningly conspicuous.)

With Segni consolidated the advance continued. McCreery had decreed that the enemy should be allowed no rest and as the 17th/21st Lancers Group advanced from Segni they fired into buildings to prompt the surrender of many German soldiers. The group seized the bridge near Gallo within ninety minutes of leaving Segni, cutting Highway 64, the Bologna-Ferrara road. Orders then came from HQ 26 Armoured Brigade:

Push on with two squadrons and your infantry to Póggio Renatico (MO178). This is the chance of a lifetime. Leave one squadron on the bridge at Gallo and hold it at all costs until relieved.[22]

Such an order was like manna from heaven to a cavalry unit; for almost the first time in the campaign the Death or Glory Boys could demonstrate true cavalry élan. The war diary of 26 Armoured Brigade records that ffrench-Blake's men 'tore into Póggio Renatico down the main road with C Squadron leading and firing literally as they went', ignoring the normal practice of advancing parallel to a road rather than on it to avoid possible mines. En route they took a heavy toll of German guns and vehicles and although, for the last 2,000 yards of their advance, the Shermans were under fire from 88s none was hit;[23] the enemy gunners were flak men unused to firing at ground targets. Nightfall saw the group at Póggio Renatico, four miles from Gallo, where, blocking every exit, they cut the only alternative road from Bologna to Ferrara. Since it had moved off the group had advanced an impressive eleven miles.[24]

Val ffrench-Blake's men were ahead of the remainder of the division, a situation that caused concern at divisional HQ, especially when 1st Welch Regiment, of 1 Guards Brigade, was forced to withdraw after crossing the Fossa Cembalina in the face of opposition from enemy infantry and armour, the latter apparently including Tigers. However, 17th/21st Lancers were fighting isolated groups of Germans, some of whom fought determinedly and received the attentions of the Rifle Brigade to effect their surrenders. Although success seemed assured at corps and army HQs the situation was somewhat different on the ground:

in the dark, under the walls of Póggio Renatico the Regiment felt very insecure. There had been heavy expenditure of ammunition on a large number of targets and possible enemy positions during the advance, petrol was down to below twenty-five miles, and there was no prospect of replenishment until the route was cleared of the enemy.[25]

But a second successful attack by the Welch, followed up by 3rd Grenadiers, and a reckless advance to Bondeno by the Lothians helped stabilize matters. En route to Bondeno the Lothians lost eleven tanks with two of their Shermans crossing the Panaro on reaching the town in the afternoon, only to be followed across the bridge by two German tanks, after which the bridge was blown. Val ffrench-Blake's group mopped up at Póggio, took some 200 prisoners and moved on to San Agostino, shooting up columns of German transport making for the Po, after which B Squadron advanced to Pilastrello where the leading Shermans saw tanks approaching from the south and opened fire. Fortunately, that first round – a 17-pounder – missed. The other tanks were American, of 1st Armored Division.

Meanwhile the 16th/5th Lancers/1 KRRC Group passed the flank of ffrench-Blake's group as they made for the second key objective along the Panaro, Finale Emilia, reaching there early on 23 April. The Lothians had struck northward towards the Po and while 17th/21st Lancers/7th Rifle Brigade were taking San Agostino the

16th/5th Battlegroup was making contact with II US Corps at Finale Emilia. How fitting was that name and how fitting also the fact that the formation from II US Corps with which 6th Armoured made contact was 6th South African Armoured Division. It has to be recorded that there might have been a tragedy instead of a happy meeting as 6th Armoured had intercepted a German convoy and called down an air strike before learning the American corps was about to attack Finale. But the air strike was called off, as was an artillery bombardment intended to cover 12 South African Brigade's attack on Finale.

There were still mopping-up operations to be carried out by the battlegroups as some determined Germans remained. In the course of one such operation Lieutenant Colonel John Hope DSO MC and Bar, CO of 1 KRRC, was conferring with Denis Smyly, CO of 16th/5th Lancers, alongside a Stuart reconnaissance tank when he was shot by an enemy sniper.[26] Corporal Stanley Waring, the Stuart's commander, went to give John Hope first aid but was also shot dead. Hope, a highly respected officer who had assumed command of his battalion on 1 March 1945, had been commissioned in the King's Royal Rifle Corps in 1940 and had served with the 1st Battalion throughout the war; he was one of the very few veterans of the original Eighth Army to have survived to this point in the war, making his death all the more poignant.

Although the destruction of the bridge at Bondeno had allowed many Germans to escape the war in Italy was all but over. Sixth Armoured's role was also almost finished, although the Derbyshire Yeomanry set off for the Po as the divisional spearhead.[27] There was certainly a degree of confusion as 17th/21st Lancers discovered to their cost when:

On the last day after the main fighting was over, our two Honey light tanks, carrying ammunition and fuel, were attacked by American fighters, and two men were killed, while coming back up to us. Both other armoured regiments were attacked by the same party of aircraft, which had mistaken the Po for the Adige, and were sixty miles south of their bomb line.[28]

The battlegroup's two units differed in their identification of the attackers, 17th/21st Lancers' war diary recording the attackers as RAF Spitfires while 1 KRRC's diary identified them as American Mustangs, an identification that the Lancers' diary later noted as correct.[29]

The Germans had lost cohesion almost completely and, although they were withdrawing to another defensive line, there was little chance of an effective defence. British and American armour had done what armour can best achieve, and cut off the head of the enemy forces. Negotiations were under way for an armistice and, on 2 May, German forces in Italy and certain provinces of Austria surrendered to Field Marshal Alexander. By then 6th Armoured Division had reached Udine and was soon to enter Austria but its experiences there are beyond the scope of this book. However, the division had lived up to the symbolism of its divisional sign of a mailed fist by delivering a crushing blow to the enemy.

Notes

This chapter is based on Jackson, *The Mediterranean and Middle East, Vol VI*, Pts II and III from the Official History of the War, Ford, *Mailed Fist*, Liddell Hart, *The Tanks (Vol II)*, Macksey, *A History of the Royal Armoured Corps*, and the war diaries of Eighth Army, V, X, and XIII Corps, 1st and 6th Armoured Divisions, their constituent brigades and some individual units. Information on the development of artillery and tanks is from Hogg, *British and American Artillery of World War 2* and Hogg and Weeks, *Illustrated Encyclopaedia of Military Vehicles* and other sources are:

1. Doherty, *In The Ranks of Death*, pp.266–8
2. ffrench-Blake, *The History of the 17th/21st Lancers*, p.187
3. Wilson, *Unusual Undertakings*, p.75
4. Doherty, *Ireland's Generals in the Second World War*, p.121
5. Horsfall, *Fling Our Banner to the Wind*, p.199
6. Wilson, op cit, p.75
7. Donovan, *A Very Fine Commander*, p.172
8. Blumenson, *Mark Clark*, p.229
9. Roberts, *From the Desert to the Baltic*, p.136
10. Quoted in Jackson, *The Mediterranean and Middle East*, Vol VI Pt II, p.232; NA Kew, WO170/398 war diary 1 Armd Div, 1944
11. Bidwell & Graham, *Tug of War*, p.359
12. Joslen *Orders of Battle*, p.148
13. NA Kew, CAB44/145, p.147
14. Donovan, op cit, p.177
15. Ibid, p.178
16. Ibid, p.180
17. NA Kew, WO170/4336, war diary 6 Armd Div, Jan–Apr 1945
18. Blaxland, *Alexander's Generals*, p.268
19. ffrench-Blake, Italian War Diary, p.48
20. Ibid
21. Blaxland, op cit, p.268
22. NA Kew, WO170/4456, war diary 26 Armd Bde, 1945
23. ffrench-Blake, Italian War Diary, p.51
24. NA Kew, WO170/4629, war diary, 17/21L, 1945
25. ffrench-Blake, *A History of the 17/21L*, p.222
26. Blaxland, op cit, p.270
27. Jackson, op cit, Pt III, pp.288–94; Blaxland, op cit, p.273
28. ffrench-Blake, Italian War Diary, p.52
29. NA Kew, WO170/4629, op cit & WO 170/5026, war diary 1 KRRC, 1945

Epilogue

The war in Europe was over and attention turned to the Far East, but no British armoured division was committed to operations there. For the divisions in Europe there were many tasks with 6th Armoured involved in settling frontiers in Austria while Guards, 7th, 11th and 79th deployed on occupation duties in Germany. Changes were on the way, the first coming on 12 June 1945 when Guards Armoured was redesignated as Guards Division and its armoured role ceased. The Desert Rats led the Victory Parade along Berlin's Charlottenburg Chaussée on 21 July and remained in Germany as part of the British Army of the Rhine (BAOR) until 1958 when it ceased to be an armoured formation on being redesignated 5th Division. Although 11th Armoured Division was disbanded in January 1946 it was re-formed in 1950 but converted to 4th Infantry Division six years later. Hobart's 79th Armoured Division disbanded on 31 August 1945 but its rich legacy lived on. While 6th Armoured Division moved back to Italy from Austria in September 1945 it was also disbanded, only to re-form in 1951, assigned to BAOR until final disbandment in 1958.

In the war's closing days the first six production models of a new British 'heavy cruiser' were sent to Germany but arrived too late to see any action. The new tank, Centurion, resulted from a War Office specification laid down in 1943 for a tank with powerful armament and armour to cope with the German 88mm gun, as well as reliability, crew comfort and the dimensions to be able to cross a standard Bailey bridge. These requirements were refined in February 1944 when the final specification for A41, as the tank was known, was set out, calling for a 17-pounder main gun, a Rolls Royce Meteor engine and a weight of over 40 tons. The first mock-up was ready and approved by May 1944 and twenty trials models were ordered. A new classification was also applied to Centurion: no longer was it a heavy cruiser but a universal tank.[1] (Although Montgomery had written to the War Office after the Ardennes battle setting out the case for a 'capital tank' he had no part in the development of Centurion which was well under way when he penned his letter. It was in this letter that Montgomery claimed that 'If we had the German armour we could not have reached Antwerp as fast as we did. If they had had ours they would have reached the Meuse in 36 hours and broken through beyond.' Little illustrates his ignorance of armour better than this comment.)[2]

Had Centurion been available a year earlier it would have made a real difference to the British armoured divisions giving them a tank that allowed them to meet any enemy tank on equal terms. But the specification for Centurion had been set only four months before D Day and the armoured formations had to soldier on with Shermans, Cromwells and, later, Comets. Even the last-named would have been a significant asset had it been available in early-1944. But it took time to design a tank. Minimum development time was a year but this could lead to problems, as happened with Cavalier, for which the specification was issued in January 1941 with the first pilot model appearing in January 1942. Cromwell was the result of a 1941 specification that also led, via Challenger, to Comet with its 77mm gun but, although available in September 1944, Comet was not issued to front-line units until March 1945. It could have been in use earlier had not the German Ardennes offensive interrupted 11th Armoured Division's re-equipment programme. The gestation time of these wartime developments contrasts with that of Covenanter which took three years from concept in 1937 to delivery in 1940, and still failed to be a good tank. A major problem plaguing British tank development was the co-ordination of tank and gun. Earlier tanks, cruiser and infantry, were equipped with the 2-pounder which was rapidly outclassed and it was some time before a British tank mounted a 6-pounder, since most could not be up-gunned. There was also the difficulty of finding a tank gun that could fire both HE and AP shot as the requirements for each conflicted: the former's ideal muzzle velocity was 1,500 feet per second (fps) against the minimum velocity of 2,600fps for an AP round.

While valid comments on the development of British tanks and guns, the foregoing may also be seen as excuses for a deeply flawed doctrine and outlook on armoured warfare. There are, of course, other examples elsewhere in wartime British design and production of weapons and weapon systems. The aviation industry got it wrong with the Manchester bomber but reworked its sound basic design into the superlative Lancaster, but little could be done with the awful Lerwick flying boat other than to withdraw it from service and the Albemarle bomber was another design that never met expectations. Even the much-vaunted Typhoon fighter-bomber had been less than successful in its original interceptor role, but was reworked as the outstanding Tempest. However, success stories far outweighed the failures in the British aviation industry, a comment that cannot be made for the tank industry. Nonetheless, there were very successful military industrial projects, including the excellent 3.7-inch heavy anti-aircraft gun that provided the backbone of UK anti-aircraft defences throughout the war. Coupled with gun-laying (GL) radar the 3.7 enabled Anti-Aircraft Command to take a heavy toll of the Luftwaffe and defeat the V-1 flying bomb in the last year of war. The GOC-in-C Anti-Aircraft Command was General Sir Frederick (Tim) Pile who adopted a policy of working closely with industry and research scientists to obtain what his gunners needed. A Great War gunner veteran, Pile had transferred to the Tank Corps in the 1920s, later commanding a tank battalion before going on to command the Suez Canal Brigade in Egypt. Although an outstanding armoured commander, and identified as a potential leader of armoured forces, he returned to the Royal Artillery in 1937 as an anti-aircraft divisional commander. In his memoirs Pile reflected on the influence he had had with industry and on the benefits that might have accrued to British armour had a similar system existed there.

I doubt if there has been a Command in war which had so much influence on the type of equipment it was eventually armed with. The producers heard once a month, without fail, what we required and why. I am also in no doubt that a similar committee on which would have sat, if not the Commander-in-Chief in the field, anyway his deputy, would have resulted in far better tanks and anti-tank guns than we possessed, even at the Armistice.[3]

Although there was co-operation between industry the abolition of HQ RAC in September 1942 had not helped the development of British armour.[4] Martel noted that he 'had stressed the necessity for producing tanks that were one step ahead of the enemy in armour and guns'[5] and that the RAC had argued unsuccessfully for the earlier introduction of 6-pounder and 75mm tank guns. Thus the armour did not have as beneficial a relationship with industry as did Pile's command. Martel made much the same point when he commented that 'when you do away with the head you cannot expect … things to be thought out and directed properly'.[6]

Martel also argued that greater attention ought to have been given to the role of armour in north-west Europe with much closer co-operation between all Allied commanders, and that operations in Russia provided a better model for what to expect on the plains of Europe than what had happened in Tunisia, Sicily and Italy where the anti-tank gun had dominated.[7] However, he found that the British general staff view was that 'the power of the tank was on the wane, and that the anti-tank gun had the measure of the tank'.[8] In a meeting with Brooke on 23 March 1944 he was told that campaigns such as those in Poland, France and Russia could not be fought again in the same way with tanks as, by 1944, 'everyone had plenty of these guns'.[9] (Following an exercise in 1931 Major Eric Dorman-Smith made the point that unsupported tanks could be dealt with effectively by anti-tank guns. He felt that Hobart resented his comment.)[10] Thus British armoured commanders were left to a less-defined role than might otherwise have been the case and, in the view of one writer, were left to work out for themselves questions such as the tactical employment of the Sherman with its 75mm gun capable of firing both AP and HE.[11] The same writer comments that experience in Normandy, with little opportunity for mobile operations and involvement in setpiece attacks on well-defended positions led to 'a complete re-organization of the division to allow intimate armour-infantry co-operation'.[12] In fact the battlegroup system to which Place refers was first introduced in 7th Armoured Division within days of arriving in Normandy and was in use at Villers Bocage.

French writes that:

Until 1942 the British fought with tanks that were so mechanically unreliable that they often undermined their doctrinal commitment to mobile operations, that were sometimes adequately armoured, but sometimes not, and that were equipped with a gun that had a diminishing ability to destroy enemy tanks and almost no ability to damage soft targets. In the middle of the war they did succeed in introducing better vehicles with better guns. But by July 1943 the

DRAC believed that existing designs of cruiser and infantry tanks had almost reached the limits of their development because their suspension systems could not carry any more weight. However, the development of completely new designs would take between 18–24 months, an option precluded because Churchill and the Chiefs of Staff had by then agreed that no weapons should be developed which were not likely to be in service when they expected the war to end, by December 1944.[13]

(The development of the Centurion suggests that French is not entirely right in his comment since the specification was not drafted until February 1944 although the concept dated back to 1943. He also exaggerates the unreliability of British tanks, presumably classing them all with Crusader.)

Much criticism of British armour in the Second World War suggests that tradition-bound cavalry officers were responsible for many of its failings. The apportionment of blame on cavalry officers is surely misplaced for many of the best armoured commanders came from the old cavalry regiments and the role of an armoured division was a twentieth-century heavy cavalry role incorporating both breakthrough and exploitation. Men such as Richard McCreery, Michael O'Moore Creagh, Roger Evans and Herbert Lumsden were cavalrymen who made the transition to armoured warfare without difficulty while infantrymen such as Brian Horrocks, Richard O'Connor and Gerald Templer showed that they too could master the art of armoured warfare. And there were also gunners and engineers, as well as those commissioned in the Royal Tank Corps with Pip Roberts the most outstanding example of the Tank Corps men.

There may also have been something in the ethos of a rifle or light infantry regiment that made for a good commander of armour as shown by John Harding, Vyvyan Evelegh and Horatius Murray. Equally, of course, a man's military background may have had less to do with his ability to handle armour than with his own ability as a leader. As the war progressed most infantry divisions were supported by a brigade of tanks, either cruiser or infantry, and divisional commanders became all-arms commanders, which was much to be desired. Those who commanded armoured divisions found that they handled an extremely flexible instrument.

So flexible is an armoured division and so good are its communications that temporary alterations of internal structure can be effected quickly and smoothly. This fact is worth emphasizing, for its implications are not easily acceptable. The notion of regrouping is normally associated with complicated movements undertaken as a result of deliberate and studied instructions and occupying several days. 'General _____'s forces have been withdrawn to rest and regroup.' 'The ____th Army is regrouping in preparation for a resumption of the offensive.' The prevalence of expressions of this kind show how unfamiliar is the idea that a formation may be able to regroup in the middle of an engagement. Yet such was repeatedly and unavoidably our practice. A few words by the General to his brigades on the wireless; a few similar and resultant words on their own networks; the quick establishment of communication between the units and their new masters – that is all. In thirty minutes the reorganization is complete.[14]

That flexibility owed much to good radio communications, which was evident throughout the war. In the Great War the bane of commanders had been losing contact with their soldiers, except by runners, once battle commenced, but this problem had been resolved between the wars and during the Second World War radio became more and more reliable. One of the great examples of the potential of radio for controlling units and formations in battle had been Charles Broad's manoeuvring of 1 Tank Brigade in front of the Army Council in 1931, only two years after an official trial had concluded that wireless contact between moving vehicles was impossible. But good communications were not restricted to contact between ground-based forces. Air and ground forces could also communicate, as was shown in the desert from 1941 onwards and to spectacular effect in north-west Europe in 1944–45.

Throughout that final campaign in north-west Europe, especially after the breakout from Normandy, armoured divisions had demonstrated flexibility time and again and by the end of the campaign virtually every division in 21 Army Group was, to some extent, an armoured formation, such was the degree of contact and co-operation between infantry divisions and their supporting armoured or tank brigades. Examples include the advance out of Normandy across France, the 'Great Swan', and the final advances through Germany. Even the dash by 7th Armoured Division that ended at Villers Bocage exemplifies this flexibility as the Desert Rats had pushed deep into enemy-held territory, led by a squadron/company battlegroup, a tactic not to be adopted generally until almost two months later. (Of the criticisms of 7th Armoured in Normandy, Lord Carver told this author that he did not agree with them. Perhaps the Desert Rats provided a convenient scapegoat?)

Perhaps the greatest example of flexibility was demonstrated by Richard McCreery's Eighth Army in Operation BUCKLAND with 78th (Battleaxe) Division, 2 and 9 Armoured Brigades, 25 Tank Brigade and 6th Armoured Division. McCreery can fairly be said to have been the greatest British armoured commander of the war.

In Lombardy as in north-west Europe the tank crews showed their mettle and their confidence in their new 76mm Shermans, 77mm Comets and Sherman Fireflies as they tackled enemy tanks with gusto. In Italy most of the Tigers and Panthers had been lost, sacrificed in isolated actions supporting infantry, and the main enemy tank was the Mark IV but Mark IV after Mark IV was lost to the fire of 76mm and 17-pounder Shermans as British tankmen showed the Germans that they had learned their lessons and were now masters of the armoured battlefield.

Notes

With the exception of material on the Centurion, information on the development of tanks and armament is drawn from Hogg and Weeks. Information on the backgrounds of commanders is taken from Smart, *British Generals of the Second World War*. Other sources are as follows:

1. Dunstan, *Centurion Universal Tank*, pp.4–8
2. Macksey, *A History of the Royal Armoured Corps*, pp.170–1
3. Pile, *Ack-Ack*, p.165
4. Martel, *Our Armoured Force*, p.292
5. Ibid, p.183
6. Ibid, p.294
7. Ibid. p.300
8. Ibid, p.298
9. Ibid, p.295
10. Macksey, *Armoured Crusader*, pp.99–100
11. Place, *Military Training in the British Army*, p.97
12. Ibid, p.92
13. French, *Raising Churchill's Army*, p.104
14. Anon, *Taurus Pursuant*, p.92

Appendix 1

Divisional Orders of Battle

Guards Armoured Division
(Formed 17 June 1941)

5 Gds Armd Bde (15 Sep 41–11 Jun 45): 2 (Armd) Gren Gds; 1 (Armd) Cldm Gds; 2 (Armd) I Gds; 1 (Motor) Gren Gds

6 Gds Armd Bde (17 Sep 41–3 Jan 43): 4 (Armd) Gren Gds; 3 (Armd) S Gds; 2 (Armd) W Gds; 4 (Motor) Cldm Gds

Gds Support Group (16 Sep 41–31 May 42): 5 Gren Gds; 5 Cldm Gds; 4 S Gds

32 Gds Inf Bde (1 Jun 42–11 Jun 45): 5 Gren Gds (1 Oct 41–4 Jun 42); 5 Cldm Gds (1 Oct 41–31 Aug 45); 3 I Gds (5 Sep 43–21 Feb 45); 1 W Gds (4 Jun 42–22 Mar 45); 2 S Gds (20 Feb–31 Aug 45); 2 W Gds (20 Jun–31 Aug 45); 32 Bde Support Gp (18 Sep 43–12 Mar 44)

Divisional Reconnaissance: 2 HCR (15 Sep 41–27 Feb 43); 2 W Gds (13 Apr 43–11 Jun 45)

Divisional Artillery: 153 Fd Regt (1 Jun 42–11 Jun 45); 55 Fd Regt (8 Jun 42–11 Jun 45)

21 A/T Regt (1 Jun 42–29 May 45); 75 A/T Regt (1–11 Jun 45)

94 LAA Regt (1 Jun 42–11 Jun 45)

Divisional Engineers: 14 Fd Sqn (4 Aug 41–11 Jun 45); 15 Fd Sqn (4 Aug 41–28 Feb 43); 615 Fd Sqn (1 Mar 43–11 Jun 45)

148 Fd Park Sqn (4 Aug 41–11 Jun 45)

11 Brdg Tp (18 Jun 41–11 Jun 45)

Divisional Signals: Guards Armd Divisional Signals (18 Jun 41–11 Jun 45)

Machine-Gun/Support: 1 Ind MG Coy (RNF) (24 Mar 44–11 Jun 45)

This division had only two GOCs, being formed under Major General Sir Oliver Leese Bt who handed over command to Major General Sir Allan Adair Bt on 12 September 1942.

1st Armoured Division (formerly The Mobile Division)
(Formed September 1939 as 1st Armoured)

2 Lt Armd Bde (3 Sep 39–13 Apr 40): Bays; 10 H; 9 L

1 Hy Armd Bde (3 Sep 39–13 Apr 40): 2 RTR; 3 RTR; 5 RTR

2 Armd Bde (14 Apr 40–25 Sep 44): Bays (14 Apr 40–26 Jun 42; 2 Aug 42–25 Sep 44); 10 H (14 Apr 40–4 Jul 42; 2 Aug 42–25 Sep 44); 9 L (14 Apr–30 Jun 40; 13 Jul 42–25 Sep 44); 3/5 RTR (7 Jul–1 Aug 42); 3 CLY (7–13 Jul 42); 6 RTR (7 Jul–1 Aug 42); 1 KRRC (7 Jul–1 Aug 42; 22 Jun 43–29 Jun 44; 16 Aug–25 Sep 44); 9 KRRC (13–20 Aug 42); 1 RB (31 Oct 40–19 Jun 42); Yks D (9 KOYLI 24 Aug–18 Dec 42); (19 Dec 42–22 Jun 43)

3 Armd Bde (14 Apr–4 Oct 40): 2 RTR (14 Apr–11 Aug 40); 5 RTR

22 Armd Bde (14 Oct 40–7 Nov 41): 2 RGH; 3 CLY; 4 CLY

1 Support Gp (3 Sep 39–11 Feb 42): 1 RHA (3 Sep–20 Oct 39); 2 RHA (3 Sep–20 Oct 39; 31 Jan 42–11 Feb); 11 RHA (9 Aug 40–29 Jan); 60 A/T Regt (22 Dec 39–41 Feb 40); 76 A/T Regt (1 Nov 40–29 Jan 42); 102 (NH) A/T Regt (29 Jan–11 Feb 42); 61 LAA Regt (1 Nov 40–26 Jan 42); 82 LAA Regt (26 Jan 42–11 Feb 42); 101 LAA/A/T Regt (15 Feb–31 Oct 40); 1 Fd Sqn (3 Sep 39–31 Jan 40); 1 Fd Pk Tp (3 Sep 39–31 Jan 40); 1 RB (3 Sep 39–24 Apr 40); 2 KRRC (3 Sep 39–24 Apr 40; 2 Aug 41–11 Feb 42); 9 Foresters (29 Jan–2 Aug 41)

200 Gds Bde Gp (12 Feb 42): see 201 Gds Bde Gp

201 Gds Bde Gp (21 May–14 Jun 42): 2 S Gds (to 14 Jun 42); 3 Cldm Gds (to 20 Jun 42); 9 RB (to 4 Jun 42)

7 Motor Bde (23 Sep 42–19 Jul 43): 2 KKRC (to 18 Dec 42); 2 RB (to 1 Jul 43); 9 KRRC (to 24 Jul 42); 7 RB (to 1 Jul 42); 1 KRRC (15 Jan–22 Jun 43); 9 KOYLI (22 Jun 43–4 Oct 44)

18 Lorried Inf Bde (20 Jul 43–16 Feb 44): see 7 Motor Bde

18 Inf Bde (5 Oct 43–16 Feb 44; 17 Aug–24 Oct 44): see 7 Motor Bde

42 Gurkha Lorried Inf Bde (21 Jul–28 Oct 44) 2/6 GR; 2/8 GR; 2/10 GR

Divisional Reconnaissance: 12 L (1 Nov 40–12 May 42; 13 Sep 42–6 Apr 44); Royals (12 May–13 Sep 42); 4 H (23 May–25 Sep 44)

Divisional Artillery: 2 RHA (24 Aug 42–26 Sep 44); 4 RHA (21 Sep 42–25 Oct 43); 11 (HAC) RHA (24 Aug 42–26 Sep 44)

60 A/T Regt (1 Apr–26 Sep 44); 76 A/T Regt (22 Sep 42–31 Mar 44)

42 LAA Regt (26 Sep 42–5 Oct 44)

Divisional Engineers: 1 Fd Sqn (1 Feb 40–4 Feb 42; 2 Sep 42–29 Sep 44); 7 Fd Sqn (23 Oct 40–19 Mar 42); 1 Oct 42–20 Aug 44); 627 Fd Sqn (21 Aug–29 Sep 44)

1 Fd Pk Sqn (3 Jul 40–25 Aug 44); 631 Fd Pk Sqn (26 Aug–29 Sep 44); 1 Fd Pk Tp (1 Jun–2 Jul 40)

27 Brdg Tp (18 Oct 43–25 Aug 44)

Divisional Signals: 1st Armd Divisional Signals (3 Sep 39–17 Dec 44)

The division ceased to be operational in Italy on 28 October 1944 and its HQ disbanded on 11 January 1945. It had several GOCs including Major General Roger Evans, Willoughby Norrie, Herbert Lumsden, Alex Gatehouse, Raymond Briggs, Alex Galloway, and Richard Hull.

2nd Armoured Division
(Formed 15 December 1939)

1 Lt Armd Bde (19 Jan–13 Apr 40) 1 KDG; 3 H; 4 H

22 Hy Armd Bde (15 Jan–13 Apr 40)

1 Armd Bde (14 Apr 40–27 Feb 41) 1 KDG; 3 H (14 Apr–14 Aug 40); 4 H; 3 RTR (11 Aug–28 Oct 40; 13–27 Feb 41); Rangers (25–27 Feb 41)

22 Armd Bde (15 Apr–12 Oct 40) 2 RGH; 3 CLY; 4 CLY

3 Armd Bde (5 Oct 40–31 Jan 41 & 20 Mar–8 Apr 41) 3 RTR (29 Oct 40–25 Jan 41); 5 RTR 3 H (20 Mar–8 Apr 41); 6 RTR (20 Mar–8 Apr 41)

2 Support Gp (5 Feb 40–8 Apr 41) 2 RHA (11 Jul 40–25 Feb 41); 12 RHA (19 Apr–7 Aug 40); 104 RHA (from 26 Mar 41) 102 (NH) A/T Regt (7–23 Feb 41)

Divisional Reconnaissance: 1 KDG (24 Jan–9 May 41)

Divisional Artillery: included in Spt Gp

Divisional Engineers: 3 Fd Sqn (10 Jun 40–26 Feb 41); 142 Fd Pk Tp (10 Jun 40–6 Feb 41); 142 Fd Pk Sqn (7–26 Feb 41)

Divisional Signals: 2nd Armd Divisional Signals (4 Mar 40–8 Apr 41)

The division was disbanded in Egypt on 10 May 1941. Its first GOC, Major General Frederick Hotblack, suffered a stroke in April 1940 and was succeeded by Willoughby Norrie as acting GOC. The next GOC, Major General Justice Tilly, was killed in an accident in Egypt on 5 January 1941. Brigadier H. B. Latham held the reins until Major General Michael Gambier-Parry took over on 12 February 1941. He was captured by Axis forces on 8 April 1941.

6th Armoured Division
(Formed 12 September 1940)

20 Armd Bde (16 Oct 40–23 Apr 42) 1 RGH; 1 NY; 2 NY

26 Armd Bde (9 Nov 40–31 Aug 45) 16/5 L; 17/21 L; 2 Lothians; 2 THR (16 Oct 40–14 Jan 41); 10 RB (15 Jan 41–29 May 44)

38 (Irish) Bde (9 Jun 42–16 Feb 43) 6 Innisks; 1 RIrF; 2 LIR

1 Gds Bde (24 Mar 43–31 Aug 45) 3 Gren Gds; 2 Cldm Gds (to 3 Mar 45); 2 Hamps (to 1 Jun 41; 10 Oct 41–25 Nov 42; 18–22 Feb 43); 3 W Gds (to 31 Aug 45); 1 Welch (9 Mar–23 Jun 45)

61 Bde (29 May 44–31 Aug 45) 2 RB; 7 RB; 10 RB (to 20 Mar 45); 1 KRRC (from 8 Mar 45)

6 Support Gp (1 Nov 40–31 May 42) 12 RHA; 72 A/T Regt; 15 LAA Regt (15 Jan 41–31 May 42); 9 RWK (3 Feb 41–24 Apr 42)

Divisional Reconnaissance: 1 DY (10 Nov 40–31 Aug 45)

Divisional Artillery: 12 (HAC) RHA (1 Jun 42–31 Aug 45); 152 Fd Regt (15 Jun 42–31 Aug 45) 72 A/T Regt (1 Jun 42–31 Aug 45); 51 LAA Regt (1 Jun 42–3 Nov 44)

Divisional Engineers: 5 Fd Sqn (19 Nov 40–6 Mar 44); 8 Fd Sqn (15 Dec 40–31 Aug 45); 625 Fd Sqn (7 Mar 44–31 Aug 45); 144 Fd Pk Sqn (19 Nov 40–31 Aug 45); 8 Brdg Tp (25 Dec 43–31 Aug 45)

Machine Gun/Support: B Hy Spt Gp Mx Regt (19 Dec 44–11 Feb 45); 1 Hy Spt Coy Mx Regt (12 Feb–31 Aug 45)

The first GOC was Major General John Crocker, who was succeeded by Herbert Lumsden. Charles Gairdner relieved Lumsden but it was Charles Keightley who took the Division to war in Tunisia in late 1942. In December 1943 Vyvyan Evelegh became GOC and was succeeded by Gerald Templer who was injured badly in August 1944, command passing to Horatius Murray on 21 August.

7th Armoured Division
(Formerly The Mobile Division, Egypt, redesignated The Armoured Division in September 1939; redesignated as 7th Armoured Division on 16 February 1940)

Lt Armd Bde (Egypt) (3 Sep 39–15 Feb 40) see 7 Armd Bde

Hy Armd Bde (Egypt) (3 Sep 39–15 Feb 40) see 4 Armd Bde

4 Hy Armd Bde see 4 Armd Bde

4 Armd Bde (16 Feb 40–29 Jul 41; 1 Nov–19 Dec 41; 4 Jan–25 Jun 42) 1 RTR (to 10 Apr 40; 3 Jun–7 Jul 42) 2 RTR (13 Oct 40–16 Apr 41); 4 RTR (5 May–27 Jul 41); 5 RTR (3 May–27 Jul 41; 31 Jul 41–7 Jun 42); 6 RTR (to 19 Jan 41; 7 Jun–7 Jul 42); 7 RTR (4 May–11 Jul 41); 7 H (10 Apr 40–3 May 41); 8 KRIH (17 Apr–3 May 41; 4 Jan–8 Feb 42; 14 Feb–2 Jun 42); 44 RTR (1–27 Jul 41); (from 7 Jun 42); 1 KRRC (1 Feb–7 Jul 42)

7 Lt Armd Bde see 7 Armd Bde

7 Armd Bde (16 Feb–18 May 40; 2 Jul 40–30 Apr 41; 20 May 41–27 Nov 41) 3 H (10 Oct 40–22 Jan 41); 7 H (to 10 Apr 40; from 7 Jul 41); 8 KRIH (to 19 Jan 41; 7 Mar–16 Apr 41); 11 H (to 14 Apr 40); 1 RTR (10 Apr 40–3 Apr 41); 2 RTR (16 Apr–10 Jul 41; from 6 Sep 41); 4 RTR (16 Apr–8 May 41); 6 RTR (from 8 Jun 41); 2 RB (16–30 Apr 41)

1 Army Tank Bde (29 Jul–9 Nov 41) 8 RTR (from 1 Sep 41); 44 RTR

22 Armd Bde (4 Jan–8 Feb 42; 26 Jul 42–31 Aug 45) 2 RGH (to 16 Sep 42); 3 CLY (to 16 Sep 42); 4 CLY (to 29 Jul 44); 1 RTR (17 Sep 42–31 Aug 45); 5 RTR (17 Sep 42–31 Aug 45); 5 R Innisk DG (29 Jul 44–31 Aug 45); 1 RB (26 Jul 42–31 Aug 45)

131 Lorried Infantry Bde (1 Nov 42–3 Mar 44) see 131 Inf Bde

131 Infantry Bde (4 Mar 44–31 Aug 45) 1/5 Queen's; 1/6 Queen's (to 3 Dec 44); 1/7 Queen's (to 3 Dec 44); 2 Devon (1 Dec 44–31 Aug 45); 9 DLI (2 Dec 44–31 Aug 45)

7 Support Gp: (22 Jan 40–12 Apr 41; 6 Jun 41–4 Jan 42; 19 Jan–8 Feb 42) see 7 Motor Bde

7 Motor Bde: (9 Feb–26 Jun 42; 5 Jul–11 Sep 42) M Bty 3 RHA; C Bty 4 RHA; 1 LAA Bty; 3 RHA; 4 RHA; 38 LAA Bty; 1 LAA Regt; 1 KRRC; 2 RB; 9 KRRC; 7 RB (from 11 Aug 42)

Divisional Reconnaissance: 11 H (10 Apr 40–3 Nov 43); 8 KRIH (16 Dec 43–31 Aug 45)

Divisional Artillery: 1 RHA (24 Aug–13 Sep 42); 3 RHA (24 Aug 42–31 Aug 45); 4 RHA (24 Aug–21 Sep 42); 5 RHA (1 Dec 42–31 Aug 45); 4 Fd Regt (18 Sep–10 Dec 42); 74 Fd Regt (13–18

Sep 42); 97 Fd Regt (13 Sep– 1 Dec 42); 146 Fd Regt (10 Dec 42–6 Nov 43); 65 A/T Regt (13 Sep 42–29 May 45); 21 A/T Regt (21 Jun–31 Aug 45); 15 LAA Regt (2 Aug 42–31 Aug 45)

Divisional Engineers: 4 Fd Sqn (17 May 41–14 Mar 42; 24 Aug 42–31 Aug 45); 21 Fd Sqn (4 Oct 42–13 Aug 43); 621 Fd Sqn (14 Aug 43–31 Aug 45); 143 Fd Pk Sqn (17 May 41–31 Aug 45); 7 Brdg Tp (6 Dec 43–31 Aug 45)

Divisional Signals: 7th Armd Divisional Signals

Machine Gun/Support: 3 Ind MG Coy RNF

As The Mobile Division, Egypt, the division was formed under Major General Percy Hobart, who was relieved of his command; Major General Sir O'Moore Creagh succeeded him. In September 1941 Major General W. H. E. 'Strafer' Gott was appointed GOC and held that appointment until 5 February 1942 when he was succeeded by Major General J. C. 'Jock' Campbell VC, who was killed in a car crash on 23 February. Brigadier Alex Gatehouse acted as GOC until Major General Frank Messervy took up post on 9 March. Messervy, in turn, was succeeded by Major General J. W. M. Renton who handed over to Major General A. F. 'John' Harding on 14 September. When Harding was wounded on 19 January 1943 Brigadier G. P. B. Roberts took temporary command, handing over to Major General G. W. E. J. Erskine on the 24th. Erskine was GOC until 4 August 1944 when Major General G. L. Verney took command. On 22 November 1944 Major General L. O. Lyne became the last wartime GOC of the Desert Rats.

8th Armoured Division
(Formed 4 November 1940)

23 Armd Bde (22 Nov 40–11 Jul 42) 40 RTR; 46 RTR; 50 RTR; 1 LRB (2 Dec 40–18 Jan 41); 7 RB (from 19 Jan 41)

24 Armd Bde (22 Nov 40–6 Nov 42) 41 RTR; 45 RTR; 47 RTR; 1 QW (1 Dec 40–31 Jan 41); 11 KRRC (from 1 Feb 41)

8 Support Gp: (7 Nov 40–22 Jul 42) 5 RHA (18 Dec 40–17 Jul 42); 56 LAA Regt (from 24 Jan 41); 73 A/T Regt (from 8 Nov 40); 14 Foresters (from 30 Nov 40)

Divisional Reconnaissance: 2 DY (27 Nov 40–20 Aug 42)

Divisional Artillery: 5 RHA (19 Sep–11 Nov 42); 11 (HAC) RHA (12–20 Aug 42); 104 RHA (13–26 Sep 42); 146 Fd Regt (19 Sep–6 Nov 42); 73 A/T Regt (25 Sep–26 Oct 42); 56 LAA Regt (23 Jul–6 Nov 42)

Divisional Engineers: 6 Fd Sqn (27 Nov 40–9 Nov 42); 9 Fd Sqn (15 Jan 41–11 Jul 42; 15 Sep–9 Nov 42); 145 Fd Pk Sqn (27 Nov 40–9 Nov 42)

Divisional Signals: 8th Armd Divisional Signals

The first GOC of the Division was Major General Richard McCreery, although Brigadier A. G. Kenchington acted as GOC on formation. McCreery commanded from 14 December 1940 until handing over to Major General Charles Norman on 15 October 1941. The last GOC was Major General Charles Gairdner who assumed the post on 24 August 1942. The division was broken up with its constituent formations under other commands and was disbanded on 1 January 1943.

9th Armoured Division
(Formed 1 December 1940)

27 Armd Bde: (4 Dec 40–11 Jun 42) 4/7 RDG; 13/18 H; 1 ERY

28 Armd Bde: (4 Dec 40–9 Jul 44) 5 R Innisk DG; 15/19 H; 1 FFY; 2 QVR (to 14 Jan 41); 8 KRRC (from 15 Jan 41)

9 Support Gp: (4 Dec 40–11 Jun 42) 6 RHA; 54 LAA Regt (from 10 Mar 41); 74 A/T Regt (from 12 Dec 40)

7 Inf Bde: (12 Jun 42–31 Jul 44) 6 R Sussex; 2/6 Surrey; 2 SWB (to 1 Mar 44)

Divisional Reconnaissance: Inns of Court Regt (23 Jan 41–15 Jan 43); 1 RGH (16 Jan 43–10 Jan 44)

Divisional Artillery: 6 RHA (12 Jun 42–10 Jul 44); 141 Fd Regt (12 Jun 42–10 Jul 44); 74 A/T Regt (12 Jun 42–6 Nov 43); 92 A/T Regt (12 Nov 43–10 Jul 44); 54 LAA Regt (12 Jun 42–2 Mar 44); 150 LAA Regt (2 Mar–10 Jul 44)

Divisional Engineers: 10 Fd Sqn (16 Mar 41–24 Jul 44); 11 Fd Sqn (15 Mar 41–1 Mar 43); 611 Fd Sqn (1 Mar 43–24 Jul 44); 146 Fd Pk Sqn (16 Mar 41–25 Jul 44); 9 Brdg Tp (1 Oct 43–25 Jul 44)

Divisional Signals: 9th Armd Divisional Signals

Major General Montagu Burrows was the first GOC of 9th Armoured Division, handing over to Brian Horrocks on 20 March 1942. The third, and final, GOC was Major General John D'Arcy, who took over as acting GOC in August 1942 before being promoted major general the following month. The division was disbanded in the UK on 31 July 1944, without ever deploying on active service.

10th Armoured Division
(Formed 1 August 1941 in Palestine by re-designating 1st Cavalry Division)

8 Armd Bde: (1 Aug 41–16 Feb 42; 27 Mar–30 Jun 42; 17 Jul–21 Nov 42) Notts Y; Staffs Y; Greys (to 30 Jun 42); 3 RTR (from 12 Jul 42)

9 Armd Bde: (9 Oct 41–25 Mar 42; 14 Nov 42–27 May 43) R Wilts Y; Warwick Y; Yks H (to 13 Mar 42); 3 H; 14 Foresters (to 9 Dec 42); 11 KRRC (from 9 Dec 42)

7 Armd Bde: (3 Jun 43–11 Apr 44) 2 RTR; 6 RTR; 8 RTR (from 29 Jan 44); 2 RB (from 26 Sep 43; 19 Dec 43–20 May 44)

23 Armd Bde: (1–14 Jun 44) 40 RTR; 50 RTR; 11 KRRC

7 Motor Bde: (12–23 Sep 42) 2 KKRC; 2 RB; 7 RB

133 Lorried Infantry Bde: (29 Sep–25 Nov 42) 4 Buffs; 2 R Sussex; 4 R Sussex; 5 R Sussex

201 Guards Motor Bde: (9 Jan–1 Feb 43) 6 Gren Gds; 3 Cldm Gds; 2 S Gds

Divisional Reconnaissance: 1 HCR (9 Oct 41–13 Mar 42; 14 Jan–5 Nov 43); 2 DY (21 Aug–10 Sep 42); Royals (22 Sep–31 Oct 42); 7 H (5 Nov 43–25 Apr 44)

Divisional Artillery: 1 RHA (13 Sep 42–27 May 43; 13 Nov 43–25 Apr 44); 14 RHA (3 Jun–8 Nov 43); 104 RHA (27 Sep 42–3 May 44); 98 Fd Regt (19 Sep–29 Dec 42); 84 A/T Regt (13 Sep 42–20 May 44)

53 LAA Regt (2 Sep–2 Nov 42); 101 LAA Regt (11 Oct 43–30 Apr 44)

Divisional Engineers: 2 Fd Sqn (21 Nov 41–10 Jun 43); 3 Fd Sqn (22 Sep–31 Oct 42); 622 Fd Sqn (11 Jun 43–31 May 44); 141 Fd Pk Sqn (20 Nov 41–1 Apr 44); 6 Brdg Tp (20 Nov 43–1 Apr 44)

Divisional Signals: 10th Armd Divisional Signals

Major General John Clark, GOC of the Cavalry Division became the first GOC 10th Armoured Division and was succeeded, on 26 June 1942, by Major General Alex Gatehouse who remained in command until December when Major General Charles Norman took over briefly before Horace Birks became the final GOC on 12 January 1943. The division was disbanded in Egypt on 15 June 1944.

11th Armoured Division
(Formed 9 March 1941)

29 Armd Bde: (9 Mar 41–31 Aug 45) 24 L (to 6 Feb 44); 23 H; 2 FFY (from 7 Jun 41); 3 RTR (from 6 Feb 44); 8 RB

30 Armd Bde: (9 Mar 41–20 Apr 42) 22 D; W Dgns; 1 Lothians; 2 QW (to 25 Mar 41); 12 KRRC (from 26 Mar 41)

11 Support Gp: (9 Mar 41–31 May 42) 13 RHA; 58 LAA Regt (from 7 May 41); 75 A/T Regt

159 Infantry Bde: (1 Jun 42–31 Aug 45) 4 KSLI; 3 Mon (to 3 Apr 45); 1 Hereford; 1 Cheshire (from 6 Apr 45)

Divisional Reconnaissance: 27 L (10 Mar 41–25 Mar 43); 2 NY (25 Mar 43–17 Aug 44); 15/19 H (17 Aug 44–31 Aug 45)

Divisional Artillery: 13 RHA (1 Jun 42–31 Aug 45); 151 Fd Regt (1 Jun 42–31 Aug 45); 75 A/T Regt (1 Jun 42–2 Jun 45); 65 A/T Regt (2 Jun–31 Aug 45); 58 LAA Regt (1 Jun 42–31 Aug 45)

Divisional Engineers: 12 Fd Sqn (16 Mar 41–1 Jan 43) 13 Fd Sqn (16 Mar 41–31 Aug 45); 612 Fd Sqn (1 Jan 43–31 Aug 45); 147 Fd Pk Sqn (16 Mar 41–31 Aug 45); 10 Brdg Tp (1 Oct 43–31 Aug 45)

Divisional Signals: 11th Armd Divisional Signals

Machine Gun/Support: 2 Ind MG Coy RNF

Major General Percy Hobart, the first GOC of 11th Armoured Division, was relieved of command on medical grounds when it was planned to deploy the division to North Africa. Montagu Burrows took command from 15 October 1942 until 'Pip' Roberts assumed command on 6 December 1943. Roberts was GOC throughout the campaign in north-west Europe.

42nd Armoured Division
(Formed 1 November 1941 by converting 42nd Infantry Division)

10 Armd Bde: (1 Nov 41–13 May 42) 108 RAC; 109 RAC; 145 RAC; 13 HLI (from 17 Nov 41)

11 Armd Bde: (1 Nov 41–13 May 42) 107 RAC; 110 RAC; 111 RAC; 1 HLI

30 Armd Bde: (13 May 42–16 Oct 43) 22 D; W Dgns; 1 Lothians; 12 KRRC

42 Support Gp: (1 Nov 41–31 May 42) 147 Fd Regt; 93 LAA Regt (from 26 Jan 42); 53 A/T Regt

71 Infantry Bde: (14 Jun 42–16 Oct 43) 1 E Lancs; 1 HLI; 13 HLI (to 30 Jul 42); 1 Ox & Bks (from 30 Jul 42)

Divisional Reconnaissance: 112 RAC (17 Nov 41–24 Feb 43); 1 NY (18 Apr–16 Oct 43)

Divisional Artillery: 86 Fd Regt (10 Jun 42–3 May 43); 147 Fd Regt (1 Jun 42–23 Sep 43); 191 Fd Regt (3 May–7 Oct 43); 53 A/Tk Regt (1 Jun 42–7 Oct 43); 93 LAA Regt (1 Jun 42–23 Sep 43)

Divisional Engineers: 16 Fd Sqn (3 Nov 41–17 Sep 43); 17 Fd Sqn (3 Nov 41–1 Mar 43); 617 Fd Sqn (1 Mar–17 Sep 43); 149 Fd Pk Sqn (3 Nov 41–17 Sep 43)

Divisional Signals: 42nd Armd Divisional Signals

This division was disbanded on 17 October 1943, less than two years after formation. Only two GOCs, Major Generals Miles Dempsey and John Aizlewood, were appointed, Dempsey commanding from formation until 1 December 1942 and Aizlewood from then until disbandment.

79th Armoured Division
(Formed 14 August 1942)

(In April 1943 the division was re-organized to become the parent formation for all specialized armour and to take responsibility for developing such armour. Only the original organization is shown.)

27 Armd Bde: (8 Sep 42–13 Apr 43) 4/7 RDG; 13/18 H; 1 ERY; 7 KRRC

185 Infantry Bde: (8 Sep 42–12 Apr 43) 2 Warwick; 1 Norfolk; 2 KSLI

Divisional Reconnaissance: 162 RAC (10 Sep 42–10 Jan 43); 2 NY (10 Jan–25 Mar 43)

Divisional Artillery: 142 Fd Regt (11 Sep 42–20 Apr 43); 150 Fd Regt (16 Sep 42–27 Mar 43)

Divisional Engineers: 18 Fd Sqn (10 Sep 42–2 Mar 43); 19 Fd Sqn (8 Sep 42–25 Mar 43); 508 Fd Pk Sqn (10 Sep 42–12 Feb 43)

Divisional Signals: 79th Armd Divisional Signals

Brigadier G. McI. Bruce was acting GOC on formation, handing over to Percy Hobart who commanded the division in both standard and specialized roles until the end of the war.

Appendix 2

Armoured Commanders

Major General Sir Allan Adair Bt GCVO CB DSO MC*: Commissioned in the Grenadier Guards in 1916 with whom he earned the MC in France, he was appointed GOC Guards Armoured Division on 12 September 1942, succeeding Major General Sir Oliver Leese. Adair commanded the division throughout the war, in the Normandy battles, the advance into Belgium, the liberation of Brussels, the attempt to relieve 1st Airborne Division at Arnhem and the final advance from the Rhine into Germany. Montgomery tried to have him removed from command in Normandy but Sir Richard O'Connor, his corps commander, refused to write an adverse report on him and was justified, as Adair proved a competent and very popular commander.

Major General John Aldam Aizlewood MC: Commissioned in 4th Royal Irish Dragoon Guards in 1914 he commanded his regiment, by then 4th/7th Royal Dragoon Guards, and was promoted to brigade command in India. He became commander 30 Armoured Brigade in 1942 and GOC 42nd Armoured Division in December 1942. When the division was disbanded he moved to district and command posts and retired in 1945.

Major General Horace Leslie Birks CB DSO: Enlisted in the London Rifle Brigade in 1915 and commissioned in the Machine Gun Corps in 1917. Having been wounded he transferred to the Tank Corps and was given a regular commission in the Worcestershire Regiment in 1918 but transferred again to the Tank Corps. On the staff of the Mobile Division (Egypt) he was appointed deputy commander 4 Armoured Brigade in 1940 and fought in the COMPASS campaign. Served with his brigade in Tobruk during the siege of 1941 after which he returned to the UK to command 11 Armoured Brigade in 42nd Armoured Division. In 1943 he was promoted and appointed GOC 10th Armoured Division which was disbanded in late-1944, after which Birks served as an armoured adviser in Italy.

Major General Raymond Briggs CB DSO: A volunteer in 1914 he was commissioned in 1915 and transferred to the Machine Gun Corps in 1917 and to the Tank Corps in 1920 with which he remained. In 1939 he was an adviser on AFVs with GHQ BEF and later helped evacuate British personnel from France. In 1941 he was promoted and appointed commander of 2 Armoured Brigade in 1st Armoured Division with which he served in North Africa, being appointed GOC 1st Armoured in August 1942 which he commanded during the final battle of El Alamein. In May 1943 he was wounded near Tunis and came home to become Director RAC at the War Office.

Field Marshal Lord Alanbrooke KG GCB OM GCVO DSO: Commissioned in the Royal Artillery in 1902 Brooke served throughout the Great War. An outstanding and innovative gunner officer, he was six times Mentioned in Despatches and appointed DSO; he introduced the creeping bombardment to the British and Canadian armies. In 1937 he was appointed GOC Mobile Division, later 1st Armoured Division and retained an interest in armoured warfare although not regarded as a tank enthusiast. Having commanded a corps in France in 1940 he later became C-in-C Home Forces and was quick to point out errors in the handling of armour. As CIGS from December 1941 until after the war he promoted officers who had impressed him, including some who served under him in the Mobile Division. It was Brooke who asked Hobart to accept command of 79th Armoured Division as a parent formation controlling all British specialized armour.

Lieutenant General Montagu Brocas Burrows CB DSO MC: Commissioned in 5th Dragoon Guards in 1914 he was taken prisoner during the retreat from Mons. He served with the North Russian Expeditionary Force in 1918–19, was appointed DSO, awarded the MC and twice Mentioned in Despatches. In the early 1930s he was brigade major of 1 Cavalry Brigade and then served in the War Office before becoming military attaché in Rome, Budapest and Tirana. A protégé of Brooke, he was promoted major general in 1940 and appointed GOC 9th Armoured Division but was transferred to 11th Armoured in 1942. In December 1943 he handed the division over to Roberts and had no further connection with armour as he was appointed head of the UK Military Mission to Moscow.

Major General John Charles (Jock) Campbell VC DSO* MC: Enlisted in the Honourable Artillery Company in 1914 and commissioned in the Royal Artillery in 1915. He was wounded twice and earned the MC in the course of the Great War. By 1939 he was a major but was promoted to command 3rd Regiment RHA in 1940, distinguishing himself during the Italian attack on the Egyptian frontier in September 1940. Creating small mobile columns of infantry and artillery, known as Jock Columns, he led the enemy to believe that British strength was greater than it really was. During the 1941 CRUSADER battles he commanded 7th Armoured Division's Support Group and earned the VC for his leadership at the battle of Sidi Rezegh. Promoted major general and appointed GOC 7th Armoured Division he was killed when his staff car crashed and overturned on the Halfaya Pass.

Lieutenant General John George Walters Clark CB MC: Commissioned in 16th (Queen's) Lancers in 1911 he served in France during the Great War where he was wounded, three times Mentioned in Despatches and awarded the MC. He later commanded his regiment, now 16th/5th Lancers, and, having commanded an infantry brigade, was promoted and appointed GOC 1st Cavalry Division in Palestine. After helping suppress the Rashid Ali rebellion in Iraq he was switched to staff jobs when his division was mechanized to become 10th Armoured Division.

Major General Sir Michael O'Moore Creagh KBE MC: Commissioned in 7th (Queen's Own) Hussars in 1911, Creagh served in France during the Great War earning a Mention in Despatches and the MC. He transferred to 15th/19th Hussars in 1925 and commanded the regiment in the mid-30s. On the outbreak of war he was Inspector Royal Armoured Corps at the War Office before being sent to Egypt to succeed Hobart as GOC Mobile Division Egypt). As the first GOC 7th Armoured Division he led it throughout much of the COMPASS campaign. After the failure of BATTLEAXE in June 1941 he was held responsible for the defeat and recalled to Britain where Dill, the CIGS, suggested to Brooke, as C-in-C Home Forces, that he be appointed GOC 42nd Armoured Division but Brooke chose not to do so and Creagh's career was at an end in spite of his having been knighted and twice Mentioned in Despatches in 1941.

General Sir John Crocker GCB KBE DSO MC: Enlisting in the Artists Rifles in 1915 Crocker served in France and was commissioned in the Machine Gun Corps with which he earned the MC and was appointed DSO. Although he left the Army in 1919 he rejoined the next year, was commissioned in the Middlesex Regiment and transferred to the Royal Tank Corps. In 1934 he was appointed brigade major of 1 Tank Brigade and by 1939 was commander 3 Armoured Brigade in 1st Armoured Division with which he saw active service in France in 1940. In September 1940 he was appointed as the first GOC 6th Armoured Division before promotions took him to command 2 Armoured Group and then IX Corps. He later commanded I Corps throughout the north-west Europe campaign in which his son, Lieutenant Wilfred Crocker, was killed while serving with 5th Royal Inniskilling Dragoon Guards.

Lieutenant General John Conyers D'Arcy CB CBE MC: Commissioned in the Royal Garrison Artillery in 1913 D'Arcy served in France during the Great War and was wounded twice and earned the MC. He received a third wound on the North-West Frontier in 1931. In August 1942 he was appointed acting GOC 9th Armoured Division and was subsequently promoted major general and confirmed in his appointment. Although he spent two years training his troops the division was not sent to war but was disbanded in July 1944 at which stage D'Arcy was promoted lieutenant general and appointed GOC British Troops, Palestine.

General Sir Miles Dempsey GBE KCB DSO MC: Commissioned in the Royal Berkshire Regiment in 1915 Dempsey served in France where he earned a Mention in Despatches and an MC as well as being wounded and later gassed. He commanded 1st Royal Berkshires from 1938 and was promoted to command 13 Brigade in 5th Division in France in 1939. Appointed DSO for his role in France he later served with the Canadians and was promoted major general and appointed GOC 46th Division before Montgomery had him transferred to the new 42nd Armoured Division in June 1942. Montgomery then had him appointed commander XIII Corps after El Alamein and he continued to command that corps until early in the Italian campaign when he was again called upon by Montgomery, this time to command Second Army which he did throughout the north-west Europe campaign. Although he had commanded an armoured division, and had armour under his command as both a corps and army commander, Dempsey showed no flair as an armoured commander, nor any deep appreciation of armour's role.

General Sir George Erskine GCB KBE DSO: Commissioned in the King's Royal Rifle Corps in 1918 he was CO of its 2nd Battalion in 1940–41 before being promoted to command 69 Brigade in North Africa in 1942. After staff jobs at XIII Corps and HQ Eighth Army he was promoted major general and appointed GOC 7th Armoured Division. Erskine led the division in the final phase of the Tunisian campaign, in the early part of the Italian campaign and in the Normandy campaign. He was removed from his post by Montgomery and appointed head of the SHAEF Mission to Belgium.

Major General Roger Evans CB MC: Commissioned in 7th (Queen's Own) Hussars in 1907 Evans served in Mesopotamia in 1917–18, was Mentioned in Despatches and awarded the MC. He commanded 5th Royal Inniskilling Dragoon Guards from 1929 to 1933 and was promoted major general in 1938, being appointed GOC Mobile Division. He was then appointed Deputy Director of Military Operations at the War Office before being appointed GOC 1st Armoured Division with which he was ordered to France in 1940. Evans was removed from his command in August 1940 and appointed Commander Aldershot District. His son, Michael, a lieutenant in the Household Cavalry, died on active service in Syria in December 1942.

Major General Vyvyan Evelegh CB DSO OBE: Commissioned in the Duke of Cornwall's LI in 1917 he served in France and then with the Allied Relief Force in north Russia, where he was wounded. By 1939 he was commanding a battalion in the BEF but was posted home as an instructor at Camberley before the German attack. Appointed OBE he was promoted to command 11 Brigade before being promoted major general in 1942. After a brief spell back at Camberley he was appointed GOC 78th Division and took his new command to Tunisia as part of First Army. An outstanding divisional commander he suffered from having been in First Army when 78th Division was transferred to Eighth Army and was passed over for corps command by both Montgomery and Leese. He was given 6th Armoured Division in February 1944 but was removed from command in July after the division's perceived slowness in exploitation after the Hitler Line battles.

Major General Sir Evelyn Dalrymple Fanshawe KBE CB CBE: Commissioned in the Queen's Bays in 1914 Fanshawe saw service in France, Egypt, Palestine, Mesopotamia, Persia, Russia and Syria and was also seconded to the Royal Flying Corps. He served with 20 Mechanized Cavalry Brigade in 1939 before being appointed to command 20 Armoured Brigade the following year, during which he was also acting GOC 6th Armoured Division. Promoted major general in 1942 he was appointed to command the RAC Training Establishment and held that post until the end of the war.

General Sir Charles Henry Gairdner GBE KCMG KCVO CB: Commissioned in the Royal Artillery in 1916 and wounded in France he transferred to the cavalry after the war and rose to command 10th Royal Hussars from 1937 to 1940. He then served on the staff of 7th Armoured Division and was Deputy Director of Plans, Middle East, before being recalled to the UK where he was promoted major general and appointed GOC 6th Armoured Division. Less than six months later he was appointed Commandant of the Higher Commanders' School at Sarafand. In August 1942 he was appointed GOC 8th Armoured Division. However, the division did not see action as a formation, its elements being attached to other formations at El Alamein and, although there had been talk of it taking part in the pursuit of Panzerarmee Afrika, it was disbanded in January 1943. Briefly CGS North Africa he was removed by Montgomery and later became Major General AFVs, India, before being promoted lieutenant general.

Lieutenant General Sir Alexander Galloway KBE CB DSO MC: Commissioned in the Cameronians (Scottish Rifles) in 1914 he served in Gallipoli, Egypt, Palestine and France and was awarded the MC in France in 1918. When war broke out again in 1939 he was commanding 1st Cameronians but was appointed Commandant of the new Middle East Staff College at Haifa in February 1940. He worked as a staff officer on the plans for COMPASS and was later CGS to Cunningham in Eighth Army. In July 1943 he was appointed GOC 1st Armoured Division and spent months training his command but was not to lead them in action. Instead he was sent to Italy as temporary GOC 4th Indian Division while awaiting 1st Armoured's arrival in Italy. However, he was hospitalized due to ill health and returned to the UK with command of the division passing to Richard Hull. Although he served on the staff of 21 Army Group and commanded 3rd Division briefly in 1945 he never had the opportunity to lead an armoured division in action. His temperament and his quick thinking would have fitted him for the role.

Major General Michael Denman Gambier-Parry MC: Commissioned in the Royal Welsh Fusiliers in 1911 he served in Gallipoli and Mesopotamia and was Mentioned in Despatches six times as well as being awarded the MC. He transferred to the Royal Tank Corps in 1924 and was appointed commander of the Malaya Infantry Brigade in 1938. Promoted major general in 1940 he was appointed GOC 2nd Armoured Division in Cyrenaica in February 1941 in tragic circumstances after the accidental death of Major General Justice Tilly. Tilly had been appointed to succeed Major General Frederick Hotblack who had suffered a stroke. Not only had 2nd Armoured suffered the loss of two GOCs in a very short time but it had deployed to Cyrenaica as little more than a weak brigade just as Rommel was attacking from Tripolitania. Not surprisingly, the division was overwhelmed and Gambier-Parry, with most of his staff, was captured by Afrika Korps in April 1941. Released in 1943 he returned to the UK in mid-1944 and retired from the Army soon after.

Major General Alexander Hugh Gatehouse DSO MC: Commissioned in the Northumberland Fusiliers in 1915 he transferred to the Tank Corps the following year and was awarded the MC at Cambrai in 1917. By the outbreak of the Second World War he was deputy commander 7 Armoured Brigade. The brigade was part of 7th Armoured Division and Gatehouse took part in the actions of the COMPASS campaign, his brigade leading the attack on Sidi Barrani and being at the battle of Beda Fomm. He took command of 4 Armoured Brigade in 1941, leading it in Operation BATTLEAXE. He also commanded during the CRUSADER battles and was appointed DSO, receiving a Bar within weeks. In June 1942 he was appointed GOC 10th Armoured Division and was praised for his defence at Alam el Halfa. However, with Lumsden, he incurred Montgomery's ire at El Alamein for what Montgomery saw as poor leadership but was really a clear understanding of what armour could do, an understanding Montgomery did not share. He was relieved of his command in November 1942 and served in a series of staff appointments for the remainder of the war. It was Gatehouse's view that Montgomery had allowed Rommel to retire from El Alamein in good order.

General Sir Reade Godwin-Austen KCSI CB OBE MC: Commissioned in the South Wales Borderers in 1909 and served in Gallipoli, Palestine and Mesopotamia during the Great War, earning two Mentions in Despatches and the MC. By 1939 he was commanding an infantry brigade and, in that year, was promoted major general and appointed GOC 8th Division. Commanded the withdrawal from Somaliland and then was GOC 2nd African Division in the Abyssinian campaign and the conquest of Italian Somaliland. Appointed commander XIII Corps in the newly-created Eighth Army in September 1941 and played a major part in the success of Operation CRUSADER. However, during Rommel's subsequent offensive he asked to be relieved of his command having reacted vociferously to orders from Ritchie, the Army Commander, to counter-attack. Although he served only in staff posts thereafter he remained in the Army until 1947.

Lieutenant General William Henry Ewart Gott CB CBE DSO* MC: Commissioned in the King's Royal Rifle Corps in 1915 he served in France where he earned the MC and was wounded. By 1938 he was CO of 1st King's Royal Rifle Corps which was in the Mobile Division, then commanded by Brooke. Posted to Egypt in 1939 his battalion became the hub of the support group for the Mobile Division (Egypt) and, by 1940, Gott, then a brigadier and commander of the support group, played a major part in the COMPASS campaign, acquiring the soubriquet 'Strafer'. In September 1941 he was appointed GOC 7th Armoured Division and led it through the CRUSADER battles, for which he was appointed DSO. He succeeded Godwin-Austen as commander XIII Corps and earned the respect of officers and men alike during the difficult battles of 1942 and the retreat to the El Alamein line. In August 1942 he was selected to be the new commander Eighth Army but the plane carrying him back to Cairo was shot down en route and Gott was killed.

Field Marshal Sir John Harding (Allan Francis, The Lord Harding of Petherton) GCB CBE DSO** MC: Enlisted in the London Regiment in 1914 and served with the Machine Gun Corps in Gallipoli, Egypt and Palestine, was wounded and earned the MC having been commissioned into the Somerset LI. He remained with the Machine Gun Corps until it was disbanded in 1921 when he returned to the Somersets and, in 1939, became CO of the 1st Battalion. Sent to Egypt he was a staff officer to O'Connor during Operation COMPASS and was BGS to XIII Corps in 1941–42; he was also appointed DSO. In September 1942 he was appointed GOC 7th Armoured Division and led it through the El Alamein battle, for which he received a Bar to his DSO. Badly wounded in January 1943 during the pursuit to Tripoli he was invalided home but returned to operational service in Italy in December as Alexander's Chief of Staff. He played a major part in the planning for Operation DIADEM in May 1944 and was knighted in the field by King George VI. In March 1945 he was appointed commander XIII Corps in Italy.

Major General Sir Percy Hobart KBE CB DSO MC: Commissioned in the Royal Engineers in 1904 and saw service in India before the Great War. During that war he served in France, earning the MC, and in Mesopotamia. Appointed DSO in 1916 he also received six Mentions in Despatches. Transferring to the Tank Corps in 1923 he became an advocate of armoured warfare and one of the leading thinkers on the subject. Between the wars he commanded a battalion of the Royal Tank Corps, was Inspector RTC and commander 1 Tank Brigade before becoming Deputy Director Staff Duties at the War Office. Promoted major general he was then appointed Director of Military Training but was passed over in favour of Brooke for command of the Mobile Division. In 1938 he was posted to Egypt to command the Mobile Division (Egypt) but was subsequently relieved and sent back to the UK where he joined the Home Guard as a lance corporal. However, he was brought out of retirement at Churchill's behest and was appointed GOC of the newly-formed 11th Armoured Division. Relieved of that command as he was considered too old for active service he was appointed GOC 79th Armoured Division and retained his command when that formation was re-organized to control all the specialized AFVs for 21 Army Group. His skill in training and innovative thinking ensured that the division and its 'Funnies' became an integral part of ground operations on D Day and throughout the subsequent campaign. He was knighted in 1943 and was appointed Commandant of the Specialized Warfare Experimental Establishment when 79th Armoured Division was disbanded.

Lieutenant General Sir Brian Horrocks KCB KBE DSO MC: Commissioned in the Middlesex Regiment in 1914 he was captured in October 1914. After the war he served with the Military Mission in Vladivostok and was awarded the MC but again was taken prisoner. Horrocks represented the UK in the modern pentathlon in the 1924 Olympiad. As the new CO of 2nd Middlesex in 1940 he arrived at the battalion HQ as the Germans were sweeping through Belgium. He commanded with distinction and was appointed to command 11 Brigade in France. By mid-1941 he was GOC 44th Division and, in March 1942, was appointed GOC 9th Armoured Division. He found the division well trained, thanks to his predecessor, Burrows. That August he was sent to Egypt to command XIII Corps which he led through the El Alamein battle before assuming command of X Corps, in which his experience with armour was of great advantage. In Tunisia he commanded IX Corps but was wounded badly in a strafing attack in June and invalided home. He returned to service in France in August 1944 as commander XXX Corps, leading the corps in the failed attempt to relieve the airborne at Arnhem. In March 1945 he led XXX Corps in the Rhine crossing and thereafter until the German surrender.

Major General Frederick Elliott Hotblack DSO MC: Commissioned in the Royal Dragoons in 1907 he served in France during the Great War and was wounded five times, Mentioned in Despatches, awarded the MC and appointed DSO and Bar, having been transferred to tanks. In 1925 he transferred to the Royal Tank Corps and served in a number of staff posts. Having been in France with the BEF he was recalled in December 1939 and appointed GOC 2nd Armoured Division. Unfortunately, he suffered a stroke in 1940 and was never again fit enough for military duties although he had been seen as a man of outstanding promise.

Field Marshal Sir Richard Amyatt Hull KG GCB DSO: Commissioned in the 17th/21st Lancers in 1928 he was CO of his regiment in 1941 before serving on the staff of 5th Canadian Armoured Division and of 2 Group RAC. In 1942 he commanded Blade Force in First Army in Operation TORCH and led his command to the outskirts of Tunis. Appointed DSO he became appointed deputy commander 26 Armoured Brigade assuming command of the brigade towards the end of the Tunisian campaign, having briefly commanded 12 Infantry Brigade. He returned to the UK as Deputy Director Staff Duties in December 1943, was promoted acting major general in 1944 and appointed GOC 1st Armoured Division in May. His division was disbanded after the battles on the Gothic Line but Hull went on to rise to the very top of the Army, having been one of the youngest divisional commanders of the Second World War.

General Sir Charles Frederic Keightley GCB CBE DSO: Commissioned in 5th Dragoon Guards in 1921 he was appointed to the staff of 1st Armoured Division in May 1940 and served in the brief campaign. He then commanded 30 Armoured Brigade before being promoted major general in charge of RAC training. In May 1942 he was appointed GOC 6th Armoured Division and led that formation throughout the Tunisian campaign, helping stem the Axis attack at Kasserine. In December 1943 he took command of 78th Division and in August 1944 became commander V Corps, which he commanded until after the war.

Lieutenant General Sir Oliver William Hargreaves Leese KCB CBE DSO: Commissioned in the Coldstream Guards in 1914 he served in France where he was wounded three times, Mentioned in Despatches twice and appointed DSO. In 1936 he assumed command of 1st Coldstream after which he was chief instructor at the Staff College Quetta. When he returned from India he was appointed to command 32 Brigade in the BEF in France and after Dunkirk took command of 29 Brigade. Promoted major general in 1941 he spent much time training troops and commanded both West Sussex County and 15th (Scottish) Divisions before being appointed the first GOC Guards Armoured Division. Montgomery asked for his presence in Egypt where he became commander XXX Corps which he commanded at El Alamein. In December 1943 he was appointed to command Eighth Army with which he remained until promoted to land forces commander in South-East Asia. He was dismissed from the latter post in April 1945 and became GOC Eastern Command in the UK before retiring from the Army in 1946.

Lieutenant General Herbert Lumsden CB DSO MC: Commissioned in the Royal Artillery in 1915 he served in France where he earned the MC. In 1923 he transferred to 12th Royal Lancers, rising to command the regiment, now an armoured car unit, in 1938 and helped cover the retreat to Dunkirk in 1940 for which he was appointed DSO. Promoted brigadier he commanded a tank brigade before being appointed GOC 1st Armoured Division in November 1941. Carver considered him a leader of exceptional quality and Montgomery appointed him to command X Corps in September 1942. Accused by Montgomery of not pushing his armour hard enough at El Alamein he was sacked in December. Later in the war Churchill sent Lumsden to be his representative on General MacArthur's staff in the Pacific. In January 1945 he was observing the US Navy's bombardment of Lingayen Gulf from the bridge of the battleship USS *New Mexico* when a Kamikaze aircraft crashed on the ship's bridge, killing him.

Major General Lewis Owen Lyne CB DSO: Commissioned in the Lancashire Fusiliers in 1921 he had seen service in France towards the end of the Great War. In 1940 he commanded 9th Lancashire Fusiliers in the BEF and was chief instructor at a senior officers' school before being appointed to command 169 Brigade which he led in the UK, Iraq, North Africa and Italy, being appointed DSO for his service at Monte Camino in late 1943. On returning to the UK he was promoted major general and appointed successively as GOC 59th (Staffordshire), 50th (Northumbrian) and 7th Armoured Divisions in north-west Europe. He commanded the Desert Rats from November 1944 until the end of the war, including the Rhine crossing and the advance through Germany.

General Sir Richard Loudon McCreery GCB KBE DSO MC: Commissioned in 12th Lancers in 1915 he was wounded badly in France where he earned the MC in 1918. Rising to command his regiment from 1935 to 1938 he was then on the staff of 1st Division and went to France with the BEF where he was appointed to command 2 Armoured Brigade in 1940. Appointed DSO for his conduct of operations in France he was promoted major general and appointed GOC 8th Armoured Division in November. Brooke sent him to Cairo as an armoured adviser but he and Auchinleck did not agree and his advice was ignored. However, he was appointed chief of staff to Alexander when the latter became C-in-C, Middle East in August 1942. Although not favoured by Montgomery he was appointed to command X Corps in Fifth (US) Army and led the corps through the Salerno landings and the first year of the Italian campaign after which he was appointed to command Eighth Army. Knighted in the field by King George VI he reinvigorated Eighth Army and prepared it for the final successful offensive in Italy in which McCreery's understanding of armoured warfare was a major factor.

Lieutenant General Sir Giffard le Quesne Martel KCB KBE DSO MC: Commissioned in the Royal Engineers in 1909 he served in France during the Great War, transferring to the Tank Corps with which he was Mentioned in Despatches five times, earned the MC and was appointed DSO. In the interwar years he showed a flair for innovation and was instrumental in the adoption of the Christie suspension system in British cruiser tanks. Having commanded 50th (Northumbrian) Division in France in 1940 he was then appointed Commander RAC. He fell out with some of his colleagues, including Hobart, and annoyed Brooke who abolished the post of Commander RAC. As Head of the British Military Mission in Moscow he studied the Red Army in action, especially its use of armour, passing his knowledge on for the use of western Allied commanders.

General Sir Frank Walter Messervy KCSI KBE CB DSO*: Commissioned in the Indian Army in 1913 he served in France, Palestine and Syria with Hodson's Horse during the Great War and in Kurdistan in 1919. He commanded 13th (Duke of Connaught's) Lancers in 1938 and 1939 when he was sent to the Sudan and the staff of 5th Indian Division. Messervy served with distinction in Ethiopia, was appointed to command 9 Brigade, which he led in the Battle of Keren, and was then promoted major general and sent to Egypt where he was appointed GOC 4th Indian Division. For his part in the CRUSADER battles he was appointed DSO. As a cavalryman he was appointed GOC 1st Armoured Division in January 1942 but was taken off balance by Rommel's offensive in which his division suffered heavily. Sent back to India he was recalled to Egypt as GOC 7th Armoured Division but was sacked by Ritchie, Eighth Army's commander, after a counter-attack at Tobruk had failed with the loss of about two-thirds of his tanks. He recovered his reputation as a divisional commander with 7th Indian Division in Burma and was promoted to command IV Corps during the re-conquest of Burma.

General Sir Horatius Murray GCB KBE DSO: Commissioned in the Cameronians (Scottish Rifles) in 1923 he commanded 1st Gordon Highlanders in 51st (Highland) Division at El Alamein and 152 Brigade in Tunisia, Sicily and Normandy, being appointed DSO in 1943. Promoted major general and appointed GOC 6th Armoured Division in August 1944 he led the division through the difficult autumn and winter of 1944–45 and proved an excellent leader and commander in the final offensive in April 1945 when his battlegroups did great service in the destruction of the German armies in Italy.

General Sir Cameron Gordon Graham Nicholson GCB KBE DSO MC: Commissioned in the Royal Artillery in 1915 he served in France during the Great War where he was wounded and awarded the MC and Bar. In 1939 he was appointed to the staff of 45th Division and was subsequently appointed DSO for his work with Sickleforce in Norway. Other staff jobs followed before he became CO of 42nd Support Group in 1941, going on to become deputy GOC 6th Armoured Division in 1942. Having served on the staff of First Army he was promoted major general and appointed GOC 44th Indian Armoured Division but, at his own request and in order to command in the field, later became GOC 2nd Division in Burma. (None of the three Indian armoured divisions saw active service although it is believed that 44th was to be sent to Italy; its lorried infantry brigade, 43 Gurkha, served with 1st Armoured Division.)

Major General Charles Wake Norman CBE: Commissioned in the 9th (Queen's Royal) Lancers in 1913 he was wounded and captured in the early days of the Great War. In 1936 he became CO of his regiment and converted it to armour during his tenure in command. Promoted colonel in 1938 he commanded 1 Armoured Reconnaissance Brigade in the BEF in France and was

Mentioned in Despatches. Promoted major general in 1941 he was appointed GOC 8th Armoured Division but relinquished his command when the formation reached Egypt.

Lieutenant General Sir Charles Willoughby Moke Norrie GCMG GCVO CB DSO MC*: Commissioned in 11th Prince Albert's Own Hussars in 1913 he served in France during the Great War, transferring to the Tank Corps. During his service he was wounded four times, Mentioned in Despatches twice, awarded the MC and Bar and appointed DSO. CO of 10th Royal Hussars (Prince of Wales's Own) from 1931 to 1935 he commanded 1 Cavalry Brigade in 1937–38, overseeing its conversion to armour. In 1938 he became commander 1 Armoured Brigade and then Inspector RAC before being appointed GOC 1st Armoured Division. However, when he arrived in Egypt in November 1941 he was immediately appointed commander XXX Corps in succession to Vyvyan Pope who had been killed. He commanded XXX Corps with distinction in the CRUSADER battles of late-1941 but his command suffered disastrously at Knightsbridge in May 1942 and he was blamed on account of his cavalry background when, in fact, the army commander, Ritchie, was the main culprit. Although he regained control of his corps' situation and appreciated the importance of the Alamein line, he was sent back to the UK where he became Commander RAC in 1943.

General Sir Richard O'Connor GCB DSO MC: Commissioned in the Cameronians (Scottish Rifles) in 1910 he served in France and Italy in the Great War, earning nine Mentions in Despatches and the MC and being appointed DSO; he was also decorated by the Italian government. Having commanded the Peshawar Brigade in India he was appointed GOC 7th Division in Palestine in 1938, transferring to command 8th Division in Egypt on the outbreak of war in 1939. As Commander Western Desert Force he launched Operation COMPASS in December 1940. Intended as a five-day raid the operation led to the destruction of the Italian Tenth Army and the conquest of Cyrenaica. O'Connor had shown himself a gifted commander of a mobile corps with an astute understanding of armour. Captured in April 1941 he finally escaped captivity and returned to the British lines in Italy in December 1943. Appointed commander VIII Corps for the invasion of Europe, he led his corps with distinction in Normandy, especially in the very trying Operation GOODWOOD. He was later relieved of his command by Montgomery in a vindictive act and transferred to India.

Lieutenant General Vyvyan Vavasour Pope CBE DSO MC: Commissioned in the North Staffordshire Regiment in 1912 he served in France where he was wounded twice and had his right arm amputated. Commanding a battalion at the end of the war, he had been awarded the MC, appointed DSO and been Mentioned in Despatches five times. He received a further Mention in 1919 for service in Russia. Having commanded an armoured car brigade in Egypt he transferred to the Tank Corps in 1923 and was seen as a rising star, commanding the Mobile Force in Egypt in 1936. As a corps staff officer under Brooke he was appointed commander 3 Armoured Brigade in November 1939 but, before the brigade saw action, had moved on to be Inspector RAC and was assigned as an adviser on AFVs to Brooke after the fall of France. As Director AFVs at the War Office he was seen as one of the RTR's most able officers and was appointed commander XXX Corps in August 1941, as that corps was intended to control the armour of the newly-created Eighth Army. He and many of his staff were killed in a plane crash near Cairo in October. Lord Carver wrote that few were better suited for the command of XXX Corps.

Major General James Malcolm Renton CB DSO OBE: Commissioned in the Rifle Brigade in 1916 he served in France, suffering severe wounds. In 1940 he was appointed to command 2nd Rifle Brigade and took part in the COMPASS campaign as a result of which he was appointed DSO and made commander 7 Motor Brigade Group. In June 1942 he was appointed GOC 7th

Armoured Division and demonstrated tactical *nous* and courage at Alam el Halfa but he argued with Montgomery for which he was sent back to the UK in September.

Major General George Philip Bradley Roberts CB DSO MC**: Commissioned in the Royal Tank Corps in 1936 he was serving with 6 RTR in Egypt when war broke out in 1939. He became Brigade Major 4 Armoured Brigade and was appointed to the staff of 7th Armoured Division and then XXX Corps. Awarded the MC he commanded 3 RTR and 22 Armoured Brigade and was appointed DSO. Acting GOC 7th Armoured Division, after Harding was wounded, in 1943 he commanded 26 Armoured Brigade of 6th Armoured Division in Tunisia. Returning to the UK he commanded 30 Armoured Brigade before being appointed GOC 11th Armoured Division, which formation he took to France and led throughout the campaign in north-west Europe. Often considered the best of the British armoured commanders.

Field Marshal Sir Gerald Walter Robert Templer KG GCB GCMG KBE DSO: Commissioned in Princess Victoria's (Royal Irish Fusiliers) in 1916 he served in France during the Great War. During the 1920s he transferred to the Loyal (North Lancashire) Regiment with which he served in Palestine where he was appointed DSO. After a spell in Military Intelligence he became a staff officer at GHQ BEF in France, and commanded an infantry battalion after Dunkirk before being appointed to command 210 Brigade. Promoted major general in April 1942 he was appointed GOC 47th (London) Division and later commanded, in succession, II and XI Corps. At his own request he reverted to major general to command in the field and was appointed GOC 1st Division before taking command of 56th (London) Division in Italy in 1943. In the Anzio beachhead in 1944 he had, for a time, both divisions under his command. In July 1944 he was appointed GOC 6th Armoured Division but was badly injured in August and evacuated to the UK. As an outstanding trainer and inspiring commander he had the attributes of a good armoured commander.

Major General Justice Crosland Tilly DSO MC: Commissioned in the Leicestershire Regiment in 1908 he served in France during the Great War with the Machine Gun Corps and was wounded, Mentioned in Despatches, awarded the MC and appointed DSO. Having transferred to the West Yorkshire Regiment in 1919 he transferred again, this time to the Royal Tank Corps, in 1927. He commanded 5 RTC, was chief instructor at the RTC Central School, Bovington and at the Gunnery Wing of the Army AFV School at Lulworth. Tilly commanded 1 Tank Brigade in 1939–40 and was appointed GOC 2nd Armoured Division in May 1940. He was killed in an accident in January 1941.

Major General Gerald Lloyd Verney DSO MVO: Commissioned in the Grenadier Guards in 1919 he transferred to the Irish Guards in 1939 and, after service with the BEF in France, commanded 2nd Irish Guards in the UK before commanding, in succession, 1 Guards Brigade (6th Armoured Division), 6 Guards Tank Brigade and 32 Guards Brigade (Guards Armoured Division). In August 1944 he was appointed GOC 7th Armoured Division in succession to Erskine but was relieved of command in November. He subsequently wrote the history of 7th Armoured Division.

Major General Robert Harley Wordsworth CB CBE: Commissioned in 6th Lancers (Watson's Horse) in 1918 he had served with the Australian Imperial Force in Egypt and France during the Great War. CO of Watson's Horse on the outbreak of war he was subsequently appointed GOC of, first, 31st Indian Armoured Division and then 43rd and 44th Indian Armoured Divisions. In 1944 he was appointed Major General AFVs at GHQ, India.

Bibliography

Alanbrooke, Field Marshal Lord (edited by Danchev, Alex and Daniel Todman), *War Diaries 1939–1945* (Weidenfeld & Nicolson, London, 2001)

Alexander, Field Marshal Sir Harold, *Memoirs*, John North (ed), (Cassell, London, 1962)

Anderson, Richard C., *Cracking Hitler's Atlantic Wall: The 1st Assault Brigade Royal Engineers on D-Day* (Stackpole, Mechanicsburg, PA, 2009)

Anon, *Destruction of an Army: The First Campaign in Libya Sept. 1940–Feb. 1941* (HMSO, London, 1941)

Anon, *A Short History of XXX Corps in the European Campaign, 1944–1945* (BAOR, Hanover, 1945)

Anon, *Finito! The Po Valley Campaign 1945* (HQ 15 Army Group, 1945)

Anon, *History of 7th Armoured Division: June 1943–July 1945* (BAOR, 1945)

Anon, *Taurus Pursuant: A History of 11th Armoured Division* (BAOR, 1945)

Anon, *The History of 61 Infantry Brigade: May 1944–June 1945* (HQ 61 Brigade, Klagenfurt, 1945)

Barnes, B. S., *Operation Scipio: The 8th Army at the Battle of Wadi Akarit, 6 April 1943* (Sentinel Press, York, 2007)

Barnett, Correlli, *The Desert Generals* (George Allen, London, 1960 and 1983)

Bates, Peter, *Dance of War: The Story of the Battle of Egypt* (Leo Cooper, London, 1992)

Battistelli, Pier Paolo, *Erwin Rommel* (Osprey Publishing, Botley, 2010)

Baynes, John, *The Forgotten Victor: General Sir Richard O'Connor KT GCB DSO MC* (Brassey's, London, 1989)

Beale, Peter, *Death by Design. British Tank Development in the Second World War* (The History Press, Stroud, 2009)

Bellamy, Bill, *Troop Leader. A Tank Commander's Story* (Sutton, Stroud, 2005)

Bidwell, Shelford and Dominick Graham, *Tug of War: The Battle for Italy, 1943–45* (Hodder & Stoughton, London, 1986)

——, *Coalitions, Politicians and Generals. Some Aspects of Command in Two World Wars* (Brasseys, London, 1993)

Birks, Maj H. L., *Armoured Operations in Italy* (AFHQ, Italy, 1945)

Blaxland, Gregory, *The Plain Cook and the Great Showman: The First and Eighth Armies in North Africa* (William Kimber, London, 1977)

——, *Alexander's Generals: The Italian Campaign 1944–45* (William Kimber, London, 1979)

Blumenson, Martin, *Mark Clark* (Jonathan Cape, London, 1985)

Boardman, Captain C. J., *Tracks in Europe: The 5th Royal Inniskilling Dragoon Guards 1939–1946* (City Press Services, Salford, 1990)

Butler, J. R. M., *Grand Strategy*, Vols II and III (HMSO, London, 1957 and 1964)

Carver, Field Marshal Lord, *El Alamein* (B. T. Batsford, London, 1962)

——, *Harding of Petherton: A Biography* (Weidenfeld and Nicolson, London, 1978)

——, *The Apostles of Mobility. The Theory and Practice of Armoured Warfare* (Weidenfeld and Nicolson, London, 1979)

——, *Dilemmas of the Desert War* (B. T. Batsford, London, 1986)

——, *Out of Step. The Memoirs of Field Marshal Lord Carver* (Hutchinson, London, 1989)

——, *Britain's Army in the Twentieth Century* (Macmillan, London, in association with the Imperial War Museum, 1998)

Churchill, Sir Winston, *The Second World War* (Cassell, London, 1951)

Close, Maj Bill, MC, *A View from the Turret. A History of the 3rd Royal Tank Regiment in the Second World War* (Tewkesbury, 1998)

Connell, John, *Auchinleck: A Biography of Field Marshal Sir Claude Auchinleck GCB GCIE CSI DSO OBE LlD* (Cassell, London, 1959)

Cooper, Matthew, *The German Army, 1933–1945: Its Political and Military Failure* (Macdonald and Jane's, London, 1978)

Copp, Terry, *Fields of Fire: The Canadians in Normandy* (University of Toronto Press, Toronto, 2003)

Daglish, Ian, *Operation GOODWOOD. The Great Tank Charge, July 1944* (Pen and Sword Military, Barnsley, 2004)

Daniels, Maj M. J., *Innovation in the Face of Adversity: Major General Sir Percy Hobart and the 79th Armoured Division* (US Army Staff & Command College, Ft Leavenworth, KS, 2003)

Darby, Hugh, and Cunliffe, Marcus, *A Short Story of 21 Army Group* (Gale and Polden, Aldershot, 1949)

de Butts, Freddie (with David Hunt), *Now the Dust has Settled* (Tabb House, Padstow, 1995)

D'Este, Carlo, *Decision in Normandy* (London, 1983)

Delaforce, Patrick, *Taming the Panzers: Monty's Tank Battalions: 3 RTR at War* (Sutton, Stroud, 2000)

Doherty, Richard, *Clear The Way! A History of 38 (Irish) Brigade, 1941 to 1947* (Irish Academic Press, Dublin, 1993)

——, *A Noble Crusade: The History of Eighth Army 1941 to 1945* (Spellmount Publishers, Staplehurst, 1999)

——, *Normandy 1944: The Road to Victory* (Spellmount Publishers, Staplehurst, 2004)

——, *Ireland's Generals in the Second World War* (Four Courts Press, Dublin, 2004)

——, *Eighth Army in Italy 1943–45: The Long Hard Slog* (Pen and Sword, Barnsley, 2007)

——, *In The Ranks of Death: The Irish in the Second World War* (Pen and Sword, Barnsley, 2010)

——, *Hobart's 79th Armoured Division at War: Invention, Innovation and Inspiration* (Pen and Sword Military, Barnsley, 2011)

Donovan, John (Ed), *'A Very Fine Commander': The Memoirs of General Sir Horatius Murray GCB KBE DSO* (Pen & Sword Military, Barnsley, 2010)

Douglas, Keith, *Alamein to Zem Zem* (Faber and Faber, London, 1992)

Dunstan, Simon, *Centurion Universal Tank 1943–2003* (Osprey Publishing, Botley, 2003)

——, *Mechanized Warfare* (Compendium Publishing, London, 2005)

Eisenhower, Gen Dwight, *D Day to VE Day: General Eisenhower's Report, 1944–45* (HMSO, London, 2000)

Ellis, Maj L. F., *The War in France and Flanders (History of the Second World War – UK Military Series)* (HMSO, London, 1953)

——, *Victory in the West. Vol I: The Battle of Normandy (History of the Second World War – UK Military Series)* (HMSO, London, 1962)

——, *Victory in the West. Vol II: The Defeat of Germany (History of the Second World War – UK Military Series)* (HMSO, London, 1968)

Evans, Major General Roger, *The Fifth Royal Inniskilling Dragoon Guards* (Gale & Polden, Aldershot, 1951)

Farrar-Hockley, Anthony, *The War in The Desert* (Faber and Faber, London, 1969)

Fitzgerald, Desmond, *History of the Irish Guards in the Second World War* (Gale & Polden, Aldershot, 1949)

Fletcher, David, *Crusader Cruiser Tank 1939–1945* (Osprey Publishing, Botley, 1995)

——, *Cromwell Cruiser Tank 1942–50* (Osprey Publishing, Botley, 2008)

——, *Sherman Firefly* (Osprey Publishing, Botley, 2008)

Ford, Ken, *Mailed Fist: 6th Armoured Division at War, 1940–1945* (Sutton Publishing, Stroud, 2005)

——, *Gazala 1942: Rommel's Greatest Victory* (Osprey Publishing, Botley, 2008)

Forty, George, *The Royal Tank Regiment. A Pictorial History* (Spellmount Publishing, Tunbridge Wells, 1989)

——, *The First Victory. General O'Connor's Desert Triumph, December 1940–February 1941* (Spellmount Publishing, Tunbridge Wells, 1990)

——, *Tank Action. From the Great War to the Gulf* (Sutton, Stroud, 1995)

——, *World War Two Tanks* (Osprey, London, 1995)

——, *British Army Handbook* (Sutton, Stroud, 1998)

——,(Ed), *Tanks Across the Desert: The War Diary of Jake Wardrop* (Sutton, Stroud, 2003)

Foss, Christopher F., *The Illustrated Encyclopedia of the World's Tanks and Fighting Vehicles* (Salamander Books, London, 1977)

Fraser, David, *And We Shall Shock Them: The British Army in the Second World War* (Hodder & Stoughton, London, 1983)

——, *Knight's Cross: A Life of Field Marshal Erwin Rommel* (HarperCollins, London, 1993)

ffrench-Blake, R. I. V., *A History of the 17th/21st Lancers 1922–1959* (Macmillan, London, 1962)

French, David, *Raising Churchill's Army. The British Army and the War against Germany 1919–1945* (Oxford University Press, Oxford, 2000)

Gorman, Sir John, *The Times of My Life* (Pen and Sword, Barnsley, 2002)

Graham, Andrew, *Sharpshooters at War. The 3rd, the 4th and the 3rd/4th County of London Yeomanry 1939 to 1945* (The Sharpshooters Regimental Association, London, 1964)

Graham, Dominick and Bidwell, Shelford, *Coalitions, Politicians and Generals: Some Aspects of Command in Two World Wars* (Brasseys, London, 1993)

Guderian, Maj Gen Heinz, *Achtung – Panzer!* (Arms and Armour Press, London, 1992)

Hamilton, Nigel, *Monty: The Making of a General 1887–1942* (Hamish Hamilton, London, 1981)

Hamilton, Stuart, MC, *Armoured Odyssey* (Spellmount, Staplehurst)

Harris, J. P., *Men, Ideas and Tanks. British Military Thought and Armoured Forces 1903–1939* (University Press, Manchester, 1995)

Hart, Stephen Ashley, *Colossal Cracks. Montgomery's 21st Army Group in Northwest Europe, 1944–45* (Stackpole Books, Mechanicsburg, PA, 2007)

Hogg, Ian V., *British and American Artillery of World War 2* (Arms & Armour Press, London, 1978)

——, and Weeks, John, *The Illustrated Encyclopedia of Military Vehicles* (London, 1980)

Horrocks, Lt Gen Sir Brian, *A Full Life* (Collins, London, 1960)

Horsfall, John, *Fling Our Banner to the Wind* (The Roundwood Press, Kineton, 1978)

Humble, Richard, *Crusader: The Eighth Army's Forgotten Victory, November 1941–January 1942* (Leo Cooper, London, 1987)

Jackson, Gen Sir William, *The Mediterranean and the Middle East. Vol VI, Part II – June to October 1944* (HMSO, London, 1986)

——, *The Mediterranean and the Middle East. Vol VI, Part III – November 1944 to May 1945* (HMSO, London, 1986)

Jarymowycz, Roman Johann, *Tank Tactics from Normandy to Lorraine* (Boulder, CO, 2001)

Joslen, Lt Col H. F., *Orders of Battle Second World War 1939–1945* (London, 1996)

Kershaw, Robert, *Tank Men: The human story of tanks at war* (Hodder & Stoughton, London, 2008)

Kesselring, Field Marshal Albert, *Memoirs* (Greenhill Books, London, 2007)

Kippenberger, Maj Gen Sir Howard, *Infantry Brigadier* (OUP, London, 1949)

Lester, J. R., *Tank Warfare* (George Allen and Unwin Ltd, London, 1943)

Lewin, Ronald, *Montgomery as Military Commander* (B. T. Batsford, London, 1971)

——, *Man of Armour: A Study of Lieut General Vyvyan Pope CBE DSO MC and the development of armoured warfare* (Leo Cooper, London, 1976)

——, *The Life and Death of the Afrika Korps* (B. T. Batsford, London, 1977)

Liddell–Hart, Basil H. (Ed), *The Rommel Papers* (Harcourt Bruce, New York, 1953)

——, *The Tanks: The History of The Royal Tank Regiment and Its Predecessors* (Cassell, London, 1959)

Macksey, Kenneth, *Armoured Crusader: The Biography of Major General Sir Percy 'Hobo' Hobart, one of the most influential military commanders of the Second World War* (Hutchinson, London, 1967, & Grub Street, London, 2004)

——, *Rommel: Campaigns and Battles* (Arms and Armour Press, London, 1979)

——, *The Tank Pioneers* (Jane's Publishing Ltd, London, 1981)

——, *A History of The Royal Armoured Corps and its Predecessors 1914 to 1975* (Newtown Publications, Beaminster, 1983)

——, *Technology in War. The Impact of Science on Weapon Development and Modern Battle* (Grub Street, London, 1986)

——, *Tank Versus Tank. The Illustrated Story of Armoured Battlefield Conflict in the Twentieth Century* (Grub Street, London, 1988)

——, and Woodhouse, William, *The Penguin Encyclopedia of Modern Warfare: From the Crimean War to the Present Day* (Viking, London, 1991)

MacLeod Ross, G., *The Business of Tanks: Help Britain Finish The Job* (Arthur H. Stockwell Ltd, Ilfracombe, 1976)

Mallinson, Allan, *The Light Dragoons. The Making of a Regiment* (Leo Cooper, London, 1993)

——, *The Making of the British Army: From the English Civil War to the War on Terror* (Bantam Press, London, 2009)

Marie, Henri, *Villers-Bocage, Normandy 1944* (Editions Heimdal, Bayeux, 2003)

Martel, Lt Gen Sir Giffard le Q., *Our Armoured Forces* (Faber & Faber Ltd, London, 1945; reprinted MLRS Books, nd)

Mellenthin, Maj Gen Frido von, *Panzer Battles* (Cassell Ltd, London, 1955)

Merewood, Jack, *To War with The Bays. A Tank Gunner Remembers 1939–1945* (1st The Queen's Dragoon Guards, Cardiff, 1996)

Messenger, Charles, *The Last Prussian: A Biography of Field Marshal Gerd von Rundstedt* (Pen & Sword, Barnsley, 2011)

Montgomery of Alamein, Field Marshal the Viscount, *The Memoirs of Field Marshal Montgomery* (Collins, London, 1958)

Mileham, Patrick, *The Yeomanry Regiments* (Spellmount Publishing, Staplehurst, 2003)

Neillands, Robin, *The Desert Rats: 7th Armoured Division 1940–45* (Weidenfeld and Nicolson, London, 1991)

Nicholson, Lt Col G. W. L., *The Canadians in Italy 1943–1945: Official History of the Canadian Army in the Second World War Vol II* (Ministry of National Defence, Ottawa, 1957)

Oliva, Gianni, *Soldati e Ufficiali. L'Esercito Italiano dal Risorgimento a Oggi* (Arnaldo Mondadori, Milano, 2009)

Perrett, Brian, *Seize and Hold. Master Strokes on the Battlefield* (Arms and Armour Press, London, 1994)

——, *Iron Fist: Classic Armoured Warfare Case Studies* (Arms and Armour Press, London, 1995)

Pile, General Sir Frederick, *Ack Ack. Britain's Defence Against Air Attack during the Second World War* (Harrap, London, 1949)

Place, Timothy Harrison, *Military Training in the British Army, 1940–44: From Dunkirk to D–Day* (Frank Cass, London, 2000)

Playfair, Maj Gen I. S. O., et al, *The Mediterranean and the Middle East. Vol I: The Early Successes against Italy [to May 1941] (History of the Second World War – UK Military Series)* HMSO

——, *The Mediterranean and the Middle East. Vol II: The Germans come to the help of their Ally [1941] (History of the Second World War – UK Military Series)* HMSO

——, *The Mediterranean and the Middle East. Vol III: British Fortunes reach their Lowest Ebb [September 1941 to September 1942] (History of the Second World War – UK Military Series)* HMSO

——, *The Mediterranean and the Middle East. Vol IV: The Destruction of the Axis Forces in Africa (History of the Second World War – UK Military Series)* HMSO

Reid, Brian A., *No Holding Back. Operation TOTALIZE, Normandy, August 1944* (Robin Brass Studio, Toronto, 2005)

Reynolds, Michael, *Steel Inferno: I SS Panzer Corps in Normandy* (Spellmount Ltd, Staplehurst, 1997)

——, *Sons of The Reich: II SS Panzer Corps: Normandy, Arnhem, Ardennes, Eastern Front* (Spellmount Publishers, Staplehurst, 2002)

Roberts, G. B. P., *From the Desert to the Baltic* (London, 1987)

Ross, Peter, *All Valiant Dust: An Irishman Abroad* (Lilliput Press, Dublin, 1992)

Rosse, Capt the Earl of, and Hill, Col D. R., DSO, *The Story of Guards Armoured Division* (Geoffrey Bles, London 1956)

Routledge, Brigadier N. W., *Anti-Aircraft Artillery, 1914–55* (Brasseys, London, 1994)

Ryder, Rowland, *Oliver Leese* (Hamish Hamilton, London, 1987)

Short, Neil, *German Defences in Italy in World War II* (Osprey Publishing, Botley, 2006)

Smart, Nick, *Biographical Dictionary of British Generals of the Second World War* (Pen and Sword, Barnsley, 2005)

Stacey, *The Victory Campaign: The Operations in North-West Europe 1944–1945: Official History of the Canadian Army in the Second World War Vol III* (Ministry of National Defence, Ottawa, 1960)

Tedder, Lord, *With Prejudice: The War Memoirs of Marshal of the Royal Air Force Lord Tedder GCB* (Cassell, London, 1966)

Verney, Maj Gen G. L., DSO MVO, *The Desert Rats. The 7th Armoured Division in World War II*

Verney, Peter, *The Micks: The Story of The Irish Guards* (Peter Davies, London, 1970)

Young, Desmond, *Rommel: The Desert Fox* (Collins & Co., Glasgow, 1950)

Warner, Philip, *Firepower: From Slings to Star Wars* (Grafton Books, London, 1988)

Wilson, Edward, *Press On Regardless: The Story of the Fifth Royal Tank Regiment in World War Two* (Spellmount Publishing, Staplehurst, 2003)

Wilson, Lt Gen Sir James, *Unusual Undertakings. A Military Memoir* (Pen and Sword, Barnsley, 2002)

Unpublished

Bredin, CB DSO** MC*, Major General H. E. N. (Bala), 'An Account of the Kangaroo Army'

ffrench-Blake DSO, Colonel R. L. Valentine, 'Italian War Diary 1944–45'

Skellorn, John, 'What Did You Do In The War Grandpa?' (An account of his service with 16th/5th Lancers)

Wingfield, DSO MC, Brigadier A. D. R., 'Memoirs 1930–1948' (IWM, London: PP/MCR/353)

Royal Armoured Corps Weapon Training: Military Training Pamphlet No. 34: Part 4: Fire Tactics for Tank Commanders and Troop Leaders (War Office, May 1940)

Army Training Instruction No. 3: Handling of an Armoured Division (War Office, May 1941)

Troop Training for Cruiser Tank Troops (Military Training Pamphlet No. 51) (War Office, September 1941)

The tactical handling of the Armoured Division and its Components (Military Training Pamphlet No. 41 Part 2) (War Office, February 1943)

The tactical handling of the Armoured Division and its Components (Military Training Pamphlet No. 41) (War Office, July 1943)

Newspapers etc.

The Daily Telegraph
The London Gazette
The Times
Britain at War

National Archives, Kew
National Archives, Kew, Richmond, Surrey
CAB23/75: Conclusions of Cabinet Meeting 16 (33), 15 March 1933
CAB24/251: Report of the Committee on German Re-armament to the Cabinet, 18 December 1934
CAB24/273: Committee of Imperial defence: Memorandum by the Minister for Co-ordination of Defence: Comparison of the strength of Great Britain with that of certain other nations as at January 1938
CAB44/97: War histories: draft chapters: Middle East, operations, battles and campaigns: German assault on the Gazala position.
CAB44/145: War histories: draft chapters: Middle East, Europe and Russia: Gothic Line 24 Aug to 30 Sep 1944.
CAB66/11/19: War Cabinet: The Munitions Situation, Memorandum by the Minister of Supply, 29 August 1940.
CAB66/24/8: War Cabinet: Post-protocol supplies to Russia, memorandum by the Minister of Production, 26 April 1942.
CAB66/26/2: War Cabinet: Operations in Cyrenaica. Note by the Secretary, 27 June 1942
CAB97: Records of the Cabinet Office
CAB106/1061: War histories: notes re Operation GOODWOOD; conversations between Gen Sir Miles Dempsey, Lt Col G. S. Jackson and Capt Basil Liddell Hart.
CAB195/1/14: Debate in the House of Commons, 24 June 1942.
WO32/2847: Cavalry Re-organization: Introduction of a Mobile Division: Experiments by 3rd Hussars in 1936.
WO32/2852: General Situation of Tank Units at Home and in Egypt: Reorganization, 1932
WO32/3347: New designs of armoured cars, 1934
WO32/9392: Operations of 1st Armoured Division in France, 1940

WO166/6662: war diary, 26 Armoured Brigade, Jan-Nov 1942
WO166/796: war diary, G Branch 1st Armoured Division, Sep 1939–Apr 1940
WO166/799: war diary, Support Group 1st Armoured Division, Sep 1939–Dec 1941
WO166/819: war diary, Support Group 2nd Armoured Division, 1 Feb-31 Oct 1940
WO166/836: war diary, Support Group 8th Armoured Division, 1941
WO166/869: war diary, Support Group 11th Armoured Division, 1941
WO166/6578: war diary, 32 Guards Brigade, 1942
WO166/6596: war diary, 131 (Queen's) Brigade, Jan-May 1942
WO166/6621: war diary, 159 Brigade, 1942
WO166/6655: war diary, 5 Guards Armoured Brigade, 1943
WO166/6660: war diary, 23 Armoured Brigade, Jan-Mar 1942
WO166/6661: war diary, 24 Armoured Brigade, Jan-Apr 1942
WO166/6665: war diary, 29 Armoured Brigade, 1942
WO166/10737: war diary, 29 Armoured Brigade, 1943
WO166/10792: war diary, 159 Brigade, 1943
WO167/16: war diary, GHQ BEF, AFV, Sep 1939–May 1940
WO167/334: war diary, G Branch 1st Armoured Division, May-Jun 1940
WO167/336: war diary, Support Group 1st Armoured Division, May-Jun 1940
WO167/419: war diary, 2 Armoured Brigade, May-Jun 1940
WO167/421: war diary, 3 Armoured Brigade, May-Jun 1940
WO169/86: war diary, G Branch 2nd Armoured Division 1940
WO169/95: war diary, Support Group 2nd Armoured Division, 1 Nov-31 Dec 1940
WO169/102: war diary, G Branch 7th Armoured Division, Aug 1939–Aug 40
WO169/103: war diary, G Branch 7th Armoured Division, Sep-Dec 1940
WO169/114: war diary, Support Group 7th Armoured Division, 1940

WO169/122: war diary, 4 Armoured Brigade, Sep 1939–Dec 1940

WO169/123: war diary, 7 Armoured Brigade, Aug 1939–Dec 1940

WO169/441: war diary, G Branch 7th Armoured Division, 1940

WO169/1134: war diary, G Branch 1st Armoured Division, Aug-Dec 1941

WO169/1146: war diary, G Branch 2nd Armoured Division, Apr-May 1941

WO169/1147: war diary, G Branch Advanced 2nd Armoured Division, Jan-Feb 1941

WO169/1173: war diary, G Branch 7th Armoured Division, Jan-Aug 1941

WO169/1174: war diary, G Branch 7th Armoured Division, Oct-Nov 1941

WO169/1175: war diary, G Branch 7th Armoured Division, Dec 1941

WO169/1185: war diary, Support Group 7th Armoured Division, Jan 1941–28 Feb 1942

WO169/1278: war diary, 3 Armoured Brigade, 1941

WO169/1281: war diary, 4 Armoured Brigade, 1941

WO169/1282: war diary, 7 Armoured Brigade, 1941

WO169/1284: war diary, 8 Armoured Brigade, Jul-Dec 1941

WO169/1286: war diary, 9 Armoured Brigade, Aug-Dec 1941

WO169/1294: war diary, 22 Armoured Brigade, Aug-Dec 1941

WO169/4053: war diary, G Branch 1st Armoured Division, Jan-Jun 1942

WO169/4054: war diary, G Branch 1st Armoured Division, Aug-Dec 1942

WO169/4068: war diary, G Branch 7th Armoured Division, Jan-Jun 1942

WO169/4087A: war diary, G Branch 7th Armoured Division, Jul-Oct 1942

WO169/4087B: war diary, G Branch 7th Armoured Division, Nov-Dec 1942

WO169/4102: war diary: G Branch 8th Armoured Division, 1942

WO169/4117: war diary, G Branch 10th Armoured Division, 1942

WO169/4218: war diary, 4 Armoured Brigade, 1942

WO169/4222: war diary, 7 Armoured Brigade, Sep-Dec 1942

WO169/4226: war diary, 7 Motor Brigade, 1942

WO169/4230: war diary, 8 Armoured Brigade, 1942

WO169/4233: war diary, 9 Armoured Brigade, 1942

WO169/4251: war diary, 22 Armoured Brigade, 1942

WO169/4260: war diary, 23 Armoured Brigade, Jul-Sep 1942

WO169/4266: war diary, 24 Armoured Brigade, May-Dec 1942

WO169/4261: war diary, 23 Armoured Brigade, Nov 1942

WO169/4276: war diary, 131 (Queen's) Brigade, Jun-Dec 1942

WO169/4307: war diary, 200 Guards Brigade, 1942

WO169/4426: war diary, 7 Motor Brigade, 1 Feb-31 Dec 1942

WO169/8866: war diary, 7 Armoured Brigade, 1943

WO169/8869: war diary, 7 Motor Brigade, 1 Jan-31 Jul 1943

WO169/8903: war diary, 22 Armoured Brigade, 1943

WO169/8943: war diary, 131 (Queen's) Brigade, 1943

WO170/398: war diary, G Branch 1st Armoured Division, 1944

WO170/437: war diary, G Branch 6th Armoured Division, Jan-Jun 1944

WO170/438: war diary, G Branch 6th Armoured Division, Aug-Oct 1944

WO170/439: war diary, G Branch 6th Armoured Division, Nov-Dec 1944

WO170/514: war diary, 1 Guards Brigade, Jan-Jun 1944

WO170/515: war diary, 1 Guards Brigade, Jul-Dec 1944

WO170/571: war diary, 18 Lorried Infantry Brigade, 1944

WO170/594: war diary, 26 Armoured Brigade, 1944

WO170/4336: war diary, G Branch 6th Armoured Division, Jan-Apr 1945

WO170/4337: war diary, G Branch 6th Armoured Division, May-Dec 1945

WO170/4404: war diary, 1 Guards Brigade, 1945

WO170/4456: war diary, 26 Armoured Brigade, 1945

WO171/376: war diary, G Branch Guards Armoured Division, Jan-Sep 1944

WO171/438: war diary, G Branch 7th Armoured Division, Jan-May 1944
WO171/439: war diary, G Branch 7th Armoured Division, Jun-Jul 1944
WO171/440 – 3: war diaries, G Branch 7th Armoured Division, Aug to Dec 1944
WO171/456: war diary, G Branch 11th Armoured Division, 1944
WO171/601: war diary, 4 Armoured Brigade, 1944
WO171/605: war diary, 5 Guards Armoured Brigade, 1944
WO171/619: war diary, 22 Armoured Brigade, Jan-Jun 1944
WO171/620: war diary, 22 Armoured Brigade, Jul-Dec 1944
WO171/627: war diary, 29 Armoured Brigade, 1994
WO171/638: war diary, 32 Guards Brigade, 1944
WO171/662: war diary, 131 (Queen's) Brigade, 1944
WO171/691: war diary, 159 Brigade, 1944
WO171/839: war diary, 5th Royal Inniskilling Dragoon Gds, 1944
WO171/843: war diary, 8th King's Royal Irish Hussars, 1944
WO171/853: war diary, 2nd Fife & Forfar Yeomanry, 1944
WO171/856: war diary, 4th County of London Yeomanry, 1944
WO171/860: war diary, 2nd Northants Yeomanry, 1944
WO171/866: war diary, 3rd Royal Tank Regt, 1944
WO171/867: war diary, 5th Royal Tank Regt, 1944
WO171/1253: war diary, 1st Grenadier Gds, 1944
WO171/1254: war diary, 2nd Grenadier Gds, 1944
WO171/1256: war diary, 2nd (Armd) Bn Irish Guards, 1944
WO171/1260: war diary, 2nd Welsh Gds, 1944
WO171/4103: war diary, G Branch Guards Armoured Division, Jan-Feb 1945
WO171/4104: war diary, G Branch Guards Armoured Division, Mar-Apr 1945
WO171/4105: war diary, G Branch Guards Armoured Division, May-Aug 1945
WO171/4170: war diary, G Branch 7th Armoured Division, Jan-Mar 1945
WO171/4171: war diary, G Branch 7th Armoured Division, Apr-Jun 1945
WO171/4184: war diary, G Branch 11th Armoured Division, Jan-Nov 1945
WO171/4314: war diary, 4 Armoured Brigade, 1945
WO171/4318: war diary, 5 Guards Armoured Brigade, 1945
WO171/4340: war diary, 22 Armoured Brigade, Jan-Jun 1945
WO171/4345: war diary, 29 Armoured Brigade, 1945
WO171/4357: war diary, 32 Guards Brigade, 1945
WO171/4394: war diary, 131 (Queen's) Brigade, 1945
WO171/4426: war diary, 159 Brigade, 1945
WO175/146: war diary, G Branch 6th Armoured Division, 1942–43
WO175/186: war diary, 1 Guards Brigade, Nov 1942–Jun 1943
WO175/203: war diary, 24 Guards Brigade, Jan-Jun 1943
WO175/210: war diary, 26 Armoured Brigade, Dec 1942–May 1943
WO175/216: war diary, 38 (Irish) Brigade, Nov 1942–Jun 1943
WO201/530B: 201 Guards Brigade: Reports on operations near Agedabia, 1 Jan-30 Apr 1942
WO373: gallantry decorations, awards etc.

Websites

www.cwgc.org Commonwealth War Graves Commission Debt of Honour Register
www.army.mod.uk/corps&regiments Brief regimental histories
www.archives.research.arc US National Archives
www.libraryandarchives.canada Canadian National Archives
www.tankmuseum.org.uk The Tank Museum, Bovington

Index

Military Formations/Units

Individuals

General